ELEMENTARY FORMAL LOGIC

ELEMENTARY FORMAL LOGIC

G. N. Georgacarakos, Ph.D.

Robin Smith, Ph.D.

Assistant Professors of Philosophy
Kansas State University

McGraw-Hill Book Company
New York St. Louis San Francisco Auckland Bogotá Düsseldorf Johannesburg
London Madrid Mexico Montreal New Delhi Panama Paris São Paulo Singapore
Sydney Tokyo Toronto

Library of Congress Cataloging in Publication Data

Georgacarakos, G   N
    Elementary formal logic.

    Includes index.
    1. Logic. I. Smith, Robin, joint author.
II. Title.
BC50.G43   160   78-16151
ISBN 0-07-023051-X

ELEMENTARY FORMAL LOGIC

1 2 3 4 5 6 7 8 9 0 DODO 7 8 3 2 1 0 9 8

This book was set in Electra by Monotype Composition Company, Inc.
The editors were Richard R. Wright and Barry Benjamin;
the designer was Charles A. Carson;
the production supervisor was Leroy A. Young.
R. R. Donnelley & Sons Company was printer and binder.

To Sharon and Carolyn,
and to our parents

Contents

Preface

This text is designed with two objectives in mind. First, it is an introduction to logic as that subject is actually studied today. In this vein, certain subjects traditionally included in introductory texts have been omitted, most notably any treatment of inductive arguments and fallacies. It is the view of the authors that the former subject is really more appropriate to courses in epistemology or the philosophy of science. As for fallacies, we feel that this subject is best regarded as an historical remnant rather than an important part of logic. Generally speaking, there is no strong connection between a study of fallacies and the rest of a course in logic, and there is no connection between fallacies and what actually concerns logicians.

Our second objective has been to make this a truly elementary text without compromising its theoretical content. Since we give a treatment of first-order logic with identity, this entails some difficulties. Generally, we have tried to accomplish this objective by detailed and, at times, repetitive, explanation. Particular attention has been paid to the process of formalizing natural-language statements and arguments in Chapters 2, 3, 4, 8, and 9. Whenever formal procedures of any complexity at all are introduced (such as the construction of semantic trees or deductions or even the construction of truth-tables), the techniques are presented in step-by-step examples which should be intelligible to a student without classroom explanation. This necessarily lengthens the text, but we think it is more profitable for a student to read a long chapter and understand it than to read a short one and be left with a host of questions.

This text can be used in a number of possible formats. In a one-semester introductory logic course, the most natural choice would be to cover the first eight chapters, which give a treatment of statement logic and monadic singly-general predicate logic. Alternatively, in order to include a fuller treatment of predicate logic in such a course, Chapters 1 through 6 and Sections 8.1 through 8.6 and 9.1 through 9.4 could be used (this plan omits deductions). A third possibility is to combine this text with an informal treatment of arguments. In such a course, we would suggest using Chapters 1, 2, 3, 4, and Sections 5.1, 6.1 through 6.3.1,

8.1 *through 8.3.2, and 9.1 through 9.2. We would suggest Michael Scriven's text* Reasoning *for the informal treatment in such a course. Finally, our text could be used in a second course in logic; in this case, it should be possible to cover all the chapters in one semester.*

In keeping with our aim of theoretical soundness, we have sharply distinguished between the semantical and the syntactical correlates of the logical concepts we study throughout the text. We introduce the technique of tree construction as a semantical device, the aim of which is to discover counterinterpretations for invalid argument forms. Many authors regard trees as syntactical devices, and of course in a sense they are (they involve manipulation of symbols). However, for us the purpose of tree construction is semantical in that we always use it as a device to find possible counterinterpretations.

We develop truth-value semantics (the substitution interpretation) for predicate logic simply because of its pedagogical advantages. Since this is an introductory text, we pass over some of the theoretical difficulties to which this semantical interpretation gives rise. In particular we assume that we are always dealing with finite sets of statement forms.

We would like to thank Richard Greechie, who made a number of useful suggestions; Michael P. O'Neil, who offered much helpful criticism; Caren Rhodes, who assisted in the early stages of manuscript preparation; Marilyn Samore and Renee Cunningham, who worked tirelessly at typing the manuscript; and our wives, who tolerated a not inconsiderable degree of disruption of their own lives.

G. N. Georgacarakos
Robin Smith

chapter 1
The Subject of Logic

1.1
WHAT THIS BOOK IS ABOUT

We'd like to say that this book is about logic, but in a way that won't quite do, for a surprising variety of subjects have been studied under that title. Instead, we are going to say that this book is about logic in one particular sense of the term, which it is the business of this chapter to explain. We will say nothing about anything else that may have been, or somewhere may still be, included under the name *logic*. This may seem arrogant and narrow-minded, but it can be defended in two ways. First, the subject that we are calling logic happens to be what logicians (those who specialize in the study of logic) actually concern themselves with nowadays. Second, the subject which we are defining as logic has a certain sort of independence. Other things which have been called logic often turn out to be part of some other study—for instance, part of psychology, rhetoric, the philosophy of science, or the theory of knowledge. However, we want to claim that logic, as we define it, is an independent study with its own set of problems to solve and its own methods for solving them. One of the purposes of this book is to make this claim convincing. Consequently, it's important that we take some time to explain carefully just what logic, as we conceive it, is. As a first approximation, we may say that logic begins with the *study of arguments*. Now, what's an argument?

ARGUMENTS

First, let's explain what we don't mean by *argument*. One thing we don't mean is a dispute, or a difference of opinion, or a disagreement, even though it is perfectly good English to apply the word *argument* to such situations. Instead, we are more concerned with the sense of the word *argument* in such examples as these: "I tried to convince him, but he wouldn't accept my arguments." "He presented his case with clear and persuasive arguments." "You haven't proved your point, because your argument isn't any good." In these examples, an argument is something involved in *reasoning* with someone, *convincing* someone of something, or *persuading* someone to believe something. But we need to be more precise here, and in fact the cases we have described might include all sorts of different activities. We can reason out the answer to a problem by just sitting down and thinking about it. We can convince people of something by showing them a picture or looking it up in an encyclopedia. We can persuade people to believe something by appealing to their prejudices. What we mean by *argument* is one particular thing we can use in these activities of reasoning, convincing, or persuading—specifically, something we can *say* to someone. As we are using the term, an argument is a piece of language.

1.2.1 Arguments and Justifications

Arguments, as we conceive them, arise most naturally in the context of justifying beliefs or claims. To illustrate the sort of justification we're talking about, let's consider an example. Imagine that a detective who has been investigating a burglary claims to have solved the case: "Smith," he tells us, "took the money." Not wishing simply to take him at his word, we ask him to defend his claim. He responds something like this:

> **Example 1:** We have established that the money was locked in the safe at 5 P.M. and that it was missing from the safe at 9 A.M. the next day. No one entered the building between those times except Jones, Smith, and Garcia. Jones did not know the combination to the safe, but Smith and Garcia did. Moreover, the safe was moved from its hiding place behind the desk before it was opened, a job that required lifting the heavy desk out of the way. Garcia, as we have discovered, had a weak back. From all these facts, it follows that Smith took the money.

Suppose we agree with the detective that these are all the facts but we want him to defend his claim further: why, we ask, does it follow? He might respond:

From the facts, it follows that the money was taken between 5 P.M. and 9 A.M. Since only Smith, Garcia, and Jones entered the building between those times, one of them must have taken it. Since Smith and Garcia were the only two who knew the combination to the safe, it must have been one of them. Finally, since Garcia could not have moved the safe, it must have been Smith.

Now, the detective has added some further claims. However, these are not really new facts: instead, he has indicated why his claim that Smith took the money follows from all the evidence. It follows, according to him, because a number of other things follow from the facts from which, in turn, it follows that Smith took the money. Of course, we might not be satisfied even with this. Suppose we ask the detective to defend his claim even further. He might respond:

The money must have been taken between 5 P.M. and 9 A.M. for the following reasons. If it was in the safe at 5 and not in the safe at 9, then it must have been taken out between 5 and 9. In fact, it was in the safe at 5 and it wasn't there at 9; therefore, it was taken out between 5 and 9. Whoever took the money must have been in the building when the money was taken. The money was taken between 5 P.M. and 9 A.M. Therefore, whoever took the money must have been in the building between 5 P.M. and 9 A.M. Smith, Garcia, and Jones—and no one else—were in the building between 5 and 9. Therefore, whoever took the money must have been one of those three. Whoever took the money must have known the combination to the safe. Jones did not know the combination, and therefore Jones did not take the money. Smith and Garcia, however, did know the combination. Therefore, since whoever took the money must have been one of Smith, Garcia, and Jones, and since it wasn't Jones, it must have been either Smith or Garcia. Whoever took the money must have moved the safe and the desk. Therefore, no one with a weak back could have taken the money. Garcia had a weak back. Therefore, Garcia didn't take the money. Either Smith or Garcia took the money. Therefore, Smith took the money.

Here the process of justification is in fact carried one step further. Someone who failed to see the detective's first or second defenses as sufficient to justify his claim would surely find this one convincing (assuming, of course, that one and only one person took the money). However, the last claim does not involve the introduction of any new facts into evidence. Instead, all that the detective has done is to explain *how* his claim that Smith took the money follows from the evidence. As we might put it, he has *deduced* that claim from the evidence. Notice that the important thing is just what is said, not who says it or how it is expressed. We might say that the justification which it provides is an *objective* justification. Our project in studying logic is to understand just how arguments understood in this way work.

1.2.2 Some Definitions: *Statement, Argument, Premise,* and *Conclusion*

Let's look again at Example 1. First, the argument consists of a sequence of sentences, as does almost any piece of language. The sentences in the argument are of a particular sort, however. It would make sense to ask this question about any of these sentences: Is it true or false? Not all sentences are like this. For instance, consider the question "What time is it?" If you were to ask this and someone were to respond "Yes" or "That's true," you would decide that the person had not understood you. It simply makes no sense to call a question true or false. Similarly, it makes no sense to say that a command like "Close the door, please" is true or false. We'll want a term to refer to sentences which have this property of being either true or false, and so we will call them *statements*. Notice that we are not trying to define the English word *statement*. Instead, we are giving that word a special definition for our purposes in this book. To make our definition explicit:

> **Definition of *Statement*:** A *statement* is a sentence that is either true or false.

With this definition in mind, we can say that our argument consists of statements. Now, one of those statements—*Therefore, Smith took the money*—stands in a certain relation to the others. We could describe this relation in several ways. The point of the argument is to *prove* this statement, to *establish* it, or to give *reasons* for it. Or, to put it another way, this statement is supposed to *follow from*, or to be *supported by*, the other statements. Or, to put it still another way, the argument *concludes* that Smith took the money. Consequently, we will give this statement a special name: it is the *conclusion* of the argument. We will also give a special name to the other statements: each of them is a *premise* of the argument. The entire argument will then consist of (1) *premises* and (2) a *conclusion* which is supposed to follow from them. To summarize all this in a definition:

> **Definition of *Argument*:** An *argument* is a sequence of statements, one of which (called the *conclusion*) is supposed to follow from the others (each of which is called a *premise*).

With these two definitions, we have indicated what we're going to study. Now, we need to explain how we're going to study it. Before we do that, however, we need to explain two ways in which we will not study arguments.

1.2.3 Arguments and Persuasion

As we have indicated, arguments may be used to persuade or convince people to believe statements. It might seem that the next step to take would be an investigation of what sorts of arguments actually do persuade people. If we did that, we would have to take into account the many different sorts of people that there are and the effects that arguments have on different people. It might be that some arguments were quite effective in persuading certain types of people but totally ineffective for other types. A scientific account of what is persuasive in this sense would thus have to take account of these different effects, and that would mean studying various sorts of psychological tendencies and probably also cultural differences. However, logic is not the study of what sort of language will get what sort of person to believe what sort of statement: a better name for that subject is *rhetoric*. Whether the conclusion of an argument follows from its premises is not something to be determined by taking a poll. It's quite possible that there could be an argument which convinced practically everyone to believe its conclusion even though that conclusion did not follow from the premises. It is also possible that there could be an argument which convinced practically nobody even though its conclusion did follow from its premises. We need to explore this relation of premises to conclusion more thoroughly, but at least we can see that there is more to arguments than the mere facts of persuading and not persuading.

1.2.4 Logic and Rules for Reasoning

The discussion of the last section suggests that there are certain arguments which ought to persuade people and certain arguments which ought not to. This might lead us to view logic as the study of how we ought to construct arguments. Our conception of logic will have some relation to this view, but that's not the whole story. Instead, logic is for us a theoretical study with some practical benefits. An example will help explain our point. Mathematics has a good many practical uses, as in engineering, for instance, and many people study mathematics only because they want to use it for some purpose. Obviously, that's an important side of mathematics. However, that's not the primary reason that mathematicians study mathematics. Instead, they are interested in mathematics for its own sake, and any practical applications of their mathematical discoveries are, in effect, something extra. We might explain this by saying that mathematicians have a *theoretical* interest in their subject: they study it out of sheer intellectual curiosity. The same thing is true of logicians. They aren't simply interested in providing practical rules to reason or argue by; they also want to develop a theoretical understanding of the nature of argument. Of course, this theoretical study often has practical consequences, just as with mathematics. However, we don't want just to present rules: we also want to develop a theoretical understanding of *why* those rules are the right ones.

1.3
GOOD AND BAD ARGUMENTS

Now that we've identified what we're going to study—arguments—we need to say how we're going to do it. The first thing we need to do is to distinguish good arguments from bad ones. There are two distinct things that can be wrong with an argument. The first is suggested by our definition of an argument: in an argument, the conclusion is *supposed* to follow from the premises. Sometimes, this doesn't actually happen. This fault is the most important one for our study of logic. Consequently, instead of the imprecise term *good argument*, we'll introduce a technical term, *valid argument*, defined as follows:

> **Definition of Valid Argument**: A *valid argument* is one in which the conclusion follows from the premises.

If an argument isn't valid in this sense, we'll call it *invalid*.

Now, the second sort of fault an argument might have is illustrated by this example:

> **Example 2:** If Wichita is the capital of Kansas, then Topeka isn't. However, Wichita is in fact the capital of Kansas. Therefore, Topeka isn't.

If you reflect on this argument for a while, you'll probably see that it's valid: the conclusion really does follow from the premises. However, there's something else wrong with it. One of the premises, namely the statement *However, Wichita is in fact the capital of Kansas*, happens to be false. This is the second fault an argument might have—namely, it might have one or more false premises. Thus, we could also add something to our notion of a good argument. Usually, the technical expression *sound argument* is defined as follows:

> **Definition of Sound Argument**: A *sound argument* is a valid argument in which all the premises are true.

If an argument isn't sound, it's called *unsound*. Notice, incidentally, that all invalid arguments are automatically unsound but that some valid arguments (such as our example) are unsound, too.

There's an important difference between soundness and validity from the standpoint of logic. In order to tell if an argument is valid, all you have to do is determine if the conclusion really follows from the premises. This is the sort of thing that logic is able to decide. However, in order to tell if an argument is sound, you must also be able to tell if its premises are all true. That, unfortunately, goes far beyond the capabilities of logic: the premises of an argument might be statements about anything whatsoever. Consequently, in order to tell whether an argument is sound, you might have to know something about its subject—chemistry, Chinese history, baseball, or Mars. Since logicians don't make any special claims to know everything, we really have to admit that deciding if an argument is sound isn't part of the business of logic, except in certain special cases. Accordingly, in what follows we'll be interested only in determining if arguments are valid. Notice, however, that there are important differences at the practical level between valid and sound arguments. Most important, just knowing that an argument is valid doesn't tell you whether it has a true conclusion, since if it's valid but unsound it might have a false conclusion.

1.3.1 One Aspect of Validity: Deducibility

One way to explain what *follows from* means in our definition of valid argument is to say that it means *is deducible from:* in a valid argument, the conclusion is *deducible from* the premises. To explain what we mean by *deducible from* here, we will consider an example from a different area, namely mathematics. Suppose you were asked to check the following addition:

```
   269
   547
 + 994
 ─────
  1810
```

You would begin with the right-hand column of digits, saying (or thinking) "9 and 7 and 4 are 20; put down 0, carry 2; now, 2 and 6 and 4 and 9 are 21; put down 1, carry 2;" and so on. Now, it is important to see that what you are doing here is following some rules for manipulating symbols. You could very well have worked out the same mathematical problem with different symbols using different rules. For instance,

```
   CCLXIX
   DXLVII
 + CMXCIV
 ─────────
   MDCCCX
```

The rules for manipulating these Roman numerals are completely different from those for our Arabic numerals. Romans would begin, for instance, by canceling I's before X's or V's with I's in other places. They would use similar rules for X's and C's, and then they would simply write down all the symbols left as the answer, simplifying as needed by replacing five I's with a V, two V's with an X, etc. The point is that the rules you learned when you learned arithmetic in elementary school are actually rules for manipulating symbols: they permit you to *deduce* an answer (which is a symbol) from other symbols. As a matter of fact, you don't need to understand why these manipulations of these symbols work. We might compare them to an electronic calculator. You don't need to know anything about how the internal machinery of a calculator operates in order to use it. All you need to know is the rules for pushing its buttons. Likewise, all you need to know about mathematical symbols in order to use them to solve problems is the rules for manipulating them.

There are similar rules involved in arguments. Consider, for instance, this example.

> **Example 3:** If Jones has not left town, then she must not know the police are after her. Jones hasn't left town. Therefore she must not know the police are after her.

This is obviously a valid argument. We might explain why it is valid in this way. It has a certain *form*, namely,

> If A, then B.   A.   Therefore, B.

The letters "A" and "B" here are intended as placeholders for parts of the argument. (We will have more to say about the use of such letters later.) Thus, in Example 3, "A" and "B" are replaced by *Jones hasn't left town* and *she must not know the police are after her*, respectively.

You might appeal to this form to explain why this argument is valid. A justification might run something like this: "The premises of Example 3 have these forms: *If* A, *then* B; and A. From premises of those forms, a conclusion—the form B—does follow. Therefore, Example 3 is a valid argument." This justification makes an implicit appeal to a rule of a certain sort when it says that a certain form of conclusion follows from premises of certain forms. Since the process of passing from the premises of an argument to a conclusion is often called *inference*, we will use the term *rule of inference* for such a rule. We will have a good deal more to say about rules later on. Now we want to convey only something of what we mean by a rule of inference: it is a rule which states that a conclusion of a certain form is deducible from a set of premises having certain forms.

1.3.1.1 Deductions

Rules of inference in effect allow us to show how the conclusion of a valid argument follows from its premises. This is illustrated in the expanded form of Example 1. What that expanded form does is to show in a satisfactory way just how the conclusion of that argument follows from its premises. The process of expanding an argument in this way can be compared to the process of working out a mathematical calculation. Suppose that you ask someone what the product of 237 and 685 is and that person tells you it is 162,345. To check this out, you might work out the product as follows:

$$
\begin{array}{r}
237 \\
\times\ 685 \\
\hline
1185 \\
1896 \\
1422 \\
\hline
162,345
\end{array}
$$

This calculation includes the two numbers with which you started (237 and 685) and the number you obtain as the answer (162,345). However, it also includes all the intermediate steps used in obtaining that answer. Unless you are exceptionally good at multiplying in your head, you would need all these steps to get the answer. However, they are not simply a practical aid, for even if you got the answer in some other way (say by working it out on a calculator), the worked-out multiplication above shows clearly that 162,345 is indeed the correct answer. If your calculator gives another answer, it's not working properly.

The additional steps added to Example 1 serve the same sort of function: they show *how* the conclusion follows from the premises, and they do so in a convincing and certain way. We will call an argument which has been expanded in this way—by the addition of intermediate steps which show how the conclusion follows from the premises—a *deduction*. The notion of deducibility ultimately rests on the notion of a deduction. The conclusion of an argument is said to be *deducible from* the premises if *it is possible to construct a deduction of the conclusion from the premises*. We will have much more to say about deductions in Chapter 7.

1.3.2 Another Aspect of Validity: Entailment

There is a quite different way we might explain what *follows from* means in our definition of valid argument. Reconsider Example 2. Someone might say of it, "Even though the premises are not all true, nevertheless if they were all true together, then the conclusion would also have to be true. Obviously, if Wichita were the capital of Kansas, and if the other premise of the example were true (which in fact it is), then it would have to be true that Topeka isn't the capital of Kansas." The reasoning involved in this justification of the validity of Example 2 makes use of a different sort of connection between the premises and the conclusion of an argument, one which we shall call *entailment*. Briefly, the premises of an argument are said to *entail* the conclusion if *the conclusion must be true whenever the premises are all true*. Another way to put this would be to say that the premises of an argument entail the conclusion whenever it is impossible for the conclusion of that argument to be false when all its premises are true. With this concept of entailment, we can give another description of the relation between the premises and the conclusion of a valid argument: in a valid argument, the premises *entail* the conclusion.

1.3.3 Some Remarks on the Two Aspects of Validity

Why have we offered two different explanations of what it means for the conclusion of an argument to follow from its premises? The full answer to this question can come only with a comprehensive study of logic. We can, however, cite some of the reasons why validity must be studied under both these aspects. The first reason is that each of these notions— deducibility and entailment—seems naturally involved in our intuitive concepts of what arguments are valid. We sometimes appeal to certain sorts of rules or patterns of argumentation to justify our reasoning, and we also appeal to claims about the connection between the truth of the premises of an argument and the truth of its conclusion for the same purpose. However, we regard these not as two different properties of arguments, but rather as two aspects of the one property of validity. We tend to suppose that any argument whose conclusion is deducible from its premises is one whose conclusion is entailed by its premises and conversely. This conviction that deducibility and entailment are two sides of the same coin is not one that should go untested. One of our principal aims in the study of logic is to gain a deeper understanding of the relation between these two notions. Ideally, we would want not only to show that deducibility and entailment go hand in hand but also to explain why this is the case.

The notions of deducibility and entailment also differ in their applications to arguments in certain practical ways. In order to determine if the conclusion of an argument is deducible from the premises, we must try to produce a deduction. If we succeed, then we have shown that the argument is valid. However, if we fail, that may only mean that we haven't been sufficiently clever to construct an appropriate deduction. This suggests that the concept of deducibility may be more effective in showing why valid arguments are valid than in detecting invalid arguments. On the other hand, to determine if the premises of an argument entail the conclusion, we need to show that the conclusion cannot be false if all the premises are true. This might be quite difficult in certain sorts of cases. However, if we can think of even a single case in which the premises are all true and the conclusion is false, then we know that the argument is invalid. This suggests that the concept of entailment may be more effective in detecting invalid arguments than in showing which arguments are valid.

1.4

LANGUAGE, TRUTH, AND MEANING[1]

Our further study of logic will be largely an examination of the concept of validity, and we will approach that subject by investigating the relation between entailment and deducibility. In order to proceed with that, first we must investigate some related concepts. Since we are talking about arguments, which are composed of language, we will need to clarify a few points about what a *language* is. We have already mentioned the truth (and falsehood) of statements several times, especially in discussing entailment. Thus we need to investigate the concept of *truth*. These investigations will, in turn, lead us to the concept of *meaning*. Obviously, in this introduction we can offer only a few sketchy remarks about what are really three vastly complex subjects.

1.4.1 Language and Syntax

Let's begin with some remarks about what a language is. Actually, we aren't going to offer any definition of what an actual human language like English is. Instead, we want to consider some of what a language consists of and some of what is involved in our understanding of our own language. Now, people who speak a language can, most of the time, tell instantly whether something said by someone else is in the language they speak. What is it that we make use of when we do this? The first thing which might come to mind is *vocabulary*: people who speak English recognize English when they hear it because they recognize the English words of which it is composed. Obviously, this is part of the answer. But there is more. Imagine, for instance, that someone came up to you and said (with apparent conviction), "Between Thursday up I two possible or." That utterance is indeed a string of English words, but it's hardly an English sentence; it's simply nonsense. In addition to the vocabulary of a language, there are rules about putting the elements of that vocabulary together to make sentences, and "sentences" not formed according to those rules are not sentences of the language. We will give the name *rules of formation* to the rules that describe how sentences may be composed. Notice, incidentally, that we're not talking about rules set up by any sorts of grammatical authorities for the proper use of the language.

[1] The standpoint we take in this section depends on the work of a number of contemporary logicians and philosophers, most importantly the great Polish logician Alfred Tarski. The account of meaning in Section 1.4.3 is modeled after that given by a well-known American philosopher, Donald Davidson, in his paper "Truth and Meaning," *Synthèse* 17(1967), pp. 304–23.

Instead, we're talking about the rules that everyone who speaks a language must in some sense already know, even if unconsciously. Recent investigations in linguistics have suggested that the rules which people follow in speaking a language are enormously complicated. Nevertheless, anyone who can speak a language, even a young child, is able to speak in accordance with these rules.

The vocabulary and the rules of formation of a language determine what counts as a sentence in that language. *My brange has a broken glorb* is not an English sentence because it contains elements not in the vocabulary of English. *I went to but, nevertheless, I correctly that is* is not an English sentence since it does not follow the rules of formation of English. There is a certain sort of reaction we have when we hear a remark of either of these two types: we feel that somehow nothing has been said, that the remark is meaningless, that it would not make any sense to try to decide whether it was true or false or what to do in response to it. To some extent, the converse of this is also true: when we hear an utterance that consists of elements of the vocabulary of our language, put together in accordance with the rules of formation, at least we do not feel that what we have heard is nonsense of that former sort. There is, consequently, some connection between the vocabulary and the rules of formation of a language, on the one hand, and what is meaningful in that language, on the other. We will explore this further below, but for now we may at least note that anything which does not conform to the rules of formation and the vocabulary of a language is meaningless in the language.

For convenience, we will use the term *syntax* to mean the combination of vocabulary and rules of formation: the *syntax* of a language is the vocabulary of that language together with its rules of formation. The syntax of a language determines all the possible sentences in that language. The study of syntax is called *syntactics*.

1.4.2 Truth and Semantics

We have talked about truth in this book in only one context—the truth (or falsehood) of statements. It's important to remember that this is the only use of the term *true* which interests us in this text, even though there are many other uses for this word in ordinary speech. We also need to make it clear that we're not trying to explain what *true* means as if we didn't already know. After all, *true* is a perfectly ordinary word which anyone who speaks English understands and can use. We've already appealed to this ordinary understanding by defining a statement as a sentence which is true or false. What we want to do now is to deepen and build on this ordinary understanding so that we can bring out more clearly the connections of the concept of truth with other concepts of importance to us.

The sentence *There are no pink pine trees growing on the other side of the moon* is a correctly formed English sentence. You can tell this simply on the basis of the syntax of English. It's also a true sentence. However, the fact that it's true *does* depend on something other than purely syntactical matters: the reason that the sentence is true is that, as a matter of fact, there aren't any trees—pink, pine, or otherwise (or anything else for that matter)—growing on the other side of the moon. If the moon had turned out to be a different sort of place, the sentence might have been false. Thus, to tell whether a sentence is true, you must know about something other than the language itself. To put the matter simply, you must know something about what the world is like.

Any language that can be used has connections with the world, or reality, or things, or whatever sort of term you may prefer for what there is outside of language. These connections are what determine whether statements are true or false. A statement is true if it connects up with the way things are in the appropriate way—if it describes things as they are. On the other hand, a statement that doesn't link up with the world in the appropriate way is false: it doesn't describe things as they are. In order to tell whether a statement is true or false, we must be able to determine whether it has the proper relation with things. The rules describing how a language connects with, or refers to, the world are called the *semantics* of the language. (Note here that this use of the term *semantics*, which is customary among logicians, is not at all the same as its use in ordinary English: the two should not be confused.) With this term at our disposal, we can now say that *truth is a semantic concept*.

An illustration may help here. Consider a simple English statement like *There are six red apples in the basket*. If you hear this statement said by someone who's pointing at a basket, you might proceed to determine whether it is true in the following way. You examine the basket to see if there is anything in it. If you find that there is, you examine the contents of the basket to see whether they include any apples, and in particular any red ones, and more specifically six of those. After you have completed your investigation, you pronounce the statement *There are six red apples in the basket* true if and only if you found six things, each of them an apple and red, in that particular basket. What you are doing in this investigation is trying to determine whether certain conditions are satisfied, namely, those conditions under which the statement in question is true. Let us call these the *truth conditions* of the statement. Since, as we have said, truth is a semantic notion, these truth conditions will necessarily be semantic.

What we have said about truth here may seem to be excessively simpleminded. As a matter of fact, what we have said is very simple, but that doesn't mean that it's trivial or unimportant. In fact, the development of a formal study of semantics is one of the most important aspects of twentieth-century logic. Let's reiterate briefly the difference between semantics and syntax in order to make the distinction clear. *Syntax* is the *vocabulary and rules of formation of a language*, and syntax concerns only *the linguistic forms in isolation*. On the other hand, *semantics* is the *rules connecting the language with the world or reality*. Since truth necessarily involves reference to something outside the bare forms of the language itself, *truth is a semantic notion*.

1.4.3   Meaning

We can further clarify the connections between syntax and semantics and their relation to validity by investigating the concept of *meaning*. As with the concept of truth, we are concerned with meaning in a strictly limited sense: the meanings of *statements*. What we have in mind is something necessarily involved in the process of understanding a language. To understand a statement is to know what that statement means. Of course, we are accustomed to talk about the meanings of statements in ordinary discourse quite freely, and we tend to suppose that we know perfectly well the meanings of the sentences we use. However, some serious philosophical problems arise when we try to consider what sorts of things meanings might be. Are they things that somehow exist independently of language and those who use it? What sorts of things could those be? Do we want to suppose that meanings are somehow thoughts or ideas in the minds of people using language? In that case, we'll run into more difficulties. If you and I mean the same thing by a statement, do we have the same idea in our minds? What does "same idea" mean, when one idea is in my mind and another is in yours? In fact, what sort of thing is an idea anyway? The problem of the nature of meanings in this sense has caused considerable difficulty to philosophers for many years. We are not going to try to solve those difficulties here. Instead, we are going to suggest a way around them.

Instead of asking the question "What is the meaning of a statement?" we are going to ask a related question that will be easier for us to answer: What must you know in order to know what a statement means? Our answer to this question is this: in order to know what a statement means, you must know under what circumstances that statement would be true. In other words, recalling the discussion of the last section, *in order to know what a statement means, you must know its truth conditions*. Let's explain what we mean with an example.

Consider once again the sentence *There are six red apples in that basket*. Anyone who speaks English, of course, understands the meaning of that sentence. How could you describe *what* you understand, when you understand that sentence? We want to say that your explanation might go like this: "The speaker of this sentence would be claiming that the following state of affairs is the case: there are, in the basket indicated, six objects, each of which is red and each of which is an apple. If that state of affairs is in fact the case, then what the speaker is saying is true; otherwise, it is false." In this explanation, the meaning of the sentence is explained by describing what conditions must be satisfied in order for the sentence to be true. Now it may appear that this is a rather trivial account of meaning, since we seem to have explained the meaning of a sentence by just repeating the sentence in a sort of modified and elaborated version. But suppose that the speaker is French, and suppose that person said, "Il y a six pommes rouges dans ce panier-là." Not speaking French, you ask a friend, "What does that mean?" Your friend replies, "What was said is true if and only if there are six red apples in that basket." What your friend has done is to give you the truth conditions of the French sentence just uttered; but hasn't your friend also told you what it means?

We don't want to claim that the meanings of statements can be completely accounted for in terms of their truth conditions, although we also don't want to claim that this is not the case—we'd rather leave that question open. This much, however, seems fairly clear: in order to understand a statement, you must *at least* understand the truth conditions of that statement. This really amounts to saying that in order to understand a statement, you must understand what it is like for it to be true. We might compare the meaning of a statement to a picture of what things might be like. If the picture matches what things are really like, then the statement is true. Otherwise, it's false. Of course, this talk about pictures cannot be taken too literally, but the point is that understanding what a statement means necessarily involves knowing what it would be like for it to be true, or under what conditions it would be correct to call the statement true.

1.4.4 Meaning, Syntax, and Semantics

Our discussion of meanings indicates that they are tied up with the *semantics* of language: knowing the meaning of a statement is knowing what the world would have to be like for that statement to be true. In discussing syntax, we also noted that in order to be meaningful, a statement must conform to the syntax of a language. So far we have talked about syntax and semantics in isolation from each other, but they are *both* necessary to the working of a language.

We use language to talk about things. In order to apply language to things, we must have semantic rules for that application. We use syntactic rules to construct statements. If the language is to be of any use to us, the syntactic rules must be connected with semantic rules so that the statements will be associated with specific truth conditions. Thus a language can be said to consist of a syntax, which determines what the statements of the language are, and a semantics, which determines what those statements are to be interpreted to mean. The meaning of a statement is consequently a product of both the syntax and the semantics of its language.

Obviously, this is a very simplified account of language. Moreover, it says nothing about any use of language except the making of statements, and that's obviously not the only use of language. Nevertheless, it is an important beginning, and it will be enough for our study of logic.

1.4.5 Syntax, Semantics, and Validity

Now we will try to explain what all this discussion of language has to do with arguments. We said that there were two aspects of validity: deducibility and entailment. We can now say that *deducibility is a syntactic concept*, while *entailment is a semantic concept*. To determine whether the conclusion of an argument is deducible from the premises, we need rules of inference which tell us that certain statements can be deduced from others. These rules will be syntactic: they will refer only to the forms of sentences and not to their meanings. It would be quite possible for someone to make use of such rules without actually understanding a language at all. All that you would have to do is apply the rules to the linguistic forms. On the other hand, to determine whether the conclusion of an argument is entailed by its premises, we need to see whether the conclusion must be true whenever all the premises are. In order to do this, we need to understand the semantics of the language. Now if, as we have argued, the syntax and the semantics of a language are connected, it becomes evident why deducibility and entailment are two sides of the same coin, or at least why they ought to be. With the right relation between syntax and semantics, the conclusion of an argument would be deducible from its premises only if it were entailed by those premises.

This, finally, is what our study of logic is about. We want to determine what it is that makes arguments valid. We have analyzed validity into two components, deducibility and entailment, that reflect each other. We will study arguments from the perspectives of syntax and of semantics in turn, in order to understand better the nature of this relationship. The importance of this can be seen in plain terms in this way. An argument is supposed to be a justification for its conclusion. If the premises of the argument are granted, then the conclusion ought to follow. From our perspective, we can interpret this to mean that the truth of the premises of an argument ought to be sufficient to establish the truth of the conclusion. A valid argument is one in which the premises really are sufficient to do this, and consequently it is an argument that we can really rely on. A study of the semantics of a language would tell us which arguments are reliable in this sense—those whose premises entailed their conclusions. We could then determine rules of inference for producing reliable arguments. The situation is exactly like that of learning to work problems in arithmetic. You learn certain rules for the manipulation of symbols, and those rules are so constructed that they always give you the correct solutions to problems. You could, of course, get by without such rules: you could, for instance, add numbers just by counting on your fingers. However, it is enormously more convenient to have rules for manipulating symbols (try to add 269, 547, and 994 just by counting on your fingers), and the rules of inference are rather like that. As a matter of fact, the rules children learn for manipulating number symbols in simple arithmetic are always reliable, but in school you simply accept this on faith. In order to understand the nature of mathematics, you must learn why those rules always work. Similarly, our purpose in logic is not simply to give rules for argument that will always produce valid arguments but to explain why such rules work.

1.5
ARTIFICIAL LANGUAGES

In this introduction, we have been talking about natural human languages, mostly English. Ideally logic should try to account for arguments in natural languages, but there are obstacles to this. First, natural languages— by which we mean languages that people actually speak—are enormously complex. No linguist today would pretend to have a complete understanding of the syntactic or semantic rules of any natural language. We would also have great difficulty in determining what the rules of inference of English are, for a variety of reasons. There is no official list of them written down anywhere, and different investigators would have very different ideas about what, if anything, would be included on such a list. In view of all this, we will make use of an *artificial language.* The advantage of such an artificial language is that we can make all its syntax and semantics completely explicit. Consequently, we can study the relation between deducibility and entailment with greater clarity and precision.

It might seem that an investigation of the validity of "arguments" in an artificial language which can't be used to say anything in ordinary communication has little relevance to the study of arguments in natural language. However, our artificial language is designed to reflect certain fundamental structural aspects of natural languages. We are, in effect, studying arguments in abstract form—the skeletons of arguments, you might say. Obviously, we cannot pretend that such a study will tell the whole complicated story of how and why some arguments in natural languages are valid and others invalid. But we will be able to say many important things about the nature of our everyday arguments.

REVIEW EXERCISES FOR CHAPTER 1

1 Discuss and define the following terms as used in this chapter.
   (a) Argument   (f) Deducibility
   (b) Statement   (g) Entailment
   (c) Premise   (h) Logic
   (d) Conclusion   (i) Semantics
   (e) Valid argument   (j) Syntax

2 Discuss whether each of the following is a statement.
   ²*(a) Has it quit raining yet?
   (b) I wouldn't do that if I were you.
   *(c) If it's raining, close the door, please.
   (d) Oh!
   (e) That hurts.
   (f) Unless some means is found to deal with the problem of overpopulation, there will be worldwide famine in the twenty-first century.
   (g) The sum of 2 and 3 is 6.
   *(h) Colorless green ideas sleep furiously.
   (i) Have be thus middle Oregon not.
   *(j) 2 + 3 = 5.
   *(k) Saturday is in bed.

3 Can you understand what a statement means without knowing whether it's true or false?

---

² Throughout the text, asterisks indicate exercises for which answers appear in the back of the book.

chapter 2
Statements

2.1
STATEMENTS AND CONNECTING WORDS

Since arguments are composed of statements, our study of what makes
an argument valid naturally begins with a study of statements. As we
have said, by *statement* we mean a *sentence that is true or false*. If we
tried to study statements in this sense from all possible aspects, we would
soon be involved in some very complex linguistic investigations. However,
we don't need to examine all the properties of statements. Instead, it
turns out that certain comparatively simple notions will take us quite a
long way. One particularly important collection of properties of statements
depends largely on the ways in which statements can be combined to
make other statements. This chapter will be concerned with just these
relations among statements made up of other statements (in ways we'll
explain below) and with nothing else. Consequently, its subject matter
is what we call *statement logic*.

Let's begin by distinguishing between compound and atomic statements. A *compound statement* is a statement which contains one or more
constituent statements as parts. Examples of compound statements
containing only one statement are the following:

> It is false that the sun is shining.
> It is possible that John will attend the meeting.
> I am certain that nobody will get hurt.

The single constituent statements in each case are

> The sun is shining.
> John will attend the meeting.
> Nobody will get hurt.

Quite obviously these constituents are themselves statements because each is either true or false.

Many compound statements contain two constituent statements, such as the following:

> If the Kansas City Chiefs go to the Super Bowl, then everybody will be surprised.

Its constituent statements are

> The Kansas City Chiefs go to the Super Bowl.
> Everybody will be surprised.

Another compound statement containing two constituent statements is

> Almost everybody likes money even though it is the root of all evil.

The constituent statements are, of course,

> Almost everybody likes money.
> Money is the root of all evil.

Notice that *it* in the second constituent refers to *money* in the first constituent. In fleshing out the constituent statements comprising compound statements, it is often important to specify what the pronouns stand for.

Some compound statements contain as many as three constituent statements:

> John will attend the meeting if Mary does; otherwise, he will go home.

The constituent statements in this case are

> John will attend the meeting.
> Mary attends the meeting.
> John will go home.

Notice that *Mary does* is an abbreviated way of saying *Mary attends the meeting*. We shall have more to say about abbreviated constituent statements occurring in compound statements below. Notice also that *he* in the third constituent statement refers back to *John* in the first constituent statement.

Now, some compound statements can be compounds of compounds; in other words, they can contain constituent statements which are themselves compound statements. Take, for instance, the following:

I will not attend the picnic if either it rains or the temperature drops.

Its constituents are as follows:

I will not attend the picnic.
Either it rains or the temperature drops.

But notice that each of these constituent statements is compound. The first statement contains, as a constituent, the statement *I will attend the picnic*. The second statement, in turn, contains the two following constituent statements:

It rains.
The temperature drops.

A statement containing no constituent statements (except itself) is said to be *atomic*. We have already met with examples of atomic statements; they occurred as constituents in our previous examples of compound statements:

The sun is shining.
John will attend the meeting.
Nobody will get hurt.
The Kansas City Chiefs go to the Super Bowl.
Everybody will be surprised.
Almost everybody likes money.
Money is the root of all evil.
John will attend the meeting.
Mary attends the meeting.
John will go home.

In comparing atomic statements with compound ones, an important additional feature stands out. We notice that, unlike compound statements, atomic statements do not contain such words or phrases as *and*; *not*; *it is possible that*; *if . . . then*; *. . . if . . . , otherwise, . . . *; and so on. Such words or phrases which generate compound statements out of less complex statements are called *connecting words*. (If a group of several words functions as a single unit in operating on statements, we call the group a connecting word also.) In the following compound statements, the connecting words are italicized:

> *It is false that* the sun is shining.
> John will *not* attend the meeting.
> *If* the Kansas City Chiefs go to the Super Bowl, *then* everybody will be surprised.
> *Either* it rains *or* the temperature drops.
> Mary will attend the picnic *and* John will go home.
> I *doubt that* money is the root of all evil.

Notice that each of these connecting words is not itself a statement; it would be silly to ask whether *it is false that* or *if . . . then* were true or false. Their purpose is not to function as statements, but rather to *operate* on statements to create new statements. For example, the connecting word *it is false that* operates on the statement *The sun is shining* to create the new statement *It is false that the sun is shining*. In similar fashion, the connecting word *and* operates on the two statements *Mary will attend the picnic* and *John will go home* to create the new statement *Mary will attend the picnic, and John will go home*.

Sometimes connecting words, at first glance, appear to operate not on statements to create new statements but rather on the subjects of statements. Take, for instance, the following two statements:

> **1a** Tom and Mary will attend the picnic.
> **2a** Either Juan or George will substitute for the injured player.

In the first statement, it looks as though the connecting word *and* operates on the subjects *Tom* and *Mary* to create the compound subject *Tom and Mary*, but that's not the way we'll look at it. Instead, we'll say that the connecting word *and* operates on the two atomic statements *Tom will attend the picnic* and *Mary will attend the picnic* to create the following compound statement:

> **1b** Tom will attend the picnic *and* Mary will attend the picnic.

From the point of view of logic, we say that statement (1a) is a disguised form of statement (1b) and that (1b) is *more precisely what (1a) is all about*. Our justification for saying this, as we'll see subsequently, is that (1b) comes closer to revealing the *logical form* of statement (1a). The concept of logical form is one we haven't discussed yet in this book.

In fact, this isn't a very easy concept to clarify. However, it will be crucial to our study of validity, and so we need to say a little about it here.

Let's begin by noting one advantage that (1b) has over (1a). We have just shown how (1a) can be said to be composed of the two statements *Tom will attend the picnic* and *Mary will attend the picnic*. Notice that neither of those statements actually appears in (1a) in so many words. On the other hand, (1b) does explicitly present these two statements—the actual words *Tom will attend the picnic* and *Mary will attend the picnic*. In other words, in the terminology of Chapter 1, the connection between (1b) and these two statements is an obvious *syntactic* connection. Also there is obviously a connection between the meanings of *Tom will attend the picnic* and *Mary will attend the picnic* and the meaning of (1b). Therefore, there is a *semantic* connection between (1b) and these statements. Moreover, if, as we noted, (1b) and (1a) have the same meaning, then the same semantic connection will hold between the two atomic statements here and (1a). However, since the *syntactic connections* of the two statements with (1b) are obvious and easy to see, there is a way in which (1b) shows *what (1a) is all about* more clearly and explicitly.

Again, the connecting word *either . . . or* in statement (2a) appears to operate on the subjects *Juan* and *George*, creating the compound subject *either Juan or George*. However, as in the previous case, we prefer to view the connecting word *either . . . or* as operating on the two atomic statements *Juan will substitute for the injured player* and *George will substitute for the injured player*, generating this compound statement:

2b Either Juan will substitute for the injured player or George will substitute for the injured player.

As these examples show, the constituents of compound statements are not always explicitly stated in ordinary language. This is even more apparent in our next example:

3a Either Paul is a good student or Tom is.

A first glance might suggest that the connecting word *either . . . or* is operating on the two atomic statements *Paul is a good student* and *Tom is* in generating the above compound statement. However, a moment's reflection will show you this can't be right. The statement *Tom is* would mean the same as *Tom exists*. So if we treated it as a component of (3a), then (3a) would say roughly the same thing as

3b Either Paul is a good student or Tom exists.

But obviously that isn't what (3a) means. It's fairly clear that in (3a) *Tom is* is short for *Tom is a good student*. Therefore, it's more appropriate to see (3a) as a compound of the atomic statements *Paul is a good student* and *Tom is a good student*.

EXERCISE 2.1

For each of the following statements, (a) determine whether it is atomic or compound. If it is compound, identify (b) the constituent statement(s) and (c) the connecting words.

  *1   It is not the case that helium is heavier than air.
   2   I doubt that manufactured diamonds are as hard as natural ones.
   3   Tom and Jerry are interesting characters.
  *4   I don't like pickles and ice cream.
   5   Margaret will not leave the party early.
   6   The leaves are turning red.
  *7   I will attend neither the party nor the picnic.
   8   Either there are not enough books in the library or José is a fast reader.
   9   An apple a day keeps the doctor away.
 *10   I will attend the picnic only if Mary does.
  11   Anger is a very explosive emotion.
  12   I wonder whether the Kansas City Chiefs will win their next game.
 *13   If Beethoven was a great composer, then so was Mozart.
  14   It will either rain or snow.
  15   Money isn't the root of all evil.

2.2
TRUTH FUNCTIONS

Now we want to restrict our attention to a certain class of compound statements, namely those we call truth functions. We say that a compound statement is a *truth function* of its constituent statements if its *truth value* (i.e., truth or falsehood) is uniquely determined under all possible circumstances by the truth values of its constituent statements. Consider, for example, the following compound statement:

    It is false that the sun is shining.

Now, this statement would be false if its constituent statement *The sun is shining* were true; and it would be true if its constituent statement were false. Notice that the truth value of the entire compound is uniquely determined under all possible circumstances by the truth value of the constituent statement. In this case, there are only two possible circumstances:

1 The statement *The sun is shining* is false.
2 The statement *The sun is shining* is true.

Under circumstance (1), *It is false that the sun is shining* is true. Under circumstance (2), *It is false that the sun is shining* is false. Since there are two and only two possible truth values for the constituent statement, it is clear that the truth value of the compound statement *It is false that the sun is shining* is uniquely determined under *all* possible circumstances. Also notice that to find out the truth value of the compound, you need to know only the truth value of the constituent statement.

Let's look at another example:

Mary will attend the picnic and John will go home.

It's not difficult to see that there are four possible circumstances in this case:

1 The statement *Mary will attend the picnic* is true and the statement *John will go home* is true.
2 The statement *Mary will attend the picnic* is true and the statement *John will go home* is false.
3 The statement *Mary will attend the picnic* is false and the statement *John will go home* is true.
4 The statement *Mary will attend the picnic* is false and the statement *John will go home* is false.

In view of the meaning of the compound statement, we recognize that it will be true if, and only if, both constituent statements are true; otherwise, it will be false. This means that the compound statement *Mary will attend the picnic and John will go home* will be true under circumstance (1) and false under circumstances (2), (3), and (4). But notice that each circumstance determines a unique truth value for the compound. And since there are four and only four possible ways for the two constituent statements to take on truth values, the original compound statement has a unique truth value under all possible circumstances. Hence, it, too, is a truth function of its constituents.

Now, not all compound statements are truth functions. Consider the following statement:

Jim doubts that money is the root of all evil.

There is only one component statement in this compound and hence only two possible circumstances:

1 The statement *Money is the root of all evil* is true.
2 The statement *Money is the root of all evil* is false.

In this case, it is easy to see that neither circumstance determines a unique truth value for the compound; whether or not money is the root of all evil, Jim might or might not doubt it. Knowing the truth value of *Money is the root of all evil* tells us very little about the truth value of *Jim doubts that money is the root of all evil*. What we need to know is something about Jim's doubts; that can't be gained by means of our natural intuitions concerning language use. In any event, we see that the truth value of *Jim doubts that money is the root of all evil* is not uniquely determined under all possible circumstances.

Let's look at another statement:

Paul knows that Maria loves him.

Here again there are two possibilities for the constituent statement of this compound:

1 The statement *Maria loves Paul* is false.
2 The statement *Maria loves Paul* is true.

Under the first circumstance, the truth value of *Paul knows that Maria loves him* is uniquely determined—it must be false. After all, if Maria does not in fact love Paul, then Paul cannot *know* that she does love him. However, under the second circumstance, where the constituent is true, the truth value of the compound is not uniquely determined. If, in fact, Maria does love Paul, he might know it or he might not. In order to determine the truth value of *Paul knows that Maria loves him*, we would have to know something about Paul's knowledge—and so we need to know more than just the meaning of the sentence plus the truth values of its constituents. As we will say, we need to appeal to *extralinguistic considerations* (considerations outside of language). This example, then, is a case where the truth value of the compound sometimes does and sometimes does not depend on the truth values of its constituents. However, since the truth value of the compound is not uniquely determined under *all* possible circumstances, it is not a truth function.

Let's now consider a compound composed of two constituent statements:

Life is absurd because people are alienated from themselves.

The two constituents are, of course, *Life is absurd* and *People are alienated from themselves*. Now this compound would undoubtedly be false if both its constituents were false. Hence there exists at least one circumstance under which the truth value for the compound is uniquely determined by the truth values of its constituents. However, if both constituents were true, the compound could be either true or false. So its truth value is not *uniquely* determined. Even if it were the case both that life is absurd and that people are alienated from themselves, it might or might not be true that life is absurd *because* people are alienated from themselves. The connecting word *because*, in this case, appears to express a *causal* relationship, and the knowledge of such relationships involves extralinguistic considerations.

We'll say that a *connecting word* is *truth-functional* when any compound statement composed by it is a truth function. When a connecting word is not truth-functional, we'll call it *intensional*. Thus, *it is false that* and *and* are usually truth-functional, whereas . . . *doubts that*, . . . *knows that*, and *because* are intensional. We also call statements formed with intensional connecting words *intensional compounds*. The determination of whether a connecting word is truth-functional will generally have to rely upon our intuitive understanding of the meaning of language.

EXERCISE 2.2

Determine whether the following compound statements are truth functions of their constituents.

*1 Plato believed that virtue is its own reward.
 2 It is not the case that Venus has any oxygen in its atmosphere.
*3 Both John and Jim love music.
 4 I will not visit Mary tomorrow.
*5 Jim will turn off the lights before going to bed.
 6 I think that Descartes was a rationalist.
*7 Either Descartes was a rationalist or he was an empiricist.
 8 I wonder whether the next President of the United States will be a Democrat.
*9 It is very likely that the earth was once visited by astronauts from outer space.
10 Roses are red and violets are blue.

2.3
STATEMENT CONSTANTS AND SYMBOLIC ABBREVIATIONS

In order to reveal the logical forms of compound statements clearly, we will study how they are built up from atomic statements and connecting words. To help do this, we'll introduce the notion of a statement constant. Essentially, a *statement constant* is an abbreviation for a statement. By replacing the atomic statements in a group of statements with statement constants, we'll get a clearer picture of the structures of those statements. We'll also get the additional benefit that the resulting *symbolic abbreviations*, as we'll call them, are shorter. It will become clearer what symbolic abbreviations are and how statement constants work in them as we explain the details of the process.

We will use capital letters for statement constants. Thus we can symbolically abbreviate the following statement:

It is false that the sun is shining.

as

It is false that S.

where "S" abbreviates the statement *The sun is shining*. Similarly, we can symbolically abbreviate

Mary will attend the picnic and Juan will go home.

as

M and J.

where "M" abbreviates the statement *Mary will attend the picnic* and "J" abbreviates the statement *Juan will go home*.

Notice that statement constants reveal, in precise fashion, how compound statements are built up from connecting words and atomic statements. Thus, in the above example, we get a clear view of the fact that the connecting word *and* operates on the two atomic statements *Mary will attend the picnic* and *Juan will go home* in generating the compound.

In any particular context, of course, we will have to choose different capital letters to abbreviate different atomic statements. Likewise, we always use the same letter for a given atomic statement if it's repeated in a given context. For example, consider the following group of statements:

1 Either Mary will attend the picnic or Juan will go home.
2 Juan will go home although the sun is shining.
3 Juan will go home.

Now, in this group of statements, there are three different atomic statements, so we use three different statement constants in abbreviating them. However, it is also necessary to use the same constant each time a given statement is repeated. Thus we obtain the following symbolic abbreviations where "M" abbreviates *Mary will attend the picnic*, "J" abbreviates *Juan will go home*, and "S" abbreviates *The sun is shining:*

1 Either M or J.
2 J although S.
3 J.

Of course, we will not always use the letters "M," "J," and "S" to abbreviate the statements *Mary will attend the picnic, Juan will go home,* and *The sun is shining,* respectively. Such invariability extends only throughout a given context. In a different context, these letters could be used to abbreviate completely different statements; but of course they would remain constant throughout that context (hence the name *statement constant*).

It should now be clear that a *symbolic abbreviation* is what results when the atomic statements occurring in a compound statement are uniformly abbreviated by statement constants. It's arbitrary which capital letters are used for abbreviating atomic statements, although it's helpful for the memory to pick out the first letter of some key word in the statement being abbreviated.

2.3.1 Monadic and Dyadic Connecting Words

A particular connecting word normally joins a fixed number of statements. Most, but certainly not all, connecting words occurring in ordinary language are either monadic or dyadic. A *monadic* connecting word operates on only *one* statement at a time. Thus the connecting words occurring in these compounds are monadic:

1a *It is not the case that* the sun is shining.
2a Mary will *not* attend the picnic.
3a *I believe that* Juan will go home.

Now, in symbolically abbreviating compounds containing monadic connecting words, we'll adopt the convention of always placing the monadic connecting word directly *in front of* (to the left of) the symbolization used to abbreviate the statement it operates on, whether it occurs in front of the original unabbreviated statement or not. Consequently, we symbolically abbreviate the above statements in the following manner:

1b It is not the case that S.
2b Not M.
3b I believe that J.

Notice that in statement (2a) the connecting word *not* occurs *within* the atomic statement it operates on; nevertheless, in symbolically abbreviating it, we place the connecting word in front of the statement constant employed. Thus, it's not correct to symbolically abbreviate (2a) as M *not*.

A *dyadic* connecting word operates on *two* statements at a time. Dyadic connecting words are employed in the following compound statements:

4a   Mary will attend the picnic *and* Juan will go home.
5a   *Although* Juan will go home, Mary will attend the picnic.
6a   *Unless* the sun is shining, Juan will go home.

We will also adopt the convention of always placing dyadic connecting words *between* the symbolizations used to abbreviate the statements they operate on, whether they occur between the original unabbreviated statements or not. Now, since the connecting word in (4a) already is between the two constituent statements, we can symbolically abbreviate it in a straightforward way:

4b   M and J.

In (5a) and (6a), however, the connecting words occur at the beginnings of the compounds. But, quite obviously, they could be rewritten, without changing what they mean, in the following fashion:

5b   Mary will attend the picnic *although* Juan will go home.
6b   Juan will go home *unless* the sun is shining.

Symbolically abbreviating them is now straightforward:

5c   M although J.
6c   J unless S.

Often it is quite appropriate to use the same statement constant to abbreviate two different statements, so long as both statements have the same sense. Consider, for example, the following two statements:

7a   Plato taught Aristotle.
7b   Aristotle was taught by Plato.

In most contexts, it would be permissible to symbolically abbreviate these two statements with the same statement constant. From a purely syntactic point of view, they are different statements. However, we could use either statement for conveying the *same information*; consequently, the statements are, for all practical purposes, the same.

There is another important restriction we must place on our symbolic abbreviations in view of the system of logic we will develop. Our system of logic will deal exclusively with truth functions. Consequently, we will not be able to investigate the logical forms of intensional compounds. Therefore, we will usually *treat all intensional compounds as atomic statements*. Thus, instead of symbolically abbreviating (3) above as *I believe that J*, we will agree to regard it as atomic and abbreviate it as

3c   B.

EXERCISE 2.3.1

Symbolically abbreviate the following statements.

*1   Even though Leibniz was a rationalist, he was a great philosopher.
 2   Both Descartes and Spinoza were rationalists.
*3   If John Locke was an empiricist, then so was David Hume.
 4   If and only if life is absurd are people alienated from themselves.
*5   Either I will attend the picnic or Mary will.
 6   Plato was a remarkable philosopher.
*7   Arthur loves cats, but Otto hates them.
 8   I will not do my logic exercises.
*9   Unless Leif Ericson discovered America, Columbus did.
10   Tom can attend the party only if he is a member of the club.

2.4
STATEMENT VARIABLES, CONNECTIVES, AND STATEMENT FORMS

Consider the following two compound statements:

1a   Cats are felines and apes are simians.
2a   Physics is a natural science and zoology is a biological science.

Obviously, these two statements are different. However, if we symbolically abbreviate them, we see that they share a common feature:

1b   C and A.
2b   P and Z.

What these two statements have in common is that they both have the following structure:

3   ———— and ————

Now, (1a) and (2a) are statements, (1b) and (2b) are symbolically abbreviated statements, but (3) is not a statement at all. In fact, (3) obviously lacks content; all it does is show the structure or form of statements (1a) and (2a). Consequently, we might call (3) a *statement form*. As the following sections will make clear, our real interest in studying statement logic will be to see the connections among different statement forms, not just actual statements. There are two reasons for this. First, since they have no content, statement forms are, in a way, more general: one statement form can stand for an infinite number of statements. Second, we can see much more clearly the relations among statements if we analyze them into statement forms. However, indicating the form of a statement by means of blanks isn't an easy procedure to use. Aside from the complications involved with keeping track of what goes where, there are more difficult problems involved if we keep ordinary-language connecting words in our statement forms. Therefore, we'll develop an artificial language that consists of *nothing but* statement forms. Having done that, we can proceed to examine statement forms in the abstract, as you might call it. We will introduce this symbolic language in an informal manner; in Chapter 5 we'll reintroduce it in more rigorous fashion.

We call this symbolic language that we are going to construct *Symbolic Language* S. This language is merely a set of symbols. Incidentally, the English language could also be viewed as a set of symbols. Fortunately, Symbolic Language S is a far less complicated language than English. It is composed of only three kinds of symbols: *statement variables*, *connectives*, and *punctuation marks*.

Statement variables are used in the same way that we used blanks to display the logical forms of statements. We'll use the lowercase letters p, q, r, s, t, . . ., and so on for statement variables. We imagine that we have an infinite stock of such symbols. It is important to understand that statement variables are not abbreviations for statements, as symbolic abbreviations are. Symbolic abbreviations are merely notational expedients for writing English statements in shorthand; statement variables, however, are totally devoid of content.

To produce statement forms in S, we need some additional symbols which function analogously to the way connecting words do in English. This is where connectives come in. A connecting word is a word or phrase which operates on statements to create new statements; analogously, then, a *connective* is a symbol which operates on statement forms to create new statement forms. Notice, incidentally, that whereas statements and connecting words belong to English, statement variables and connectives belong to S. Unlike the English language, which has an enormous number of connecting words, S has only five connectives. Of course, this suggests that S has many limitations that English does not have—and indeed it does.

The connectives in S are the following: $\sim$, $\wedge$, $\vee$, $\supset$, and $\equiv$. The first symbol is called the *tilde*; the second, the *inverted wedge*; the third, the *wedge*; the fourth, the *horseshoe*; and the fifth, the *triple bar*. These connectives will be used to symbolize connecting words. Actually, they don't precisely symbolize connecting words. S is, in fact, an artificial language with its own rules; it is not some sort of abstract shorthand for English. When we symbolize, what we're really doing is a sort of translating, although since S is purely formal, everything we translate will lose something (usually a great deal) in the translation. We're going to define the connectives of S in such a way that they correspond more or less to certain English connecting words. Exactly what this correspondence comes to, will be explained throughout the rest of this chapter. The translation procedure can be broken down into two main steps:

Step 1 *Symbolically abbreviate* the statement.
Step 2 Translate the symbolic abbreviation into S (we call this *formalization*).

Step 2 involves two different operations. First, we replace statement constants with statement variables. Next, we replace connecting words with connectives. In order to make this procedure clearer, we'll often make use of some hybrid expressions we call *quasi-statement forms:* these are what you get if you replace the statement constants in a symbolic abbreviation with statement variables. We call them hybrids since they don't really belong to either S or natural language, and we will use them only as steps in formalization. To see what we mean by a quasi-statement form, consider the statement

Mares eat oats and little lambs eat ivy.

We can symbolically abbreviate it as

M and L.

Now, in order to formalize, we'll first replace the statement constants with statement variables, which gives us the *quasi-statement form*

p and q.

To turn this into a statement form, we need to replace the connecting word *and* with a connective. As we'll see later, the inverted wedge is often useful for formalizing *and*. So our quasi-statement form is fully formalized as

$p \wedge q$

To review, the steps will be as follows:

Step 1 *Symbolically abbreviate* the statement.
Step 2 *Formalize* the symbolic abbreviation.

    a Assign a statement variable to each statement constant (this yields a quasi-statement form).
    b Assign a connective to each connecting word (this yields the final statement form).

Notice that our example shows something about the connection between a statement and its formalization in S. If we took any other statement that consisted of two atomic statements joined by *and*, for instance,

Dogs eat meat and cows eat grass.

and then symbolically abbreviated it, in this case perhaps as

D and C.

we'd arrive at the same statement form as formalization. We can now explain a little more of what we mean by *logical form*. Statements which can be formalized in S with the same statement form have the *same logical form with respect to statement logic*. For instance, our two examples above have the same logical form, since each is formalized as $p \wedge q$. We can generalize this to give a definition of logical form: from the standpoint of statement logic, the *logical form* of a statement is its formalization in S.

The third group of symbols of S are the *punctuation marks*. The symbols of this group are (,), [,], {, and }. We refer to these symbols, respectively, as left and right *parentheses*, left and right *brackets*, and left and right *braces*. Their purpose is to remove the ambiguity that the combination of statement variables and connectives of S might otherwise have. Consider, for example, the following string of symbols:

$p \wedge q \vee r$

This is intrinsically ambiguous. However, punctuation marks can resolve the confusion. Thus, we could group them as

$(p \wedge q) \vee r$

or as

$p \wedge (q \vee r)$

This resembles the use of such marks in arithmetic to accomplish the same purpose, for example, in distinguishing

$(2 + 3) \times 5$

from

$2 + (3 \times 5)$

Before we proceed to the details of formalizing, let's take note of the role of S in evaluating arguments. Arguments are the sorts of things which occur in natural language. Now, since arguments play a major role in those areas of life where rationality is important, we often need to evaluate them. However, this requires standards or criteria. One of the purposes of logic is to develop these criteria. One way—and perhaps the best way—to develop these standards is to construct artificial languages like S which are easier to deal with because of their simple and orderly nature. By viewing the statements occurring in natural language as instances of the statement forms in S, we can use S in determining the validity of arguments in natural language. Consequently, *logical form* is an abstract feature of natural language resulting from our viewing certain statements, for certain purposes, as instances of statement forms occurring in S.

2.4.1 The Meanings of Connecting Words

We said earlier that we would define the connectives of S so that to some extent they would correspond to certain connecting words in ordinary language. Now we need to explain how that can be accomplished. To define something, we need to give its meaning, and so we have to assign meanings to our connectives that correspond to the meanings of various English connecting words. In order to do that, first we have to discuss the meanings of connecting words in an ordinary language.

Let's recall briefly what we said about meaning in Chapter 1. We said that to give an account of the meaning of a statement, it is necessary at least to give an account of the conditions under which the statement is true. This gave us some account of the meaning of a statement. At the moment, we're concerned with the meanings of *connecting words*, which aren't statements and which therefore aren't true or false. How could we extend our account of meaning to individual words?

Let's first present a bad theory of the meanings of words, just to get it out of the way. It's tempting to think that the meaning of a word must be some sort of thing that the word refers to or names. For instance, if someone asked you what *dog* means, you might answer by pointing to a dog and saying "It means that." However, if you think about it, you'll realize that you don't exactly want to say that the dog you are pointing to is the meaning of *dog*. After all, there are other dogs. Perhaps you meant to say that *dog* means an animal *like* the one you pointed to. But *how* like it? Suppose the person who asked you what *dog* means sees a cat and says, "There's another dog." You'd want to explain, "No, *dog* doesn't mean just any small, furry four-legged creature, only certain ones." Now, if you went on to explain which ones, you'd find yourself giving some sort of instructions explaining under what circumstances it's correct to call an animal a dog. In other words, you'd give a semantic account of the truth conditions of *That's a dog*.

You might look at this in a more general way. In explaining the meaning of *dog*, as we have sketched it here, you'd have to explain how the word *dog* affects the truth conditions of a statement in which it occurs. Of course, in the case of a noun like *dog*, that account will just be some sort of description of the things to which that word can be applied correctly. So it's not all *that* misleading to say that you give the meaning of the word by pointing to some things. However, as a general account of the meanings of words, this won't do at all. It breaks down obviously in the case of connecting words: what do you point to if you want to explain the meaning of *and?* Nevertheless, connecting words obviously are meaningful, even though it's nonsense to imagine pointing to what they mean. Consequently, we'll try to explain their meanings by looking at how they affect the truth conditions of statements containing them.

Let's restrict our attention to the connecting words we'll be concerned with in this chapter: truth-functional connecting words. If you remember, we defined a truth-functional connecting word as one that combined statements into a statement which is a truth function of the original statements. That, in turn, means that the compound statement depends for its truth value only on the truth values of the constituent statements. Of course, we weren't being completely explicit in that last statement. Actually, the truth value of a compound statement depends on *two* considerations: the truth values of its constituents *and* the connecting word that combines them.

Here's what we mean. Take the statements *Yvette speaks German* and *Hans speaks French*. We can combine these atomic statements with truth-functional connecting words. Two such connecting words are *or* and *and*. So, let's combine these two statements using each of these connecting words:

1 Yvette speaks German or Hans speaks French.
2 Yvette speaks German and Hans speaks French.

It's fairly apparent that (1) and (2) are both truth functions of the two atomic statements *Yvette speaks German* and *Hans speaks French*: all you need to know in order to tell whether (1) or (2) is true is whether Yvette speaks German and whether Hans speaks French. However, it's equally obvious that (1) and (2) have different meanings. Let's restate that in terms of our account of meaning: (1) and (2) have different truth conditions. In other words, there exist circumstances under which one of them would be true and the other false. For example, suppose that Yvette does speak German but Hans doesn't speak French. Then, as you can see, (1) would be true and (2) would be false.

Let's briefly review the situation here. We have two statements—(1) and (2)—each of which is composed from the same atomic statements. These two statements are both truth functions of those atomic statements. However, (1) and (2) don't have the same meaning. Since the only thing different about them is the connecting words they contain, obviously the difference in meaning must come from those connecting words. Finally, since we can discuss differences in meaning in terms of differences in truth conditions, we can say that the difference between these two statements is the difference between the *way* their truth values depend on the truth values of their constituents. Now, the connecting words *or* and *and* have precisely this function: they determine the ways that (1) and (2) depend for their truth values on the truth values of their constituents. Consequently, the contribution to the meaning of the compound statement which is made by the connecting word is this: a truth-functional connecting word determines *the way in which* the truth value of any compound statement containing it depends on the truth values of its constituent statements.

We can make this clearer with an example. In Section 2.2, we discussed the truth-functional connecting word *and*. Let's see how this word works in example (2) above. The statement

    2   Yvette speaks German and Hans speaks French.

is a compound of the two atomic statements *Yvette speaks German* and *Hans speaks French*. Since this statement has two atomic constituents, there are four possible combinations of truth values for these constituents, as indicated in the following table:

Yvette speaks German	Hans speaks French
true	true
true	false
false	true
false	false

Now, let's complete the table by adding a third column that gives the truth value of (2) under each of these circumstances:

Yvette speaks German	Hans speaks French	Yvette speaks German and Hans speaks French
true	true	true
true	false	false
false	true	false
false	false	false

This table shows the relationship between three statements: statement (2) and its two atomic constituents. However, we could also make up a similar table for *any other* compound statement consisting of two atomic statements joined by the word *and*. In fact, our table doesn't say anything about the meanings of the atomic statements over the first two columns. All it says is that the compound statement over the third column is true if both of the constituents (whatever they may be) are true, and it is false otherwise.

Suppose, now, that we symbolically abbreviated (2) as Y *and* H and write our table as follows:

Y	H	Y and H
true	true	true
true	false	false
false	true	false
false	false	false

If we understand Y and H as abbreviations of the two constituents of (2), then this is a sort of abbreviation of the full table above. However, we could use Y and H to abbreviate *anything we wished*. That means we could get our second table from *any* statement containing a truth-functional *and*. In that case, what does the table really show? It shows the *meaning* of the word *and*. We could construct a similar table for any truth-functional connecting word, and that table would give its meaning. Since we'll make considerable use of tables like this, we'll need a name for them: we will call them *truth tables*.

2.4.2 The Meanings of Connectives in S

We could proceed to study all the truth-functional connecting words in English by developing truth tables for them. Unfortunately, most connecting words in natural languages are more complex in their meaning than that. It turns out that a great many of them are not simply truth-functional, although part of their meaning is. Moreover, many of them (including *and*) are truth-functional on some occasions and not on others. We'll make things easier for ourselves here by abandoning the complexities of natural language in favor of our simple and well-behaved artificial language S. However, since we'll want to use S for the purpose of formalizing natural-language arguments, we'll define its connectives so that they correspond to certain truth-functional connecting words in English. The major difference between these definitions and any attempted definitions of natural-language connecting words is that in S a connective always has precisely the meaning we assign to it, whereas in a natural language the same connecting word may have slightly (or even not so slightly) different meanings on different occasions.

It may sound a little odd to talk about giving meanings to symbols in an artificial language. Actually, it *is* just a bit odd: it's important that we make clear just what we have in mind here, for a number of misunderstandings are possible. One thing we don't want to suggest is that we're going to define the connectives by giving English words that *mean the same thing*. Even though we'll *translate* certain English connecting words with certain connectives, still we recognize that the truth-functional definitions of the connectives don't always capture the full meanings of the English words. Beyond that, a connective is a symbol in an artificial language that doesn't have any role outside its limited function within that language. Consequently, you shouldn't get the idea that somehow the connectives of S are better than or superior to English connecting words or that they give the "real" meanings of those words. They are, in fact, simpler and more orderly than natural-language connecting words, but they're not *better* except in the sense that they are easier to study.

Our method of giving meaning to the connectives in S is simple: we *define* each connective by *assigning a truth table to it*. The five truth tables are as follows:

Tilde			Wedge				Inverted Wedge		
p	$\sim p$		p	q	$p \vee q$		p	q	$p \wedge q$
T	F		T	T	T		T	T	T
F	T		T	F	T		T	F	F
			F	T	T		F	T	F
			F	F	F		F	F	F

Horseshoe			Triple Bar		
p	q	$p \supset q$	p	q	$p \equiv q$
T	T	T	T	T	T
T	F	F	T	F	F
F	T	T	F	T	F
F	F	T	F	F	T

In these tables, T and F are used as abbreviations of *true* and *false*. The significance of these tables will become apparent as we discuss each connective in the sections that follow.

Let's return now to the procedure for translating a statement into a statement form of S. If the statement in question is atomic, it gets formalized as a single statement variable. Therefore, recalling our definition of the logical form of a statement as its formalization in S, *all atomic statements have the same logical form*. Obviously, this means that, as far as our system of logic is concerned, *The sun rises in the east and 7 is the square root of 49* are of the same form: either could be formalized as *p*. Consequently, we don't pay any attention to the difference in meaning between these two statements. The reason is that S is designed as a language for statement logic, and no aspect of the meaning of a statement is important to statement logic except its truth value. In effect, the statement variables of S are like statements which have lost everything but the barest minimum of significance: all that they have is truth values.

Since, therefore, all that matters about atomic statements for truth-functional logic is their truth values, we'll ignore the rest. We'll assign truth values to our statement forms solely on the basis of assignments of truth values to their constituent statement variables and assignments of truth tables to the connectives. In Chapter 6, we'll be more precise about what this procedure amounts to and what its purpose is.

In the next five sections, we will explain the truth table for each connective. We will also discuss the formalization of English connecting words with connectives of S. In these formalizations, it is important to remember that we are producing approximations at best. Most (though not all) connecting words in ordinary language have more than just a truth-functional meaning, and we won't be able to capture the intensional components of any connecting words in our limited logic.

2.4.2.1 Negation: The Tilde

The simplest truth table defines the tilde, the only monadic connective of S:

p	$\sim p$
T	F
F	T

Here is what this table means: If a statement form is assigned the value *true*, then the same statement form with a $\sim$ in front of it is assigned the value *false*; and if a statement form is assigned the value *false*, then the same statement form with a $\sim$ in front of it is assigned the value *true*. It's important to realize that we are, in effect, using the statement variable *p* here as a representative of *any* statement form whatever. For example, we could substitute something complicated like $[q \lor (r \land s)] \supset t$ for *p* in the table and get the following table:

$[q \lor (r \land s)] \supset t$	$\sim\{[q \lor (r \land s)] \supset t\}$
T	F
F	T

Our truth table, then, defines the meaning of ~ no matter where it occurs.

Let's see now how this truth table allows us to translate English connecting words into connectives of S. What the tilde does is invert or reverse the truth value of its constituent. Any English connecting word that takes a single constituent statement and produces a new statement which has the opposite truth value to the original statement will then have roughly the same *meaning* as the tilde. When a compound statement is derived from another statement by means of such a connecting word, we call it a *negation*.

Connecting words behaving in this way in English include *not*, *it is false that*, *it is not the case that*, and others. We say that such connecting words *express negation*, and therefore we symbolize them with the tilde. Actually, negations are the most obvious truth functions in natural language.

Consider the following compound statement:

Peter is not Melissa's brother.

Using P as an abbreviation for *Peter is Melissa's brother*, we symbolically abbreviate the above statement as

Not P.

Formalizing it by putting p for P and ~ for *not* yields the following statement form:

$\sim p$

Now consider this statement:

It is not the case that it is raining.

Symbolically abbreviating it yields

It is not the case that R.

Formalizing it gives us

$\sim p$

Similarly, it is easy to see that each of the following statements

Jim wo*n't* attend the picnic.

Mary does*n't* love Tom.

It isn't true that I attended the picnic.

Julio *never* drinks alcoholic beverages.

is formalized as ~*p* since each of these compound statements is the negation of an atomic statement.

2.4.2.2 Conjunction: The Inverted Wedge

The truth-functional definition for the inverted wedge—a dyadic connective—is given by the following truth table:

p	q	$p \wedge q$
T	T	T
T	F	F
F	T	F
F	F	F

Perhaps the best example of a connecting word that approximates the definition of the inverted wedge is *and*. In Section 2.4.1, we saw that the sentence *Yvette speaks German and Hans speaks French* has a truth table resembling that for $\wedge$. We may symbolically abbreviate this as

Y and H.

Formalizing it gives us

$p \wedge q$

Now consider the following statement:

Monkeys and dogs are animals.

Using M this time as an abbreviation for *Monkeys are animals* and D for *Dogs are animals*, we obtain the following symbolic abbreviation:

M and D.

Formalizing it will again give us

$p \wedge q$

Any compound statement which is true when and only when both its constituent statements are true (and false otherwise) is said to be a *conjunction* of the two constituent statements. The two constituent statements in such cases are called *conjuncts*. Thus the compound

statement *Monkeys and dogs are animals* is a conjunction of the constituent statements *Monkeys are animals* and *Dogs are animals,* and the
latter two statements are the conjuncts of the conjunction.

Sometimes the connecting word *and* is accompanied by the word
both, as in the following example:

Both Pericles and Strange Ways are cats.

The connecting word *both . . . and* usually expresses conjunction, and
so this compound would also be formalized as $p \wedge q$.

Not all uses of *and* express conjunction, especially since *and* is not
always truth-functional. Perhaps you have noticed that when a use of
and does express conjunction, the order of the conjuncts is not important.
For example, if the statement *Monkeys are simians and dogs are canines*
were true, then *Dogs are canines and monkeys are simians* would also be
true. But the order of the constituent statements in the next example is
of some consequence:

They got married and had a child.

To see this, compare it with

They had a child and got married.

We wouldn't be at all surprised if the married couple involved insisted
that the first statement was true but the second false. Actually, the first
of these statements is really equivalent to

They got married and then had a child.

The connecting word *and then,* which expresses a temporal sequence,
is intensional and so not amenable to a truth-functional analysis. Consequently, it would be more appropriate to treat this statement as atomic.

An example of another use of *and* that does not express conjunction
in the truth-functional sense is

Tom and Jerry are friends.

At first glance, this statement appears similar to

Tom and Jerry are cartoon characters.

The latter statement is obviously an abbreviated version of

Tom is a cartoon character and Jerry is a cartoon character.

But the former statement obviously isn't equivalent to

Tom is a friend and Jerry is a friend.

Tom and Jerry are friends expresses something that *Tom is a friend and Jerry is a friend* does not—namely, that Tom and Jerry are friends of each other. The *and* in *Tom and Jerry are friends* is being used to conjoin two subjects in the same statement rather than two atomic statements. Consequently, it seems more appropriate to view *Tom and Jerry are friends* as atomic.

Many other connecting words in English express conjunction. Consider, for example, the following statement:

Tom is overweight but agile.

What this statement seems to assert is

1   Tom is overweight and Tom is agile.
2   That's not what you would expect.

The use of *but* instead of *and* serves to emphasize that we would not ordinarily expect someone who is overweight to be agile as well. As a consequence, if we were to symbolize *but* by ∧, the statement would lose part of its meaning—that part of its meaning expressed in (2). In other words, *but* appears to express something more than just truth-functional meaning. Nevertheless, for our purposes it would be permissible to translate *but* by means of the inverted wedge since that at least captures the truth-functional meaning expressed in (1).

Now consider this statement:

The picnic is still being held although it is raining.

The connecting word *although* functions in similar fashion to the connecting word *but*. This statement means

1   The picnic is still being held and it is raining.
2   That's not what you would expect.

Again, in viewing this statement as being a conjunction of its components, we lose a lot of the meaning expressed in (2); nevertheless, we do capture its truth-functional meaning.

There are still other connecting words besides *and*, *but*, and *although* which often express conjunctions. Letting C and D be any statement constants you please, we list some of them as follows.

C though D	not only C but also D
C even though D	C albeit D
C whereas D	C, for D
C despite the fact that D	C; moreover, D
C, while D	C no sooner than D

Now there will clearly be some contexts where rendering these as conjunctions just simply won't do. The decision of whether to symbolize certain connecting words by means of the inverted wedge often will have to be made on a case-by-case basis, relying on our linguistic intuitions and our "feel" for the context.

2.4.2.3 Disjunction: The Wedge

We define the wedge—a dyadic connective—by the following truth table:

p	q	$p \vee q$
T	T	T
T	F	T
F	T	T
F	F	F

An example of a connecting word in natural language approximating the definition of the wedge is *or*. However, the word *or* actually has two common uses in ordinary language, usually distinguished as the *inclusive* and the *exclusive* senses. Consider the following statement:

Peter will play with his toys or Melissa will tease her brother.

Now, if the connecting word *or* is being used in the *inclusive* sense (sometimes expressed with *and/or*) in this statement, it asserts the following: either Peter will play with his toys, or Melissa will tease her brother, or both Peter will play with his toys and Melissa will tease her brother. Clearly, the above statement would then be true if any one of these three conditions should obtain. As you can see by inspecting the truth table above, it is the inclusive sense of *or* that the wedge approximates most in meaning.

Any compound statement which is true when and only when either one or both of its constituent statements are true (and false when both constituents are false) is said to be an *inclusive disjunction* of the two constituent statements. The two constituent statements in such cases are called *inclusive disjuncts*. Hence the compound statement *Peter will play with his toys or Melissa will tease her brother* is an inclusive disjunction of the inclusive disjuncts *Peter will play with his toys* and *Melissa will tease her brother*.

Letting P abbreviate *Peter will play with his toys* and M abbreviate *Melissa will tease her brother*, we symbolically abbreviate the compound in the following fashion:

P or M.

Formalizing it yields

$p \lor q$

In contrast to the inclusive sense of *or*, there is also an *exclusive* sense of *or*. An example of a statement making use of the exclusive sense of *or* is the following:

Dinner at this restaurant includes either soup or salad.

This statement informs the customer that the price of dinner will include either soup or salad but not both. Accordingly, we should expect that this statement will be false not only if both the atomic statements *Dinner at this restaurant includes soup* and *Dinner at this restaurant includes salad* are false, but also if both are true. The connective that would more appropriately capture the meaning of the exclusive sense of *or* is not the wedge, but rather a connective having the following truth-functional definition:

p	q	$p\ ?\ q$
T	T	F
T	F	T
F	T	T
F	F	F

We call compound statements like our second example *exclusive disjunctions*. The constituent statements of exclusive disjunctions are called *exclusive disjuncts*. Hence the compound statement *Dinner at this restaurant includes either soup or salad* is an exclusive disjunction of the exclusive disjuncts *Dinner at this restaurant includes soup* and *Dinner at this restaurant includes salad*.

Letting S abbreviate the first exclusive disjunct and A abbreviate the second one, we symbolically abbreviate the above statement as

S or A.

However, at present there is no way for us to formalize this symbolic abbreviation, since S does not contain a connective with the appropriate truth table. Actually, there is a way of formalizing exclusive disjunctions, as we will see in Chapter 3.

The essential way in which the two senses of disjunction differ is indicated by the first row of each truth table. An inclusive disjunction is true if both disjuncts are true, whereas an exclusive disjunction is false under these conditions. This difference between the two senses of disjunction makes the inclusive sense *weaker* than the exclusive sense. The terms *stronger* and *weaker* are often used by logicians to compare truth-functional connectives. We may define them as follows: one connective is *stronger* than another if the truth table for the first (stronger) connective has F everywhere that the second (*weaker*) connective has F and also has F in at least one place that the other has T. In other words, one connective is stronger than another if it is false whenever that other one is false and false somewhere else besides. Now if the following statement

Jim will attend the party with Mary or Cathy.

is treated as an inclusive disjunction, then it would be false under one possible circumstance, viz., only if Jim attends the party with neither Mary nor Cathy. However, if we view this statement as an exclusive disjunction, then it would be false not only if Jim fails to attend the party with either Mary or Cathy, but also if he attends the party with both. Consequently, the exclusive sense of disjunction imposes the additional stipulation that both disjuncts cannot be true.

Appealing to the context where the statement is asserted is the only surefire way of determining which sense of *or* is intended. It often happens, however, that we simply cannot decide which sense of *or* is correct. In such cases, it will be our practice to assume that the inclusive sense is intended. In fact, we shall *always assume that the inclusive sense is intended unless there exists strong evidence that the exclusive sense is being employed*. Then, even if it turns out that we're mistaken, at least we've captured that part of the meaning that the two senses have in common, namely that both disjuncts are not false.

Of course, just the way a disjunction is asserted will sometimes indicate quite clearly which sense is intended. For example, consider the following statement:

Jim will attend the party with Mary or Cathy, or with both.

Now there is absolutely no doubt that the inclusive sense of *or* is intended. Clearly, then, this statement would be formalized as

$p \vee q$

As for the exclusive sense of *or*, it is often expressed in this way:

Jim will attend the party with Mary or Cathy, but not with both.

Quite obviously, this statement would be false if both the exclusive disjuncts were true.

Sometimes the word *or* in statements expressing disjunctions is accompanied by the word *either*, as in the following example:

Jim will attend the party with either Mary or Cathy.

This can be symbolically abbreviated, using M for *Jim will attend the party with Mary* and C for *Jim will attend the party with Cathy*, as

Either M or C.

and formalized, when *either . . . or* is interpreted as expressing inclusive disjunction, as

$p \vee q$

Or also occurs in the connecting word *whether or not*, as in the following statement:

Peter will play with his toys whether or not Melissa teases her brother.

Symbolically abbreviating this statement yields

P whether or not M.

It might be suspected that this statement is formalized by means of the wedge, but that isn't so. To see this, let's consider what this statement actually asserts. When one says *P whether or not M*, one is really saying *No matter whether M is true or not, P is going to be the case*. Hence P is going to be true no matter what the truth value of M. So, to say *P whether or not M* is tantamount to saying simply *P*. Consequently, an alternative way of symbolically abbreviating *Peter will play with his toys whether or not Melissa teases her brother* is

P.

Now formalizing it is straightforward; we simply replace the statement constant by a statement variable and obtain

p

2.4.2.4 Material Conditional: The Horseshoe

The horseshoe—a dyadic connective—is defined in the following way:

p	q	$p \supset q$
T	T	T
T	F	F
F	T	T
F	F	T

Notice that in this truth table, when the two constituent statement forms have different truth values, it makes a difference which has the T and which the F. When the *first* is T and the *second* F, the value for the compound is F; but when the *first* is F and the *second* T, the value for the compound is T. In this respect, the horseshoe is unlike the other dyadic connectives of S. Since the two constituents differ in this respect, we'll give them different names. The *first* constituent is called the *antecedent*, and the *second* is called the *consequent*.

In a sense, the horseshoe is strictly a logician's invention. There's no difficulty in understanding the truth conditions associated with its truth table: the statement form $p \supset q$ receives the value *false* when p is *true* and q is *false*, and under all other circumstances it gets the value *true*. There wouldn't seem to be any trouble finding an English connecting word that corresponds to this. If nothing else, we could make up a complex one, for instance, *It is not the case that both . . . and not . . .* , as in

It is not the case both that it is raining and that there are no clouds in the sky.

A little reflection will show that this statement is false only under the circumstance that *It is raining* is true and *There are clouds in the sky* is false. Consequently, we could write its logical form as

$p \supset q$

However, the horseshoe as a logical symbol has been associated with another class of statements, namely, what are called *conditionals*. Typically, conditionals in English are statements containing the dyadic connecting word *if . . . then*. What is peculiar about using the horseshoe in formalizing conditional statements is that most, if not all, conditionals in natural language are intensional and consequently don't have truth tables.

Whatever prompted logicians to use a truth-functional symbol for the formalization of intensional connecting words? What reason is there for using the horseshoe to formalize statements that don't seem to be truth-functional at all? We'll try to answer each of these questions, but it will take some time. To begin, let us note here that in fact intuitions prompted logicians to use this symbol as a formalization of *if . . . then*. However, the intuitions in question are what might be called *logical intuitions*—intuitions, or unsystematic first guesses, about the logical relationships among certain sentences. As we'll see, the real significance of the truth table for the horseshoe is in the deductive relationships it determines. Logicians have really been interested in this aspect of conditionals more than anything else, and surprisingly enough logicians in three widely separated historical periods all came up with something like the truth table for the horseshoe as an account of conditionals: the Megarian-Stoic logicians of ancient Greece, the logicians of medieval Europe, and the mathematical logicians at the beginning of this century. If nothing else, that shows that the intuitive notion that a connective like the horseshoe should represent conditionals is pretty widespread.

Now, let's consider the meaning of a simple conditional, for instance,

1   If it's raining, then there are clouds in the sky.

This statement consists of the connecting word *if . . . then* and two constituent statements:

It's raining.
There are clouds in the sky.

Using R to abbreviate the first constituent and C to abbreviate the second, we may symbolically abbreviate (1) as

If R, then C.

In order to determine whether this statement is true or false, you'd have to know the circumstances under which it's true and the circumstances under which it's false. Since (1) is a compound of R and C, perhaps the first thing to do is to investigate the significance of each possible combination of truth values of these constituents. Let's construct a table:

R	C	If R, then C
T	T	
T	F	
F	T	
F	F	

Now let's try to fill in the last column. First, consider the second line. Suppose that you discovered one day that it was raining, although there wasn't a cloud in the sky. Under those circumstances, R would be true and C false, which corresponds to the second line of the table. Now, if that were to happen, you would no doubt conclude that (1) is false. Your reasoning might be something like this: "It can't be true that if it's raining, then there are clouds in the sky. After all, here it is raining, and yet there aren't any clouds in the sky. Therefore, statement (1) is false." Now, we are appealing only to linguistic intuition here, to the feel you have for the language. Nevertheless, this seems to be a very secure intuition, and so we can confidently fill in one line of our third column:

R	C	If R, then C
T	F	F

In other words, *a conditional with a true antecedent and a false consequent is false*.

Now, let's try some other cases, beginning with the third line. Suppose one day you find it's not raining (that is, *It's raining* is false) and that there are clouds in the sky (*There are clouds in the sky* is true). Is (1) true or false? You would probably answer, "Since it isn't raining, I can't tell whether it's true that if it's raining then there are clouds in the sky." In other words, when the antecedent *It's raining* is false, there's some sense in which you can't say whether the conditional is true or false. Our intuitions about this case aren't as solid, but at least one thing is clear: if R were false and C were true, that would be no reason for concluding that (1) is false. We might say, "For all that we know in that circumstance, it *could* be true that if it's raining then there are clouds in the sky."

The same sort of reasoning holds for the fourth line: if it's not raining and there aren't any clouds in the sky, that just doesn't tell us whether statement (1) is true or false. To summarize, our intuitions about a conditional with a false antecedent aren't clear, but at least such circumstances don't count against it being true.

Now, let's consider the first line. We notice that it's raining and that there are clouds in the sky. Does this show us conclusively that (1) is true? Again, our intuitions are a little shaky here. "After all," we might say, "perhaps another occasion will come along in which it will be raining without any clouds in the sky." Therefore, we might be reluctant to say that (1) was certainly true when both its antecedent and consequent are true. However, we probably would consider that *some* sort of evidence that (1) was true, and we certainly wouldn't think it was evidence that (1) was false. Therefore, this circumstance also doesn't count against (1) being true (and probably counts for it, in this particular case).

If we now try to fill in the rest of our truth table, we might get something like this:

R	C	If R, then C
T	T	could be T
T	F	F for sure
F	T	could be T
F	F	could be T

As this table shows, the truth value of (1) isn't determined just by the truth values of R and C in every possible circumstance. In every case but one, knowing the truth values of the constituent statements isn't enough to tell us whether (1) is true or false. In other words, (1) is *intensional*. As we'll see, most (perhaps all) conditional sentences in natural language are intensional. However, there is at least one truth-functional aspect to (1): we definitely know that it's false if its antecedent is true and its consequent false.

If you look now at the truth table for the horseshoe, you'll notice that it gets the value F under just these circumstances. However, the horseshoe *is* a truth-functional connective, and so the truth value of a statement form containing it is truth-functionally determined in all possible circumstances. As you'll note, a statement form containing the horseshoe receives the value T in the remaining three cases. Let's pause just a moment and consider what might correspond to this in the case of natural-language conditional statements. The corresponding valuation would be to consider a conditional true unless it had a true antecedent and a false consequent—in other words, to replace *could be true* with *true* in our table above. What reason would there be for doing that? The reason is a little complex, but briefly it's this: the horseshoe corresponds to the *weakest* truth-functional component of any conditional statement. We'll explain what we mean by *weakest* below. It will help to keep in mind that our aim in all this is to see how connecting words affect relations of deducibility and entailment among statements. As we'll see later, the *minimal truth-functional meaning* of the horseshoe is closely connected with the role that conditionals play in arguments.

Let's look again at example (1). We've agreed that the minimal truth-functional meaning of this is expressed by the truth table corresponding to the horseshoe. What more is there to its meaning? Probably the best answer is that a certain *connection between antecedent and consequent* is being asserted: we're saying that there's a connection of a certain sort between *It's raining* and *There are clouds in the sky*. We can now see at least in part why conditionals are intensional. A conditional says that *whenever* its antecedent is true, its consequent is also true. Thus, it refers not only to what is presently the case but also to what would be the case under other circumstances. The reason we can't tell whether (1) is true if it's not raining is that we can't tell, based on that circumstance, what *would* happen if it *were* raining—and that is important to the truth or falsity of (1). Likewise, the reason we can't tell for sure whether (1) is true just in view of a circumstance in which R is true and C also true is that (1) takes account of *all* the occasions on which R is true. Obviously, then, (1) isn't only truth-functional.

Now it's time to explain in more detail why we choose the horseshoe to formalize the connecting words in conditionals, even though most, if not all, conditionals contain intensional connecting words. Essentially, the answer is that all conditionals share the same *minimal truth-functional meaning:* any of them would be false if it had a true antecedent and a false consequent. Under other combinations of truth values of their constituents, conditionals are not truth-functional: they could be true or false. Now, earlier we introduced the notion of one truth-functional connective being *weaker* than another. Roughly, one connective is weaker than another when it is true under every combination of truth values for which the other connective is true and also true for some combination of truth values for which the other is false. The horseshoe is only false for one combination of truth values; consequently, it's weaker than any other connective which has the value F for the combination of truth values T and F. This is why we describe the truth-functional meaning of the horseshoe as the *minimal* truth-functional meaning of all conditionals: it's the *least* truth-functional component that any conditional must have. Therefore, one reason for using the horseshoe to formalize conditionals is that we're making the smallest supposition about them: we're saying only that they are false with true antecedents and false consequents. Since, as far as the other cases are concerned, the conditional *could* be true, we assign the value T to the other three possibilities.

This supposition may sound like more than we ought to make. After all, if we really want to say the minimum possible, then we ought not to put *any* truth value in the other lines of our truth table for the horseshoe. There's an element of truth in this criticism, but two things prevent us from doing this. First, the structure of S requires that all its connectives be truth-functional, and therefore they all must be defined by truth tables. Consequently, we've got to fill in every line of the truth table for the horseshoe. Putting an F in some row besides the second would result in a stronger connective than we wanted, one that wouldn't, in fact, fit some conditionals. However, as it will turn out, putting T's in these other places is comparatively harmless. The second point is that it's really the second line of the truth table that specifies the deductive properties we need for the conditional. As we'll explain in more detail in Chapter 6, the definition of the horseshoe is intimately related to our concept of valid argument, and it's the second line of its truth table that is important in that connection.

Now, let's attempt to clarify a little further the relation between the horseshoe and conditional statements. At the beginning of this section, we said that we could imagine a truth-functional connecting word with the same truth table as the horseshoe. Since the connecting word *if* . . . *then* already has several uses, let's just propose one more, in this case one which corresponds *exactly* to the horseshoe. We'll call this the *material if . . . then*, and we'll call conditional statements formed with it *material conditionals*. A material conditional, then, is false if its antecedent is true and its consequent false, and true otherwise.

Are there any material conditionals in English? If there are, they will certainly appear a bit odd. After all, a material conditional will be strictly truth-functional, so that its truth value will depend *only* on the truth values of its constituents and not at all on any connection between them. In fact, we could combine *any* two statements into a material conditional. Moreover, whatever those statements might be, unless the antecedent were true and the consequent false, our material conditional would be true. For instance,

> If 2 + 3 = 5, then Jimmy Carter is the thirty-ninth President of the United States.

would be an example of a material conditional given that there is apparently no connection between its antecedent and its consequent. Also notice that, taken as a material conditional (since both the antecedent and the consequent are true), this statement must be regarded as true.

The results of our consideration of the last example may sound somewhat paradoxical—and, in fact, they are often regarded as being so. The difficulty, of course, is that material conditionals don't often, if ever, occur in natural languages. Perhaps the closest thing to a material conditional is a certain sort of conditional with both antecedent and consequent false, for instance,

> If the moon is made of moldy cheese, then I am a monkey's uncle.

Of course, if we interpret this statement as expressing a material conditional, we would have to count it as true (the antecedent is false). However, when using such assertions, we do not ordinarily intend to express conditionals of any kind; rather we wish to deny the antecedent by adducing an obviously ludicrous consequent. In fact, our intention is not only to deny the antecedent but also to emphasize how ridiculous it is. Thus, to say

> If the moon is made of moldy cheese, then I am a monkey's uncle.

amounts to saying

> It is ridiculous to say that the moon is made of moldy cheese.

Another kind of conditional often used in ordinary contexts is the *counterfactual* conditional. An example of this kind of conditional is the following:

If Booth had not killed Lincoln, then someone else would have.

Counterfactual conditionals are packed with so much intensional meaning they cannot be formalized by means of the horseshoe. To see why this is so, compare the above counterfactual conditional with the following one:

If Booth had not killed Lincoln, then nobody else would have.

We wouldn't ordinarily consider both these conditionals true; yet, since both have false antecedents, both would have to be true by definition if they were treated as material conditionals. The best policy, given our purposes, is to treat them, along with other intensional compounds, as atomic statements.

It is a rather simple matter to formalize conditionals. Consider the following statement:

If Jim attends the meeting, then Tom will attend the meeting.

Letting J abbreviate *Jim attends the meeting* and T abbreviate *Tom will attend the meeting*, we symbolically abbreviate this statement as

If J, then T.

Using the horseshoe for *if . . . then*, the symbolic abbreviation is formalized as

$p \supset q$

Sometimes the *then* in the connecting word *if . . . then* is suppressed, as in the following statement:

If Raoul swallows 25 grams of arsenic, he will die.

Abbreviating *Raoul swallows 25 grams of arsenic* as A and *Raoul will die* as D, we obtain the following symbolic abbreviation:

If A, D[1].

---

[1] In this one case, we won't follow our usual policy of placing the connecting word between its constituents.

Formalizing yields

$p \supset q$

Conditionals are often expressed in the following way as well:

Everybody will be surprised if the Kansas City Chiefs go to the Super Bowl.

Symbolically abbreviating *Everybody will be surprised* by E and *The Kansas City Chiefs go to the Super Bowl* by C, we obtain

E if C.

This obviously says the same thing as *If C, then E*. Notice that the antecedent C is *second* in the original statement and the consequent E is *first*. Hence it is formalized as

$q \supset p$

Conditionals are also expressed with *only if*, as in the following example:

Patti can vote only if she is a citizen.

This statement says the same thing as:

If Patti can vote, then she is a citizen.

Formalizing therefore gives us

$p \supset q$

The connecting word *when* is often employed like *if* in expressing conditionals, as in

It snows when the temperature drops.

This tends to say the same thing as

It snows if the temperature drops.

Consequently, it is formalized as $q \supset p$.

There are many other connecting words which we haven't mentioned that are often used to express conditionals; some of them, which are formalized in exactly the same way as *if . . . then*, are *provided that . . . then, on the condition that . . . then, in the circumstance that . . .*

then, in the event that . . . then, in case . . . then, assuming that . . . then, on the supposition that . . . then, granting that . . . then, and *given that . . . then.* Note that, like *if . . . then,* these connecting words can also be used with a suppressed *then.* That is, instead of *provided that p, then q* we can have *provided that p, q.* They may also be used with a suppressed *then* in reverse order, as in *p provided that q.* Quite obviously, this behaves just like *p if q* and hence would be formalized as $q \supset p$.

One more connecting word worth mentioning is *even if,* which resembles *whether or not.* To see this, note that in asserting *p even if q,* we are not only asserting that *p if q* but also *p if not q;* thus we are really asserting *p whether or not q.* Consequently, *p even if q* is simply formalized as *p.*

2.4.2.5   Biconditional: The Triple Bar

The triple bar—a dyadic connective—is defined in the following manner:

p	q	$p \equiv q$
T	T	T
T	F	F
F	T	F
F	F	T

An example of a connecting word in natural language approximating rather closely the definition of the triple bar is *if and only if,* as in the following statement:

The temperature will drop if and only if it rains.

Letting T abbreviate *The temperature will drop* and R abbreviate *It rains,* we symbolically abbreviate this statement as follows:

T if and only if R.

Formalizing it yields

$$p \equiv q$$

Any compound statement which is true when and only when both its constituent statements have the *same truth value* (and is false otherwise) is said to be a *biconditional* of the two constituent statements. The two constituent statements are called *equivalents.* Thus the compound statement *The temperature will drop if and only if it rains* is a biconditional of the two equivalents *The temperature drops* and *It rains.* The equivalents occurring in biconditionals are often said to be *materially equivalent* to one another. In terms of our definition of the triple bar, this simply means that they have the same truth value.

The biconditional actually amounts to the conjunction of two conditionals with antecedents and consequents interchanged. For example, the statement

The temperature will drop if and only if it rains.

is essentially equivalent to

The temperature will drop if it rains, and the temperature will drop only if it rains.

Much of what has been said about the conditional applies to the biconditional.

2.4.2.6 A List of Connecting Words

In this section we list the connecting words discussed in the preceding subsections along with a few additional ones not discussed. The column on the left is composed of quasi-statement forms displaying the various connecting words, and the column on the right shows how each of them is usually formalized. You might find it helpful to refer to this list from time to time while doing exercises concerning the formalization of statements and arguments.

Below this list is a table summarizing the truth-functional definitions of the five connectives of S.

Group 1: Conjunctions

p and q	$p \wedge q$
p but q	$p \wedge q$
p despite the fact that q	$p \wedge q$
p although q	$p \wedge q$
p though q	$p \wedge q$
p even though q	$p \wedge q$
p despite that q	$p \wedge q$
p, while q	$p \wedge q$
p; moreover, q	$p \wedge q$
not only p but also q	$p \wedge q$
p, albeit q	$p \wedge q$
p, whereas q	$p \wedge q$
p, for q	$p \wedge q$
p no sooner than q	$p \wedge q$
p; still, q	$p \wedge q$
p; besides, q	$p \wedge q$
p; on the other hand, q	$p \wedge q$

Group 2: Negations

It is false that p	$\sim p$
It is not the case that p	$\sim p$
It is not true that p	$\sim p$
It is impossible that p	$\sim p$
It is absurd that p	$\sim p$
Not p	$\sim p$
Never p	$\sim p$

Group 3: Disjunctions

p or q (inclusive)	$p \vee q$
Either p or q (inclusive)	$p \vee q$
p or q or both	$p \vee q$
p, or alternatively q	$p \vee q$

Group 4: Conditionals

If p, then q	$p \supset q$
If p, q	$p \supset q$
Provided that p, then q	$p \supset q$
On the condition that p, then q	$p \supset q$
In the circumstance that p, then q	$p \supset q$
In the event that p, then q	$p \supset q$
In case p, then q	$p \supset q$
Assuming that p, then q	$p \supset q$
On the supposition that p, then q	$p \supset q$
Granting that p, then q	$p \supset q$
Given that p, then q	$p \supset q$
p only if q	$p \supset q$
p if q	$q \supset p$
p when q	$q \supset p$
p so long as q	$q \supset p$
p provided that q	$q \supset p$
p on the condition that q	$q \supset p$
p in the circumstance that q	$q \supset p$
p in the event that q	$q \supset p$
p in case q	$q \supset p$
p assuming that q	$q \supset p$
p on the supposition that q	$q \supset p$
p granting that q	$q \supset p$
p given that q	$q \supset p$

Group 5: Biconditionals

p if and only if q	$p \equiv q$
p when and only when q	$p \equiv q$
p if q, otherwise not	$p \equiv q$
p just in case q	$p \equiv q$

Group 6: Connecting Words Formalized by One Variable

p whether or not q	p
p even if q	p

Group 7: Complex Connecting Words

Neither p nor q	$\sim(p \vee q)$ or $\sim p \wedge \sim q$
p unless q (inclusive)	$\sim q \supset p$
p except if q (inclusive)	$\sim q \supset p$
p or q (exclusive)	$(p \vee q) \wedge \sim(p \wedge q)$
p or q, but not both	$(p \vee q) \wedge \sim(p \wedge q)$
p unless q (exclusive)	$(p \vee q) \wedge \sim(p \wedge q)$
p except if q (exclusive)	$(p \vee q) \wedge \sim(p \wedge q)$
p if q; otherwise, r	$(q \supset p) \wedge (\sim q \supset r)$
p unless q, in which case r	$(p \vee q) \wedge (q \supset r)$
p if q; otherwise, not	$(q \supset p) \wedge (\sim q \supset \sim p)$
p if q; otherwise, neither	$(q \supset p) \wedge [\sim q \supset \sim(p \vee q)]$
p if q, in which case r	$(q \supset p) \wedge (p \supset r)$
p rather than q	$p \wedge \sim q$
p instead of q	$p \wedge \sim q$
p without q	$p \wedge \sim q$

Notice that most of the connecting words in Group 7 have not been discussed yet. They will be dealt with in the next chapter. We list them here so that you need only refer to a single list when formalizing statements and arguments.

Summary Table of the Connectives of S

p	q	$\sim p$	$p \wedge q$	$p \vee q$	$p \supset q$	$p \equiv q$
T	T	F	T	T	T	T
T	F		F	T	F	F
F	T	T	F	T	T	F
F	F		F	F	T	T

EXERCISE 2.4

Symbolically abbreviate and then formalize each of the following statements.

*1 Mary will attend the picnic only if Jim does.
2 Tom has gone to the beach even though it is raining.
*3 The President of the United States is not only the Chief Executive but also the Commander in Chief of all the military forces.
4 Miguel will attend the seminar this summer even if he gets a summer job.
*5 Margaret will be elected provided that she promises to appoint a new director of the committee.
6 Boston will win the World Series on the condition that Cincinnati loses the pennant.

*7 The unexamined life is not worth living.
 8 If and only if the sun is shining will I go to the beach.
*9 Nancy will relax when she hears from Larry.
10 I will go if you will go.
*11 Hitler lost the war despite the fact that he invaded England.
12 I will go given that everybody else does.

REVIEW EXERCISES FOR CHAPTER 2

1 Define each of the following:

Compound statement   Symbolic abbreviation
Atomic statement   Quasi-statement form
Connecting word   Monadic connecting word
Truth function   Dyadic connecting word
Truth-functional connecting word   Statement form
Intensional connecting word   Statement variable
Logical form   Truth table
Statement constant

2 Formalize the following statements.
  (a) This statement is false.
  *(b) If George III had not been king in 1776, then there would not have been an American Revolution.
  *(c) Mary had a ham and cheese sandwich and a cup of coffee for lunch.
  (d) While I was walking down the street, I saw an accident.
  (e) In the twenty-first century, all that we'll have left to eat is reprocessed garbage; still, we'll have plenty of that.
  *(f) Assuming that that's an oak tree, we'll have ham sandwiches for lunch.
  (g) In the event that the world ends, this insurance policy is canceled.
  (h) If there is any way to do it wrong, Roger will.
  (i) We can go anywhere you want for dinner if you pay.
  *(j) There is no free lunch.
  (k) Either Tom or Mary will go to the ball game.
  (l) We'll make the trip even if it rains.

3 Discuss each of the following.
  (a) If most connecting words in natural language are not truth-functional, then what good is S?
  (b) Do you think that there could be any material conditionals in English? If so, what would they be like?
  (c) What is the difference between a statement form and a symbolic abbreviation?

chapter 3
Complex Statements and Truth Table Construction

3.1
MORE COMPLEX STATEMENTS

There are many compound statements whose constituent statements are themselves compound. An example is the following:

If Tom is a bachelor, then Tom is not married.

Now this compound statement is a conditional having an atomic antecedent but a compound consequent. Letting B abbreviate *Tom is a bachelor* and M abbreviate *Tom is married*, the statement is symbolically abbreviated in the following way:

If B, then not M.

Formalizing it will yield

$p \supset \sim q$

When one connecting word is part of a statement on which another operates, we say that the first connecting word is *within the scope* of the second; thus, in our example above, *not* is within the scope of *if . . . then*. Now, obviously, if one connecting word is within the scope of a second connecting word, the second operates on a larger piece of the statement than the first. In a compound statement with compound constituents, we can distinguish the scopes of different occurrences of connecting words and determine which word has the largest scope—that is, which one has all the others within its scope. This connecting word, which operates on the largest constituent (or constituents) of the statement, is the *main connecting word*. In our example, the main connecting word is *if . . . then*. We also distinguish the main connective of a complex statement form in the same way. Thus, in the last example the main connective is the horseshoe.

Sometimes, in formalizing we need punctuation to indicate which is the main connective. Consider this example:

If both Tom and Mary love music, then both Mary and Tom love music.

This, too, is a conditional statement and hence compound, but its antecedent and its consequent are themselves also compound statements. Letting T abbreviate *Tom loves music* and M abbreviate *Mary loves music*, the compound is symbolically abbreviated in the following fashion:

If both T and M, then both M and T.

If we formalize this without punctuation, we get

$$p \wedge q \supset q \wedge p$$

However, this is ambiguous, since we can't tell which is the main connective. The original statement is a conditional, and so the main connective should be the horseshoe. We indicate this by punctuating as follows:

$$(p \wedge q) \supset (q \wedge p)$$

Actually, the kind of logical punctuation we are discussing is often employed in natural language as well; both punctuation symbols (for instance, commas) and certain words (for example, *either* and *both*) serve this function. In English the following statement, in certain contexts, could be ambiguous:

1   It is not true that Mary will attend the picnic or Jim will go home.

It could mean either

2a   Either it is not true that Mary will attend the picnic or Jim will go home.

or

3a It is not true that either Mary will attend the picnic or Jim will go home.

Notice that the ambiguity is avoided simply by the appropriate use of the word *either*. In (2a) the word *either* is placed before the connecting word *it is not true that*, whereas in (3a) the word *either* is placed immediately after the connecting word *it is not true that*. Hence (2a) is a disjunction of the disjuncts *It is not true that Mary will attend the picnic* and *Jim will go home*, where the first inclusive disjunct is a negation of the atomic statement *Mary will attend the picnic*. Statement (3a), on the other hand, is a negation of the disjunction *Either Mary will attend the picnic or Jim will go home*. Clearly, then, (1) is ambiguous because we cannot be sure whether it is to be viewed as a disjunction or a negation. The appropriate use of the word *either*, however, resolves the ambiguity in favor of either (2a) or (3a). The *main connecting word* in (2a) is *either . . . or*, whereas in (3a) the main connecting word is *it is not true that*.

Letting M abbreviate *Mary will attend the picnic* and J abbreviate *Jim will go home*, we symbolically abbreviate (2a) as

Either it is not true that M or J.

and (3a) as

It is not true that either M or J.

We formalize each, respectively, as

2b $\sim p \vee q$
3b $\sim (p \vee q)$

The *main connective* of (2b) is the wedge, whereas the *main connective* of (3b) is the tilde.

You might think that, strictly speaking, (2a) should be formalized as

$(\sim p) \vee q$

but a well-established convention among logicians lets us omit the parentheses enclosing the first constituent. So, we can write this statement form as

$\sim p \vee q$

The convention in question is the following: unless parentheses indicate otherwise, *the tilde always takes the shortest possible scope*. In other words, if no parentheses specify on what a tilde operates, it's understood

---

to operate on the shortest well-formed statement form following it. Two examples will clarify the rule. First, in

$$\sim\sim p \supset q$$

the scope of the first tilde is the shortest statement form following it, which is $\sim p$. The scope of the second tilde is p, and so this statement form is the equivalent of

$$[\sim(\sim p)] \supset q$$

Now consider

$$\sim(p \supset q) \vee r$$

The scope of the tilde is $(p \supset q)$, because that's the shortest statement form following it [the sequences $(p$ and $(p \supset$ aren't statement forms]. Therefore, this is the equivalent of

$$[\sim(p \supset q)] \vee r$$

We have seen that one way of avoiding ambiguities in statements in natural language is by the appropriate use of certain words. Sometimes this is also accomplished by the use of commas and semicolons. For example, the following ambiguous statement

4a Mary will attend the picnic and Jim will go home or George will go fishing.

could mean either

5a Mary will attend the picnic and Jim will go home, or George will go fishing.

or

6a Mary will attend the picnic, and Jim will go home or George will go fishing.

Statement (4a) is ambiguous because we don't know whether to view it as a disjunction or a conjunction. Consequently, the formalization

4b $p \wedge q \vee r$

would also be ambiguous, since it isn't possible to decide whether its main connective is an inverted wedge or a wedge. Statement (5a), however, uses a comma to make a disjunction out of the whole compound and a conjunction out of the first disjunct. Thus (5a) is formalized as

5b $(p \land q) \lor r$

Here the main connective is the wedge, and the connective in the first disjunct is the inverted wedge. Statement (6a), on the other hand, uses the comma to make the whole compound into a conjunction having a second conjunct which is a disjunction. Then (6a) is formalized in the following way:

6b $p \land (q \lor r)$

Its main connective is, of course, the inverted wedge, and the connective in the second conjunct is the wedge.

Natural language often employs compound statements composed of three or more disjuncts (or three or more conjuncts), as in the following statement:

7 Mary will attend the picnic or Jim will go home or George will go fishing.

Statements like these are not ambiguous. Nevertheless, when formalized, they must be punctuated because the wedge and the inverted wedge are by definition dyadic connectives: they must operate on exactly two constituents. Consequently, statement (7) cannot be formalized as

$p \lor q \lor r$

but must be formalized as either

$(p \lor q) \lor r$

or

$p \lor (q \lor r)$

It doesn't matter which, since the choice of punctuating in either way is arbitrary.[1] The same remarks apply to statements composed of three or more conjuncts.

The negation of any compound statement other than a negation always requires punctuation:

[1] Strictly speaking, from the point of view of S as a formalized language, it isn't arbitrary: we should prove that the two forms are equivalent (in fact, we've made use of what are called the *associative laws* of $\land$ and $\lor$ here). However, this needn't concern us here, since as far as formalization is concerned, these statement forms are interchangeable.

8a   Tom and Mary won't both attend the picnic.
9a   Neither Sue nor George will go fishing.

These statements are formalized, respectively, in the following fashion:

8b $\sim(p \wedge q)$
9b $\sim(p \vee q)$

So far our formalizations have made use only of parentheses. Some formalizations, however, require the use of both parentheses and brackets, as in the following statement:

If Gladys goes fishing, then either Mary will attend the picnic or Jim and Tom will both go home.

Letting G abbreviate *Gladys goes fishing*, M abbreviate *Mary will attend the picnic*, J abbreviate *Jim will go home*, and T abbreviate *Tom will go home*, we can symbolically abbreviate the above statement in the following way:

If G, then either M or both J and T.

Formalizing it will then yield

$p \supset [q \vee (r \wedge s)]$

Notice that we pair off first the parentheses and then the brackets. Of course, we could have formalized the above statement as

$p \supset (q \vee (r \wedge s))$

using only parentheses. Using brackets as well, however, makes the statement form easier to read.

    The formalizations of some compound statements require the use of all three kinds of punctuation symbols. Consider, for example, the following statement, which is merely the negation of the one considered above:

It is not the case that if Gladys goes fishing then either Mary will attend the picnic or Jim and Tom will both go home.

This statement is formalized in this way:

$\sim\{p \supset [q \vee (r \wedge s)]\}$

Notice that in formalizing this statement, we pair off first the parentheses, then the brackets, and then the braces. But what if more than three pairs of punctuation are required? Well, we begin all over again; that is, we always pair off in the following manner:

$$\ldots \{ [(\{ [( )] \})] \} \ldots$$

Finally, note that compound statements can be compounded out of a single atomic constituent statement, as in the following:

Either it is raining or it isn't.

If we let R abbreviate *It is raining*, this compound statement is symbolically abbreviated in this way:

Either R or not R.

Formalizing it will yield

$$p \lor \sim p$$

Sometimes only one of the constituent statements is repeated, as in

If Mary attends the picnic, then Jim will; but if she doesn't, Tom will.

Letting M abbreviate *Mary attends the picnic*, J abbreviate *Jim will attend the picnic*, and T abbreviate *Tom will attend the picnic*, we symbolically abbreviate this statement as

If M, then J; but if not M, then T.

Formalizing will now yield

$$(p \supset q) \land (\sim p \supset r)$$

EXERCISE 3.1

1 Punctuate each of the following ambiguous forms in at least two different ways.
*(a) $p \lor q \land r \supset s$
 (b) $p \equiv q \land r \supset \sim s \lor \sim t$
*(c) $p \supset q \land \sim (r \equiv s)$
 (d) $p \supset q \supset p$
 (e) $p \land q \supset \sim t \lor s \land t$

2 Formalize each of the following statements.

— *(a)* Roses are red and violets are blue, but some tulips are purple.

(b) If it neither rains nor snows, then Paul will have to go to work.

(c) The senator will carry the rural areas only if she attracts the farm vote; but if she doesn't carry the farm vote, then not only will she lose the election but her political career will also be short-lived.

(d) Assuming that Jones enters the primary, then he will lose even if big business backs him.

(e) Water will boil on the condition that it is heated to 100°C. •

(f) We will either go swimming or boating given that the weather is suitable; but if it isn't, then we will stay home and play Monopoly.

— *(g)* If Sartre is a philosopher, then he is either an existentialist or a Marxist.

(h) Jones will run for election even though she doesn't have a chance of winning.

(i) It's not at all obvious that John's argument is valid; moreover, I cannot possibly be persuaded by it, for I reject his premises.

(j) Although logic is fascinating, many students do not recognize its significance.

(k) If love is what makes the world go round, then, given that hate does not prevent it from going round, hate cannot be the opposite of love.

(l) Gonzales was not invited to the reception unless Jones was; but, as a matter of fact, Jones was not even though Smith thought that she was.

(m) The investigation will uncover the facts of the case only if all the investigators work diligently.

(n) Either Paul is not telling the truth or Melvin is not cooperating.

— *(o)* Unless the President declares this community a disaster area, the victims of the flood will not be eligible to receive federal funds.

(p) If both Nancy and Carol are invited to the reception, then neither Tom nor Jim will attend; but Jorge will attend despite the fact that Mary won't.

(q) Jim will go swimming provided that the temperature doesn't drop, but Lucy will go swimming if and only if both the temperature drops and Jim doesn't go.

(r) A material conditional is not true when and only when both its antecedent is true and its consequent is false.

(s) A material conditional is true if and only if either its antecedent is false or its consequent is true.

(t) If a conjunction is true when and only when both the first conjunct is true and the second conjunct is true, then the negation of a conjunction is true when and only when either the first conjunct is false or the second conjunct is false.

3.2

CONSTRUCTING TRUTH TABLES

After constructing Symbolic Language S, we defined its connectives. This enabled us to compare their meanings with the meanings of connecting words in natural language, thereby making it possible for us to decide which connectives to use for formalizing compound statements.

Actually, our definitions for the connectives of S permit us to determine the truth-functional meaning of any statement form whatsoever. But why should this interest us? There are several reasons. First, as we shall see in Section 3.2.1, certain statements are *logically equivalent* to other statements, and one way of deciding which statements are logically equivalent is by determining the truth-functional meanings of their formalizations. Another reason, as we'll see in Section 3.4, is that statements possess certain kinds of semantic properties, which we can investigate by determining the truth-functional meanings of their corresponding statement forms. Still another reason, as we'll see in Chapter 6, is that determining whether an argument is valid, at least from a semantic point of view, is intimately connected with truth-functional meaning.

These are some of the reasons it's important to determine the truth-functional meanings of statements. In this section, we show how to do this for any statement form whatever. Let's begin with an example. Suppose we were interested in knowing the possible circumstances under which the following statement is true:

It is false that either George is going fishing or Alice is going hunting.

The first thing we would do, of course, is formalize it:

$\sim(p \lor q)$

Now that we have exposed its logical form, we first determine how many *different* statement variables there are in the formalization. In this case there are two: p and q. The first phase of our truth table construction for $\sim(p \lor q)$ involves setting up a column for each statement variable. Then we list the possible combinations of truth values for both p and q:

p	q
T	T
T	F
F	T
F	F

Being satisfied that we have listed all the possible combinations of T's and F's, we systematically break down the original statement form into its constituents, and break down those constituents into their constituents, until we arrive at single statement variables. In the process, we set up a column for the original statement form and for each constituent, moving from right to left. We begin by writing the original statement form at the far right of the table:

p	q		$\sim(p \lor q)$
T	T		
T	F		
F	T		
F	F		

Now, we *locate the main connective* (in this case $\sim$) and set up a column for the constituent(s) on which it operates:

p	q	$p \lor q$	$\checkmark$ $\sim(p \lor q)$
T	T		
T	F		
F	T		
F	F		

Here, of course, there is only the single constituent $p \lor q$. Since we've now finished taking apart $\sim(p \lor q)$, we put a check mark by it. Now, we proceed in the same manner with $p \lor q$. However, its constituents are the statement variables p and q, and we already have columns for those, so we're finished dissecting our statement form.

Now all that we have to do is fill in the two empty columns with T's and F's. Let's begin with the column for $p \lor q$. This column is filled in, row by row, from the columns for p and q in accordance with the definition of the wedge:

p	q	$p \lor q$	$\sim(p \lor q)$
T	T	T	
T	F	T	
F	T	T	
F	F	F	

In fact, the first three columns look just like the truth table definition for the wedge. Finally, we fill in the column for $\sim(p \lor q)$, row by row, from the column for $p \lor q$ in accordance with the definition of the tilde:

p	q	$p \lor q$	$\sim(p \lor q)$
T	T	T	F
T	F	T	F
F	T	T	F
F	F	F	T

Recall that, according to the definition of the tilde, when a statement form has the value T, placing a tilde in front of it gives it the value F. Note that the first three rows of the column for $p \lor q$ have the value T, and the final row has the value F; hence the first three rows of the column for $\sim(p \lor q)$ take the value F, and the final row takes the value T. This completes the truth table construction for the statement form $\sim(p \lor q)$. The final column gives us its truth-functional meaning. Now, where p formalizes *George goes fishing* and q formalizes *Alice goes hunting*, the truth table for $\sim(p \lor q)$ tells us that there is only one possible circumstance under which the statement *It is false that either George is going fishing or Alice is going hunting* is true, namely (look at the final row of the completed table) when both the atomic statements *George goes fishing* and *Alice goes hunting* are false.

Let's try another example. This time let's construct the truth table for the following statement form:

$$\sim(p \land \sim q) \supset (\sim p \lor \sim q)$$

We set up our truth table columns according to the procedure described above (note that although there are four *different occurrences* of statement variables, there are only two *different statement variables* in the statement form):

p	q	$\sim p$	$\sim q$	$p \land \sim q$	$\overset{\checkmark}{\sim(p \land \sim q)}$	$\overset{\checkmark}{\sim p \lor \sim q}$	$\overset{\checkmark}{\sim(p \land \sim q) \supset (\sim p \lor \sim q)}$
T	T						
T	F						
F	T						
F	F						

At this point, we have three compound statement forms unchecked: $\sim p$, $\sim q$, and $p \land \sim q$. The constituents of the first two are p and q, respectively, and we already have columns for those statement variables. The constituents of $p \land \sim q$ are p and $\sim q$, and we already have columns for each of those, too. Consequently, we're now ready to begin filling in the truth table.

(1)	(2)	(3)	(4)				
p	q	$\sim p$	$\sim q$	$p \land \sim q$	$\sim(p \land \sim q)$	$\sim p \lor \sim q$	$\sim(p \land \sim q) \supset (\sim p \lor \sim q)$
T	T	F	F				
T	F	F	T				
F	T	T	F				
F	F	T	T				

The truth values for columns 3 and 4 come from columns 1 and 2, respectively, in accordance with the definition of the tilde: when p has the value F, $\sim p$ takes the value T, and similarly for $\sim q$.

(1)	(2)	(3)	(4)	(5)			
p	q	$\sim p$	$\sim q$	$p \land \sim q$	$\sim(p \land \sim q)$	$\sim p \lor \sim q$	$\sim(p \land \sim q) \supset (\sim p \lor \sim q)$
T	T	F	F	F			
T	F	F	T	T			
F	T	T	F	F			
F	F	T	T	F			

The truth values for column 5 come from columns 1 and 4 in accordance with the definition of the inverted wedge. The reasoning involved for each row is as follows:

First Row: When the first conjunct has the value T and the second conjunct has the value F, then the conjunction of the two conjuncts takes the value F. (This corresponds to the *second* row of the truth table definition of the inverted wedge.)

Second Row: When both conjuncts have the value T, then the conjunction of the two conjuncts takes the value T. (This corresponds to the *first* row of the truth table definition of the inverted wedge.)

Third Row: When both conjuncts have the value F, then the conjunction of the two conjuncts takes the value F. (This corresponds to the *fourth* row in the truth table definition of the inverted wedge.)

Fourth Row: When the first conjunct has the value F and the second conjunct has the value T, then the conjunction of the two conjuncts takes the value F. (This corresponds to the *third* row of the truth table definition of the inverted wedge.)

Now we proceed to the next column:

(1)	(2)	(3)	(4)	(5)	(6)		
p	q	$\sim p$	$\sim q$	$p \wedge \sim q$	$\sim(p \wedge \sim q)$	$\sim p \vee \sim q$	$\sim(p \wedge \sim q) \supset (\sim p \vee \sim q)$
T	T	F	F	F	T		
T	F	F	T	T	F		
F	T	T	F	F	T		
F	F	T	T	F	T		

The truth values for column 6 come from column 5 in accordance with the definition of the tilde. Now, for the next column:

(1)	(2)	(3)	(4)	(5)	(6)	(7)	
p	q	$\sim p$	$\sim q$	$p \wedge \sim q$	$\sim(p \wedge \sim q)$	$\sim p \vee \sim q$	$\sim(p \wedge \sim q) \supset (\sim p \vee \sim q)$
T	T	F	F	F	T	F	
T	F	F	T	T	F	T	
F	T	T	F	F	T	T	
F	F	T	T	F	T	T	

The truth values for column 7 come from columns 3 and 4 in accordance with the definition of the wedge. The reasoning involved for each row is as follows:

First Row: When both disjuncts have the value F, then the disjunction takes the value F. (This corresponds to the *fourth* row of the truth table definition of the wedge.)

Second Row: When the first disjunct has the value F and the second disjunct has the value T, then the disjunction takes the value T. (This corresponds to the *third* row in the truth table definition of the wedge.)

Third Row: When the first disjunct has the value T and the second disjunct has the value F, then the disjunction takes the value T. (This corresponds to the *second* row of the truth table definition of the wedge.)

Fourth Row: When both disjuncts have the value T, the disjunction takes the value T. (This corresponds to the *first* row of the truth table definition of the wedge.)

Now we turn to the final column:

(1) p	(2) q	(3) $\sim p$	(4) $\sim q$	(5) $p \wedge \sim q$	(6) $\sim(p \wedge \sim q)$	(7) $\sim p \vee \sim q$	(8) $\sim(p \wedge \sim q) \supset (\sim p \vee \sim q)$
T	T	F	F	F	T	F	F
T	F	F	T	T	F	T	T
F	T	T	F	F	T	T	T
F	F	T	T	F	T	T	T

The truth values for column 8 come from columns 6 and 7 (in that order) in accordance with the definition of the horseshoe. The reasoning involved for each row is as follows:

First Row: When the antecedent has the value T and the consequent has the value F, then the material conditional takes the value F. (This corresponds to the *second* row of the truth table definition of the horseshoe.)

Second Row: When the antecedent has the value F and the consequent the value T, then the material conditional takes the value T. (This corresponds to the *third* row of the truth table definition of the horseshoe.)

Third Row: When both the antecedent and consequent have the value T, then the material conditional takes the value T. (This corresponds to the *first* row of the truth table definition of the horseshoe.)

Fourth Row: The reasoning is the same as for the third row.

This completes the truth table construction for the statement form $\sim(p \wedge \sim q) \supset (\sim p \vee \sim q)$; its truth-functional meaning is indicated by column 8. Notice that it informs us that the only possible circumstance under which a statement having this logical form is false is when both of its atomic constituents are true.

The truth table for any statement form is constructed similarly. We need only follow the procedure outlined below:

1   Determine the number of different statement variables in the given statement form and set up a column for each statement variable.
2   List all the possible combinations of truth values in the columns for each of the statement variables.
3   Find the main connective of the statement form and take it apart into its constituents, setting up a column for each constituent. Continue in this manner with any constituents that are compound until you reach single statement variables.
4   Fill in each row of all the remaining empty columns with the appropriate truth values. The appropriate truth values are determined by the main connectives of the statement forms appearing in each column.

Following these four steps will always result in the desired truth table for any statement form of S.

When we turn to forms with three or more statement variables, the procedure remains the same. However, we need a procedure for determining the number of possible circumstances for step 2. With one statement variable there are two possibilities. When we add a second, we divide each of these into two, giving 2×2, or 4, combinations. When we add a third variable, each of *these* is divided into two cases, giving $(2 \times 2) \times 2$, or 8, possibilities. So, for any n statement variables, there will be $2 \times 2 \times \cdots \times 2$ (n times), or 2^n, combinations of truth values. Consequently, the number of rows required to exhaustively list all their truth-value combinations will be 2^n. Thus, if there is one statement variable in a given statement form, the number of rows required to state its possible truth-value combinations will be $2^1 = 2$; if two, then the number of rows will be $2^2 = 4$; if three, then the number of rows will be $2^3 = 8$; and so on.

Now, to ensure that every possible combination of truth values is listed without any repetitions, let's adopt the following convention: write one-half T's and one-half F's for the first statement variable; then write one-quarter T's, one-quarter F's for the second statement variable; and continue this sort of halving procedure until the last statement variable has a column consisting of alternating T's and F's. Halving in this way will always efficiently result in a complete listing of all possible combinations.

Suppose we have arrived at step 2 in our procedure for constructing a truth table for a given statement form composed of three different statement variables. Our formula tells us that our truth table will require eight rows. Using the halving procedure mentioned above, we list the truth values for the columns in the following fashion:

p	q	r
T	T	T
T	T	F
T	F	T
T	F	F
F	T	T
F	T	F
F	F	T
F	F	F

Before concluding this section, we give the truth tables for two more statement forms. The first one is

$$[(p \equiv q) \wedge r] \vee (\sim q \supset r)$$

Its completed truth table is as follows:

p	q	r	$p \equiv q$	$\sim q$	$(p \equiv q) \wedge r$	$\sim q \supset r$	$[(p \equiv q) \wedge r] \vee (\sim q \supset r)$
T	T	T	T	F	T	T	T
T	T	F	T	F	F	T	T
T	F	T	F	T	F	T	T
T	F	F	F	T	F	F	F
F	T	T	F	F	F	T	T
F	T	F	F	F	F	T	T
F	F	T	T	T	T	T	T
F	F	F	T	T	F	F	F

The second statement form is

$$\sim\{p \supset [q \vee (r \wedge s)[\}$$

and its completed truth table is as follows:

p	q	r	s	$r \wedge s$	$q \vee (r \wedge s)$	$p \supset [q \vee (r \wedge s)]$	$\sim\{p \supset [q \vee (r \wedge s)]\}$
T	T	T	T	T	T	T	F
T	T	T	F	F	T	T	F
T	T	F	T	F	T	T	F
T	T	F	F	F	T	T	F
T	F	T	T	T	T	T	F
T	F	T	F	F	F	F	T
T	F	F	T	F	F	F	T
T	F	F	F	F	F	F	T
F	T	T	T	T	T	T	F
F	T	T	F	F	T	T	F
F	T	F	T	F	T	T	F
F	T	F	F	F	T	T	F
F	F	T	T	T	T	T	F
F	F	T	F	F	F	T	F
F	F	F	T	F	F	T	F
F	F	F	F	F	F	T	F

EXERCISE 3.2

1 Construct truth tables for each of the following statement forms.
   (a) $(p \supset \sim q) \equiv (\sim p \lor q)$
   (b) $[(p \land \sim q) \lor r] \supset (q \land \sim r)$
   *(c) $\sim p \land (q \lor p)$
   (d) $(p \lor \sim q) \supset (p \equiv q)$
   (e) $(p \supset \sim p) \lor (p \land p)$
   *(f) $[(p \lor \sim q) \land r] \supset [(\sim q \lor \sim p) \land \sim r]$
   *(g) $[p \supset (p \land q)] \supset \sim p$
   (h) $[p \land (q \lor r)] \supset (s \lor \sim q)$
   (i) $[(p \equiv \sim q) \equiv r] \lor [\sim s \land (t \supset q)]$
   (j) $\sim p \land \sim q$

2 Under what possible circumstances are each of the following statements true?
   (a) John Locke was an empiricist only if George Berkeley was a rationalist.
   (b) If God doesn't exist, then even though there is a devil, everything is possible.
   *(c) Mary will attend the picnic on the condition that neither Jim nor Tom attends.
   (d) If Venus is the closest planet to the earth, and if Mercury is the closest planet to Venus, then Pluto is the farthest planet from the earth.
   *(e) It is both raining outdoors and not raining outdoors.

3.2.1 Logical Equivalence

Now that we know how to construct truth tables for any statement form, we can introduce the notion of logical equivalence. We will say that two statements are *logically equivalent* (with respect to statement logic) if and only if their corresponding statement forms in S have the same truth-functional meaning, that is, *have the same final columns in their respective truth tables*. In order to see just what logical equivalence amounts to, consider these statements:

1 If Jim attends the meeting, then Tom will attend the meeting.
2 It is false that both Jim attends the meeting and Tom doesn't.

To see if these are logically equivalent, we first formalize (1):

$p \supset q$

Its truth table will, of course, be

p	q	$p \supset q$
T	T	T
T	F	F
F	T	T
F	F	T

Formalizing (2) will yield

$\sim(p \land \sim q)$

Its truth table is

p	q	$\sim q$	$p \land \sim q$	$\sim(p \land \sim q)$
T	T	F	F	T
T	F	T	T	F
F	T	F	F	T
F	F	T	F	T

Note that the final columns of these tables are the same, and so statements (1) and (2) are logically equivalent. This doesn't mean that these two statements mean the same thing in any sense except a truth-functional one. In fact, (1) is a conditional and therefore has an intensional component to its meaning that (2) lacks. Nevertheless, their truth-functional meanings are the same. (Incidentally, this further illustrates the difference between the material conditional and ordinary conditionals.)

Beginners in logic sometimes mistakenly believe that $\sim(p \lor q)$ and $\sim p \lor \sim q$ are equivalent statement forms. To see why this isn't so, let's first construct the truth table for $\sim(p \lor q)$:

p	q	$p \lor q$	$\sim(p \lor q)$
T	T	T	F
T	F	T	F
F	T	T	F
F	F	F	T

Now the truth table for $\sim p \lor \sim q$ is as follows:

p	q	$\sim p$	$\sim q$	$\sim p \lor \sim q$
T	T	F	F	F
T	F	F	T	T
F	T	T	F	T
F	F	T	T	T

The final columns in this case are not the same; hence $\sim(p \lor q)$ does not have the same truth-functional meaning as $\sim p \lor \sim q$, and so any statements with these logical forms in natural language would not be logically equivalent.

Although $\sim(p \lor q)$ is not logically equivalent to $\sim p \lor \sim q$, it is logically equivalent to $\sim p \land \sim q$. To see this, let's construct the truth table for $\sim p \land \sim q$:

p	q	$\sim p$	$\sim q$	$\sim p \wedge \sim q$
T	T	F	F	F
T	F	F	T	F
F	T	T	F	F
F	F	T	T	T

Sometimes in using truth tables to determine whether certain statement forms are logically equivalent, it proves convenient—and certainly less time-consuming—to construct only one truth table that incorporates the two statement forms being tested. Thus, in determining whether $\sim(p \vee q)$ and $\sim p \wedge \sim q$ are logically equivalent, we could construct a single truth table:

p	q	$\sim p$	$\sim q$	$p \vee q$	$\sim(p \vee q)$	$\sim p \wedge \sim q$
T	T	F	F	T	F	F
T	F	F	T	T	F	F
F	T	T	F	T	F	F
F	F	T	T	F	T	T

Inspecting the two final columns shows that the two statement forms are logically equivalent.

EXERCISE 3.2.1

Construct truth tables to determine whether the following pairs of statement forms are logically equivalent.

1 $\sim(p \vee q)$ $\sim p \vee . \sim q$

*2 $\sim(p \supset q)$ $\sim p \supset \sim q$

3 $p \equiv q$ $\sim p \equiv \sim q$

4 $p \equiv q$ $(p \supset q) \wedge (q \supset p)$

5 $p \wedge (q \vee r)$ $(p \wedge q) \vee (p \wedge r)$

6 p $\sim\sim p$

*7 $\sim(p \equiv q)$ $\sim p \equiv q$

8 $p \supset q$ $\sim p \vee q$

*9 $p \vee q$ $\sim(\sim p \wedge \sim q)$

10 $\sim p \equiv q$ $p \equiv \sim q$

3.2.2 Complex Connecting Words

In Section 2.4.2.3 we pointed out that a connective that would capture the meaning of the exclusive sense of *or* would have the following truth table:

p	q	$p ? q$
T	T	F
T	F	T
F	T	T
F	F	F

S doesn't have a connective with this truth table. Nevertheless, we can still capture the logical forms of exclusive disjunctions in S. To see how, consider the following statement:

Jim will attend the party with Mary or Cathy.

Now if this statement is an exclusive disjunction, it could more explicitly be expressed as

Jim will attend the party with Mary or Cathy, but not with both.

Letting M abbreviate *Jim will attend the party with Mary* and C abbreviate *Jim will attend the party with Cathy*, we symbolically abbreviate the latter statement as

M or C, but not both M and C.

Formalizing this symbolic abbreviation yields

$(p \lor q) \land \sim(p \land q)$

Clearly, then, we do have a way of formalizing exclusive disjunctions in S. To show that it does indeed work, we construct a truth table for $(p \lor q) \land \sim(p \land q)$:

p	q	$p \land q$	$p \lor q$	$\sim(p \land q)$	$(p \lor q) \land \sim(p \land q)$
T	T	T	T	F	F
T	F	F	T	T	T
F	T	F	T	T	T
F	F	F	F	T	F

The final column of this truth table shows that the truth-functional meaning of $(p \lor q) \land \sim(p \land q)$ is identical to that of the exclusive sense of *or*.

Connecting words requiring more than one connective of S in their formalizations are called *complex* connecting words. In its exclusive sense *or* is a complex connecting word. Several other representative complex connecting words are given under Group 7 of the list of connecting words in Section 2.4.2.6. Let's consider some of these. The connecting word *neither . . . nor* often is used to indicate the negation of a disjunction. For example, the statement

Jim will attend the party with neither Mary nor Cathy.

which we symbolically abbreviate as

Neither M nor C.

can be formalized as either

$\sim(p \lor q)$

or

$\sim p \land \sim q$

As we saw in the last section, these are equivalent. However, it cannot be formalized as

$\sim p \lor \sim q$

Again, we saw why in the previous section.

Another complex connecting word is *unless*, as in the following statement:

Mary will attend the meeting unless Tom asks her out.

It is not difficult to see that this statement asserts the same thing as the following conditional:

If Tom does not ask Mary out, then Mary will attend the meeting.

Letting T stand for *Tom asks Mary out* and M stand for *Mary will attend the meeting*, we can symbolically abbreviate this as

If not T, then M.

Formalizing, of course, gives us

$\sim p \supset q$.

Consequently, any statement having the form of the quasi-statement form *p unless q* can be formalized as $\sim q \supset p$. Actually, as you can verify yourself, this statement form is logically equivalent to $p \lor q$, and so we could also treat it as an inclusive disjunction. Similar remarks apply to the connecting word *except if*.

Just as *or* has both an inclusive and an exclusive sense, so do *unless* and *except if*. These exclusive senses are formalized exactly like exclusive *or* (see Group 7 in the list of connecting words).

Another connecting word listed under Group 7 is . . . *if* . . . ; *otherwise, not* which occurs in the following statement:

George will go fishing if Robin will; otherwise not.

Let G abbreviate *George will go fishing* and R abbreviate *Robin will go fishing*. Thus we obtain

G if R; otherwise, not.

Quite obviously this means the same as

G if R; but not G if not R.

Formalizing, then, yields

$(q \supset p) \land (\sim q \supset \sim p)$

which is how Group 7 instructs us to formalize the connecting word . . . *if* . . . ; *otherwise, not*. Note that it is also more simply formalized under Group 5 as $p \equiv q$. Either way is correct, as you can verify for yourself.

A connecting word which resembles *p if q; otherwise, not* is *p if q; otherwise, r*. A peculiar feature of the latter connecting word is that it is *triadic*: it operates on *three* different statements in creating a compound statement. Although S contains no triadic connectives, we can still formalize it. Consider the following statement:

John will attend the meeting if Maria does; otherwise, he will go home.

Now this asserts the same as

If Maria attends the meeting, then John will; but if she doesn't, then John will go home.

Its formalization is

$(p \supset q) \land (\sim p \supset r)$

which is the formalization suggested by Group 7.

Another triadic connecting word is

p unless q, in which case r.

It is not difficult to see that this is equivalent to

If not q, then p; but if q, then r.

Formalizing it yields

$(\sim q \supset p) \wedge (q \supset r)$

Group 7, however, renders its formalization as

$(p \vee q) \wedge (q \supset r)$

We leave it to you to verify that the two statement forms are logically equivalent.

Three more connecting words appearing under Group 7 are *without*, *rather than*, and *instead of*. Each of these has the same meaning as *but not*; that is, each of

p without q.

p rather than q.

p instead of q.

amounts to saying

p but not q.

Hence each of these quasi-statement forms will be formalized as

$p \wedge \sim q$

To see this, let's first consider *without*:

Tina went to work without going home.

Obviously, this means the same as

Tina went to work, but she didn't go home.

Next, consider *rather than*:

Tina went to work rather than going home.

Again, it is easy to see that this statement asserts the same as this one:

Tina went to work, but she didn't go home.

Another example illustrates *instead of*:

Tom went to the movies instead of the museum.

This obviously means the same as

Tom went to the movies, but he did not go to the museum.

EXERCISE 3.2.2

How would you go about justifying that *p whether or not q* and *p even if q* can be formalized simply by *p*? Can you do it?

3.2.3 Tautologies, Contradictions, and Contingencies

Consider the following statement:

Either it is raining out or it isn't.

Almost everybody would agree that this statement must be true—in fact, so true that it appears trivial. The formalization of this statement is, of course,

$p \lor \sim p$

Its truth table is

p	$\sim p$	$p \lor \sim p$
T	F	T
F	T	T

This truth table informs us that no matter what the truth value of *It is raining out*, the compound statement *Either it is raining out or it isn't* must be true. Statements of this sort are called *tautologies*. In general, we say that a statement is a tautology if and only if the truth table of its formalization has T's in every row of its final column. Thus, any statement having the logical form $p \lor \sim p$ is a tautology (is *tautological*).

Tautologies are also known as *logical truths* or *laws of logic*, since such statements are true solely in virtue of their logical forms. We don't need to make any empirical observations to determine that a logical truth is true. For example, notice that we were able to determine that the statement *Either it is raining out or it isn't* was true solely by constructing a truth table for its corresponding statement form. Thus logical analysis alone was sufficient to determine that the above statement had to be true; we didn't have to look outside.

Logicians have given special names to many of the logical truths. The statement form $p \lor \sim p$ expresses what is often called the *law of the excluded middle*. In abstract terms, it asserts that every statement is either true or false. Since we have defined a statement as a sentence which is either true or false, this law seems quite trivial; it doesn't inform us of anything we didn't already know. As a matter of fact, this is quite correct. However, although tautologies are, in a way, trivial, this doesn't mean that they are not important. We'll see subsequently that tautologies are intimately connected with the concept of entailment.

Another well-known law of logic is the *law of noncontradiction*, which asserts that no statement is both true and false. The statement form which is taken to express this law is

$\sim(p \land \sim p)$

That this is a tautology is demonstrated by its truth table:

p	$\sim p$	$p \land \sim p$	$\sim(p \land \sim p)$
T	F	F	T
F	T	F	T

Another example is

$[(p \supset q) \land (q \supset r)] \supset (p \supset r)$

Its truth table is

p	q	r	$p \supset q$	$q \supset r$	$p \supset r$	$(p \supset q) \land (q \supset r)$	$[(p \supset q) \land (q \supset r)] \supset (p \supset r)$
T	T	T	T	T	T	T	T
T	T	F	T	F	F	F	T
T	F	T	F	T	T	F	T
T	F	F	F	T	F	F	T
F	T	T	T	T	T	T	T
F	T	F	T	F	T	F	T
F	F	T	T	T	T	T	T
F	F	F	T	T	T	T	T

Now some statements, unlike tautologies, are never true under any possible circumstances, no matter what the truth values of their constituent statements are. An example of such a statement is

José is both tall and not tall.

Formalizing it yields

$p \wedge \sim p$

Its truth table is:

p	$\sim p$	$p \wedge \sim p$
T	F	F
F	T	F

We call such statements *contradictions*. In general, we say that a statement is a contradiction if and only if the truth table of its formalization has F's in every row of its final column. Thus any statement having the logical form $p \wedge \sim p$ is a contradiction (is *contradictory*).

Contradictions are also called *logical falsehoods* since they are false by virtue of their logical forms. As in the case of tautologies, we don't need to make any empirical observations to determine that a contradiction is false. Notice, for example, that in the above contradictory statement, logical analysis alone (constructing a truth table) was sufficient to decide that the statement had to be false; we didn't have to look at José.

An example of another contradictory statement form is

$(p \supset \sim q) \equiv (p \wedge q)$

Its truth table looks like this:

p	q	$\sim q$	$p \supset \sim q$	$p \wedge q$	$(p \supset \sim q) \equiv (p \wedge q)$
T	T	F	F	T	F
T	F	T	T	F	F
F	T	F	T	F	F
F	F	T	T	F	F

Any statement which is neither a tautology nor a contradiction is said to be *contingent*. Thus, as we might expect, a contingent statement is one whose truth table has both T's and F's in its final column. Good examples of contingent statements are atomic ones. Take, for example, the following:

Tom and Mary often make love.

Its formalization would, of course, be

p

As we know, its truth table is

p
T
F

Since this truth table has both a T and an F, the statement must be contingent. Quite obviously, every atomic statement is contingent. The negations of atomic statements are always contingent as well.

Although logical analysis can tell us which statements are contingent, it can never tell us what their actual truth values are. If we wish to learn whether the above atomic statement is true, logical analysis will not be sufficient. We must do something more. Either ask Tom or Mary, or make some unusual observations.

Of course, compound statements can be contingent as well. Take, for example, the following statement:

If George doesn't go fishing, then Larry won't go either.

Its formalization is

$\sim p \supset \sim q$

Needless to say, its truth table is

p	q	$\sim p$	$\sim q$	$\sim p \supset \sim q$
T	T	F	F	T
T	F	F	T	T
F	T	T	F	F
F	F	T	T	T

Notice that although this truth table tells us under what circumstances the compound is either true or false, it doesn't tell us which circumstance actually obtains. That can be determined only by extralogical means.

EXERCISE 3.2.3

Using truth tables, determine whether the following statement forms are tautological, contradictory, or contingent.

*1 $p \supset \sim p$
 2 $[p \supset (q \wedge \sim q)] \supset \sim p$
*3 $\sim p \supset (p \wedge \sim p)$
 4 $(p \wedge q) \wedge (\sim p \vee \sim q)$
*5 $(p \vee q) \supset (\sim q \supset \sim p)$
 6 $(p \wedge q) \equiv (q \wedge p)$
*7 $[(p \wedge q) \supset r] \supset [p \supset (\sim r \supset \sim q)]$
 8 $(p \supset q) \wedge (p \wedge \sim q)$
*9 $(p \supset q) \vee [(q \wedge \sim p) \supset r]$
10 $p \supset p$

REVIEW EXERCISES FOR CHAPTER 3

1 Formalize the following statements.
   (a) If Mary goes home rather than stopping at the store, then unless Sam remembered to thaw the roast, they won't have any dinner.
   *(b) Instead of eating lunch, we'll go to see the historic old fort unless it's raining, in which case we'll stay home and play bridge if Arthur doesn't mind.
   *(c) Tom won't go home without having another drink unless he's quit being as obnoxious as he used to be.
   (d) I went to town and bought myself some new shoes, but on the way home I stepped into a hole and broke both my legs.
   (e) Even if the weather seems to be suitable, we won't go boating without checking the forecast.
   *(f) If we go to dinner with Jones, then unless we go somewhere cheap, he'll claim he lost his wallet if we ask him to pay his share of the bill.
   (g) Joe is a liar, a cheat, a thief, and a boor; but at least, if you ask him, he'll admit that he is.
   (h) It is not the case that if the moon shines in your mouth, then you'll go mad.
   *(i) If we get to Tucson before six o'clock, then Mary will drive from there to Phoenix unless it begins to rain, in which case Felipe will take over if we can wake him up.

2 Construct truth tables for the following statement forms.
   (a) $(p \wedge q) \vee [\sim r \vee (\sim p \supset q)]$
   *(b) $p \equiv [q \wedge \sim(r \supset \sim p)]$
   (c) $[p \vee (q \equiv \sim p)] \vee (p \supset q)$
   *(d) $[p \wedge (p \supset q)] \vee [p \wedge (\sim q \wedge p)]$
   (e) $[(p \wedge q) \vee (r \wedge s)] \supset [(q \vee \sim s) \wedge (p \vee \sim r)]$

3 Construct truth tables for the formalizations of (a), (c), (e), and (h) of problem 1.

4 Construct truth tables to determine which of the following pairs of statement forms are logically equivalent.
   *(a) $p \wedge q$ $\sim(p \supset \sim q)$
   (b) $p \supset (q \supset r)$ $q \supset (p \supset r)$
   *(c) $(p \vee q) \supset r$ $(p \supset r) \wedge (q \supset r)$
   (d) $p \supset (q \wedge r)$ $(p \supset q) \vee (p \supset r)$
   *(e) $p \supset q$ $\sim p \supset \sim q$
   (f) $(p \supset q) \wedge (p \supset \sim q)$ p

5 Determine whether each of the following statement forms is a tautology, a contradiction, or contingent.
   *(a) $\{[p \supset (p \wedge \sim p)] \supset (p \wedge \sim p)\} \supset p$
   (b) $(p \supset q) \supset \sim(p \supset \sim q)$
   *(c) $\sim(p \supset \sim p)$
   *(d) $(p \supset q) \wedge (\sim p \supset q)$
   *(e) $[(p \supset q) \supset p] \supset p$
   (f) $[(p \supset q) \wedge (q \vee r)] \wedge \sim(p \supset r)$
   *(g) $(p \supset q) \vee (q \supset r)$
   (h) $[(p \equiv q) \vee (q \equiv r)] \vee (p \equiv r)$

chapter 4
Arguments

4.1
ARGUMENTS

In the previous chapters we discussed the representation of statements as statement forms in S. In this chapter, we extend this method to the representation of arguments. In Chapter 1, you will remember, we defined an argument as a group of statements of which one (the conclusion) is supposed to follow from the others (the premises). For the purposes of introduction this was adequate, but it's now time to introduce certain refinements. The principal difficulty concerns the relation between the premises and the conclusion. In this chapter, we want to develop procedures for studying the forms of any arguments whatsoever, regardless of validity. Here, we run into a difficulty. In our definition above, we described the relation between the premises and the conclusion by saying that the conclusion is supposed to follow from the premises. What should we understand by *supposed to follow?* Perhaps the most natural thing is to take this as a psychological claim about the person presenting the argument: the speaker intends the conclusion to follow from the premises. Unfortunately, the result is that we can tell whether a group of statements constitutes an argument only if we know something about the motives of the person who utters them, and obviously logic does not attempt to deal with psychological questions like this. What alternative might we find?

4.1.1 Some Examples

Let's investigate this problem by considering some examples. The following argument is quite clearly valid:

> All whales are mammals, and all mammals have hearts.
> Moreover, every creature with a heart has kidneys.
> Therefore, all whales have kidneys.

Now, in such an argument, it's irrelevant to the question of validity what the person who uttered it might have had in mind. If the premises of the argument, namely,

> All whales are mammals, and all mammals have hearts.
> Moreover, every creature with a heart has kidneys.

are both true, then it's impossible for the conclusion, namely,

> Therefore, all whales have kidneys.

to be false. In fact, this argument is valid even if the person who happens to utter it on some occasion thinks that it's invalid. The conclusion just *does* follow from the premises, no matter whether anyone intends it. Thus validity doesn't have anything to do with psychological questions like the motives or intentions people might have when presenting arguments.

Now, consider the following argument:

> Everyone who got an A on the final exam passed the course. George, however, got only a C on the final. Consequently, George must have failed.

This is, as you have perhaps recognized, an invalid argument. Nothing in the premises says that *only* those who got A's on the final passed. Now, although this argument is invalid, you might imagine someone thinking that it's valid. It might happen that someone would be persuaded by it to accept the conclusion or would use it to try to prove the conclusion. Clearly, you could intend the conclusion to follow from the premises, even though it doesn't. Therefore, we will want to call this an argument, but an invalid one, and we want our definition of *argument* to include this example as well.

Now, consider another argument:

> God is love. Love is blind. Therefore, God is blind.

Obviously, this argument is no good at all. We won't discuss just what's wrong with it here, but you can easily see that there is no connection at all between the premises and the conclusion. Nevertheless, the difference between this argument and the last example is only a matter of degree: even if one is more likely to pass for valid than the other, they are both equally invalid (an argument is either valid or it isn't). Since it's not our purpose to say how bad an argument has to be in order not to fool anyone, we should define *argument* so that this example too is included.

Transparently bad as our last example is, the following attempt at argument is much worse:

> Hot dogs are traditionally eaten at baseball games, as everyone knows. Moreover, there was an eclipse of the moon last year. Consequently, in view of the well-known fact that earthquakes are more frequent in Los Angeles than in Kansas City, it will probably snow in Denver next Thursday.

This argument is, of course, ridiculous. In fact, although it has the appearance of an argument, we might be inclined to say that it is no argument at all. However, as we indicated above, the difference between this and our previous examples of invalid arguments is one of degree.

4.1.2 Common Features of Arguments

The point we are trying to suggest here is that if we want to define argument in such a way that both valid and invalid arguments are included, we can't say just how ridiculous or implausible a purported argument has to sound before it is no longer an argument. It would be better, in fact, to include as many sorts of arguments as possible under our definition, since in that way we extend the subject of our investigation more widely. Ultimately, our aim is to separate the valid arguments from the others, and so perhaps it's not of any great consequence if we formulate a definition that includes some doubtful cases. Now, if we consider the above four examples of arguments from the point of view of logic, we will pay attention to only those details that the logician is competent to study. Since logic is not psychology, we won't concern ourselves with the attitudes people might have toward these arguments or the motives people might have in propounding them. Instead, we will consider only the language contained in them. What, from that point of view, do they all have in common?

4.1.3 Definition of *Argument*

Aside from the fact that each of our examples consists of premises and a conclusion, there is nothing that they appear to have in common. Therefore, we will define *argument* in the following way:

> **Definition of *Argument***: An *argument* is a set of statements (each of which is called a *premise*) and a statement (called the *conclusion*).

This definition makes use of the term *set* in a somewhat technical sense which must be explained. A set is a collection, aggregate, or group of things. The most important thing about sets is that once we have determined what things are in a set (what its *elements* are, as we say), then we have completely identified that set. Because of this, we can define what it is for two sets to be the same or different: two sets are the same set if, and only if, they contain exactly the same elements.

Now, let us look back at our definition of argument and see how the notion of set functions in it. We have defined an argument as a set of premises and a conclusion, that is, as a set of statements and a statement. According to this definition, then, two arguments will be the same if they have the same premises and the same conclusion. However, the order of the premises of an argument makes no difference, as far as our definition is concerned. Another point is that our definition makes no reference to the connection between the premises and the conclusion. The reason for this is quite simple: the only sort of connection we are interested in is that which occurs when the conclusion follows from the premises—the connection between the premises and the conclusion of a valid argument. If this connection is not present, then in a sense there is no connection between premises and conclusion. Thus, although some invalid arguments may seem to involve such a connection and thus be persuasive (remember our examples above), nevertheless for our purposes one invalid argument is no better than another. This means that, according to our definition, the following is an argument:

2 and 2 is 4.
Australia is in the Southern Hemisphere.
I'm hungry.   (premises)
The moon is made of green cheese.
You owe me $5.   (conclusion)

As a final note, we should point out that nothing in our definition requires that an argument have several premises. There are, in fact, many examples of arguments having only one premise, such as

He has pneumonia. Therefore, he isn't healthy.

Indeed, the notion of set does not even require that a set have *any* elements. If this seems strange, consider this expression: *the set of all people who have been king of the United States of America.* As a matter of fact, there are no such people. Then, should we say that there is no such set? Perhaps we might, but we'll find it more convenient to speak of a set which has no elements. We call this set the *null set*, and we also use the symbol $\emptyset$ to represent it. Now, should we admit arguments with only a conclusion and no premises? For this chapter, let's just note that there is nothing in our definition to exclude such arguments. We'll return to the notion of an argument without premises later.

4.2
ARGUMENTS AND ARGUMENT FORMS

An *argument form* is to an argument as a statement form is to a statement. We derive an argument form from an argument by replacing the statements of the argument with their corresponding statement forms. Since we have studied the latter process in the previous chapters, we only have to add certain details to have a complete account of the process of formalizing arguments. First, let us give a definition of argument form analogous to our definition of argument:

> **Definition of *Argument Form:*** An *argument form* is a set of statement forms (each of which is called a *premise*) and a statement form (which is called the *conclusion*).

Obviously, this is simply our definition of *argument* with *statement form* and *argument form* substituted for *statement* and *argument*, respectively.

In determining the forms of arguments, we will use a procedure like that we used on statements: first we'll symbolically abbreviate the statements of the argument, and then we'll derive statement forms of S from those abbreviations. However, we must have a way of indicating which of the statements in the argument is the conclusion and which are premises. There are two aspects to this problem. First, we must be able to identify the premises and conclusions of arguments. Second, we must have a way of representing this in our argument forms. The second of these problems is quite easily solved. Since an argument is just a set of statements and a statement, all we have to do is list the statements contained in the argument and somehow mark one of them as the conclusion. Any other statement must obviously be one of the premises. The method is straightforward. We will list the premises of an argument or an argument form vertically, then draw a horizontal line, and then list the conclusion below this line:

Premise 1
Premise 2
Premise 3
_____

Conclusion

However, the conclusion of an argument is often found in the middle or even at the beginning of it instead of at the end. Therefore, we'll sometimes have to do a little shifting around to get the conclusion at the end before we proceed with formalizing. We will make this a part of the procedure of symbolic abbreviation.

4.2.1 Finding the Conclusion

As far as possible, we want to be able to accomplish our symbolic abbreviations mechanically: we want rules that we can simply apply to natural-language arguments in a straightforward way without having to worry about problems of interpretation. This is, of course, an ideal that cannot be reached at anything like our elementary level of study here, as we have seen in dealing with statements. When we come to finding the conclusions of arguments, we find some more difficulties of this sort. Sometimes, we can find the conclusion of an argument with no difficulty at all, clearly marked as a separate statement. At other times, we have to extract the conclusion by interpreting the argument in certain ways; we may have to divide a statement into parts or simply guess the intentions of the argument. Naturally, we want to avoid this when possible, and so let's begin with simple cases.

4.2.1.1 Conclusion Indicator Words

Certain words mark the conclusions of arguments. A familiar example is *therefore*, as in the following argument:

> If Juan passed the course, then either he got an A on the final or his term average was at least B. He did pass the course. However, he did not get an A on the final. *Therefore*, his term average must have been at least B.

In this argument, obviously the conclusion is *His term average must have been at least B*. As it appears in this argument, this statement is preceded by the word *therefore*. Clearly, then, the only function of *therefore* here is to indicate that what follows it is the conclusion. Many other *conclusion indicator words* are used in this way, including the following:

As a result

Consequently

Ergo

Hence

It follows that

So

Therefore

Thus

Whence

Wherefore

If you substitute any of these words for *therefore* in the example above, it won't affect the sense of the argument at all. There are other conclusion indicator words that work somewhat differently from these. The largest such group includes those which indicate conclusions coming at the beginnings of arguments. We may use one of them, *since*, to recast our last example:

> Juan's term average must have been at least B, *since* he didn't get an A on the final. If he passed the course, then either he got an A on the final or his term average was at least B. He passed the course.

It isn't hard to see that this is the same argument as our previous example. However, here the conclusion is the statement which is *followed* by *since* and which comes at the *beginning* of the argument. Also, notice that *since* has another peculiarity: it combines the conclusion with one of the premises into a single statement. Thus, when we come to analyze this argument, we'll separate the first statement in it, namely,

> Juan's term average must have been at least B, since he didn't get an A on the final.

into two statements:

> Juan's term average must have been at least B.   (conclusion)
> He didn't get an A on the final.   (premise)

4.2.1.2 Premise Indicator Words

In addition to words which mark conclusions, there are other words which mark statements as premises of arguments. Consider the italicized words in the following example:

> If German technology had lived up to its potential, then Germany would have won the second World War. *However*, many German scientists emigrated for political reasons. *Moreover*, Hitler himself was distrustful of some important inventions. *Indeed*, some sophisticated weaponry, such as jet aircraft and rocket bombs, did not appear until late in the war, although it could have been available sooner. *Finally*, the German economy was not really able to sustain the necessary research expenses or to produce some of what could be made. Germany did, *of course*, lose the war. Therefore, German technology did not live up to its potential.

In this rather lengthy argument, the word *therefore* in the last statement obviously marks the conclusion. What about the words *however, moreover, indeed, finally,* and *of course* in the various premises? First, note that these words are not really necessary to the argument (you can see this by reading through it and omitting those words). They do have a use, however: they indicate that the statements containing them are premises of an argument. Of course, most of these words have other shades of meaning (consider the contrast between *however* and *moreover*). However, just as we ignored the non-truth-functional components of meaning in interpreting connecting words in the last two chapters, we'll also disregard these shades of meaning here.

Obviously, premise indicator words are useful in finding the conclusion. If we know that a particular statement is a premise of an argument, we know that it isn't the conclusion. At least, then, these words help us eliminate certain statements as possible conclusions.

The following words are common premise indicators:

After all	In addition
And	Indeed
As a matter of fact	In fact
Besides	Moreover
By contrast	Nevertheless
Even so	Now
Finally	Of course
For	On the one hand
Furthermore	On the other hand
Fortunately	Similarly
However	Unfortunately

4.2.1.3 Arguments without Indicator Words

As some of our examples indicate, arguments usually don't have a premise indicator word attached to every premise and a conclusion indicator word attached to the conclusion. Most often, only the conclusion and a premise or two will be marked with indicators, leaving the rest to the interpretation of the listener. Sometimes no indicator words at all are found in an argument, as in the following example:

> Wars will always be with us. There has never been a time when men were not engaged in fighting other men somewhere. Man's very nature contains aggressive tendencies that can be satisfied only in the conflict of war. The

scarcity of resources and population pressures create situations of conflict and tension that are capable of no other resolution than war. Some societies even support war as a major occupation and probably could not survive at peace.

This passage is, as you can probably see, an argument with the conclusion *Wars will always be with us*. How can we tell that this is the conclusion? Actually, there is no explicit indication of this in the argument itself. Instead, as we read it, we recognize that the statements after the first all seem to be the sorts of things someone might offer in support of that conclusion. Obviously, what this amounts to is guessing the motives of the person presenting the argument. And equally obviously, there is no very sure method for this sort of thing. In practice, such an intuitive procedure works pretty well: when someone presents us with an argument, we generally pick out the conclusion without difficulty, even if we can't explain how it is that we do it. However, it is part of our aim in studying logic to make everything explicit. What, then, are we to say about this sort of argument?

Actually, it turns out that it will not make any difference for our study of *argument forms* whether we can always correctly pick out the conclusion of a given *argument*. What we can do with such an argument is simply pick out any statement we like and let it be the conclusion. Then, taking the remaining statements as premises, we can test the argument for validity. The point is this: if one statement of a group of statements follows from the rest, then an argument with that statement as conclusion and all the rest as premises will in fact be valid, quite independently of anyone's intentions. Therefore, if we come across something which appears to be an argument, we can perfectly well go ahead and examine it to determine whether the "conclusion" really does follow from the rest of the statements in it. We could, in fact, take every statement in turn as the conclusion and test each argument that resulted in that way.

EXERCISE 4.2

Identify the premises and the conclusion of each of the following arguments.

*1 There is absolutely no doubt that Mr. Pickwick murdered the butler. After all, he was seen arguing with the butler about the condition of the silverware only hours before. Moreover, he surely knew what was going on between his wife and the butler, even if he never said so. Finally, it was with Mr. Pickwick's prized revolver that the butler was shot—and Pickwick himself admits that he alone knew where the gun was kept.

2 In view of the fact that it's raining, the picnic must have been canceled, since we agreed not to go if it rained.

*3 Alice promised to rent her apartment to her sister while she took a vacation.

However, her sister doesn't want to live there, although Alice doesn't know that. Consequently, she'll have to find someone else to live there while she's away. After all, her lease doesn't expire for six months.

4 Doing logic exercises is considerably more interesting than removing cabbage worms from cabbage leaves. But then, so are a lot of other things. Therefore, even though we won't remove any cabbage worms from cabbage leaves this afternoon, we still won't do any logic exercises.

* 5 John probably isn't going to quit his job after all. He really doesn't want to give up all that money, even though he hates his boss. Besides, if he did quit, then he'd have to move and his wife would have to quit her job, and she doesn't want to do that. He's also too old to look for a new job now.

4.3

SYMBOLIC ABBREVIATION OF ARGUMENTS

In symbolically abbreviating arguments, we'll begin with the symbolic abbreviation of statements. Generally, this proceeds as outlined in Chapter 2 and 3. However, there are certain additional rules we must follow. The most important rule is this:

If a certain letter is used for the symbolic abbreviation of a certain atomic statement in an argument, that same letter must be used for that same statement wherever else it occurs in that argument, and that letter must not be used for any other atomic statement.

The reason for this rule should be obvious. Consider the first example in Section 4.2.1.1. The first premise is

If Juan passed the course, then either he got an A on the final or his term average was at least B.

We could symbolically abbreviate this as

If P, then either F or T.

where P is *Juan passed the course*, F is *Juan got an A on the final*, and T is *Juan's term average was at least B*. Now, the second premise is

He (Juan) did pass the course.

Suppose that we symbolically abbreviated this as

T

since it is an atomic statement. This gives rise immediately to two confusions. First, we have also used the letter T in our symbolic abbreviation of the first premise of the argument as an abbreviation for *Juan passed the course*. Thus, using T again for this premise would fail to indicate that these atomic statements were different. Second, as a matter of fact, the second premise occurs as a constituent statement in the first premise, as you can easily see. However, we used the letter P to symbolically abbreviate this statement in our first abbreviation. Therefore, by using T for the second premise, we have failed to indicate this relation between the two premises. If we had followed the rule above, we wouldn't have used T for the second premise since we had already used it for a constituent of the first premise that is not the same statement as the second premise. Furthermore, since we used P for *Juan passed the course* in abbreviating the first premise, our rule would have required us to use P again for this same atomic statement when it occurred as the second premise.

In giving this rule, we are actually indicating an application of a principle given in Chapter 2: the same statement letter is always to be used for the same atomic statement *within a given context*. All that we have done here is to indicate what one such context is.

In addition to this rule, we need one other rule that is more a matter of convenience than anything else:

Remove all premise and conclusion indicator words and other stylistic words.

These words, in fact, do not affect the logical structure of the argument.

We can now give a step-by-step description of the procedure, with an example. We'll take the following argument:

If Juan passed the course, then either he got an A on the final or his term average was at least B. He did pass the course. However, he did not get an A on the final. Therefore, his term average must have been at least B.

We begin by arranging the premises and conclusion in the proper form:

If Juan passed the course, then either he got an A on the final or his term average was at least B.

He did pass the course.

However, he did not get an A on the final.

Therefore, his term average must have been at least B.

Next, we remove all premise and conclusion indicator words:

If Juan passed the course, then either he got an A on the final or his term average was at least B.

He did pass the course.

He did not get an A on the final.

His term average must have been at least B.

Before we proceed with our abbreviation, two observations about style need to be made. First, the pronoun *he* appears in place of the proper name *Juan* everywhere except once in the first premise. We treat this just as we did in the case of statements, except that we now have pronouns that have antecedents in other sentences, not just earlier in the same sentence. Second, notice the following pairs of atomic statements:

Juan *passed* the course (premise 1).
Juan *did pass* the course (premise 2).

His term average *was* at least B (premise 1).
His term average *must have been* at least B (conclusion).

These statements differ slightly in the form of verb that appears in them. However, we'd like to keep our atomic statements straight, and so we'll ignore such differences. We might, if we wished, rewrite the statements in question:

If Juan passed the course, then either Juan got an A on the final or Juan's term average was at least B.

Juan passed the course.

Juan did not get an A on the final.

Juan's term average was at least B.

Now, we can proceed with the symbolic abbreviation of the statements in the argument, following our rule about letters as stated above. We abbreviate the first premise with

If P, then either A or T.

where P is *Juan passed the course*, A is *Juan got an A on the final*, and T is *Juan's term average was at least B*. When we proceed to abbreviate the next premise, we check the atomic statements appearing in the first premise to see if any of them occurs in the second. If so, we use the same letter as in the first premise. If not, we choose a letter different from any already used. (For a long and complex argument, it might be useful actually to write out a list of atomic statements and letters used.) In the present case, the next premise, *Juan passed the course*, is the same statement we've already symbolically abbreviated with P, so we use this letter again:

If P, then either A or T.
P.

Continuing in this manner, we arrive at the symbolic abbreviation for the entire argument:

If P, then either A or T.
P.
Not A.
_____

T.

To derive an argument form from this abbreviation, we proceed exactly as we did in the case of individual statements, again being careful to use one and only one statement variable for one and only one statement constant. The form corresponding to this argument will be

$p \supset (q \lor r)$
p
$\sim q$
_____

r

We now give a summary of rules for formalizing arguments:

Step 1 *Find the conclusion*, using indicator words, intuition, or whatever.
Step 2 *Arrange* the premises one after another in a list, with a line under the last premise and the conclusion under the line.
Step 3 *Remove* all indicator words and stylistic devices.
Step 4 *Symbolically abbreviate* premises and conclusion, observing the following rule: always use the same letter for the same atomic statement.
Step 5 *Formalize* the argument by replacing symbolic abbreviations with corresponding statement forms.

EXERCISE 4.3

Symbolically abbreviate and formalize the following arguments.

1 If it doesn't stop raining soon, I'll go crazy. Now, if I go crazy, then I'll burn the house down. However, I won't burn the house down unless I can find

my lighter, in which case I'll have a cigarette. As a result, either it will stop raining or I'll have a cigarette.

*2 John has lots of money, but he's a very nasty person; besides, he hates cats. He drives an old car that barely runs, even though he owns two new Ferraris. Moreover, he insists on playing Scriabin on the piano at four in the morning—and he plays badly. Consequently, he's probably been quite mad for a good many years.

3 If unemployment decreases in the future, then only students who really want to learn will go to school. Consequently, there will be fewer students in college. After all, if only students who really want to learn go to college, there will be fewer students in college, on the assumption that the birthrate does not rise. As a matter of fact, however, the birthrate will not rise.

4 Since it's Friday the 13th, we'll go to Clancy's for lunch. We go there when Fred's in town unless it's Friday the 13th. However, even if it's Friday the 13th, we go to Clancy's on the condition that Laura pays. Laura will pay just in case Clancy's has corned beef. Now, as a matter of fact, although it's Friday the 13th, Clancy's does have corned beef.

5 I won't have another cup of coffee unless I'm not able to finish my paper by midnight. However, unless George returns my textbook, I won't be able to finish my paper by midnight. Unfortunately, George won't return my textbook, since Betty saw him selling it at the bookstore. So, I'll have another cup of coffee.

*6 Euthanasia is an acceptable practice assuming that it is not murder. Of course, it is murder if and only if it involves an intentional and unjustifiable homicide. Now, euthanasia involves an intentional and unjustifiable homicide unless some other purpose is actually sought. Therefore, so long as some other purpose is actually sought, euthanasia is an acceptable practice.

7 If religion necessarily involves belief in the supernatural, then all religious people have a concept of natural order. Now, unless primitive people construct theories of the world, it is not true that they have a concept of natural order. Primitive people, in fact, do not construct theories of the world, but they are religious. If primitive people are religious and yet do not have a concept of natural order, then it is false that all religious people have a concept of natural order. It follows that religion does not necessarily involve a belief in the supernatural.

4.4
PROBLEMS IN FORMALIZING ARGUMENTS

We've now given all the essential elements of formalizing arguments from the standpoint of statement logic. However, a number of practical difficulties can arise with respect to stylistic devices and other variations. There's no way we can give a comprehensive list of all the twists and quirks that show up in actual arguments. However, to make things easier, we've tried to assemble some of the more common problems in the following sections.

4.4.1 Stylistic Variations

Textbook examples of arguments may retain a great deal of regularity in the way the atomic constituents of compound statements are presented, but the arguments people actually use almost never do so. Moreover, some elements in an argument can be disregarded, as far as logical analysis is concerned. To illustrate what we mean, we'll go through the formalization of the following argument in detail:

> If worldwide reserves of oil are depleted in the near future, then unless nuclear power is a practical alternative, we shall have to depend on coal. According to the most authoritative estimates, we will exhaust all oil reserves comparatively soon. Now, as far as nuclear power is concerned, it cannot be called practical in view of the problems associated with it. As a result, soon we shall find ourselves dependent on coal.

Step 1 *Find the conclusion.* The last statement in this passage begins with the conclusion indicator word *as a result*, which tells us that it's the conclusion. We might also note the word *now*, which is a premise indicator word, at the beginning of the third statement.

Step 2 *Arrange premises and conclusion in order.* The following arrangement, with the premises in the same order that they occur in the original, is the most direct way to proceed:

> If worldwide reserves of oil are depleted in the near future, then unless nuclear power is a practical alternative, we shall have to depend on coal.
>
> According to the most authoritative estimates, we will exhaust all oil reserves comparatively soon.
>
> Now, as far as nuclear power is concerned, it cannot be called practical in view of the many problems associated with it.
> _____
> As a result, soon we shall find ourselves dependent on coal.

Step 3 *Remove all indicator words and stylistic devices.* The only indicator words are *now* in the third premise and *as a result* in the conclusion. There are, however, certain parts of this argument which we must treat as stylistic additions for our analysis. First, consider the phrase *according to the most authoritative estimates* in premise 2. This acts to qualify the claim that we will soon exhaust all oil reserves, but it doesn't add anything to the content of that claim. It gives only what we may call an *extralogical* reason (a reason outside the sphere of logic) for believing it. The argument would proceed the same way if this phrase were omitted, and so we omit it in preparing the argument for formalization. Next, look at the third premise. This may be regarded as a rather convoluted way of saying "Nuclear power is not practical." Now, notice that there is an atomic statement occurring as a component in the first premise which is very much like this: (unless) *nuclear power is a practical alternative*. It is quite natural to take one of these statements as a negation of the other, as far as our analysis of the argument is concerned, even though this means ignoring the mention of problems associated with nuclear power in the third premise. We will thus treat the constituent of premise 3 and the second constituent of premise 1 as the same statement, differing only stylistically. A similar relation holds between the first constituent of premise 1 and premise 2 (*comparatively soon* and *in the near future* are pretty much synonymous), and another such relationship between the last constituent of premise 1 and the conclusion. We want to modify the premises so that these different stylistic variants are replaced everywhere by identical atomic statements. The following is one such modification:

> If worldwide reserves of oil are depleted in the near future, then unless nuclear power is a practical alternative, we shall have to depend on coal.

> Worldwide reserves of oil will be depleted in the near future.

> Nuclear power is not a practical alternative.

> We shall have to depend on coal.

Step 4 *Symbolically abbreviate.* Now that we have eliminated all these stylistic variations, we can easily accomplish the symbolic abbreviation. We will use the following statement constants:

> D = Worldwide reserves of oil are depleted in the near future.
> N = Nuclear power is a practical alternative.
> C = We shall have to depend on coal.

Our symbolic abbreviation will then be

> If D, then C unless N.
> D.
> Not N.
> C.

Step 5 *Formalize.* Having accomplished the symbolic abbreviation, it is a straightforward process to derive the argument form:

$$p \supset (\sim r \supset q)$$
$$p$$
$$\sim r$$
$$q$$

This argument involved a great deal of stylistic variation in the expression of the same atomic statement on several occasions. While most of our examples in this text will not be so varied, it is actually rare in ordinary language that an argument occurs *without* such variation. Most writers, in fact, try as a matter of style never to say the same thing twice in the same way. In such cases, it's necessary to make use of a lot of interpretation and a good deal of feel for the language to identify what can count as different occurrences of the same atomic statement.

Another stylistic variation worth noting is the occurrence of sentences that are not, strictly speaking, statements. The most common sort of item in this category is the *rhetorical question*—a question whose answer is obvious. The second premise of the following example is a rhetorical question:

> Senator Jones will be reelected unless the story of his dealings with the crime syndicate is publicized. But won't the story of his syndicate dealings surely be publicized? As a result, Jones won't be reelected.

Although it's a question in form, the second sentence in this argument amounts, in this context, to an assertion that

> The story of Senator Jones's dealings with the crime syndicate will be publicized.

Rhetorical questions often expect affirmative answers, as in the previous example, and then they amount to assertions of the statements contained in them. Perhaps more frequently, they expect negative answers, as in the following argument:

> If the survivors of the wreck didn't all drown, then either someone came by to rescue them or they managed to swim all the way to shore by themselves. But surely they didn't swim all that distance by themselves, did they? Consequently, someone must have come by to rescue them.

Since the answer to the question in this argument is obviously intended to be no, it amounts to an assertion of the premise:

> The survivors didn't swim all that distance by themselves.

The conclusion of an argument might also appear as a rhetorical question:

> My client wasn't at the scene of the crime. Moreover, she didn't have any reason for committing this murder. Therefore, how can you find her guilty?

Sometimes, incidentally, you may find an argument presented in which something appears to be a rhetorical question although its answer isn't obvious. About all you can do with that sort of thing (which is an error on the part of the person presenting the argument) is to try it both ways—both affirmatively and negatively—to see if either gives a valid argument.

One of the most common stylistic devices for varying the forms of the statements in arguments is the use of *intensional idioms*—phrases that normally function as intensional connecting words—in a way that can (at least for our purposes) be interpreted truth-functionally. One kind of intensional idiom of this sort is illustrated in the following argument:

> If John Jones committed the murder, then Mary Smith is innocent. Now, I think it's pretty obvious that John Jones did commit this murder. Therefore, Mary Smith is innocent.

The second premise of this argument is, technically, an intensional compound with the atomic constituent

> John Jones did commit this murder.

and the non-truth-functional connecting word *Now, I think it's pretty obvious that*. In this context, however, this intensional idiom doesn't amount to much more than *it's true that*, which can be regarded as a truth-functional operator. As a matter of fact, *it's true that* produces a compound with the same truth value as its only constituent, and so in a sense it doesn't do anything. It's what we call a *vacuous operator*. Consequently, no truth-functional meaning will be lost if we simply omit it. Since the operator in the second premise above amounts to *it's true that*, we can omit it, too, and rewrite that premise as

> John Jones did commit this murder.

Sometimes we find intensional idioms that do affect the argument's validity. Just see what happens if we change the second premise of the argument above as follows:

> If John Jones committed this murder, then Mary Smith is innocent. Now, Mary Smith thinks it's pretty obvious that John Jones did commit this murder. Therefore, Mary Smith is innocent.

Obviously, it wouldn't be appropriate to replace the second premise here with *John Jones did commit this murder*, since what is being said is not that he did, but that Mary Smith thinks it's obvious that he did. Here, the intensional idiom is important and can't be disregarded. The only way to decide whether an intensional idiom can be treated as a vacuous operator is by considering the context.

Many intensional idioms are like the conclusion in the following example:

> If logic could be any harder than it is, then I couldn't do it at all. If I couldn't do logic at all, then I'd shoot myself in desperation. However, I won't shoot myself in desperation. Consequently, *I don't think that* logic could be harder than it is.

The conclusion consists of the atomic sentence *Logic could be harder than it is* and the intensional connecting word *I don't think that*. Now, it's fairly evident that this conclusion amounts to

> Logic couldn't be harder than it is.

which is the negation of the constituent of the conclusion as it appears. Therefore, the intensional *I don't think that* amounts to a negation. Actually, this idiom is just a negated form of the vacuous operator *I think that*, and a vacuous operator plus a negation amounts to a negation. Certain other intensional idioms also work as negations, as, for instance, *I doubt that* in the following argument:

> If the moon is made of green cheese, then there are certainly mice on the moon. However, *I doubt that* the moon has mice. Therefore, the moon isn't made of green cheese.

Of course, if we negate this intensional idiom, it becomes a vacuous operator, as in the following argument:

> If Moriarty is involved in this case, then Holmes will exert himself to the utmost and catch the culprit. According to Watson, Moriarty is definitely involved. Therefore, *I don't doubt that* Holmes will exert himself to the utmost and catch the culprit.

4.4.2 Abbreviated Premises

In arguments a special sort of abbreviation is sometimes encountered, as in the following example:

> Either it rained last night, or there's a leaking pipe in the basement. If the former, it would be in the weather report. However, if the latter, we'll have to go to the basement to see for ourselves. It wasn't in the weather report. Therefore, I guess we'll have to go to the basement to see for ourselves.

In this argument, the expressions *the former* and *the latter* are used as abbreviations for the atomic statements

> It rained last night.
> There's a leaking pipe in the basement.

In a way, these words work here much like the statement constants of our symbolic abbreviations: they abbreviate entire statements. Again, like those statement constants, it's necessary to refer to the context to tell what an abbreviation of this sort stands for.

Another, perhaps more explicit, device is the use of expressions with *ordinal numbers* (first, second, third, etc.). A common construction is illustrated in this argument:

> The picnic will be held on Saturday unless it rains or the park is closed. *In the first case* the picnic will be rescheduled, and in the second case we'll meet to determine our course of action.

The expressions *in the first/second case* function much as the antecedents of conditionals. That is, the second sentence above is, in effect, an abbreviation of

> If it rains, then the picnic will be rescheduled; and if the park is closed, we'll meet to determine our course of action.

Thus, here *in the first case* abbreviates *if it rains*. Likewise, *in the second case* functions as an abbreviation of *if the park is closed*. A few other expressions work in just this way, among them *on the first/second assumption, on the first/second alternative*.

Ordinal numbers can also be used just about in the same way as we used statement constants:

> Either John sold his car, or the bank repossessed it. The first of these, however, is false; therefore, the second is true.

Another common way of abbreviating premises is through the use of letters or numbers in parentheses to divide up compound statements. This is especially common when very complex statements are involved:

> If John doesn't get the job, then he'll either (1) get depressed, go home, and get drunk; (2) get mad, leave town, and drop out of society; or (3) try again. If (1), it will all be over in two days; but if (3), he'll probably fail again, and we'll have to go through it one more time. If (2), on the other hand, he'll give up and drop back in after two weeks.

In all cases involving abbreviated statements, the procedure is simple: substitute full statements for their abbreviations. It's generally convenient to do this while removing stylistic devices.

4.4.3 Conjoined Premises

It's not unusual, especially in spoken (as opposed to written) arguments, to find a whole argument tied together with conjunctions, perhaps with some indicator words here and there:

> John will move to Chicago unless Mary gets the job or he has trouble selling his house, but in fact he won't have any trouble selling his house, and moreover Mary isn't likely to get the job, and consequently John will move to Chicago.

Now, we could regard this as a compound statement containing three conjunctions. However, it's also natural to take this as an argument with three premises, treating *in fact* and *moreover* as premise indicator words and *consequently* as a conclusion indicator word. As we've said, which we do is a little arbitrary and depends on the context and our purpose in the analysis. As a matter of fact, there's more than one way we can break up this statement. We could, for instance, make it into an argument with one rather long premise:

> John will move to Chicago unless Mary gets the job or he has trouble selling his house, but in fact he won't have any trouble selling his house, and moreover Mary isn't likely to get the job.

> Consequently, John will move to Chicago.

(Notice that we've deleted the last *and*, leaving the conclusion as a separate statement.) We could also have analyzed this example into a three-premise argument:

> John will move to Chicago unless Mary gets the job or he has trouble selling his house.

> In fact, he won't have trouble selling his house.

> Moreover, Mary isn't likely to get the job.

> Consequently, John will move to Chicago.

(Notice here that we've removed all the occurrences of *and*, leaving only the premise and conclusion indicator words.) These aren't the only ways to dissect this example. Now, as a matter of fact, these different ways of breaking up conjunctions in an argument won't really affect the results of our procedures for determining that the argument is valid, as we'll see later. However, we need to set up some rules to follow in formalizing such arguments. There are two things we'd like to accomplish. First, we want the conclusion to be separated from the premises. Second, it's convenient to eliminate long *coordinated conjunctions* (statements of the form *A and B and C and . . .*). Consequently, we'll adopt the following rules:

1   If the conclusion is conjoined to a premise, separate them.
2   If a coordinated conjunction contains more than three conjuncts, break it up into constituents.
3   When a word can be regarded as either a conjunction or a premise indicator, treat it as a premise indicator.

4.4.4 Chained Arguments

As we've defined *argument*, an argument has exactly one conclusion. Sometimes, however, you may come across arguments like the following:

> If Colonel Blimpington hasn't returned from the Amazon yet, then unless he's gotten lost or been eaten by ants, he has no doubt found the lost kingdom of Caramba. Now, as a matter of fact, Colonel Blimpington hasn't returned from the Amazon yet. Therefore, unless he's gotten lost or been eaten by ants, he has found the lost kingdom of Caramba. Now, on a previous expedition with him, I learned that ants actually find the Colonel most distasteful, and so he hasn't been eaten by ants. Consequently, if he hasn't gotten lost, he's found the lost kingdom of Caramba.

In this argument there are three different conclusion indicator words: *therefore* at the beginning of the third sentence, *and so* in the fourth sentence, and *consequently* at the beginning of the last sentence. Does this mean that this argument has three conclusions? That won't fit with our definition of argument. However, we can't simply break it up into three separate arguments by including everything up to the first conclusion as one argument, everything from there to the second conclusion as another, and so on. To see why, look what happens if we do that. The first argument would be

> If Colonel Blimpington hasn't returned from the Amazon yet, then unless he's gotten lost or been eaten by ants, he has no doubt found the lost kingdom of Caramba. Now, as a matter of fact, Colonel Blimpington hasn't returned from the Amazon yet. Therefore, unless he's gotten lost or been eaten by ants, he has found the lost kingdom of Caramba.

There seems to be nothing wrong so far. This looks like an argument all by itself. However, the second argument would be

> Now, on a previous expedition with him I learned that ants actually find the Colonel most distasteful, and so he hasn't been eaten by ants.

We could treat this as a one-premise argument by separating *he hasn't been eaten by ants* as the conclusion. Again, this seems to be at least plausible as an argument all by itself, although we might want to say that its importance here is in its connection with the rest of the whole argument. But look at the last "argument":

> Consequently, if he hasn't gotten lost, he's found the lost kingdom of Caramba.

This is just a conclusion, and if we treat it as an argument all by itself, we'll have to consider it an argument without premises. As we pointed out in Section 4.1.3, there's nothing impossible about the notion of an argument with no premises. However, in this case it's obvious that this conclusion is intended to follow from the *entire argument*. In fact, what we have here is the sort of thing which we described in Chapter 1 as a *deduction*, or at least a partial one. The last conclusion is really the conclusion of the argument, but the intermediate conclusions are only steps along the way which show how we get from the premises to the conclusion.

When an argument includes several statements indicated as conclusions in this way, we call it a *chained argument*. Usually, chained arguments have additional premises added after some of or all the intermediate conclusions, as the above example does. Now, as we indicated, a deduction is a sort of chained argument, but not just any sort. In a deduction, all the steps necessary to make it clear that the conclusion follows from the premises have been added. Just how we determine what steps might be necessary is a subject we'll treat in Chapter 7. For the present, however, we should note that not all chained arguments are deductions: many (such as our example) include only some of the steps needed to show how the conclusion follows. For now, our problem is how to formalize chained arguments. Since the intermediate conclusions only show how the conclusion follows from the premises, they actually don't affect the validity of the argument. Therefore, for the purposes of formalizing, we should simply *omit* them. Taking our example above as an illustration, we ignore all conclusions except the last:

> If Colonel Blimpington hasn't returned from the Amazon yet, then unless he's gotten lost or been eaten by ants, he has no doubt found the lost kingdom of Caramba.
>
> Colonel Blimpington hasn't returned from the Amazon yet.
>
> On a previous expedition with him, I learned that ants actually find the Colonel most distasteful, and so[1] he hasn't been eaten by ants.
> ___
> If he hasn't gotten lost, he's found the lost kingdom of Caramba.

___

[1] Note that *and so* here is a conjunction, not a conclusion indicator word.

For practice, let's symbolically abbreviate this, say, as

If not C, then K unless L or A.
Not C.
D and so not A.

___

K if not L.

and formalize it:

$\sim p \supset [\sim(r \lor s) \supset q]$
$\sim p$
$t \land \sim s$

___

$\sim r \supset q$

___

EXERCISE 4.4

Formalize the following arguments.

1   If my client is guilty, then either he hid the money so well that no one could find it or he burned it in the furnace. But, I ask you, how could he have hidden it that well, given that he had barely three minutes in which to do it? On the other hand, do you honestly believe he would have burned up all that money? Therefore, you must conclude that my client is not guilty.

*2   I don't think the astronauts actually went to the moon. After all, if they had gotten there, in no time at all some developer would've put buildings all over it. But, as anyone can see just by looking, there's not a single building on it.

3   At Mary's party tonight, I'm quite sure that either Alfred will put a lampshade on his head or Alice will suspend herself upside down from the chandelier. In the first case Alfred's wife will get furious and go home screaming, while in the second that silly fool Martin will become hysterical and call the police. Therefore, as you can see, no matter what happens, it will be a memorable party.

*4   If we could invent a perpetual-motion machine, we'd have found a solution to the world's energy problems. Now, quite obviously, if we did that, then everybody would benefit and we'd be rich. Consequently, if we made a machine like that, we'd be rich. However, it's also true that if we could invent a perpetual-motion machine, then there'd be a free lunch; and, as everyone knows, there's no free lunch. I suppose, therefore, that we won't get rich.

5   If Juan was there, then Sam was; and if Sam was there, Mary was; but unless Alice wasn't there, Juan wasn't there; and so Mary and Alice weren't both there.

REVIEW EXERCISES FOR CHAPTER 4

Formalize the following arguments.

1　We can travel either by the main highway or by the side road. If we do the former, we won't get there before dark; on the other hand, we won't get lost either. However, while it's true that if we go by the side road, we'll get there before dark unless we get lost, nevertheless it's possible that we'll get lost if we go that way. Now, bear in mind that, in view of the fact that Fred is driving, if it's possible that we'll get lost, then we will. Furthermore, if we get lost, we certainly won't get there before dark. Consequently, it looks as if we won't get there before dark, whatever road we take.

*2　Unless I pay the rent by Friday, I'll be evicted. Now, if I'm evicted, I'll have to sell my television; and if I do that, I'll take up reading. According to what everyone tells me, if I take up reading, my grades will improve. Moreover, unless my grades improve, I won't graduate this June. Knowing myself as I do, I'm quite sure that my grades won't improve unless I sell my television, which I won't do unless I'm evicted. Consequently, if you see me graduate this June, you'll know I didn't pay the rent by Friday.

3　According to the conditions specified by King Thold, you may marry the princess if either (1) you slay the dragon and capture the citadel of Orp or (2) you solve the Riddle of Ghast and banish the ogre from the kingdom. Also note, however, that if you banish the ogre without solving the Riddle of Ghast, you can expect the ogre's sister Agnes to take her revenge, in which case you won't be able to marry the princess. On the other hand, if you succeed in slaying the dragon, then there's no doubt that you will capture the citadel of Orp. Now, I happen to know that you can't solve the Riddle of Ghast, whence I conclude that you can't marry the princess unless you slay the dragon.

*4　Your insurance policy won't pay for damage from bursting water pipes unless the pipes burst as a result of an earthquake. However, your policy pays for all damage that results from a tornado. Consequently, in my opinion, your policy will pay for damage from bursting water pipes even if they don't burst as a result of an earthquake, so long as the damage results from a tornado.

5　According to paragraph 10 of the contract, paragraph 2 is not effective unless the conditions set forth in paragraphs 4 and 5 obtain. If those conditions obtain, however, then paragraph 6 becomes effective. Paragraph 7, however, becomes effective just in case the conditions set forth in paragraphs 4 and 5 do not obtain. From all this it may be concluded that paragraphs 2 and 7 are not both effective.

*6　Unless Chuck's car is repaired by 4 P.M., he won't get home tonight without riding home with George. However, with a reckless driver like George, Chuck's life will be in danger if he rides home with him. Clearly, then, unless Chuck's car does get repaired by 4, he won't get home tonight without endangering his life. Knowing Chuck, he'll definitely get home tonight. As a result, his life will be in danger if his car is not repaired by 4.

7　Since Ferd's hamburgers are disgusting, inedible, and unspeakable, I'll quite definitely get sick if we eat there. However, if Bill comes to lunch with us, then considering how fond he is of Ferd's french fries, we'll no doubt eat there. As I'm sure you realize, if I get sick, then Ferd's will throw us out and we won't have to pay for lunch. Consequently, if Bill comes to lunch with us, we won't have to pay for it even though I'll get sick.

chapter 5
Sets and Other Technical Matters

INTRODUCTORY REMARKS

In this chapter, we need to introduce some technical details that will make our study of arguments simpler and more effective. First, we need some elementary concepts of *set theory* (with which you may already be familiar) in order to make our investigation more systematic and to give us greater generality in expression. Second, we need to introduce the technical distinction between an *object language* and a *metalanguage*. This distinction is of philosophical as well as technical importance. Philosophically, it enables us to deal with problems concerning the difference between *using* a word or expression and *mentioning* it. Technically, the object language–metalanguage distinction will allow us to express features of the syntactic and semantic theories of Symbolic Language S with both greater simplicity and increased clarity. Beyond these technical points, however, the use-mention distinction is of theoretical interest in its own right, and so we will begin with a discussion of the problems which give rise to it.

OBJECT LANGUAGE AND METALANGUAGE

Consider the following two sentences:

Topeka is the capital of Kansas.
Topeka begins with a T.

At first you might think that these both say something about the same thing (namely, Topeka), but a little reflection will show that this isn't so. The first statement says something about a city, namely the capital of Kansas, while the second says something about a word which happens to be the name of that city. Thus, the word *Topeka* in the second sentence is not being used to name the city of Topeka at all: it's being used instead to name *itself*. When a word functions as a name for itself in this way, we will say that it is *mentioned*. By contrast, when a word functions in the usual way to refer to something other than itself, we will say that it is *used* (as the word *Topeka* is in the first statement). It's sometimes of considerable importance to keep straight whether a word is being mentioned or used. In such cases, we'll use the following convention: when a word is mentioned, we'll place single quotes around it. Thus, we would use our convention to rewrite the second statement as

'Topeka' begins with a 'T.'

Sometimes it isn't clear what a sentence means unless we can tell whether certain expressions are being used or mentioned. Consider the following statement:

An inch is longer than a mile.

Obviously, this statement is false. However, the following statement is true:

'An inch' is longer than 'a mile.'

since 'an inch' has six letters while 'a mile' has only five.

The distinction between mention and use gives rise to a corresponding distinction between *object language* and *metalanguage*. Suppose that you were studying French in an American classroom. Obviously, you would talk about the French language in English. French, being the object of study, is called the *object language* here. The language used to talk about French (in this case, English) is called the *metalanguage*. Thus, although French words would occur in the metalanguage, they would be mentioned instead of used. Actually, the French words occurring in the metalanguage could be written within quotation marks to make it clear that they function as the names of French words in the object language. As an example, consider the following statement:

The word 'livre' is a noun.

This is a *metalinguistic* statement—a statement which occurs in the metalanguage. The French word written within single quotes also occurs in the metalanguage since it is the name of a word occurring in the object language. In other words,

'livre'

occurs in the metalanguage and is used as a name for mentioning the French word

livre

which occurs in the object language.

The object language and the metalanguage need not be different languages in the same way that French and English are different languages. After all, it's quite possible to study the English language in English, in which case both the object language and the metalanguage would be English. The important thing to note is that the language being used to talk about a language is at a *different level* from the language being talked about: we might say that the object language is at level one and the metalanguage is at level two. Noting the difference between object language and metalanguage involves taking notice of different levels of language.

Now, in talking about the relationship between object language and metalanguage, we have, of course, used a language at a still higher level. If the object language is at level one and the metalanguage is at level two, then the language used to talk about these two languages must be at level three. The language used to talk about the object language and the metalanguage is now called the *meta-metalanguage*. There is no limit to the number of levels which are possible.

Distinctions among various levels of language are relative. To see what we mean, consider the following statement:

1   The word 'livre' contains five letters.

Undoubtedly, this statement occurs in a metalanguage, i.e., in a language used to talk about the object language. But now suppose we wish to talk about the above metalinguistic statement. For instance, we might wish to say:

2   The statement "The word 'livre' contains five letters" contains six words.

Now (2) is in the metalanguage, and (1) is in the object language, from the point of view of the language used to assert (2). The string of words occurring between the double quotes in (2) together with the double quotes now functions as the name used to mention (1). Of course, if we are interested in preserving differences among the three different levels of language, then we would say that 'livre' occurs in the object language, (1) occurs in the metalanguage, and (2) occurs in the meta-metalanguage. Notice that in distinguishing these three different levels of language, we talked about them and so we were using a "new" metalanguage to do so.

This may all seem to be a pedantic exercise in fruitless trivialities, but it has an important point. Consider the following statement:

3   Statement (3) is false.

Let's symbolically abbreviate this statement as S. Now let's consider whether S is true or false. Clearly, if S is true, then since S asserts that S is false, it follows that S is false. On the other hand, if S is false, then since S asserts that S is false, it follows that it is false that S is false and so S must be true. It seems that we are compelled to accept the unfortunate conclusion that S is true if and only if S is false. We've come to this conclusion by what appears to be correct reasoning, and yet the conclusion itself is absurd. This sort of situation is know as a *paradox*. A paradox is effectively an affront to reason, since it appears to be impossible and at the same time true. Since we place a high value on rationality, we shouldn't allow a paradox to go unresolved.

Obviously, this paradox arises because statement (3) is *self-referential*: it is a statement used to assert something about itself. Put in our terms, the paradox arises because statement (3) occurs in an object language which attempts to serve as its own metalanguage. Given the distinction between object language and metalanguage, we can resolve the paradox by showing that if (3) means anything at all, then it does not refer to itself. Clearly, if (3) does not really refer to itself, the paradox simply disappears. Given our analysis of language in terms of ordered levels, this is easily demonstrated.

Suppose that (3) is a meaningful statement. Then it follows that it occurs in a metalanguage at a certain level. If this is so, then (3) must assert something about a statement at a lower level. In other words, the name "Statement (3)" occurring in statement (3) at linguistic level n is used to mention a particular statement at a lower level. Statement (3) is, then, a metalinguistic statement used to assert that some other statement in the object language is false. Therefore, statement (3) above does not refer to itself.

If the intention is to rid ourselves of self-referential statements because they give rise to paradoxes, then why not simply call them all meaningless rather than attempt to do away with them by drawing a pedantic distinction between object languages and metalanguages? Perhaps this objection would have some merit if it weren't for the stubborn fact that self-referential statements are not the only kinds of statements which generate paradoxes.

Consider the following two statements:

4   Statement (5) is false.
5   Statement (4) is true.

Neither of these statements refers to itself. Statement (4) ostensibly refers to statement (5), and statement (5) apparently refers to statement (4). These two statements would not be eliminated if we simply considered all self-referential statements as meaningless; consequently, they would have to be counted as legitimate ones. Nevertheless, they, too, give rise to paradoxical results.

Suppose that statement (4) is true. Then, since it asserts that statement (5) is false, (5) must be false. But if (5) is false, then since (5) asserts that (4) is true, it follows that it is false that (4) is true. Hence (4) must be false. Thus, if (4) is true, (4) is false.

Now let's assume that (4) is false. Clearly, if (4) is false, then since (4) asserts that (5) is false, it must be the case that it is false that (5) is false, in which case (5) has to be true. But if (5) is true, then since (5) asserts that (4) is true, it follows that (4) is true. Therefore, the supposition that (4) is false entails that (4) is true.

Unfortunately, we have generated another paradox: if (4) is true, then it is false; if, on the other hand, (4) is false, then it is true. In this case, of course, the paradox cannot be attributed to self-reference. Obviously, calling self-referential statements meaningless will not avoid the generation of all paradoxes. However, distinguishing between object language and metalanguage enables us to resolve even this paradox since this distinction will dismiss one of these statements as meaningless, if it is supposed that each refers to the other.

For the sake of argument, assume that statement (4) above is meaningful. In that case, since (4) asserts something about statement (5), (4) must be a metalinguistic statement used to assert that a statement in the object language is false. But if this is so, statement (5), being in the object language, cannot assert something about statement (4) in the metalanguage, since this is impossible on account of the various levels of language. Then, clearly (5) cannot be used to assert something about (4), and so (5) must be meaningless. If, however, (5) is indeed meaningful, then (5) is not being used to say that statement (4) *above* is false, but rather to say that *another* statement (4) at an even lower level is false. So, if (5) cannot meaningfully be used to make reference to statement (4), then the paradox disappears. Distinguishing between levels of language effectively eliminates this sort of "referring."

5.3

SETS

We will need a certain amount of elementary set theory to deal with our subject matter effectively in the following chapters.

As mentioned in Chapter 4, a set is a collection or aggregate of "things" in the broadest possible sense of the word. Thus, we can speak of sets of physical objects, numbers, properties, statements, and even sets of sets (after all, a set is a "thing," too, even if an "abstract thing"). When talking about sets in this book, usually we will be concerned with sets of statements or sets of statement forms. The things which are in sets are often referred to as *members* or *elements* of those sets, as we've noted before.

The notation we will use for describing sets is called the *tabular notation:* we simply list the members of a given set. Thus, the set of odd numbers between 1 and 6 is described in the following way:

$\{3,5\}$

Notice that the elements (members) 3 and 5 are separated by commas and enclosed in braces. The advantage of the tabular notation is that it shows us clearly just what the members of a set are.

If a certain thing, say x, is a member of a given set, say S (that is, if S contains x as one of its elements), then we write

$x \in S$

which can be read variously as x *belongs to* S, as x *is a member of* S, or as x *is an element of* S. Thus, if we are interested in indicating that 3 is a member of the set $\{3,5\}$, we write

$3 \in \{3,5\}$

If, on the other hand, we want to express that a certain thing x is not a member of a given set, we write:

$x \notin S$

which indicates that x is not a member of S. Quite obviously, the following is a true statement:

$$2 \notin \{3,5\}$$

Sets can be of any size. The set {Jimmy Carter} consists of only one person, and the set {'Set theory is fun.'} contains only one statement. Sets consisting of only one member are called *unit sets*. Sets that have only a finite number of members are called *finite sets*. Informally, a set is finite if and only if it consists of a specific number of different elements; that is, if you count the different members of the set, the counting process comes to an end. Some sets, however, have infinitely many members, as, for example, the set of all the positive integers.

The set with no members is called the *empty* or *null set*, and it's usually referred to by means of the symbol $\varnothing$. The set of all human beings born on earth but presently living on Jupiter is the null set. The set of all odd numbers which satisfy the equation $x^2 = 4$ is also the null set.

We say that a set S is the *same as* (or *identical to*) a set S' if and only if S and S' have exactly the same members. Note that if two sets have the same *number* of members, they still might not be the same; they must have the very *same members* if they are to be identical. Another way of stating this is to say that two sets S and S' are the same if every element which belongs to S also belongs to S' and if every element which belongs to S' also belongs to S. We denote the identity of sets S and S' by

$$S = S'$$

Thus the set of all the even numbers between 1 and 9 and the set of 2, 4, 6, and 8 are the same. Incidentally, you might note that when S and S' have no members, all the members of S also belong to S' and *vice versa*. Consequently, there is just one null set.

Various operations can be performed on sets to obtain new sets. We'll concern ourselves only with two simple ones. Given any two sets S and S', you can always combine their members into one set, called their *union*. We use the expression

$$S \cup S'$$

to name the union of the two sets. And, again given any two sets S and S', you can form their *intersection*, consisting of all the members common to the two sets. We write

$$S \cap S'$$

to name the intersection of the two sets. The union of the two sets {2,4,6} and {1,3,4,5}, namely,

{2,4,6} ∪ {1,3,4,5}

is

{1,2,3,4,5,6}

whereas their intersection

{2,4,6} ∩ {1,3,4,5}

is

{4}

EXERCISE 5.3

1   Using the tabular notation, describe the following sets.
(a)   Set of all United States Presidents since 1952.
(b)   Set of all dogs capable of doing logic.
(c)   Set of all your logic instructors.
(d)   Set of all negative integers.

2   Rewrite the following statements using set notation.
*(a)   x belongs to S.
*(b)   The set S is not a member of itself.
*(c)   The intersection of S and S' is identical to T.

3   Let $S = \{x,y,z\}$ and $S' = \{10,11,12,13\}$. State whether each of the following statements is true or false.
(a) $(S \cup S') = \{x,y,z,10,11,12,13\}$
*(b) $(S \cap S') = \{x\}$
(c) $(S \cap S') = S$
*(d) $(S \cap S') = \varnothing$
(e) $10 \notin S$
*(f) $S \neq S'$

*4   Which of these sets are the same? $\{w,x,y,x\}$, $\{y,x,w\}$, $\{w,w,x,x,y\}$, $\{w,x,y\}$.

5   Let $S = \{1,2,3,4\}$ and $S' = \{4,3,2\}$. State whether each of the following statements is true or false.
(a) $1 \in S'$
*(b) $(S \cup S') = S$
(c) $(S \cap S') = S'$
*(d) $3 \notin (S \cap S')$
(e) $(S \cap S') = \{1\}$
*(f) $(S' \cup \{1\}) = S$

SYMBOLIC LANGUAGE s

Symbolic Language s is composed of three different sets of symbols: an infinite set of statement variables, a set of connectives, and a set of punctuation marks. Employing the tabular notation, we can define each of these sets, respectively, as follows:

$$\mathbf{P} = \{p, q, r, s, t, \ldots\}$$
$$\mathbf{C} = \{\sim, \wedge, \vee, \supset, \equiv\}$$
$$\mathbf{M} = \{(, [, \{, \},],)\}$$

In Chapter 2, we introduced the notion of a statement form more or less informally. Now that we have the distinction between object language and metalanguage, we can give a precise definition of a statement form. But first a few preliminary matters.

Obviously, our object language is s. Our metalanguage is English supplemented with the names of the various symbols in s. Usually, we can get by simply by using the symbols as names for themselves, although if we wish to make it absolutely clear that a symbol is being mentioned instead of used, we can place quotes around it according to the convention of Section 5.2. Thus, although

$$r \equiv (s \wedge t)$$

$$q$$

$$p \supset q$$

$$q \vee \sim r$$

$$\sim q \supset r$$

are all statement forms in s, their names

$$'r \equiv (s \wedge t)'$$

$$'q'$$

$$'p \supset q'$$

$$'q \vee \sim r'$$

$$'\sim q \supset r'$$

are not. Of course, when the context makes it clear that a symbol is being mentioned and not used, we can omit the quotes.

However, a difficulty arises when we wish not so much to mention some particular statement form of s but to talk about statement forms in general. For these purposes, we introduce *metavariables* into the metalanguage. We use metavariables to stand for the statement forms of S, although not necessarily any specific ones. We use the following capital letters for metavariables:

A, A_1, A_2, . . .

B, B_1, B_2, . . .

C, C_1, C_2, . . .

D, D_1, D_2, . . .

. . . .

Thus, if we wish to speak generally about any statement form of S containing one and only one connective, we could express it in the following way:

> If A is any statement form having one and only one connective in it, then A is contingent.

Obviously this false statement is talking not about some particular statement form but about any statement form possessing one and only one connective; consequently, we are talking about $p \lor q$, $q \land r$, $t \supset p$, $p \equiv p$, and so on, but definitely not about p, r, $\sim q \lor s$, $p \supset (q \land r)$, and so on. A does not occur in S but rather in the metalanguage used to talk about S. In a sense, metavariables are indefinite names for the statement forms of S.

Metavariables enable us to say things about statement forms in S with much greater clarity and precision. Consider the following description:

> A statement form of S which is a conditional having as its antecedent a disjunction the first disjunct of which is a negation

This is a very cumbersome description, not at all easy to interpret. However, using metavariables, we can say the same thing simply as

> A statement form of S of the form $(\sim A \lor B) \supset C$

This expression can be used to refer to any statement form in S which can be obtained by substituting some statement form for A, some statement form (not necessarily a different one) for B, and some statement form (again, not necessarily different) for C. Thus, it could refer to any of the following:

1 $(\sim p \vee q) \supset r$
2 $[\sim(p \vee q) \vee (q \supset \sim r)] \supset (s \wedge t)$
3 $(\sim p \vee q) \supset \sim p$
4 $(\sim p \vee p) \supset p$

Example (1) can be obtained from $(\sim A \vee B) \supset C$ by substituting p for A, q for B, and r for C. Example (2) is more complex: we obtain it from $(\sim A \vee B) \supset C$ by substituting $(p \vee q)$ for A, $(q \supset \sim r)$ for B, and $(s \wedge t)$ for C. Since each of these is a statement form, $(\sim A \vee B) \supset C$ could refer to example (2). Note that in this case we have a left-hand *parenthesis* in $(\sim A \vee B) \supset C$ where there is a left-hand *bracket* in $[\sim(p \vee q) \vee (q \supset \sim r)] \supset (s \wedge t)$. We use parentheses, brackets, and braces in the metalanguage effectively as metavariables for punctuation symbols: (can refer to (, [, or {, as can [and {. Similarly,),], and } can all refer to any of),], and }. A diagram may make it clearer which parts of $(\sim A \vee B) \supset C$ refer to which parts of $[\sim(p \vee q) \vee (q \supset \sim r)] \supset (s \wedge t)$:

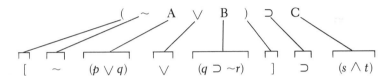

Don't be confused by the fact that p occurs twice in (3). A diagram showing the connections of $(\sim A \vee B) \supset C$ is:

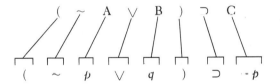

In (4), we have another situation:

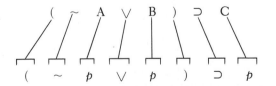

Note that A, B, and C all refer to the same symbol, namely p. However, they do not refer to the same *occurrence* of p. Nothing requires that different metavariables refer to different statement forms, although they always will refer to different occurrences of statement forms.

Notice, incidentally, that the symbols $\sim$, $\vee$, and $\supset$ in $(\sim A \vee B) \supset C$ are not really being used as symbols of S: they are metalinguistic names for the corresponding connectives in S. Thus, ~ in ~*p* is a connective in S, but ~ in ~A is the metalinguistic name of that connective and so is not in S.

Although the same statement form may be substituted for different metavariables, we cannot substitute different statement forms for different occurrences of the same metavariable. Thus, example (1) is not of the form (~A ∨ B) ⊃ A, as the following diagram shows:

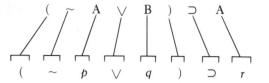

Note that the first occurrence of A would refer to *p* while the second would refer to *r*. As a result, (~A ∨ B) ⊃ A cannot refer to (~*p* ∨ *q*) ⊃ *r*.

5.4.1 Definition of *Statement Form*

S is composed of three different sets of symbols: a set **P** of statement variables, a set **C** of connectives, and a set **M** of punctuation marks. We now define a set **F** of statement forms determined by the following definition:

1 If A ∈ **P**, then A ∈ **F**.
2 If A ∈ **F**, then ~A ∈ **F**.
3 If A, B ∈ **F**, then (A ∧ B) ∈ **F**.
4 If A, B ∈ **F**, then (A ∨ B) ∈ **F**.
5 If A, B ∈ **F**, then (A ⊃ B) ∈ **F**.
6 If A, B ∈ **F**, then (A ≡ B) ∈ **F**.
7 Nothing else is in **F**.

Let's pause at this point to make certain that this definition is understood. We note that this definition specifies under what conditions a string of symbols of S is a statement form of S, that is, under what conditions a symbol or string of symbols is in **F**. Quite obviously, not just any combination of symbols counts as a statement form of S; for example,

p~

does not count as a statement form since this combination of symbols is not constructed in terms of our definition. However,

~*p*
(*p* ∨ *q*)

are statement forms of S since they are generated in accordance with parts 1, 2, and 3 of the definition.

In effect, part 1 of the definition asserts that any statement variable is a statement form; part 2 states that if A is a statement form, then so is ~A; parts 3, 4, 5, and 6 stipulate that if A and B are statement forms, then so are (A $\wedge$ B), (A $\vee$ B), (A $\supset$ B), and (A $\equiv$ B). Part 7 of the definition simply states that no other combinations of symbols count as statement forms of $\mathcal{S}$ except those which are generated in accordance with parts 1 through 6.

A cursory glance at parts 2 through 6 of our definition reveals that the following strings of symbols are not, strictly speaking, statement forms of $\mathcal{S}$:

$p \wedge q$
$p \vee q$
$p \supset q$
$p \equiv q$

After all, they are not properly punctuated in accordance with the conditions of the definition. They should be written as

$(p \wedge q)$
$(p \vee q)$
$(p \supset q)$
$(p \equiv q)$

Now this is a deviation from our practice so far in this book: it has been our policy not to use punctuation symbols except where ambiguity would otherwise result. In our definition, however, we require that the result of joining two statement forms with any of the dyadic connectives always be enclosed in punctuation marks, even if it's not the constituent of another statement form. The reason for this is that it makes our definition simpler: if these compound statement forms are always enclosed in parentheses, then ambiguities can't ever arise. If we didn't present our definition like this, then we'd have to add other clauses to differentiate between ~$p \vee q$ and ~$(p \vee q)$, for instance. However, we don't need to write the outermost pair of punctuation marks on a compound statement form if it doesn't occur as a constituent of another statement form, so we'll normally not write them.

5.4.2 Metavariables and Argument Forms

Using metavariables, we can represent any argument form as

A_1
A_2
.
.
.
A_n
___
B

where obviously $A_1, A_2, \ldots, A_n$ are the premises and B is the conclusion. In order to take up less space, we'll sometimes write this in a horizontal form, using a slash line (/) in place of the horizontal line:

$A_1, A_2, \ldots, A_n/ B$

EXERCISE 5.4

For each of the following metalinguistic expressions, tell to which of the following statement forms it could refer.

*1 $(A \supset B) \vee (\sim C \wedge \sim A)$
*2 $[A \vee (B \wedge C)] \supset (A \vee B)$
*3 $(A \supset B) \vee (C \wedge D)$

   (a) $\{(p \supset q) \vee [q \wedge (\sim p \supset r)]\} \supset [(p \supset q) \vee q]$
   (b) $[(\sim p \vee q) \supset (p \wedge r)] \vee [\sim r \wedge \sim(\sim p \vee q)]$
   (c) $[(p \wedge q) \supset r] \vee [(r \wedge \sim s) \wedge \sim t]$
   (d) $[p \supset (r \wedge s)] \vee [(r \wedge s) \wedge t]$
   (e) $\{[p \supset (q \wedge r)] \supset \sim p\} \vee \{s \wedge \sim[p \supset (q \wedge r)]\}$

REVIEW EXERCISES FOR CHAPTER 5

1 What is a set?
2 What is the difference between an object language and a metalanguage?
3 Why is it necessary to distinguish between an object language and a metalanguage?
4 What is a self-referential statement? How do self-referential statements give rise to paradoxes? How does the distinction between object language and metalanguage avoid them?
5 Why are paradoxes unwelcome?
6 Explain why each of the following statements could be considered self-referential and hence paradoxical.
   (a) Every rule has an exception.
   (b) I am a liar.
   (c) Everything is relative.
7 Imagine a barber named Herman in a small town who shaves those and only those people in the town who do not shave themselves. Does Herman shave himself? What is so peculiar about saying that he does or he doesn't?
8. What is a metavariable? Why is it needed?

chapter 6
The Semantic Side of Validity

INTRODUCTORY REMARKS

In Chapter 1, we mentioned that there were two aspects of the concept of validity: a syntactic aspect called *deducibility* and a semantic one called *entailment*. In a rough sort of way, Chapter 1 attempted to convey something of what these two concepts are all about. For example, it was noted that deducibility depends on rules of reasoning, whereas entailment is connected with truth. In this chapter, we will begin a more thorough study of the concept of validity.

There are other concepts besides validity which interest logicians. Some of these have already been introduced, for example, *law of logic* and *logical equivalence*. Another concept, which we have not yet discussed, is *consistency*. Now, these three concepts are intimately connected with the concept of validity, and they, too, have both syntactic and semantic correlates. For instance, from the syntactic side, a law of logic is called a *logical theorem*, whereas from the semantic side it's called a *logical truth*. The syntactic correlate of logical equivalence is *deductive equivalence*, whereas its semantic correlate is *semantic equivalence*. The syntactic and semantic correlates of consistency are *deductive consistency* and *semantic consistency*. Let's summarize these terms in a table:

Logical Concept	Syntactic Correlate	Semantic Correlate
Validity	Deducibility	Entailment
Law of logic	Logical theorem	Logical truth
Logical equivalence	Deductive equivalence	Semantic equivalence
Consistency	Deductive consistency	Semantic consistency

We'll investigate each of these concepts in detail in this and the following chapters.

6.2
THE SEMANTIC THEORY OF S

We have already become acquainted with the semantic theory of S. As we saw in Chapters 2 and 3, this is merely a group of truth tables defining each of the connectives. Of course, we indicated in Chapter 3 that we wanted our truth tables to work for any statement forms involving the various connectives, and in Chapter 3 we used them that way to construct truth tables for more complex statement forms. Now, however, since we've introduced metavariables, we can state the definitions of the connectives with greater generality:

A	~A
T	F
F	T

A	B	A ∧ B	A ∨ B	A ⊃ B	A ≡ B
T	T	T	T	T	T
T	F	F	T	F	F
F	T	F	T	T	F
F	F	F	F	T	T

6.2.1 Entailment and Validity

As we said in Chapter 1, the semantic side of the concept of validity is *entailment*. Entailment is a relation between sets of statement forms and single statement forms. We'll use the symbol ⊩ to express this relation. To say that a set $\{A_1, A_2, \ldots, A_n\}$ of statement forms *entails* a statement form B, we write $\{A_1, A_2, \ldots, A_n\}$ ⊩ B. Using this notation, we define the semantic side of validity as follows:

> **Definition of *Valid Argument Form*:** An argument form A_1, A_2, . . . , A_n/B is *valid* (in the semantic sense) if and only if $\{A_1, A_2, \ldots, A_n\}$ ⊩ B.

Of course, this definition isn't very useful until we explain entailment, which is our purpose in this section. However, let's first present the corresponding definition of valid argument in the semantic sense:

> **Definition of *Valid Argument*:** An argument in natural language is *valid* (in the semantic sense) *with respect to statement logic* if and only if the set of statement forms corresponding to its premises in S entails the stetement form corresponding to its conclusion in S.

In Chapter 1, we said that the premises of an argument entail the conclusion if the conclusion must be true whenever all the premises are true, that is, if it is impossible for the conclusion to be false when all the premises are true. We might use this to get our first, preliminary notion of what *entails* means:

> **Preliminary Definition of *Entailment*:** A set S of statement forms *entails* a statement form B (that is, S ⊩ B) if and only if there do not exist any circumstances under which all the members of S are true and B is false.

Now that we have an idea of what entailment is, it's possible for us to determine whether a given argument form is valid in the semantic sense. To see how we do it, consider the following argument form:

$$p \supset (q \supset r)$$
$$p \supset \sim r$$
$$\overline{}$$
$$q \supset \sim p$$

Is this argument form valid in the semantic sense? Given our definition of validity, we know that it is provided that $\{p \supset (q \supset r), p \supset \sim r\}$ ⊩ $q \supset \sim p$. In order to show that, we must show that there do not exist any circumstances under which both $p \supset (q \supset r)$ and $p \supset \sim r$ are true and $q \supset \sim p$ is false.

One way to show this is to use a truth table. First, we determine how many different statement variables appear in the entire argument form. There are three: p, q, and r. Next, we construct a truth table for all these statement forms simultaneously:

						P_1	P_2	C
p	q	r	$\sim r$	$\sim p$	$q \supset r$	$p \supset (q \supset r)$	$p \supset \sim r$	$q \supset \sim p$
T	T	T	F	F	T	T	F	F
T	T	F	T	F	F	F	T	F
T	F	T	F	F	T	T	F	T
T	F	F	T	F	T	T	T	T
F	T	T	F	T	T	T	T	T
F	T	F	T	T	F	T	T	T
F	F	T	F	T	T	T	T	T
F	F	F	T	T	T	T	T	T

Notice that in this truth table the last three columns contain the statement forms of the argument form. The final column contains the conclusion (we place a C over it to indicate this), and the two preceding columns contain the premises (P₁ indicates the first premise, and P₂ indicates the second premise). Now, a careful examination of the columns marked P₁,

P_2, and C, row by row, reveals that there does not exist any circumstance in which P_1 and P_2 are both true and C false. Clearly, then, there does not exist a circumstance among the eight possible circumstances under which the premises of the above argument form are all true and its conclusion is false. Consequently, we have demonstrated that $\{p \supset (q \supset r),\ p \supset {\sim}r\} \Vdash q \supset {\sim}p$, and so the argument form is valid in the semantic sense.

Now consider this argument form:

$p \supset q$
$r \vee {\sim}p$

$\overline{}$

${\sim}p \supset r$

In order to determine whether the premises of this argument form entail its conclusion, we again construct a truth table for the argument form:

				P_1	P_2	C
p	q	r	${\sim}p$	$p \supset q$	$r \vee {\sim}p$	${\sim}p \supset r$
T	T	T	F	T	T	T
T	T	F	F	T	F	T
T	F	T	F	F	T	T
T	F	F	F	F	F	T
F	T	T	T	T	T	T
→ F	T	F	T	T	T	F
F	F	T	T	T	T	T
→ F	F	F	T	T	T	F

By looking at the sixth and eighth rows, you can tell that there are two possible circumstances under which the premises of this argument form are both true and its conclusion false. Therefore, it is not the case that $\{p \supset q,\ r \vee {\sim}p\} \Vdash {\sim}p \supset r$, and so the argument form is invalid.

Usually, when an argument form is invalid, we show this by indicating *at least one* possible circumstance under which its conclusion is false and its premises are all true. Thus, we might say that the above argument form is shown to be invalid by the following circumstance:

p is false.
q is true.
r is false.

In other words, when the statement variables in the above argument form have these truth values, the argument form is shown not to be valid because it then has true premises and a false conclusion. Note that it is the sixth row of the above truth table which has provided us with this information. Of course, we could have shown the argument form's invalidity by the information given in the eighth row as well.

When an argument form is invalid, it is always possible to find at least one row in its truth table where the premises are all true and the conclusion false. Logicians refer to such rows as *counterinterpretations*. Hence, in order to show that a given argument form is invalid, we need only find at least one counterinterpretation for it. As we have seen, then, a counterinterpretation for

$$p \supset q$$
$$r \lor \sim p$$
$$\overline{\sim p \supset r}$$

is

p is false.
q is true.
r is false.

EXERCISE 6.2.1

Using truth tables, determine whether the following argument forms are valid. If they are invalid, list at least one counterinterpretation.

*1 $p \lor \sim q$
    q
    $\overline{}$
    $\sim p$

2 $p \supset q$
   $\sim p$
   $\overline{}$
   $\sim q$

*3 $p \supset q$
    $\sim q \lor \sim p$
    p
    $\overline{}$
    $\sim p$

4 $p \lor (q \land r)$
   $\sim p$
   $\overline{}$
   q

*5 $p \supset q$
    $\sim p \supset \sim r$
    $\overline{}$
    $r \supset q$

6 $p \supset q$
   $q \supset p$
   $\overline{}$
   $p \equiv q$

*7 $\sim(p \lor \sim q)$
    $r \supset p$
    $\overline{}$
    $r \supset s$

8 $p \supset q$
   $r \supset s$
   $\sim q \lor \sim s$
   $\overline{}$
   $p \supset \sim r$

*9 $p \supset q$
    $q \supset r$
    $\sim s \supset \sim r$
    $\overline{}$
    $\sim s \supset \sim p$

10 $\sim p \supset \sim q$
    $s \supset (p \supset r)$
    $\overline{}$
    $(q \land \sim r) \supset s$

DECISION PROCEDURES

Ideally, we would like our methods to give a determinate answer to the question "Is this argument form valid?" When a set of methods always provides such an answer, we say that they are a *decision procedure* with respect to validity. In order to be a decision procedure, the methods used to test the validity of argument forms must meet two conditions: *mechanicalness* and *effectiveness*. We call them mechanical when they give a uniform set of instructions as to how to go about determining whether a given argument form is valid. The procedures are *effective* if a finite number of applications of the set of instructions always yield a yes or no answer to the question "Is this argument form valid?" Intuitively speaking, we might say that a system is mechanical if, in principle, a machine could carry out the process and effective if the process always comes to an end.

Notice that the truth table method is a decision procedure. Given a truth table for any argument form, if it displays at least one counter-interpretation, then the argument form is invalid; otherwise, it is valid.

FORMAL SEMANTICS

You have probably noticed that employing truth tables in determining whether a given argument form is valid is, to say the least, rather tedious. This point can be appreciated once you imagine the size of the truth tables that will be required for argument forms containing five, six, or seven different statement variables. Surely we would prefer a shorter decision procedure than this, if we could find one. The next section will provide just such a decision procedure. This section aims at providing the theoretical groundwork for it.

Perhaps the best way to begin our discussion is with the concept of an *interpretation*. For our purposes, it will do to view an interpretation as roughly equivalent to a row of a truth table. Hence, the number of interpretations that a given statement form or argument form will have depends on the number of different statement variables it has. Thus, the following statement form

$$(p \lor q) \supset (\sim p \land \sim q)$$

has 2^2, or 4, interpretations, each of which is displayed by one line of the following truth table:

	p	q	$p \vee q$	$\sim p$	$\sim q$	$\sim p \wedge \sim q$	$(p \vee q) \supset (\sim p \wedge \sim q)$
I_1	T	T	T	F	F	F	F
I_2	T	F	T	F	T	F	F
I_3	F	T	T	T	F	F	F
I_4	F	F	F	T	T	T	T

The above truth table shows us that there exists one and only one interpretation on which $(p \vee q) \supset (\sim p \wedge \sim q)$ is true, namely, the one in which p and q are both false.

Now consider the following argument form:

$$(p \supset q) \supset \sim r$$
$$p \supset \sim q$$

$$\overline{}$$

$$r \supset q$$

Since this argument form has three different statement variables in it, it will have $2^3 = 8$ different interpretations, as exhibited by the following truth table:

	p	q	r	$\sim q$	$\sim r$	$p \supset q$	P_1 $(p \supset q) \supset \sim r$	P_2 $p \supset \sim q$	C $r \supset q$
I_1	T	T	T	F	F	T	F	F	T
I_2	T	T	F	F	T	T	T	F	T
I_3	T	F	T	T	F	F	T	T	F
I_4	T	F	F	T	T	F	T	T	T
I_5	F	T	T	F	F	T	F	T	T
I_6	F	T	F	F	T	T	T	T	T
I_7	F	F	T	T	F	T	F	T	F
I_8	F	F	F	T	T	T	T	T	T

Notice that interpretation I_3 is a significant one since it's on that interpretation that we have both the premises all true and the conclusion false. Consequently, I_3 constitutes a counterinterpretation, and the premises of this argument form do not entail its conclusion.

In Section 6.2.1, we gave a preliminary definition of entailment as follows:

> A set S of statement forms entails a statement form B (that is, $S \Vdash B$) if and only if there do not exist any circumstances under which all the members of S are true and B is false.

The difficulty with this definition is that it is not at all clear just what is supposed to count as a *circumstance*. In an effort to circumvent this difficulty, let's replace *circumstance* by *interpretation* in our definition. This results in our final definition of entailment:

Definition of *Entailment*: A set S of statement forms *entails* a statement form B (that is, $S \Vdash B$) if and only if there does not exist any *interpretation* on which all of the members of S are true and B is false.

It may appear that all we've done here is exchange one word for another in our two formulations of this definition. After all, if all that we mean by *circumstance* is interpretation, nothing is gained by switching the terms. However, the point here is precisely that the word *interpretation* is a technical term of our theory. We don't want to say anything more about *interpretations* than we feel is necessary in order to explain the semantic properties of S. This is what we mean when we describe the theory we are developing as *formal* semantics: we say nothing more about what counts as a circumstance than the semantic properties of S require us to, as we will explain in the rest of this section.

Now that we have the notion of an interpretation, we may, if we wish, dispense with truth tables altogether. We can view the semantic theory of S as simply a set of interpretations governed by certain rules. Of course, if we do away with truth tables, we will need to find another way of defining the connectives. To accomplish this, we define each of the connectives of S with respect to any given interpretation. We will call these definitions *interpretation rules*. The first rule is preliminary to each of the rules for the specific connectives (hence we call it IR0 for *Interpretation Rule* 0):

IR0: For any interpretation I, if $A \in \mathbf{P}$, then either A is true on I or A is false on I, and not both.

This simply reflects the fact that every statement has exactly one of two possible truth values.

From now on, instead of saying A *is true on interpretation I*, we'll write $I(A) = T$; similarly, instead of saying A *is false on interpretation I*, we'll write $I(A) = F$. Using these abbreviations, we could restate Interpretation Rule 0 as

IR0: For any interpretation I, if $A \in \mathbf{P}$, then either $I(A) = T$ or $I(A) = F$, and not both.

Now, we give interpretation rules to define each of the connectives of S. One will tell us under what conditions statement forms with that connective as their main connective are true, and the other will tell us under what conditions such statement forms are false. These rules enable us to build up the truth value of any statement form on any interpretation out of the truth values of its constituent statement variables on that interpretation.

IR1a: For any interpretation I, I($\sim$A) = T if and only if I(A) = F.

IR1b: For any interpretation I, I($\sim$A) = F if and only if I(A) = T.

What this rule says is that a statement form $\sim$A whose main connective is the tilde is true on an interpretation if and only if its constituent A is false on that interpretation, and false on that interpretation if and only if its constituent A is true on that interpretation. This, of course, corresponds exactly to the following truth table:

A	$\sim$A
T	F
F	T

Our next rules define the inverted wedge:

IR2a: For any interpretation I, I(A $\wedge$ B) = T if and only if both I(A) = T and I(B) = T.

IR2b: For any interpretation I, I(A $\wedge$ B) = F if and only if either I(A) = F or I(B) = F.

IR2a states that a statement form A $\wedge$ B is true on a given interpretation if an only if both A and B are true on that interpretation. In other words, a conjunction is true if and only if both its conjuncts are true. Obviously, this is also reflected in the truth table for the inverted wedge:

A	B	A $\wedge$ B
T	T	T
T	F	F
F	T	F
F	F	F

Notice that the only time A $\wedge$ B is true (first row) is when both A and B are true. IR2b may not appear quite as obvious as IR2a, but a little reflection will show that it, too, corresponds to the truth table definition. If you examine this truth table, you will see that when A receives the truth value F, so does A $\wedge$ B; likewise, when B receives the truth value F, so does A $\wedge$ B.

The interpretation rules for the wedge are as follows:

IR3a: For any interpreation I, I(A $\vee$ B) = T if and only if either I(A) = T or I(B) = T.

IR3b: For any interpretation I, I(A $\vee$ B) = F if and only if both I(A) = F and I(B) = F.

Looking to the truth table for the wedge, we see, of course, that IR3b is a straightforward consequence of its fourth row:

A	B	A $\vee$ B
T	T	T
T	F	T
F	T	T
F	F	F

The only time A $\vee$ B is false is when both its constituents—A and B—are false. However, there are three circumstances under which A $\vee$ B is true, and IR3a is a succinct formulation of them: when A is true (first and second rows of the table) or when B is true (first and third rows).

The interpretation rules for the horseshoe are as follows:

IR4a: For any interpretation I, I(A $\supset$ B) = T if an only if either I(A) = F or I(B) = T.

IR4b: For any interpretation I, I(A $\supset$ B) = F if and only if both I(A) = T and I(B) = F.

A glance at the truth table for the horseshoe will show that these rules are correct:

A	B	A $\supset$ B
T	T	T
T	F	F
F	T	T
F	F	T

The only time A $\supset$ B is false is when A is true and B is false (second row), which gives us IR4b. Under all other circumstances, A $\supset$ B is true, and this is what IR4a expresses: A $\supset$ B is true when A is false (rows 3 and 4) and when B is true (rows 1 and 3).

The interpretation rules for the triple bar, although a bit more complicated, are equally obvious once you consider the truth table:

IR5a: For any interpretation I, I(A $\equiv$ B) = T if and only if either both I(A) = T and I(B) = T or both I(A) = F and I(B) = F.

IR5b: For any interpretation I, I(A $\equiv$ B) = F if and only if either both I(A) = T and I(B) = F or both I(A) = F and I(B) = T.

It is an easy matter to see that these rules reflect the truth table:

A	B	A ≡ B
T	T	T
T	F	F
F	T	F
F	F	T

An even more succinct way to express these rules is as follows: I(A ≡ B) = T if and only if I(A) = I(B), and I(A ≡ B) = F otherwise.

6.5

SEMANTIC TREES AND ENTAILMENT

Now that we have reformulated the semantic theory of S in terms of interpretations, we are in a position to introduce an alternative decision procedure to the truth table method. We call this procedure the *semantic tree* method. A *semantic tree* is a diagrammatic representation of an interpretation. In order to construct semantic trees, we convert our interpretation rules for the connectives into rules for constructing semantic trees. When completed, these semantic trees consist of branching patterns (hence the name *semantic trees*) which schematically represent the possible interpretations on which certain statement forms can have certain truth values. The best way to explain semantic trees more fully is to present the rules and explain how to use them.

Since these rules correspond to our interpretation rules, there are, of course, two rules for each connective:

1a   ~A   1b   ~~~A~~
      ~~A~~   A

2a   A ∧ B   2b   ~~A ∧ B~~
        A   ⟨⟩
        B   ~~A~~   ~~B~~

3a   A ∨ B   3b   ~~A ∨ B~~
       ⟨⟩   ~~A~~
     A   B   ~~B~~

4a   A ⊃ B   4b   ~~A ⊃ B~~
       ⟨⟩   A
    ~~A~~   B   ~~B~~

5a   A ≡ B   5b   ~~A ≡ B~~
       ⟨⟩   ⟨⟩
    A   ~~A~~   A   ~~A~~
    B   ~~B~~   ~~B~~   B

You will notice that some of the metavariables in these rules have slash lines through them. This means that they refer to statement forms which are *false* on the interpretation that the tree is being constructed to represent. Statement forms without slashes are *true*. Now, these rules, when read from top to bottom, give us diagrammatic representations of interpretations. To see how this works, look at rule 1a. The topmost statement form is ~A (without a slash), and below it is the statement form A (with a slash). Since ~A appears unslashed, it is true on the interpretation represented by the tree. Now, according to IR1a, for any I, I(~A) = T if and only if I(A) = F; therefore, the statement form A must be false on this interpretation. Accordingly, below ~A we write $\cancel{A}$ to indicate that I(A) takes the value F. Similarly, 1b reflects IR1b as follows: any statement form $\cancel{\sim A}$ is false on an interpretation (first line of the rule: $\cancel{\sim A}$) if and only if the statement form A is true on the interpretation (second line of the rule: A).

The two rules for each remaining connective correspond to the interpretation rules for that connective in the same way that rules 1a and 1b correspond to IR1a and IR1b. We use these rules to construct trees from top to bottom: given that a statement form containing any of the connectives is true or false on a certain interpretation, these rules permit us to say that a certain other statement form or statement forms will have certain truth values on that interpretation.

Note that rules 2b, 3a, 4a, 5a, and 5b differ from the others in appearance: we say that these rules introduce *branching*. The significance of branching is to indicate alternative interpretations. Thus, in rule 2b, we say: if a statement form of the form A $\wedge$ B is false on an interpretation, then *either* A is false on that interpretation (left branch) *or* B is false on that interpretation (right branch). This, of course, reflects IR2b. The separate branches of the developing semantic tree represent different possible interpretations. In this case, the left-hand branch represents an interpretation on which A is false, while the right-hand branch represents one on which B is false. Notice, however, that since they both branch from $\cancel{A \wedge B}$, they both represent interpretations in which A $\wedge$ B is false. Similar remarks hold for the other branching rules.

Now that we've given some idea what the semantic tree rules are, let's see how we construct semantic trees to test the validity of argument forms. Consider the following example:

$\sim p \vee \sim q$
$r \supset q$
$s \supset p$
___

$r \supset \sim s$

By definition, this argument form is valid in the semantic sense just in case $\{\sim p \vee \sim q, r \supset q, s \supset p\} \Vdash r \supset \sim s$, that is, just in case the set of all its premises entails its conclusion. Now, in view of the definition of entailment, this will be true if there doesn't exist an interpretation on which the members of $\{\sim p \vee \sim q, r \supset q, s \supset p\}$ are all true and $r \supset \sim s$ is false. In using the semantic tree rules, we assume that there is such an interpretation and then attempt to find out what it (which will be a counterinterpretation to the argument) is. If we find a counterinterpretation, then the premises do not entail the conclusion; however, if we can show that there is no counterinterpretation, then the premises do entail the conclusion and so the argument form is valid.

Step 1 $\sim p \vee \sim q$
      $r \supset q$
      $s \supset p$
      $\cancel{r \supset \sim s}$

In step 1, we simply list the premises of the argument form in order and then list the conclusion. Notice that the conclusion is *slashed:* this means that we're assuming that there is an interpretation on which the premises are all true and the conclusion is false. Our tree so far says that this interpretation meets the following conditions:

$I(\sim p \vee \sim q) = T$
$I(r \supset q) = T$
$I(s \supset p) = T$
$I(r \supset \sim s) = F$

The construction of the tree now proceeds by the application of the tree rules to each of the statement forms in the list. Theoretically, it makes no difference with which statement form we start; here, we'll begin with $\cancel{r \supset \sim s}$:

Step 2 $\sim p \vee \sim q$
      $r \supset q$
      $s \supset p$
      $\cancel{r \supset \sim s}$ $\checkmark$
      r
      $\cancel{\sim s}$

Note that the main connective of this statement form is a horseshoe and that it has a slash through it. Since rule 4b deals with statement forms of this form, it applies here. Now, 4b says that if in a tree you have

   $\cancel{A \supset B}$

then add

   A
   $\cancel{B}$

Now, in step 2, since we have

$r \supset \sim\!s$ (crossed out)

we have added the lines

r

$\sim\!s$ (crossed out)

The check mark after $r \supset \sim\!s$ indicates that we have applied a semantic tree rule to it. When we apply a rule to a statement form, we say that we have *extended* that statement form. Thus, the check mark after $r \supset \sim\!s$ serves as a reminder that $r \supset \sim\!s$ has been extended.

Although the order in which you apply rules to statement forms in developing a tree makes no difference theoretically, often you can save a great deal of time by extending first those statement forms which require rules that don't branch. Since 4b is not a branching rule, we used it first here; all the other statement forms in the initial set require branching rules.

Step 3 $\sim\!p \lor \sim\!q$
$r \supset q$
$s \supset p$
$r \supset \sim\!s$ (crossed out) ✓
r
$\sim\!s$ (crossed out) ✓
s

The check mark to the right of $\sim\!s$ indicates that in step 3 we extended $\sim\!s$. The semantic tree rule appealed to in this step is 1b, which states that if you are given

$\sim\!\sim\!A$

add

A

Hence, since we were given $\sim\!\sim\!s$, we write s below it in the tree. Notice here that $\sim\!\sim\!s$ did not belong to the original set of statement forms. In constructing the semantic tree of an argument form, we extend *all* compound statements that occur in the tree, including those that result from extending other compound statement forms. Of course, the only statement forms which are not compound are statement variables, and so we extend everything except statement variables. We continue in this way in every branch of a tree until that branch *closes* or until we run out of statement forms to extend. To explain what we mean by *branch* of a tree and what we mean by a branch *closing*, let's continue with our example.

Step 4 $\sim p \lor \sim q$

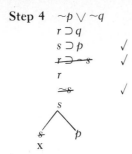

$r \supset q$

$s \supset p$ √

~~$r \supset s$~~ √

r

~~$\sim s$~~ √

s

x

Up to this point, our tree has had only one branch. Now, we have extended $s \supset p$, which required the use of a branching rule (4a). As a result, our tree now has two branches. The first one proceeds downward to s from the top of the tree, $\sim p \lor \sim q$. The second one, at the right, proceeds downward to p. Each branch includes all the steps between it and the topmost statement form in the tree.

Notice also that we placed "x" below the left-hand path. This is to indicate that this path is *closed*. We say that a path is closed when it contains some statement variable both slashed and unslashed. Notice that this path contains the statement variable s slashed at its last step and unslashed at the step immediately above that, where the tree branches. Consequently, this branch of the tree is closed. When a branch closes, we no longer add anything to that branch. The reason is that if a branch closes, there is no possible interpretation corresponding to that branch. It should be obvious why. The presence of the same statement variable both slashed and unslashed indicates that on the interpretation corresponding to that branch, that statement variable is both false and true. This, however, contradicts IR0.

We still have one open branch in our tree, namely, the branch to the right ending in p. Therefore, we continue the construction of our tree by extending the remaining statement forms into this branch. In fact, this is how we always proceed: we extend any statement form into *every* branch below it that remains open. We here extend $r \supset q$:

Step 5 $\sim p \lor \sim q$

q

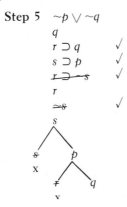

$r \supset q$ √

$s \supset p$ √

~~$r \supset s$~~ √

r

~~$\sim s$~~ √

s

s p

x

~~r~~ q

x

Here $r \supset q$ has been extended under p in accordance with semantic tree rule 4a. Again, because 4a is a rule which involves branching, two more branches have been generated in the downward construction of our tree. The first additional branch proceeds upward from ~~r~~ to $\sim p \lor \sim q$. Because this branch contains both ~~r~~ and r, we have closed it by placing an "x" below ~~r~~. The remaining additional branch proceeds upward from q through p and s to $\sim p \lor \sim q$. Inspecting this branch shows that it is still open. We have one more statement form to extend, and so we extend it into the only remaining open branch:

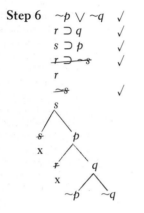

Step 6 $\sim p \lor \sim q$ ✓
  $r \supset q$ ✓
  $s \supset p$ ✓
  ~~r ⊃ s~~ ✓
  r
  ~~~s~~ ✓
  s

Here, we extended $\sim p \lor \sim q$ in accordance with semantic tree rule 3a, since the main connective of $\sim p \lor \sim q$ is the wedge. Rule 3a says that if we are given

$A \lor B$

write

  A   B

This is, of course, what we've done with $\sim p \lor \sim q$. We extended it below q in step 5. Notice that because 3a is a branching rule, two more branches have been created. The one on the left proceeds upward from $\sim p$ to $\sim p \lor \sim q$, whereas the one on the right proceeds upward from $\sim q$ to $\sim p \lor \sim q$.

Although we have now extended every statement form in our original set, we're not finished with the construction of our tree. We still have two branches open, and each of them contains a compound statement form. We first extend $\sim p$ into the left-hand branch:

Step 7

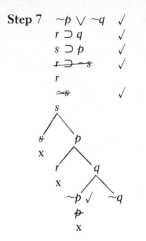

After applying 1a to ~p, we find that the branch closes, since it contains both p and p̶. Note, incidentally, that we did *not* extend ~p into the right-hand path below ~q: this is because that path is not *below* the statement form that we were extending (to get from ~p to ~q, we'd have to go *up* the tree to q and back *down* again). We can extend ~q in exactly the same way:

Step 8

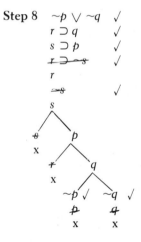

Since every branch in this tree has closed, the construction has come to an end. Furthermore, since every branch in the tree is closed, we have shown that *the argument form is valid*. But before discussing why this is so, let's first summarize the steps in the construction of any semantic tree for any argument form:

1 List the premises unslashed and the conclusion slashed.
2 Begin constructing a tree in a downward fashion by extending some compound statement form into every open branch below

it. Place a check mark after the statement form when you have extended it.

   a   If there are any branches that contain the same statement variable both slashed and unslashed, close them with an "x."
3 If there are any open branches after step 2a, then ascertain whether *all* the compound statement forms in these branches have been check-marked.
   a   If all the compound statement forms have been check-marked, the tree is completed and the argument form is invalid.
   b   If not all the compound statement forms have been check-marked, then choose one in an open branch and begin again at step 2.
4 When steps 1 through 3 have been completed, if there are no branches which remain open, then the argument is valid.

Steps 1 through 4 are a set of instructions which tell us how to construct semantic trees. Obviously, then, the semantic tree method is mechanical. Furthermore, since every construction will terminate in a finite number of steps, the semantic tree method is effective. Therefore, the semantic tree method is a decision procedure for validity. If *all* the branches of the tree for a given argument form *close*, then the argument form is valid. If *at least one* branch of the finished tree remains *open*, then the argument form is invalid.

Why does the semantic tree method work? As we have already mentioned, when we construct a semantic tree for a given argument form, we are assuming that the premises are all true and the conclusion false on some interpretation. In other words, we assume that the premises do not entail the conclusion. If, in fact, the premises don't entail the conclusion, there must be some interpretation on which the premises are all true and the conclusion false; that is, there must be a counterinterpretation for the argument. Now, if we view each branch of a tree as representing at least one potential counterinterpretation, then if a branch closes, it can't really represent a counterinterpretation. After all, no statement variable can be both true and false on an interpretation (by IR0); but a closed branch contains some statement variable both slashed (false) and unslashed (true). Obviously, then, if all the paths of a tree close, then there aren't any counterinterpretations to the argument form. However, if there aren't any interpretations on which all the premises of the argument form are true and the conclusion false, then (by the definition of entailment) the premises of the argument form entail the conclusion, and so the argument form is valid.

Any open branch of a finished tree represents a counterinterpretation. Therefore, if at least one branch of a finished tree remains open, the argument form is invalid. Later, we will show just how to construct a counterinterpretation from an open branch in a finished tree.

We said that the order in which we extend the compound statement forms in developing a tree doesn't matter. We'll show this now by constructing another tree for the argument form tested above:

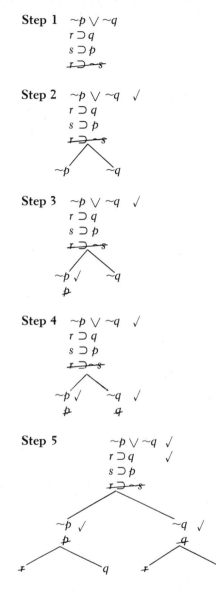

Step 1 $\sim p \lor \sim q$
          $r \supset q$
          $s \supset p$
          ~~$r \supset s$~~

Step 2 $\sim p \lor \sim q$ $\checkmark$
          $r \supset q$
          $s \supset p$
          ~~$r \supset s$~~

          $\sim p$ $\sim q$

Step 3 $\sim p \lor \sim q$ $\checkmark$
          $r \supset q$
          $s \supset p$
          ~~$r \supset s$~~

          $\sim p$ $\checkmark$ $\sim q$
          ~~p~~

Step 4 $\sim p \lor \sim q$ $\checkmark$
          $r \supset q$
          $s \supset p$
          ~~$r \supset s$~~

          $\sim p$ $\checkmark$ $\sim q$ $\checkmark$
          ~~p~~   ~~q~~

Step 5 $\sim p \lor \sim q$ $\checkmark$
          $r \supset q$ $\checkmark$
          $s \supset p$
          ~~$r \supset s$~~

          $\sim p$ $\checkmark$ $\sim q$ $\checkmark$
          ~~p~~   ~~q~~

       ~~r~~ q ~~r~~ q
                                          x

Since at step 4 two branches remained open, at step 5 we had to extend the statement form $r \supset q$ into each of these branches. Remember, you always extend a statement form into every open branch below it at that stage of the tree's construction.

Step 6

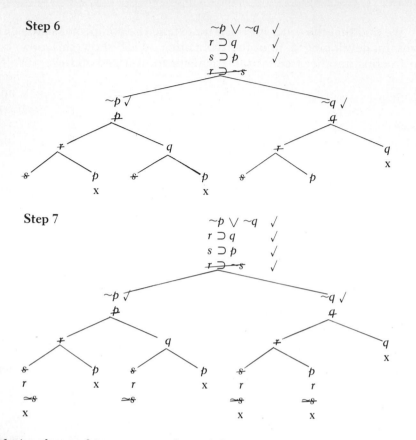

Step 7

Notice that at this stage every branch but one has closed. However, since the open branch still contains a compound statement form which is not check-marked, we proceed to step 8:

Step 8

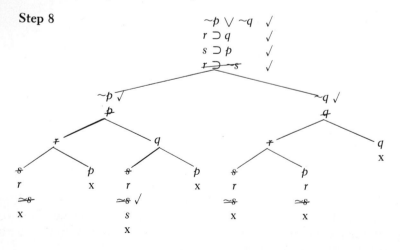

Notice that ~s in the other branches did not have to be extended, since these branches closed before we arrived at that statement form.

This should illustrate our point that, from a theoretical standpoint, it makes no difference in what order we extend the compound statement forms in a tree. However, our first tree construction was shorter and simpler than our second. The reason is that the second tree contains more branchings, because we extended statement forms that required branching rules before those that did not. No doubt, whenever possible, it's a good idea to extend statement forms which don't introduce branching before extending any others.

The semantic tree method provides a far less tedious decision procedure than the truth table method. In order to appreciate how much simpler the tree method is, just consider that the truth table for the argument form we've been dealing with requires 16 rows.

Let's look at another example:

$(p \supset q) \land (r \supset s)$
$t \land (p \lor r)$
$\sim t \supset s$
_____

$q \lor s$

That it is also valid is demonstrated by its tree (numbers to the left indicate the order in which statement forms were extended):

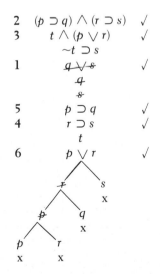

Note that $\sim t \supset s$ was never extended since all the branches closed before we got to it. Of course, this indicates that $\sim t \supset s$ is a superfluous premise: the argument form would still be valid without it. Notice that if a truth table were used to determine the validity of this argument form, 32 rows would be required.

Now, let's consider an argument form which is invalid:

$p \supset (q \wedge r)$
$(q \wedge \sim r) \supset s$
$(p \supset s) \equiv \sim r$
_____

$\sim r$

Its tree looks like this:

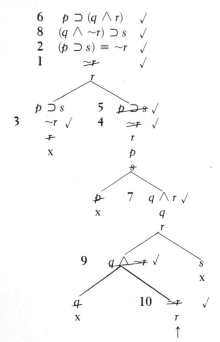

One branch of this tree remains open after we have extended every statement form; therefore, this argument form is invalid. This means that it has a counterinterpretation. Now, just what is this counterinterpretation? It's a rather simple matter to retrieve one from the tree. We select some open branch (in this case, there is only one) and collect all the statement variables which appear alone in it, noting whether they are slashed or unslashed. In this case, proceeding along the only open branch, we obtain the following set of statement variables:

r, r, q, s, p, r, r

Notice that there are four unslashed occurrences of r. Eliminating duplications, we obtain the following list, in alphabetical order:

p, q, r, s

This list tells us that any interpretation I which meets the following conditions is a counterinterpretation for this argument form:

$I(p) = T$
$I(q) = T$
$I(r) = T$
$I(s) = F$

To see this, let's construct that row of the truth table corresponding to the counterinterpretation indicated above for the tested argument form:

				C				P_1	P_2	P_3
p	q	r	s	$q \land r$	$\sim r$	$q \land \sim r$	$p \supset s$	$p \supset (q \land r)$	$(q \land \sim r) \supset s$	$(p \supset s) \equiv \sim r$
T	T	T	F	T	F	F	F	T	T	T

As the table shows, on this interpretation the premises are all true and the conclusion false.
Let's consider one more argument form:

$p \supset (q \land r)$
$s \lor \sim p$
$\sim s$
_____
$q \land r$

Its tree looks like this:

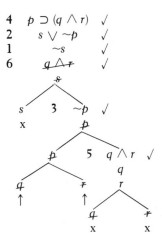

This argument form is invalid, since at least one branch (in fact, two) remains open when it is completed. In order to show that an argument form is invalid, you need only produce one counterinterpretation. So, technically, it doesn't matter from which open branch you choose to retrieve a counterinterpretation. Let's arbitrarily choose the leftmost branch. Then, collecting the statement variables from this branch, we obtain

~~q, p, p, s~~

Eliminating repetitions gives us, in alphabetical order,

~~p, q, s~~

Notice that one statement variable which appears in the argument form is missing, namely r. What this tells us is that in the branch we have selected, it doesn't matter which truth value r has. Therefore, we can add either r or ~~r~~ to this list. We might purely arbitrarily establish the convention of always adding an unslashed statement variable in a case like this. Thus, our list would become

~~p~~, ~~q~~, r, ~~s~~

Consequently, the following will be a counterinterpretation to the above argument form:

$I(p) = F$
$I(q) = F$
$I(r) = T$
$I(s) = F$

Again, to check that this is indeed a counterinterpretation, let's construct the relevant row of the truth table:

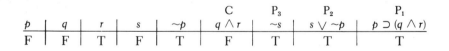

					C	P_3	P_2	P_1
p	q	r	s	$\sim p$	$q \wedge r$	$\sim s$	$s \vee \sim p$	$p \supset (q \wedge r)$
F	F	T	F	T	F	T	T	T

If we had placed ~~r~~ instead of r in our list, then we would have obtained a different counterinterpretation, as shown by the following truth table row:

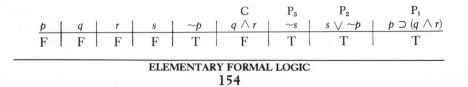

					C	P_3	P_2	P_1
p	q	r	s	$\sim p$	$q \wedge r$	$\sim s$	$s \vee \sim p$	$p \supset (q \wedge r)$
F	F	F	F	T	F	T	T	T

EXERCISE 6.5

1   Using semantic trees, determine whether the argument forms in Exercise 6.2.1 are valid. List at least one counterinterpretation for the invalid ones.

2   Using semantic trees, determine whether the argument forms listed below are valid. Give at least one counterinterpretation for each invalid form.

*(a) $r \vee (\sim p \wedge \sim q)$

$(p \supset r) \wedge (q \supset r)$

(b) $(p \wedge q) \supset r$
$p \supset q$

$\sim (p \wedge r)$

(c) $(p \wedge q) \supset r$
$(\sim s \vee t) \supset q$
$t \wedge p$

$r \wedge t$

*(d) $(p \supset q) \supset r$
$s \vee [t \supset (p \supset q)]$
$t \wedge \sim r$
$\sim s$

q

(e) $p \supset (q \supset r)$
s
$s \supset t$

$t \supset (q \supset r)$

(f) $p \supset q$
$r \supset p$
$(r \supset q) \supset q$

q

*(g) $p \supset q$
$r \supset s$
$t \vee (\sim p \supset r)$
$(q \vee s) \supset \sim r$
$\sim t$

p

(h) $(p \supset q) \wedge (p \vee \sim r)$
$\sim q$

r

*(i) $(p \wedge q) \supset (\sim r \supset s)$
$\sim s \vee \sim t$
$\sim (s \wedge t) \equiv t$

$p \supset (q \supset \sim r)$

3   Using semantic trees, determine whether the arguments in the Review Exercises for Chapter 4 are valid. For each invalid argument, list at least one counterinterpretation.

6.6

SEMANTIC CONSISTENCY

We define semantic consistency as follows:

> **Definition of *Semantic Consistency*:** A set S of statement forms is *semantically consistent* if and only if there is some interpretation on which all the members of S are true.

Given this definition, we can define a set to be *semantically inconsistent* just in case it is not semantically consistent. Of course, this would entail that if S is semantically inconsistent, there isn't an interpretation on which all the members of S are true.

These definitions seem to accord well with our logical intuitions. When we accuse someone of saying something inconsistent, what we are doing is accusing him or her of saying some things which couldn't possibly all be true. Thus, when someone says something consistent, at least we know that it *could* be true in some circumstances.

It is a simple matter to determine whether a given set of statement forms is semantically consistent by using either the truth table method or the semantic tree method. Consider the following set of statement forms:

$$\{(p \lor q) \supset \neg p, p \supset \neg q, q \lor p\}$$

If we construct a truth table for this set, we get the following:

p	q	$p \lor q$	$\neg p$	$\neg q$	A $(p \lor q) \supset \neg p$	B $p \supset \neg q$	C $q \lor p$
T	T	T	F	F	F	F	T
T	F	T	F	T	F	T	T
F	T	T	T	F	T	T	T
F	F	F	T	T	T	T	F

Inspection reveals that there does exist an interpretation on which every statement form in this set is true: when $I(p) = F$ and $I(q) = T$, we have $I(A) = T$, $I(B) = T$, and $I(C) = T$. Therefore, this set is consistent.

As in the case of argument forms, the truth table method is practical when there are not too many statement variables. However, truth tables become increasingly tedious as the number of statement variables increases. Consequently, here, too, we will make use of semantic trees for a more efficient decision procedure with respect to semantic consistency.

To use the tree method, we assume that the set is consistent—i.e., that there is an interpretation on which all the statement forms of the set are true. Then, using the tree method exactly as we did in the case of testing argument forms, we determine if, in fact, there is such an interpretation. Since an open branch in a finished tree represents an interpretation on which all the initial statement forms are true, if there is at least one open branch in the finished tree, it follows that the set of statement forms is semantically consistent. However, if every branch closes, then there is no such interpretation, and the set is semantically inconsistent.

Let's construct a tree for the set given above. First, we simply list the members of the set:

$(p \lor q) \supset \sim p$
$p \supset \sim q$
$q \lor p$

Notice that we don't slash any of these statement forms: the interpretation we want is one in which *all* of them are true. We then proceed to construct the tree:

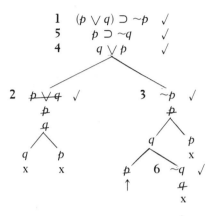

The open branch indicates that the set is consistent: when $I(p) = F$ and $I(q) = T$, the three original statement forms are all true.

EXERCISE 6.6

1 Using semantic trees, determine whether each of the following sets of statement forms is semantically consistent. List at least one interpretation for each consistent set.

*(a) $\{p \supset q, p \lor r, q \supset r, r \supset \sim p, \sim p \supset \sim r\}$
(b) $\{(p \supset q) \land (r \supset s), \sim q \land \sim s, p \lor r\}$
*(c) $\{p, (q \supset r) \supset r, r\}$
*(d) $\{p \supset (q \supset r), r \supset (q \supset s), p, \sim(s \lor \sim q)\}$
(e) $\{(p \land q) \equiv r, s \supset (t \supset \sim u), \sim(r \lor v) \supset t\}$

2 Could a person consistently assert the following statements jointly? (Justify your answer.)
(a) The senator will not seek reelection although his chief aid will, provided that the senator receives his party's presidential nomination.
(b) Assuming that either the senator does not seek reelection or Ms. Campbell enters the gubernatorial race, Mary will vote.
(c) Mary will not vote.
(d) Ms. Campbell will enter the gubernatorial race unless the senator receives his party's nomination for president.

6.6.1 Trivial Validity

Consider the following argument:

The earth is round.
On the other hand, the earth isn't round.
Therefore, the world ends next Thursday afternoon.

If we formalize it and test it for validity, we get this tree:

p
$\sim q$ $\checkmark$
$\cancel{q}$
$\cancel{p}$
x

According to the tree, this is a valid argument by our definition. In fact, if you examine the tree above, you will see that it would have closed even without the conclusion. As a result, this tree would have closed no matter what conclusion we inserted. The reason is, obviously, that the premises are inconsistent: they can't both be true at the same time. This indicates that any argument with inconsistent premises is automatically valid, no matter what its conclusion is. After all, a counterinterpretation to an argument form is an interpretation on which the premises are all true and the conclusion false. If the premises are inconsistent, there aren't any interpretations on which they are all true, and so there can't be any counterinterpretation for the argument form.

What we have just shown is a general truth about statement logic, namely that *any statement whatsoever is entailed by inconsistent premises*. We call general results like this *metatheorems*. In general, a *metatheorem* is simply a statement about some important feature of a system of logic which we can demonstrate to be true. As the name suggests, these are always statements in the metalanguage, *about* the logical system but not *in* it. Our first metatheorem is as follows:

Metatheorem: If a set S of statement forms is semantically inconsistent, then for any statement form A, S ⊩ A.

As the above example suggests, this metatheorem shows that our semantic theory for S requires us to call certain arguments valid when our intuitive reaction might be to call them silly or irrelevant. This might seem to indicate that we should change our definition of validity to exclude arguments with premises that are irrelevant to their conclusions, at least when the premises are inconsistent. However, we'll find it simpler to distinguish two classes of valid arguments. If an argument has inconsistent premises, we'll continue to call it valid, but we'll say that it is *trivially valid*. As the name suggests, trivially valid arguments don't need to be taken seriously, in a way. If a valid argument has consistent premises, we'll say that it is *nontrivially valid*.

In distinguishing between trivially and nontrivially valid arguments, we are, in effect, recognizing that the former are not on a par with the latter. Ordinarily, when we say that an argument is valid, what we intend is that if we accept the premises, then we must also accept the conclusion. Now, in the case of trivially valid arguments, the acceptance of the premises would compel us to accept *any conclusion whatever*. But—and this is the important point—no one *could* ever rationally accept the premises of a trivially valid argument since they are inconsistent. Consequently, a trivially valid argument, although valid, is in a way useless: it simply cannot provide us with a reason to believe its conclusion.

Given the semantic tree method, we can determine not only whether an argument form is valid but also, if it is valid, whether it is trivially or nontrivially valid. We set up a tree for the argument form in the usual manner; but in constructing the tree, we first extend all the premises and continue until we have completed the tree without using the conclusion. If all branches of the tree close at this point, the argument form is trivially valid. If some branch remains open, then the premises are semantically consistent, and we then test the argument for nontrivial validity by extending the conclusion into each open branch. If all branches then close, the argument is nontrivially valid. (*Note:* If the conclusion is a single statement variable, it should not be used in determining whether branches close in testing the premises for consistency.)

To see a more concrete example of this, consider the following argument:

> If the rate of inflation stabilizes only when the gross national product rises, then the rate of unemployment will decrease. But it appears that unemployment will not decrease even though the average American will not be banking his or her money over the next few months. Now either the gross national product will rise given that the rate of inflation stabilizes or the President's economic advisor will resign. Undoubtedly, if the President's economic advisor resigns, then either the rate of unemployment will decrease or the gross national product will rise. Consequently, the average American will bank his or her money over the next few months.

This argument is formalized as follows:

$(p \supset q) \supset r$
$\sim r \wedge \sim s$
$(p \supset q) \vee t$
$t \supset (r \vee q)$
_____

s

We then construct the following tree:

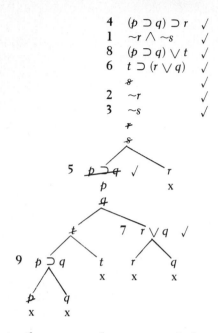

Note that we made no use of the conclusion in determining which branches close. Thus, this tree shows that the premises of this argument form are semantically inconsistent, and so this argument is trivially valid.

EXERCISE 6.6.1

1 Determine whether each of the following argument forms is valid in the semantic sense. If an argument form is valid, determine whether it is trivially or nontrivially valid; if it is invalid, give at least one counterinterpretation.

*(a) $p \vee (q \wedge r)$
$p \supset r$
$\sim r$
―――――
$s \vee \sim p$

(b) $(p \wedge q) \equiv \sim r$
$p \supset q$
$r \equiv p$
―――――
q

*(c) $(p \vee q) \supset r$
$(r \vee s) \supset t$
$\sim (\sim p \vee t)$
―――――
$u \supset r$

(d) $p \supset q$
$p \supset (q \supset r)$
$\sim s \vee (r \vee p)$
$\sim (s \wedge \sim r)$
―――――
t

(e) $(p \wedge q) \supset (r \vee s)$
$(p \supset r) \supset (q \supset s)$
$\sim q$
$\sim s$
―――――
r

*(f) $p \vee \sim q$
$q \vee \sim r$
$\sim p$
―――――
$\sim r$

2 Determine whether each of the following arguments is valid in the semantic sense. For each valid one, determine whether it is trivially or nontrivially valid. Give a counterinterpretation for each of the invalid ones.

(a) Either Mary will have an abortion or, assuming that she can get the money, she'll run away to Peru. Supposing that she'll run away to Peru only if she gets the money, then it follows that George will give her the money unless his father stops him. However, she'll have an abortion if George gives her the money, while if George's father stops him, George will kill himself. Consequently, unless Mary has an abortion, George will kill himself.

*(b) When it rains, it pours. On the other hand, when it's cloudy without raining, old men oversleep and sailors go to sea. Now, as everyone knows, sailors go to sea unless it's raining, in which case they go to the movies. From all this you can, of course, see that it pours in the event that sailors go to the movies while old men oversleep.

(c) When prices go up, the average consumer panics, but it is also true that the average consumer panics only if supply doesn't meet demand. Now, it's an undeniable fact of economics that supply has a tendency not to meet demand if and only if people spend a lot of money. Furthermore, it is well known that supply often doesn't meet demand even though the average consumer panics. As a result, people spend a lot of money whether or not prices go up.

(d) Unless Fred quits smoking, he'll surely get lung cancer. On the other hand, if he does quit smoking, he'll gain too much weight, in which case he'll develop a heart condition. Now, if he gets lung cancer, he'll die, while if he develops a heart condition, he'll also die. From all this, it appears that we must conclude that poor Fred is going to die.

*(e) If my calculations are correct, the world will end next Thursday. Of course, in that case classes will be canceled on Friday if there's anyone to cancel them. I'm afraid, however, that if the world does end then, no one will remember to cancel classes. Now, if classes aren't canceled, a lot of people will be inconvenienced, as you can readily see. Consequently, if my calculations are correct, lots of people are going to be inconvenienced.

6.7

SEMANTIC EQUIVALENCE

The semantic correlate of the concept of logical equivalence was discussed in Chapter 3. However, we didn't call it semantic equivalence there; we merely referred to it as logical equivalence. In Chapter 3, we said that two statement forms of S are logically equivalent just in case they both have the same truth-functional meaning, that is, the same truth table. Now that we have been introduced to the notion of an interpretation, we can define semantic equivalence in the following way:

> **Definition of *Semantic Equivalence*:** Two statement forms A and B are *semantically equivalent* (we write A ⇔ B) if and only if A and B are true on just the same interpretations.

In other words, two statement forms are semantically equivalent just in case whenever A is true on a given interpretation, B is also true on that same interpretation, and whenever A is false on a given interpretation, B is also false on that same interpretation. Thus we could just as well have defined semantic equivalence as follows: for every interpretation I, I(A) = I(B); that is, A and B have the same truth value on every interpretation.

It's easy to determine whether any two statement forms of S are semantically equivalent by the semantic tree method. Given any two statement forms A and B, we proceed by assuming that A and B are *not* semantically equivalent; that is, we assume that there exists some interpretation on which A and B do not have the same truth value. This involves two possibilities: for some interpretation I, either both I(A) = T and I(B) = F or both I(A) = F and I(B) = T. Now we proceed first by constructing a tree for the first possibility:

> **Step 1** A
> ~~B~~

If at least one branch of this tree remains open, then we may conclude that A and B are not semantically equivalent, since an open branch indicates that there is at least one interpretation on which A is true and B is false. However, if all the branches close, this indicates only that there is no interpretation on which A is true and B false. There still might be one on which A is false and B true. To check this, we proceed to step 2:

> **Step 2** ~~A~~
> B

Now if all the branches of the tree at step 2 close, then we may conclude that A and B are semantically equivalent since we will also have shown that there isn't an interpretation on which A is false and B is true. Of course, if at least one branch of the tree remains open at step 2, then A and B are not semantically equivalent.

Let's consider whether the following two statement forms are semantically equivalent:

$$(p \wedge q) \supset r, \quad (p \supset r) \vee (q \supset r)$$

First, we assume that they are not semantically equivalent; that is, we assume that there exists at least one interpretation on which the two statement forms have different truth values. The first possibility is that there exists at least one interpretation I on which $I[(p \wedge q) \supset r] = T$ and $I[(p \supset r) \vee (q \supset r)] = F$.

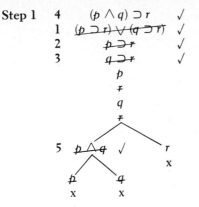

Step 1

4    $(p \wedge q) \supset r$ ✓
1    $(p \supset r) \vee (q \supset r)$ ✓
2    $p \supset r$ ✓
3    $q \supset r$ ✓
     p
     f
     q
     f

5   $p \wedge q$ ✓ r
             x

   p q
   x   x

Clearly, if $(p \wedge q) \supset r$ and $(p \supset r) \vee (q \supset r)$ are not semantically equivalent, it can't be because there is an interpretation on which $(p \wedge q) \supset r$ is true and $(p \supset r) \vee (q \supset r)$ is false.

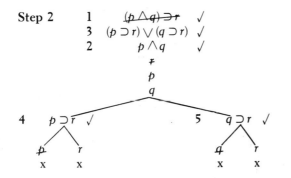

Step 2

1    $(p \wedge q) \supset r$ ✓
3    $(p \supset r) \vee (q \supset r)$ ✓
2    $p \wedge q$ ✓
     f
     p
     q

4   $p \supset r$ ✓   5 $q \supset r$ ✓

   p r q r
   x   x   x   x

Nor can it be because there is an interpretation on which $(p \wedge q) \supset r$ is false and $(p \supset r) \vee (q \supset r)$ is true. Hence the two statement forms are semantically equivalent.

Let's consider another example. Is $(p \supset q) \supset r$ semantically equivalent to $p \supset (q \supset r)$?

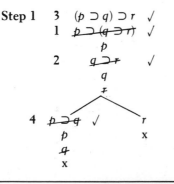

Step 1

3    $(p \supset q) \supset r$ ✓
1    $p \supset (q \supset r)$ ✓
     p
2    $q \supset r$ ✓
     q
     f

4   $p \supset q$ ✓ r
   p x
   q
   x

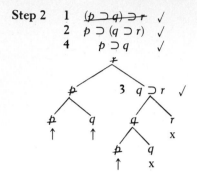

Step 2

1. $(p \supset q) \supset r$ ✓
2. $p \supset (q \supset r)$ ✓
4. $p \supset q$ ✓

The two statement forms are not semantically equivalent since step 2 makes it clear that there is an interpretation (in fact, several) on which $(p \supset q) \supset r$ is false and $p \supset (q \supset r)$ is true. By choosing the leftmost open branch, such an interpretation is

$I(p) = F$
$I(q) = T$
$I(r) = F$

This is also demonstrated by the appropriate row of the truth table for the two statement forms:

p	q	r	$p \supset q$	$q \supset r$	$(p \supset q) \supset r$	$p \supset (q \supset r)$
F	T	F	T	F	F	T

EXERCISE 6.7

1 Using the semantic tree method, determine whether the following pairs of statement forms are semantically equivalent. List a counterinterpretation for each of those pairs which are not.

(a) $\sim p \vee q$, $\sim(p \wedge \sim q)$
*(b) $p \vee (p \supset q)$, $\sim q \supset p$
(c) $p \supset (q \wedge r)$, $(p \supset r) \wedge (q \supset r)$
(d) p, $(q \supset p) \wedge (\sim q \supset p)$
*(e) $(p \wedge \sim q) \supset r$, $q \vee (\sim r \supset \sim p)$
(f) $(p \supset q) \supset q$, $p \vee q$
(g) $[\sim p \vee (q \wedge r)] \supset s$, $s \supset [(p \supset q) \wedge (r \supset p)]$
*(h) $(p \vee \sim q) \wedge r$, $(\sim p \supset r) \wedge (q \supset r)$

2   Show that the following is a metatheorem of statement logic:

A ⇔ B if and only if {A} ⊪ B and {B} ⊪ A

6.8

TAUTOLOGIES, CONTRADICTIONS, AND CONTINGENCIES

We have already studied the semantic side of the concept of a law of logic in Chapter 3. As we have seen, a tautology, or logical truth of statement logic, is simply a statement which takes the value *true* on every row of its truth table. This means, then, that the definition of a tautology in terms of our reformulated semantic theory of S would be this:

> **Definition of *Tautology*:** A statement form A of S is a *tautology* (we write ⊪ A to indicate this) if and only if A is true on all interpretations.

As we mentioned earlier, there is a difference between a tautology and a logical truth, although we have employed the terms more or less synonymously. In natural language, a tautology is a statement which is logically true with respect to statement logic, whereas a logical truth may depend on features of logical form besides those studied in statement logic. In Chapter 8 we will see that there are logical truths which are not truth-functional. However, so long as we restrict ourselves to statement logic, we may use the two terms synonymously.

We are also able to use the semantic tree method to determine whether a given statement form of S is a tautology. To do that, we assume that the given statement form is not true on at least one interpretation. If all branches of the tree for the statement form close, then the assumption is false and thus the statement form in question must be a tautology. However, should at least one branch remain open, then the assumption is true and the statement form in question is not a tautology.

As an example, consider the following statement form:

$[p \supset (q \supset r)] \supset [q \supset (\sim r \supset \sim p)]$

First, we place a slash through the statement form:

$\cancel{[p \supset (q \supset r)] \supset [q \supset (\sim r \supset \sim p)]}$

This amounts to assuming that there is at least one interpretation on which the statement form is false. Now we simply construct the tree which results from this assumption:

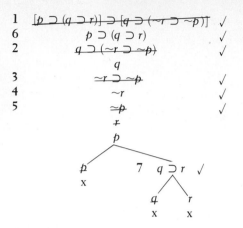

Clearly, there isn't any interpretation on which $[p \supset (q \supset r)] \supset [q \supset (\sim r \supset \sim p)]$ is false. Hence it must be true on all interpretations, and so it is a tautology.

Notice that the process of deciding whether a statement form is a tautology is just like the process of determining whether an argument is valid, except that here we have no premises. Now, in Chapter 4 we said that nothing in our definition of argument required that an argument have any premises. Although we wouldn't normally consider a conclusion without any premises to be an argument, we can extend the notion of an argument and regard a logical truth as a valid argument with no premises. Obviously, then, the following is true:

Metatheorem: ⊩ A if and only if ∅ ⊩ A.

Now consider the following statement form:

$[(\sim p \supset \sim q) \supset p] \supset p$

That it is not a tautology is demonstrated by its tree:

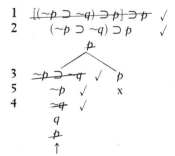

It is not a tautology because the tree indicates that there is an interpretation on which it is false, namely,

$$I(p) = F$$
$$I(q) = T$$

In Chapter 3 we saw that if a statement form is not a tautology, it must be either a contradiction or a contingency. Now the above tree surely verifies that $[(\sim p \supset \sim q) \supset p] \supset p$ is not a tautology, but it doesn't tell us whether it is a contradiction or a contingency. At first sight, it appears as if the semantic tree method is limited in a way that the truth table method isn't. But this isn't so. We can also determine whether a statement form is contradictory or contingent using semantic trees. However, first we need to redefine these two concepts. Given what we have said about them in Chapter 3, it's obvious that contradiction will be redefined in terms of the notion of an interpretation as follows:

> **Definition of *Contradiction*:** A statement form A is a *contradiction* if and only if there isn't any interpretation on which A is true.

Notice that this definition is equivalent to saying that a contradiction is a statement form that is false on every row of its truth table. We retain the definition of contingency given in Chapter 3:

> **Definition of *Contingency*:** A statement form A is a *contingency* if and only if it is neither a tautology nor a contradiction.

To determine whether a given statement form is contradictory by the semantic tree method, we assume that there is an interpretation on which it is true. Given that assumption, if every branch of its tree closes, the assumption is false and so the statement form in question must be a contradiction. If, however, at least one branch remains open, the statement form in question is not a contradiction since the assumption will have proved true. Thus, consider the following statement form:

$$(p \supset p) \supset \sim(q \supset q)$$

To determine whether it is a contradiction by means of the semantic tree method, we assume that there is an interpretation on which $(p \supset p) \supset \sim(q \supset q)$ is true. Consequently, we construct its tree *without slashing it*:

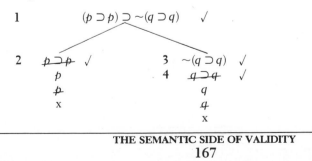

Obviously the assumption is false, and so $(p \supset p) \supset \sim(q \supset q)$ is contradictory.

Returning to $[(\sim p \supset \sim q) \supset p] \supset p$, which we have already determined is not a tautology, we now assume that there is an interpretation on which it is true. As a result, we obtain the following tree:

Obviously, we need not complete the construction of this tree since the branch at the right will never close no matter what we do with the branch at the left. Hence there is at least one interpretation on which $[(\sim p \supset \sim q) \supset p] \supset p$ is true:

$I(p) = T$
$I(q) = T$ [or $I(q) = F$]

Undoubtedly, then, $[(\sim p \supset \sim q) \supset p] \supset p$ is not contradictory either. Since it is neither a tautology nor a contradiction, it follows by the definition of contingency that $[(\sim p \supset \sim q) \supset p] \supset p$ is contingent.

EXERCISE 6.8

Determine whether each of the following statement forms is tautologous, contradictory or contingent (if contingent, list at least one interpretation on which it is true and one on which it is false):

1   $[p \lor (q \land r)] \supset [(\sim q \supset p) \land (\sim r \supset p)]$
2   $\sim p \supset p$
*3 $\sim(p \supset \sim p)$
4   $(p \supset q) \supset \sim(p \supset \sim q)$
5   $(p \supset q) \land (\sim q \land p)$
*6 $p \equiv [p \lor (p \land q)]$
7   $[(p \supset q) \supset p] \supset p$
8   $[(p \lor q) \supset r] \supset (r \supset \sim p)$
*9 $(p \supset q) \lor (q \supset p)$
10   $[(p \supset q) \land (p \supset r)] \supset [p \supset (q \land r)]$
11   $[(p \supset q) \supset q] \supset (p \land q)$
*12 $\sim(p \supset q) \land \sim(p \supset \sim q)$

6.9

ENTAILMENT AND THE MATERIAL CONDITIONAL

In Chapter 2, we saw that most (if not all) conditionals in natural language are intensional. As a rule, there is some kind of connection between their antecedents and their consequents which cannot be captured by the truth-functional definition of the horseshoe. We introduced the term *material conditional* for the kind of conditional that the horseshoe would formalize accurately. However, as we have seen, material conditionals are seldom, if ever, asserted in natural language. Nevertheless, we have chosen to formalize most conditionals by the horseshoe. Our justification for this, you will recall, was that most conditionals of natural language do share a minimum of truth-functional meaning with the material conditional. Like the material conditional, most conditionals of natural language are false if their antecedents are true and their consequents false. However, unlike the material conditional, most conditionals of natural language are not *necessarily* true under all other possible circumstances. Nevertheless, in defining the horseshoe, we made it necessarily true under all other possible circumstances. The reason cited for doing this in Chapter 2 was that we wanted the material conditional to be the weakest possible conditional we could get; otherwise, it would not fit some conditionals.

Actually there is still another reason why we made the horseshoe definitely true under all other possible circumstances: there is a connection between entailment and the material conditional. A set S of statement forms entails a statement form A just in case there isn't an interpretation on which all the members of S are true and A is false. Stated differently, an argument form is valid (in the semantic sense) if and only if it is impossible for the premises to be true and the conclusion to be false. Now, by defining the material conditional as false only when its antecedent is true and its consequent is false, but true otherwise, we have built into our definition of the material conditional our intuitions concerning entailment. In other words, we have defined the material conditional so that it reflects the semantic properties of entailment. Precisely what we mean is stated by the following metatheorem:

Metatheorem: $\{A_1, A_2, \ldots, A_n\} \Vdash B$ if and only if $\Vdash (A_1 \wedge A_2 \wedge \ldots \wedge A_n) \supset B$.

In other words, the set of all premises of an argument form entails its conclusion just in case the conditional having as its antecedent the conjunction of all the premises and as its consequent the conclusion is a tautology (a logical truth of statement logic). For example,

$$p \supset q$$
$$q \supset r$$
$$\overline{p \supset r}$$

is valid (in the semantic sense) just in case $\{p \supset q, q \supset r\} \Vdash p \supset r$. However, according to the above metatheorem, $\{p \supset q, q \supset r\} \Vdash p \supset r$

is the case if and only if $[(p \supset q) \wedge (q \supset r)] \supset (p \supset r)$ is a tautology. In order to show that this is indeed the case, we first demonstrate, by employing the semantic tree method, that $\{p \supset q, q \supset r\} \Vdash p \supset r$:

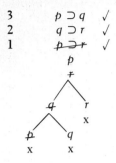

3      $p \supset q$ $\checkmark$
2      $q \supset r$ $\checkmark$
1      $\cancel{p \supset r}$ $\checkmark$

Now we show that $[(p \supset q) \wedge (q \supset r)] \supset (p \supset r)$ is a tautology:

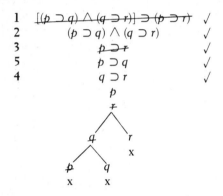

1      $\cancel{[(p \supset q) \wedge (q \supset r)] \supset (p \supset r)}$ $\checkmark$
2      $(p \supset q) \wedge (q \supset r)$ $\checkmark$
3      $\cancel{p \supset r}$ $\checkmark$
5      $p \supset q$ $\checkmark$
4      $q \supset r$ $\checkmark$

Obviously, then, the material conditional, as we have defined it, does reflect the semantic properties of entailment.

REVIEW EXERCISES FOR CHAPTER 6

1 Define the following notions.

    (a) Interpretation
    (b) Entailment
    (c) Semantic consistency
    (d) Semantic equivalence
    (e) Logical truth (tautology)
    (f) Contradiction
    (g) Contingency

2 Determine whether the following argument forms are valid in the semantic sense. List at least one counterinterpretation for the invalid ones.

*(a) $(p \lor q) \equiv r$
$\sim p$
$\sim q$
_____
$\sim(r \land s)$

(b) $\sim(p \lor q) \supset r$
$\sim q$
$p \supset s$
_____
$s \lor r$

(c) $p \supset (q \supset r)$
$s \supset \sim r$
_____
$p \supset \sim q$

*(d) $p \lor (q \land \sim r)$
$q \supset (\sim r \land p)$
_____
p

(e) $p \supset q$
$r \supset s$
_____
$(p \lor q) \supset (r \lor s)$

(f) $p \supset (r \lor s)$
$q \supset (r \supset s)$
_____
$p \lor q$

*(g) $(p \supset q) \land (r \supset s)$
$(q \lor s) \supset t$
$\sim t$
_____
$\sim(p \lor r)$

(h) $p \supset q$
$r \supset s$
$q \lor r$
_____
$p \lor s$

(i) $(p \lor q) \supset (r \supset s)$
$(\sim s \lor t) \supset (p \land r)$
_____
s

*(j) $(p \lor q) \supset (r \land s)$
$(r \lor t) \supset (\sim u \land v)$
$(u \lor t) \supset (p \land w)$
_____
$\sim u$

(k) $p \supset (q \supset r)$
$(r \lor s) \supset t$
$q \supset (\sim s \supset r)$
_____
$p \supset t$

(l) $(p \lor q) \supset [(r \lor s) \supset t]$
_____
$p \supset [(r \land s) \supset t]$

*(m) $p \equiv (q \land r)$
$s \equiv p$
$q \equiv (t \lor u)$
$t \lor u$
_____
$t \land u$

(n) $p \supset q$
$r \supset p$
r
_____
q

(o) $\sim p \supset (q \land r)$
$(s \supset \sim t) \supset (\sim q \land \sim p)$
$(t \lor s) \supset r$
_____
r

*(p) $p \supset \sim q$
$(p \supset r) \supset s$
$q \lor r$
_____
s

(q) $p \supset (q \land r)$
$\sim q$
$p \equiv s$
_____
$\sim s$

(r) $(p \lor q) \supset r$
$(s \supset p) \supset \sim t$
$r \supset (q \lor t)$
$p \supset (\sim s \supset q)$
_____
$q \equiv r$

*(s) $p \supset (q \supset r)$
$p \supset (s \supset t)$
$p \land (q \lor s)$
$\sim r$
_____
t

(t) $(p \lor q) \supset r$
_____
$\sim r \supset p$

3 Determine whether the following sets of statement forms are semantically consistent.

*(a) $\{p \supset (q \supset r), q, \sim(p \supset r)\}$
 (b) $\{p \supset \sim(q \vee \sim r), p, r \supset q\}$
*(c) $\{p, \sim q, \sim r, p \supset (s \vee t), t \supset (r \wedge q)\}$
 (d) $\{\sim p \supset q, p \supset r, p, \sim r \vee \sim q\}$
*(e) $\{p \supset q, p \vee q, \sim q\}$
 (f) $\{p \supset q, r \supset q, (p \vee r) \supset q\}$

4 Determine whether the following statements are true.

*(a) $p \supset (q \supset r) \Leftrightarrow r \supset \sim(p \wedge q)$
 (b) $p \supset \{q \supset [r \supset (s \supset t)]\} \Leftrightarrow \sim t \supset \{q \supset [p \supset (s \supset \sim r)]\}$
*(c) $p \supset (q \vee r) \Leftrightarrow (q \wedge r) \supset \sim p$
 (d) $p \vee q \Leftrightarrow (p \supset q) \supset q$
*(e) $p \wedge q \Leftrightarrow \sim q \supset p$

5 Employing semantic trees, determine whether each of the following is a tautology, a contradiction, or a contingency.

*(a) $p \equiv [p \wedge (q \supset p)]$
 (b) $(p \supset \sim p) \wedge (\sim p \supset p)$
*(c) $(p \supset q) \supset [(q \supset \sim r) \supset (r \supset \sim p)]$
 (d) $[(p \supset q) \supset p] \supset p$
*(e) $(p \supset q) \vee (q \supset p)$
 (f) $[p \supset (q \supset r)] \supset [(p \supset q) \supset r]$
*(g) $[p \vee (q \wedge r)] \equiv [(p \vee q) \wedge r]$
 (h) $(p \equiv q) \supset [(p \wedge \sim q) \vee (\sim p \wedge q)]$
*(i) $(p \supset p) \supset p$
 (j) $(\sim p \supset p) \supset p$
*(k) $p \supset (q \supset q)$
 (l) $[(p \supset q) \supset q] \supset q$
*(m) $(p \supset q) \equiv (\sim p \supset \sim q)$
 (n) $(p \supset q) \supset [(q \supset r) \supset (p \supset r)]$
*(o) $[(p \vee q) \supset r] \supset \{[(r \vee s) \supset t] \supset (p \supset t)\}$

6 Determine whether each of the following arguments is valid. If it is valid, determine whether it is trivially valid.

(a) Given that the Republicans will be unable to carry the upstate urban vote there is no question but that the next Governor of the state will be a Democrat. Hence, the next Governor will be a Democrat or I'm a monkey's uncle. After all, the Republicans will carry the urban vote only if they are able to put up an honest candidate. But, as anybody can see, they will not be able to put up an honest candidate.
(b) Either the unexamined life is not worth living or Plato was hopelessly mistaken. Certainly, the intellectual life is not worth pursuing only if the unexamined life is worth living. Furthermore, either Plato was not mistaken or some things are worth pursuing. So it follows that either the intellectual life is worth pursuing or nothing at all is worth pursuing.
(c) Undoubtedly, either there will be a depression or the housing industry will not improve. It is well known that the housing industry will improve only if interest rates do not rise. But there is no question that interest rates will rise. Moreover, it appears that unemployment will increase. Now, obviously, if both unemployment increases and interest rates rise, there will be a depression.

(d) So long as the Republicans retain control of the executive branch of the government, social programs designed to improve the human condition are not forthcoming. But then again, congressional Democrats cannot be counted on for putting forth progressive legislation except if they receive a lot of pressure from their respective constituencies. Now, as far as I am concerned, they will receive a lot of pressure from their respective constituencies only if the news media do more investigative reporting. Consequently, the Republicans will retain control of the executive branch only if the news media don't do any more investigative reporting. After all, social programs designed to improve the human condition are forthcoming even if we cannot depend on congressional Democrats to put forward progressive legislation.

(e) Assuming that speculation about the origins of the universe is meaningful, then even if the "Big Bang Theory" is correct, it is, nonetheless, undeniable that the Biblical account of creation has not been refuted. Now, I do not wish to suggest that the Big Bang Theory is incorrect; on the contrary, I am a staunch supporter of that theory. However, I must say that I staunchly support the Big Bang Theory only if speculation about the origins of the universe is indeed meaningful. Moreover, the Big Bang Theory, I believe, can be correct only if there is no God. Therefore, although the Biblical account of creation has not been refuted, God does not exist.

chapter 7
The Syntactic Side of Validity

7.1
A SYSTEM OF NATURAL DEDUCTION

In this chapter, we'll study the syntactic side of validity, or *deducibility*. Now, as we said in Chapter 1, in order to talk about deducibility, we need certain rules for deducing conclusions from premises. We call these *rules of inference*. Consequently, since S has no such rules, we need to add a set of rules in order to study deducibility. We will call the resulting system *Natural Deduction System* 𝔇.

Before we begin that, however, let's make it clear just how deductions fit into our general picture of logic. The most important point to remember is that in studying deductions, we are studying the *syntactic* correlate of validity. Consequently, as far as this chapter is concerned, semantic considerations don't matter. Instead, we will treat the symbols of 𝔇 just as symbols, without any meaning.

We will describe the construction of certain sequences of statement forms in 𝔇, which we call *deductions*, all in purely syntactic terms. Even though we have certain interpretations of the connectives in mind, we'll forget about them: officially, in this chapter, all symbols are simply meaningless formal marks. In fact, you can view 𝔇 as providing us with the rules for a game (we might call it the game of *deduction*). However, this doesn't mean that 𝔇 is necessarily trivial. It's often helpful to treat certain important matters (such as military strategy or economic planning) as games. Beyond that, even though we're now treating 𝔇 as a game, the rules for the game (the rules of inference of the system) will be chosen to make this game reflect something about actual argumentation.

The object of the game is to construct a deduction of some given statement form from some given set of statement forms. Here, a deduction is a sequence of statement forms which is constructed in accordance with certain rules. Let's state this more clearly by using some metavariables. Suppose we have a set $\{A_1, A_2, \ldots, A_n\}$ of statement forms and a statement form B. Then, a deduction of B from $\{A_1, A_2, \ldots, A_n\}$ is a sequence of statement forms $C_1, C_2, \ldots, C_p$ which is related to $\{A_1, A_2, \ldots, A_n\}$ in a certain manner (we'll explain this below) and such that C_p is B. Notice that the order of $C_1, C_2, \ldots, C_p$, unlike the order of the elements in a set, is important. Thus, when we say that C_p is B, we're saying that the *last* statement form in that sequence is B.

We'll present deductions as follows. First, we list the statement forms that the deduction is *from*, one below the other, as we would the premises of an argument form. Then, again as in an argument form, we draw a line. Below this line, we list the sequence of statement forms which constitutes the deduction, one below the other, in the appropriate order. Finally, for convenience in referring to the different lines, we number each line, beginning with the first and proceeding to the last. Using the same metavariables as above, we can present this general form as follows:

$$
\begin{array}{ll}
1 & A_1 \\
2 & A_2 \\
\cdot & \cdot \\
\cdot & \cdot \\
\cdot & \cdot \\
n & A_n \\
\hline
n+1 & C_1 \\
n+2 & C_2 \\
\cdot & \cdot \\
\cdot & \cdot \\
\cdot & \cdot \\
n+p & C_p \quad (\text{or B; } C_p = B)
\end{array}
$$

This is the form of a deduction of B from $\{A_1, A_2, \ldots, A_n\}$. Notice that we arrange A_1, A_2, etc., in an order. It actually doesn't make any difference what order we use, but once we've arranged them, we number them so that we can refer to them later. Since there are n statements (whatever number n might be) in the set, the numbers here go from 1 to n. When we reach C_1, we continue numbering: since C_1 is the next line after A_n, it receives the next number, which is $n + 1$. From here on, of course, the order is important. Note that since there are n lines up to A_n and p more lines after this up to C_p, the last line of the deduction will have the number $n + p$.

The lines $C_1, C_2, \ldots, C_p$ are added in accordance with certain rules, as we said. The rules are the following:

RULES OF INFERENCE FOR NATURAL DEDUCTION SYSTEM 𝔇

Transformation Rules

1 Simplification (Simp.)

	1a			1b	
.	.		.	.	
m	A∧ B		m	A∧ B	
.	.		.	.	
n	A	m, Simp.	n	B	m, Simp.
.	.		.	.	

2 Addition (Add.)

	2a			2b	
.	.		.	.	
m	A		m	A	
.	.		.	.	
n	A∨ B	m, Add.	n	B∨ A	m, Add.
.	.		.	.	

3 Modus Ponens (M.P.)

.	.	
l	A ⊃ B	
.	.	
m	A	
.	.	
n	B	l, m, M.P.
.	.	

4 Modus Tollens (M.T.)

.	.	
l	A ⊃ B	
.	.	
m	~B	
.	.	
n	~A	l, m, M.T.
.	.	

5 Hypothetical Syllogism (H.S.)

.	.	
l	A ⊃ B	
.	.	
m	B ⊃ C	
.	.	
n	A ⊃ C	l, m, H.S.
.	.	

6   Disjunctive Syllogism (D.S.)

	6a			6b	
l	A $\lor$ B		*l*	A $\lor$ B	
m	~A		*m*	~B	
n	B	*l, m*, D.S.	*n*	A	*l, m*, D.S.

7   Conjunction (Conj.)

l	A	
m	B	
n	A $\land$ B	*l, m*, Conj.

8   Constructive Dilemma (C.D.)

l	(A $\supset$ B) $\land$ (C $\supset$ D)	
m	A $\lor$ C	
n	B $\lor$ D	*l, m*, C.D.

Replacement Rules

1   Double Negation (D.N.)

A : ~~A

2   Implication (Impl.)

A $\supset$ B : ~A $\lor$ B

3   Transposition (Trans.)

A $\supset$ B : ~B $\supset$ ~A

4   Commutation (Com.)

a   A $\land$ B : B $\land$ A
b   A $\lor$ B : B $\lor$ A

5   Distribution (Dist.)

a   A $\land$ (B $\lor$ C) : (A $\land$ B) $\lor$ (A $\land$ C)
b   A $\lor$ (B $\land$ C) : (A $\lor$ B) $\land$ (A $\lor$ C)

6 Association (Assoc.)

a $A \wedge (B \wedge C)$: $(A \wedge B) \wedge C$
b $A \vee (B \vee C)$: $(A \vee B) \vee C$

7 Biconditionalization (Bic.)

$A \equiv B$: $(A \supset B) \wedge (B \supset A)$

8 DeMorganization (DeM.)

a $\sim(A \wedge B)$: $\sim A \vee \sim B$
b $\sim(A \vee B)$: $\sim A \wedge \sim B$

9 Exportation (Exp.)

$(A \wedge B) \supset C$: $A \supset (B \supset C)$

10 Repetition (Rep.)

a $A \wedge A$: A
b $A \vee A$: A

Assumption Rules

1 Deduction (Ded.)

i	m	A	ai
i	n	B	
i	$n + 1$	$A \supset B$	m—n, Ded.

2 Reductio ad Absurdum (R.A.)

i	m	A	ai
i	n	$B \wedge \sim B$	
i	$n + 1$	$\sim A$	m—n, R.A.

3 Reiteration (Reit.)

$i_1, \ldots, i_k$	m	A	
$i_1, \ldots, i_k, j_1, \ldots, j_l$	n	B	
$i_1, \ldots, i_k, j_1, \ldots, j_l$	$n + 1$	A	m, Reit.

Notice that there are three groups of rules: eight transformation rules, ten replacement rules, and three assumption rules. Each rule of inference says that if, in a deduction, you have already included a step of a certain form (or steps of certain forms), then you can add a step of a certain form as the next line. When a given statement form can be added in this way, then we say that it *follows from* the line or lines specified *in accordance with* the rule of inference specified. In terms of playing a game, each move in this game—that is, each line of the deduction—must be made according to two things: (1) the moves already made (the previous lines of the deduction) and (2) the rules of the game (the rules of inference).

Now that we've explained what we mean by a deduction, we can define a concept more closely related to our concept of validity, namely, *deducibility*:

> **Definition of *Deducibility*:** A statement form A is *deducible in* $\mathcal{D}$ from a set of statement forms S just in case it is possible to construct a deduction in $\mathcal{D}$ of A from S.

It's important to notice one thing about this definition: it is *relative to a particular system of deduction*. This definition, strictly speaking, defines only what it is for a statement form of $\mathcal{D}$ to be deducible *in* $\mathcal{D}$ from a set of statement forms *of* $\mathcal{D}$.

We will introduce the symbol $\vdash$ (called the *turnstile*) into the metalanguage to express symbolically the relationship of deducibility between a set of statement forms and a statement form. In using the turnstile, we put the name of the set before it (to the left) and the name of the statement form deducible from it after it (to the right). Thus, if we want to express in symbols that the statement form A is deducible from the set of statement forms S, we write

$S \vdash A$

This may be read A *is deducible from* S.

7.2
DEDUCIBILITY AND VALIDITY

Our intent all along is to explain the syntactic side of validity, which we call deducibility. Let's begin by defining *valid argument form* in $\mathcal{D}$ in terms of our definition of deducibility.

> **Definition of *Valid Argument Form*:** An argument form $A_1, A_2, \ldots,$ A_n / B is *valid* (in the syntactic sense) in $\mathcal{D}$ if and only if $\{A_1, A_2, \ldots, A_n\} \vdash B$ in $\mathcal{D}$.

Our aim in choosing the rules of inference of $\mathcal{D}$ has been to make explicit some of our logical intuitions about what follows from what syntactically with respect to statement logic. In arguing, frequently we rely on these intuitions. Sometimes, however, especially in long or complex arguments, they simply give out: we just don't know what to say about whether a particular statement follows from certain others. Perhaps even worse, there are occasions on which we find ourselves misled by our intuitions: we might be led to absurd conclusions, even though we seem to have gotten there by following our intuitions in reasoning. The best way to avoid these difficulties is to stick to the cases about which we're most certain. When we come across an argument, we should try to see if we can get from the premises to the conclusion by means of steps about which we have such a high degree of intuitive certainty that we can't imagine them ever going wrong. This is the process of constructing a deduction as described in Chapter 1. In effect, our rules of inference provide us with a list of moves to make in constructing deductions. Constructing a deduction in $\mathfrak{D}$, then, is the formalized equivalent to finding a path of such intuitively certain steps from the premises to the conclusion of an argument.

We can now give a definition of *valid argument* in the syntactic sense:

Definition of *Valid Argument* (in the syntactic sense) with respect to statement logic: An argument is *valid* with respect to statement logic (in the syntactic sense) if and only if its corresponding argument form is valid (in the syntactic sense) in $\mathfrak{D}$.

In order to justify this definition, we need to give some reasons why any and all arguments valid with respect to statement logic have valid corresponding argument forms in $\mathfrak{D}$. Our principal justification here is that each rule of inference corresponds in a way to an intuitively valid mode of reasoning. Let's look at one of the rules to see how this intuitive certainty lies behind it. Consider the following argument:

If John attended the party, then Mary did too.
John did attend the party.
_____

Therefore, Mary also attended the party.

There is no need to appeal to a system of logic to see that this argument is valid: our logical intuitions here are so secure that we simply can't conceive of this inference not being correct. Now, this argument is of the following form:

$$p \supset q$$
$$p$$
___
$$q$$

It's not hard to see that any other argument of this form will have the same high degree of intuitive certainty. This suggests that we can always rely on this pattern of argumentation. In fact, we should generalize this pattern into a rule of inference that applies whenever we come across such a pattern in the course of an argument. In effect, we do this when we make something a rule of inference of our system. Here, the rule would be as follows: If in the course of an argument we encounter a statement of the form A and another statement of the form A ⊃ B, then it will always be acceptable to infer another statement of the form B. In fact, this is the rule we call *Modus Ponens* (the third transformation rule):

l A ⊃ B

m A

n B l, m, M.P.

This is roughly the way in which we obtain our rules of inference. We single out certain simple arguments which our logical intuitions convince us must be valid. Then, we formalize them and generalize their applicability. Having done this, we are in a position to determine the validity of more complex arguments by demonstrating that the conclusions of those arguments follow from their premises by means of simple steps made in accordance with those fundamental argument patterns.

There is a problem, however, with proceeding on the basis of intuitive certainty. Possibly, we won't include every rule of inference that we should, or we might include some rules that somehow conflict with others. These difficulties become especially important in the study of systems more complex than statement logic. For the present, we'll only note that we have another test available for any rule of inference—we can check it against the semantic theory of S. That is, we can test to see if our rules of inference ever allow us to produce semantically invalid arguments. In fact, we've chosen rules which always guarantee validity in this sense: if the statement form(s) to which the rule is applied is (are) true on an interpretation, then the statement form which is inferred by the rule is true on that interpretation. For more on this subject, see Section 7.7.

7.3
DEMONSTRATING THE VALIDITY OF ARGUMENTS

Consider the following argument:

> God is omnibenevolent provided that He is perfect. If God is both perfect and the creator of the world, then there is no evil in the world. But it is an incontestable fact that there is evil in the world. Furthermore, it is usually claimed that God created the world. Therefore, either God is imperfect or He is not omnibenevolent.

Formalizing yields the following argument form:

$$p \supset q$$
$$(p \wedge r) \supset \sim s$$
$$s$$
$$r$$

$$\overline{\sim p \vee \sim q}$$

But how do we determine whether this argument form is syntactically valid? On the basis of the last section, we see that this argument form is valid on the condition that $\{p \supset q, (p \wedge r) \supset \sim s, s, r\} \vdash \sim p \vee \sim q$, that is, just in case $\sim p \vee \sim q$ is deducible from the set $\{p \supset q, (p \wedge r) \supset \sim s, s, r\}$. But now how do we determine whether $\{p \supset q, (p \wedge r) \supset \sim s, s, r\} \vdash \sim p \vee \sim q$? Given our definition of deducibility, we know that this is the case if we can find a deduction in $\mathcal{D}$ of $\sim p \vee \sim q$ from $\{p \supset q, (p \wedge r) \supset \sim s, s, r\}$. Finding such a deduction will, of course, involve producing a sequence of statement forms of $\mathcal{D}$ from $\{p \supset q, (p \wedge r) \supset \sim s, s, r\}$ to $\sim p \vee \sim q$ so that each step is justified by the rules of inference of $\mathcal{D}$. In order to show what a completed deduction looks like, we produce one below:

1	$p \supset q$	
2	$(p \wedge r) \supset \sim s$	
3	s	
4	r	
5	$\sim \sim s$	3, D.N.
6	$\sim (p \wedge r)$	2, 5, M.T.
7	$\sim p \vee \sim r$	6, DeM.
8	$\sim \sim r$	4, D.N.
9	$\sim p$	7, 8, D.S.
10	$\sim p \vee \sim q$	9, Add.

We have just demonstrated that the above argument is valid (in the syntactic sense). Of course, we haven't yet explained the deduction itself; that need not bother you for the moment since we will show how to construct deductions in the next few sections. It is essential that you understand, in view of the definitions of the previous section, why the above argument is valid. Briefly stated, this argument is valid because we have been able to construct a deduction in $\mathcal{D}$ of the formalization of its conclusion from the formalization of its premises.

7.3.1 Using the Transformation Rules

In this and the next few subsections, we will show how to use the rules of inference of $\mathcal{D}$. This subsection is concerned with the eight transformation rules. We will consider them in turn, beginning with Simplification.

In Section 7.1, the rule of Simplification is stated in the following two ways:

$$m \quad A \wedge B \qquad\qquad m \quad A \wedge B$$

$$n \quad A \qquad n, \text{Simp.} \qquad n \quad B \qquad n, \text{Simp.}$$

In words, this rule states that if at any step in a deduction we have a statement form of the form $A \wedge B$, we may write *either conjunct* as a later step of the deduction. Imagine that the following is part of a deduction:

$$m \quad p \wedge q$$

According to the rule of Simplification, we may write p at step n, thus:

$$m \quad p \wedge q$$

$$n \quad p$$

Of course, while constructing the deduction, we will want to indicate where we obtained the p; hence at the right of the step we must cite both the rule which justifies our writing p at step n and the step (or steps) to which we applied that rule.

We therefore *annotate* step n:

$$m \quad p \wedge q$$

$$n \quad p \qquad m, \text{Simp.}$$

The m indicates that we obtained p from step m, and *Simp.* indicates that the rule which justifies our writing p at step n is the rule of Simplification.

Remember that the rule applies to any statement form named by $A \wedge B$, no matter how complex. Hence, the following is a correct use of the rule of Simplification:

$$m \quad (p \supset q) \wedge [r \vee (s \equiv t)]$$

$$n \quad p \supset q \qquad m, \text{Simp.}$$

In employing the rule of Simplification (or any other rule of inference), strict adherence to the very letter of the rule is required. Any deviation, no matter how slight, constitutes a wrong move in deducing. Consequently, it might be helpful at this point to go over some misapplications and indicate why they are erroneous. Consider the following partial deduction:

$$m \quad p \supset q$$

$$n \quad p \qquad m, \text{ Simp. (Improper)}$$

This is an improper use of the rule since Simplification is applicable only to statement forms whose main connectives are inverted wedges. The main connective of step m in this example is a horseshoe.

Another misuse of the rule is the following:

$$m \quad (p \wedge q) \supset r$$

$$n \quad p \qquad m, \text{ Simp. (Improper)}$$

The difficulty here is that although the statement form at step m contains a conjunction, it is not itself a conjunction: its main connective is, in fact, the horseshoe. The rule of Simplification applies only to those statement forms whose *main* connectives are inverted wedges.

Finally, consider this misapplication of the rule:

$$m \quad (p \vee q) \supset r$$

$$n \quad p \supset r \qquad m, \text{ Simp. (Improper)}$$

Again, the reason why this is improper is that the rule has been applied to a statement form whose main connective is not an inverted wedge but (in this case) a horseshoe. We might mention that all the transformation rules must be applied only to statement forms with the appropriate *main* connectives.

We insist on a strict adherence to the letter of the rules of inference in $\mathfrak{D}$ because we want to make every detail of our deductions explicit. If at times we seem to insist on making explicit justifications for obvious steps, our reply would be that from our standpoint, *all* the rules of inference of $\mathfrak{D}$ are in a way obvious. Therefore, every step in a deduction is supposed to be obvious—so obvious, in fact, that we intuitively feel certain that it could not be wrong.

The rule of Simplification is perhaps among the most obvious of our rules of inference. Certainly, nobody would seriously question the validity of the following argument:

Maria will attend the party and Juan will go home.

Therefore, Maria will attend the party.

Our second transformation rule is Addition, which has the following two parts:

2a

m A

n A $\lor$ B m, Add.

2b

m A

n B $\lor$ A m, Add.

This rule simply states that given any statement form in a deduction, we may add as a later step of the deduction that statement form combined by means of a wedge with *any other statement form whatsoever*. Thus, the following incomplete deduction makes legitimate use of the rule of Addition:

m p

n $p \lor q$ m, Add.
$n + 1$ $p \lor (q \supset s)$ m, Add.
$n + 2$ $p \lor (p \land q)$ m, Add.

Obviously, the following use of the rule is improper:

m p

n $p \supset q$ m, Add. (Improper)

This application is illegitimate because it makes use of a connective other than the wedge.

Now consider the following incomplete deduction:

m $p \equiv \sim q$

n $(p \lor r) \equiv \sim q$ m, Add. (Improper)
$n + 1$ $p \equiv (\sim q \lor r)$ m, Add. (Improper)
$n + 2$ $(p \equiv \sim q) \lor r$ m, Add. (Correct)

Steps n and $n + 1$ are improper uses of the rule because it is not possible to append a statement form to a *part* of another statement form; you must append it to the *whole* of the other statement form, as in step $n + 2$.

The rule of Addition is also a rather obvious inference rule once we reflect on it. Consider the following argument:

It's raining outdoors.
_____

Therefore, either the sun is shining or it's raining outdoors.

If, in fact, it is raining outdoors, then it follows from this fact that either *It's raining outdoors* is true or any other statement is true. Quite obviously, the corresponding argument form of this argument is

p
_____

$q \lor p$

The rules of Simplification and Addition infer a statement form from *one* previous statement form. The remaining transformation rules, however, each infer statement forms from *two* previous statement forms. Keeping this in mind, let's proceed with the next six transformation rules, beginning with Modus Ponens:

$l \quad A \supset B$

$m \quad A$

$n \quad B \qquad l, m,$ M.P.

In words, this rule states that if you are given a statement form whose main connective is the horseshoe at some step in a deduction, and if, in addition, you are given the antecedent of that first statement form at some other step, then you can add the consequent as another step. Incidentally, in this rule, as in all other transformation rules which are applicable to two steps instead of one, the order of the two steps to which the rule is applied makes no difference. The following incomplete deduction displays Modus Ponens at work:

$k \qquad p \supset q$

$l \qquad (s \supset {\sim}r) \supset {\sim}(t \lor s)$

$m \qquad (p \supset q) \supset (s \supset {\sim}r)$

$n \qquad s \supset {\sim}r \qquad\qquad k, m,$ M.P.
$n + 1 \quad {\sim}(t \lor s) \qquad\qquad l, n,$ M.P.

An example of the misuse of Modus Ponens is given below:

$$l \quad (\sim p \supset q) \supset (r \wedge s)$$

$$m \quad \sim p$$

$$n \quad q \supset (r \wedge s) \qquad\qquad l, m, \text{M.P. (Improper)}$$

Modus Ponens, like all the other transformation rules, can be applied to only the *main* connective of a statement form.

We now turn to the rule of Modus Tollens:

$$l \quad A \supset B$$

$$m \quad \sim B$$

$$n \quad \sim A \qquad l, m, \text{M.T.}$$

This rule permits any of the inferences exhibited in the following partial deduction (again note that the order of the statement forms corresponding to $A \supset B$ and $\sim B$ is immaterial):

$$k \quad p \supset q$$

$$l \quad \sim q$$

$$m \quad \sim r \supset q$$

$$n \quad s \supset \sim r$$
$$n+1 \quad \sim p \qquad k, l, \text{M.T.}$$
$$n+2 \quad \sim\sim r \qquad m, l, \text{M.T.}$$
$$n+3 \quad \sim s \qquad n, n+2, \text{M.T.}$$

The following use of Modus Tollens, however, is incorrect:

$$l \quad (p \wedge q) \supset r$$

$$m \quad \sim r$$

$$n \quad p \wedge q \qquad l, m, \text{M.T. (Improper)}$$

A correct use of the rule here would have inferred $\sim(p \wedge q)$, not $p \wedge q$. Another incorrect use of the rule is

$l \quad p \supset q$

$m \quad \sim p$

$n \quad \sim q \qquad l, m, \text{M.T. (Improper)}$

Consider the following argument:

If God is omnibenevolent, then there is love in the world.
But there isn't any love in the world.

Therefore, God isn't omnibenevolent.

This argument is obviously valid. Note that it has the following form:

$$p \supset q$$
$$\sim q$$
$$\sim p$$

From the intuitive validity of arguments of this form, we get the rule of Modus Tollens.

Our next transformation rule is Hypothetical Syllogism; it has the following form:

$l \quad A \supset B$

$m \quad B \supset C$

$n \quad A \supset C \qquad l, m, \text{H.S.}$

This rule states that if you are given two conditionals at any two steps in a deduction such that the consequent of one is the same as the antecedent of the other, then it is permissible to combine the antecedent of the former with the consequent of the latter by a horseshoe. Thus, the following is a legitimate use of the rule of Hypothetical Syllogism:

$l \quad p \supset q$

$m \quad q \supset r$

$n \quad p \supset r \qquad l, m, \text{H.S.}$

Again, note that the order of the steps $A \supset B$ and $B \supset C$ does not matter.

Also, note that the consequent of the first conditional at step l is the same as the antecedent of the conditional at step m.

The following is also a correct use of the rule of Hypothetical Syllogism:

l $\sim(q \wedge r) \supset (\sim q \vee \sim r)$

m $\sim p \supset \sim(q \wedge r)$

n $\sim p \supset (\sim q \vee \sim r)$ $l, m,$ H.S.

Obviously, the following use of the rule is incorrect:

l $p \supset \sim q$

m $r \supset s$

n $p \supset s$ $l, m,$ H.S. (Improper)

The error here is that the consequent of the first conditional is not the same as the antecedent of the second.

The rule of Hypothetical Syllogism is a natural kind of inference which we often use. In ordinary circumstances, it takes the form of what is sometimes called "reasoning in a chain," as in the following argument:

If Mary attends the party, then so will Ted.
If Ted attends the party, Larry will too.

Therefore, if Mary attends the party, then so will Larry.

Quite obviously, the logical form of this argument is

$p \supset q$
$q \supset r$

$p \supset r$

The rule of Hypothetical Syllogism, as this example illustrates, is, of course, an intuitively valid rule of inference.

Now let's attempt to construct a deduction employing the rules studied so far. Consider the following argument form:

$[\sim(p \wedge \sim q) \vee \sim p] \supset [r \supset (\sim p \vee s)]$
$(p \wedge \sim q) \supset (r \vee p)$
$t \wedge \sim(r \vee p)$
$(\sim p \vee s) \supset \sim s$

$r \supset \sim s$

First, we number the premises. Next, in order to remind us of what we are trying to deduce, we place a diagonal line at the right and write the conclusion we want to deduce after it:

1 $[\sim(p \wedge q) \vee \sim p] \supset [r \supset (\sim p \vee s)]$
2 $(p \wedge \sim q) \supset (r \vee p)$
3 $t \wedge \sim(r \vee p)$
4 $(\sim p \vee s) \supset \sim s$ _____ / $r \supset \sim s$

We then proceed in the following way:

1 $[\sim(p \wedge \sim q) \vee \sim p] \supset [r \supset (\sim p \vee s)]$
2 $(p \wedge \sim q) \supset (r \vee p)$
3 $t \wedge \sim(r \vee p)$
4 $(\sim p \vee s) \supset \sim s$ _____ / $r \supset \sim s$
5 $\sim(r \vee p)$ 3, Simp.
6 $\sim(p \wedge \sim q)$ 2, 5, M.T.
7 $\sim(p \wedge \sim q) \vee \sim p$ 6, Add.
8 $r \supset (\sim p \vee s)$ 1, 7, M.P.
9 $r \supset \sim s$ 8, 4, H.S.

We now turn to the rule of Disjunctive Syllogism, which has the following forms:

6a			6b		
.	.			.	.
l	$A \vee B$		l	$A \vee B$	
.	.			.	.
m	$\sim A$		m	$\sim B$	
.	.			.	.
n	B	l, m, D.S.	n	B	l, m, D.S.
.	.			.	.

This rule states that given any statement form whose main connective is a wedge, along with the negation of one of the disjuncts of that statement form, it is permissible, at some later step in a deduction, to add the other disjunct of that disjunction. Thus, the following incomplete deduction makes correct use of the rule of Disjunctive Syllogism:

.   .
k $\sim q \vee p$

.   .
l $q \vee (r \wedge s)$

.   .
m $\sim p$

.   .
n $\sim q$ k, m, D.S.
$n + 1$ $r \wedge s$ l, n, D.S.
.   .

On the other hand, the following use of the rule is incorrect:

$l \quad p \lor (q \land r)$

$m \quad p$

$n \quad q \land r \qquad l, m, \text{D.S. (Improper)}$

In order for this to be correct, we would have to have $\sim p$ at step m.
Any argument having the following form is intuitively valid:

$$p \lor q$$
$$\underline{\sim p}$$
$$q$$

To see this, consider the following argument, which has this form:

Either Ramirez won the election or Yamoto did.
But Ramirez didn't win the election.

Therefore, Yamoto did.

Clearly, then, the rule of Disjunctive Syllogism is in accordance with our
logical intuitions.

Our next transformation rule is Conjunction, which has the following
form:

$l \quad A$

$m \quad B$

$n \quad A \land B \qquad l, m, \text{Conj.}$

Essentially, this rule states that give any two statement forms at any two
different lines of a deduction, it is permissible to combine both of these
items with an inverted wedge at some subsequent line of the deduction.
Note here that order does not matter: we could also have inferred $B \land A$
by the rule. The following incomplete deduction employs the rule of
Conjunction in legitimate ways:

$k \quad p$

$l \quad q$

$m \quad \sim r \supset s$

$$
\begin{array}{lll}
n & p \wedge q & k, l, \text{Conj.} \\
n+1 & (\sim r \supset s) \wedge (p \wedge q) & m, n, \text{Conj.} \\
n+2 & (p \wedge q) \wedge (\sim r \supset s) & m, n, \text{Conj.} \\
n+3 & q \wedge (p \wedge q) & l, n, \text{Conj.} \\
n+4 & (\sim r \supset s) \wedge p & k, m, \text{Conj.} \\
n+5 & [q \wedge (p \wedge q)] \wedge [(\sim r \supset s) \wedge (p \wedge q)] & n+1, n+3, \text{Conj.} \\
& \ \ \cdot &
\end{array}
$$

Note that in employing the rule of Conjunction, it is permissible to combine statement forms only by means of the inverted wedge.

Our final transformation rule is called Constructive Dilemma. It has the following form:

$$
\begin{array}{ll}
& \ \ \cdot \quad \cdot \\
l & (A \supset B) \wedge (C \supset D) \\
& \ \ \cdot \quad \cdot \\
m & A \vee C \\
& \ \ \cdot \quad \cdot \\
n & B \vee D \qquad\qquad l, m, \text{C.D.} \\
& \ \ \cdot \quad \cdot
\end{array}
$$

In some ways, this is similar to Modus Ponens. It differs, however, in that step l involves a conjunction of two conditionals and step m involves the disjunction of the antecedents of those two conditionals. The rule states that if you are given such statement forms at steps l and m of a deduction, you may at some later step n infer the disjunction of the consequents of the conditionals conjoined at step l. Thus, the following incomplete deduction makes use of Constructive Dilemma correctly:

$$
\begin{array}{ll}
& \ \ \cdot \quad \cdot \\
l & (p \supset q) \wedge (r \supset s) \\
& \ \ \cdot \quad \cdot \\
m & p \vee r \\
& \ \ \cdot \quad \cdot \\
n & q \vee s \qquad\qquad l, m, \text{C.D.} \\
& \ \ \cdot \quad \cdot
\end{array}
$$

So does the following:

$$
\begin{array}{ll}
& \ \ \cdot \quad \cdot \\
l & [(p \wedge \sim q) \supset (\sim r \vee s)] \wedge [\sim t \supset (\sim p \wedge r)] \\
& \ \ \cdot \quad \cdot \\
m & (p \wedge \sim q) \vee \sim t \\
& \ \ \cdot \quad \cdot \\
n & (\sim r \vee s) \vee (\sim p \wedge r) \qquad\qquad l, m, \text{C.D.} \\
& \ \ \cdot \quad \cdot
\end{array}
$$

We now construct a deduction for the following argument form using the rule of Constructive Dilemma:

$(p \supset q) \supset r$

$(p \lor \sim r) \land \sim q$

$\sim r \supset \sim s$

$p \supset s$

$s \lor \sim s$

We proceed in the following way:

1	$(p \supset q) \supset r$	
2	$(p \lor \sim r) \land \sim q$	
3	$\sim r \supset \sim s$	
4	$p \supset s$	

$/\ s \lor \sim s$

5	$(p \supset s) \land (\sim r \supset \sim s)$	4, 3, Conj.
6	$p \lor \sim r$	2, Simp.
7	$s \lor \sim s$	5, 6, C.D.

Constructing deductions is rather difficult until you become accustomed to it. There are no tricks involved; it is purely a trial-and-error procedure. The only surefire way of getting good at it is by prolonged practice.

EXERCISE 7.3.1

1　Annotate the following deductions.

*(a)
1	$p \supset (\sim q \supset \sim r)$
2	$p \land r$
3	$\sim \sim r$

$/\ \sim \sim q \lor \sim p$

4	p
5	$\sim q \supset \sim r$
6	$\sim \sim q$
7	$\sim \sim q \lor \sim p$

(b)
1	$p \supset [(q \land r) \supset t]$
2	$\sim t$
3	p

$/\ \sim (q \land r) \lor \sim s] \land p$

4	$(q \land r) \supset t$
5	$\sim (q \land r)$
6	$\sim (q \land r) \lor \sim s$
7	$[\sim (q \land r) \lor \sim s] \land p$

*(c) 1 $\sim r \wedge q$
      2 $p \supset [q \supset (r \vee \sim s)]$
      3 $r \supset t$
      4 p
      5 $\sim s \supset \sim s$
      6 $\sim t \wedge (q \supset r)$
      _____ / $(\sim s \vee \sim p) \wedge (\sim t \wedge q)$

      7 $q \supset (r \vee \sim s)$
      8 q
      9 $r \vee \sim s$
     10 $(r \supset t) \wedge (\sim s \supset \sim s)$
     11 $t \vee \sim s$
     12 $\sim t$
     13 $\sim s$
     14 $\sim s \vee \sim p$
     15 $\sim t \wedge q$
     16 $(\sim s \vee \sim p) \wedge (\sim t \wedge q)$

(d)   1 $\sim (p \vee r)$
      2 $\sim q \wedge (s \wedge \sim p)$
      3 $q \supset (p \vee r)$
      4 $p \vee t$
      _____ / t

      5 $\sim q$
      6 $s \wedge \sim p$
      7 $\sim p$
      8 t

(e)   1 $\sim p \wedge \sim q$
      2 $(\sim p \vee r) \supset (s \supset p)$
      _____ / $\sim s \vee q$

      3 $\sim p$
      4 $\sim p \vee r$
      5 $s \supset p$
      6 $\sim s$
      7 $\sim s \vee q$

2 Complete the following deductions in accordance with the justifications
provided at the right.

(a)   1 $(\sim p \vee q) \supset \sim q$
      2 $(p \wedge \sim r) \supset (s \supset p)$
      3 $\sim (s \supset p) \wedge t$
      4 $[\sim (p \wedge \sim r) \vee \sim p] \supset [s \supset (\sim p \vee q)]$
      _____ / $s \supset \sim q$

      5   3, Simp.
      6   2, 5, M.T.
      7 $\sim (p \wedge \sim r) \vee \sim p$ 6, Add.
      8   4, 7, M.P.
      9   8, 1, H.S.

*(b)   1 $p \supset q$
      2   r
      3   $(\sim s \vee q) \supset [(r \vee \sim p) \supset \sim t]$
      4   $t \vee \sim q$
      5   $(r \wedge p) \wedge \sim s$ _____ / $\sim p$

      6   5, Simp.
      7   $\sim s \vee q$ 6, Add.
      8   3, 7, M.P.
      9   2, Add.
     10   8, 9, M.P.
     11   4, 10, D.S.
     12   1, 11, M.T.

(c)   1 p
      2   $\sim q$
      3   $[(p \vee r) \wedge (\sim q \vee s)] \supset \sim t$
      4   $(u \wedge \sim s) \vee t$ _____ / $(u \wedge p) \wedge \sim t$

      5   $p \vee r$ 1, Add.
      6   $\sim q \vee s$ 2, Add.
      7   5, 6, Conj.
      8   3, 7, M.P.
      9   4, 8, D.S.
     10   u 9, Simp.
     11   10, 1, Conj.
     12   11, 8, Conj.

*(d)   1 $(p \wedge q) \wedge (r \vee s)$
      2   $p \supset (\sim q \vee s)$
      3   $s \supset t$
      4   $(p \wedge q) \supset (\sim q \supset \sim p)$ _____ / $\sim p \vee t$

      5   1, Simp.
      6   5, Simp.
      7   2, 6, M.P.
      8   4, 5, M.P.
      9   8, 3, Conj.
     10   9, 7, C.D.

(e)   1 $\sim(p \vee q) \wedge r$
      2   $(\sim p \vee \sim s) \supset (p \vee q)$
      3   $\sim(\sim p \vee \sim s) \supset \sim t$
      4   $t \vee \sim q$ _____ / $\sim q$

      5   1, Simp.
      6   2, 5, M.T.
      7   3, 6, M.P.
      8   4, 7, D.S.

7.3.1.1 Constructing Deductions

Some students feel that it is helpful to construct deductions by *reasoning backward*; this procedure serves to minimize the trial-and-error aspect of deduction construction. To see how reasoning backward works, consider the following valid argument form:

$$p \supset (q \lor r)$$
$$\sim(q \lor r)$$
$$q \lor s$$
$$\underline{\sim p \supset (\sim q \land t)}$$
$$s$$

Setting up in the usual fashion, we obtain

1 $p \supset (q \lor r)$
2 $\sim(q \lor r)$
3 $q \lor s$
4 $\sim p \supset (\sim q \land t)$ _____ / s

Obviously, the last step in any deduction of s from any set will be s itself. Hence, this much of the deduction is easily obtained:

1 $p \supset (q \lor r)$
2 $\sim(q \lor r)$
3 $q \lor s$
4 $\sim p \supset (\sim p \land t)$ _____ / s

n s

To fill in the rest of the steps, let's reason backward from s. Looking at the premises, we see that s appears as the second disjunct in the third premise. This means, then, that we could directly obtain s if we had $\sim q$, since s would then follow from $\sim q$ and the third premise by the rule of Disjunctive Syllogism. Thus, we could obtain s if we had $\sim q$:

1 $p \supset (q \lor r)$
2 $\sim(q \lor r)$
3 $q \lor s$
4 $\sim p \supset (\sim q \land t)$ _____ / s

$n-1$ $\sim q$
n s 3, $n-1$, D.S.

Let's again reason backward, now from $\sim q$. What would we need in order to obtain $\sim q$? Looking at the fourth premise, we see that $\sim q$ appears in the consequent of $\sim p \supset (\sim q \wedge t)$. Therefore, we could easily obtain $\sim q$ if we had $\sim q \wedge t$ alone, since $\sim q$ would follow from $\sim q \wedge t$ by the rule of Simplification. Clearly, then, we could obtain $\sim q$ if we had $\sim q \wedge t$:

$$
\begin{array}{ll}
1 & p \supset (q \vee r) \\
2 & \sim(q \vee r) \\
3 & q \vee s \\
4 & \sim p \supset (\sim q \wedge t)
\end{array} \qquad / \; s
$$

$n - 2$	$\sim q \wedge t$	
$n - 1$	$\sim q$	$n - 2$, Simp.
n	s	$3, n - 1$, D.S.

Again looking at the fourth premise, we see that we could obtain $\sim q \wedge t$ if we had $\sim p$, since it would then follow from $\sim q$ and $\sim p \supset (\sim q \wedge t)$ by Modus Ponens:

$$
\begin{array}{ll}
1 & p \supset (q \vee r) \\
2 & \sim(q \vee r) \\
3 & q \vee s \\
4 & \sim p \supset (\sim q \wedge t)
\end{array} \qquad / \; s
$$

$n - 3$	$\sim p$	
$n - 2$	$\sim q \wedge t$	$4, n - 3$, M.P.
$n - 1$	$\sim q$	$n - 2$, Simp.
n	s	$3, n - 1$, D.S.

Reasoning backward from $\sim p$, we see that $\sim p$ can be obtained immediately from the first and second premises by means of Modus Tollens:

$$
\begin{array}{ll}
1 & p \supset (q \vee r) \\
2 & \sim(q \vee r) \\
3 & q \vee s \\
4 & \sim p \supset (\sim q \wedge t)
\end{array} \qquad / \; s
$$

$n - 3$	$\sim p$	$1, 2$, M.T.
$n - 2$	$\sim q \wedge t$	$4, n - 3$, M.P.
$n - 1$	$\sim q$	$n - 2$, Simp.
n	s	$3, n - 1$, D.S.

Notice that we have now completed our deduction: we obtained $\sim p$ directly from premises of the deduction, and so we have reasoned our way all the way back to the set of premises. Therefore, we can systematically renumber the steps and arrive at the deduction in finished form:

$$
\begin{array}{ll}
1 \quad p \supset (q \vee r) & \\
2 \quad {\sim}(q \vee r) & \\
3 \quad q \vee s & \\
4 \quad {\sim}p \supset ({\sim}q \wedge t) & / \; s \\
\hline
5 \quad {\sim}p & 1, 2, \text{M.T.} \\
6 \quad {\sim}q \wedge t & 4, 5, \text{M.P.} \\
7 \quad {\sim}q & 6, \text{Simp.} \\
8 \quad s & 3, 7, \text{D.S.}
\end{array}
$$

Usually there are several ways of constructing any given deduction; that is, not every correct deduction of a given statement form from a given set of statement forms need have the same steps. The only requirement is that each of the steps in a deduction be sanctioned by the rules of inference.

EXERCISE 7.3.1.1

Construct deductions for the following argument forms (only the transformation rules are necessary for these deductions).

*1 $(p \supset q) \supset r$
   $\sim r \wedge \sim s$
   $(p \supset q) \vee t$
   $t \supset (r \vee q)$
   ─────
   q

2 $\sim(p \vee q)$
   $q \vee r$
   $\sim r \supset (p \vee q)$
   $q \supset \sim r$
   ─────
   $r \vee p$

3 $(p \vee q) \supset (q \equiv r)$
   $s \supset (p \vee q)$
   $s \wedge r$
   ─────
   $q \equiv r$

4 $p \supset q$
   $\sim q$
   $r \supset p$
   ─────
   $\sim r \wedge \sim q$

*5 $(p \vee q) \supset r$
   $\sim s$
   $(r \vee s) \supset t$
   $s \vee p$
   ─────
   t

6 $(p \supset q) \vee (r \supset s)$
   $(p \supset q) \supset (t \supset u)$
   $s \supset p$
   $\sim(t \supset u)$
   ─────
   $r \supset p$

7 $p \supset (q \supset r)$
   $(q \wedge r) \supset s$
   q
   p
   ─────
   s

8 $p \supset q$
   $(r \vee s) \vee (r \supset p)$
   $\sim t$
   $(\sim t \wedge \sim p) \supset \sim(r \vee s)$
   $\sim q$
   ─────
   $\sim r$

9 $p \vee q$
   r
   $[(r \vee p) \wedge \sim s] \supset (\sim t \wedge p)$
   $\sim s$
   $p \supset t$
   ─────
   q

10 $\sim p$
   $q \supset r$
   $s \supset p$
   $\sim s \supset (p \supset q)$
   ─────
   $p \supset r$

---

11 $p \lor q$
$(r \lor p) \supset s$
$\sim p$
$(q \lor t) \supset r$
_____
s

*12 $(p \lor q) \supset (r \land s)$
$\sim t \supset \sim (r \land s)$
$(r \land s) \supset \sim t$
_____
$(p \lor q) \supset \sim (r \land s)$

7.3.2 Using the Replacement Rules

This section concerns the use of the ten replacement rules. Now, we have seen that the transformation rules apply to an entire statement form in a deduction. The replacement rules, however, operate not only on the wholes of statement forms but also on any of their constituents. Another difference between the two kinds of rules is that with the exception of Simplification and Addition, the transformation rules all infer a statement form from *two* previous statement forms. The replacement rules, on the other hand, always infer a statement form from *one* previous statement form.

These rules are also formulated differently. As we have seen, the transformation rules are stated vertically. The replacement rules, on the other hand, are stated horizontally, with two metalinguistic expressions separated by a colon (see Section 7.1). In effect, these rules tell us when we can substitute certain expressions for others. If we find an expression in some line of a deduction which corresponds to one side of one of these rules, then we may replace it with the expression corresponding to the other side and write the result as a new step of the deduction. This applies whether the expression in question is the entire line of the deduction or a constituent of a line. Note that we may substitute the left-hand expression for the right-hand expression and conversely.

Perhaps the best way to explain how these rules are used is to present a few examples. Let's begin, then, with the rule of Double Negation (D.N.). It has the following form:

A : $\sim\sim$A

In employing the rule from left to right, we may operate on the whole of a statement form in the following way:

. .

m $p \lor [q \land (\sim r \supset s)]$
. .

n $\sim\sim \{p \lor [q \land (\sim r \supset s)]\}$ m, D.N.
. .

Examples of the use of the rule from left to right on the constituents of statement forms are provided in the following incomplete deduction:

$$m \qquad p \lor [q \land (\sim r \supset s)]$$

n	$p \lor [\sim\sim q \land (\sim r \supset s)]$	m, D.N.
$n+1$	$p \lor [\sim\sim q \land \sim\sim(\sim r \supset s)]$	n, D.N.
$n+2$	$p \lor [\sim\sim q \land \sim\sim(\sim\sim\sim r \supset s)]$	$n+1$, D.N.

Examples of the use of the rule from right to left are given below:

$$m \qquad \sim\sim[p \land (q \supset \sim\sim r)]$$

n	$p \land (q \supset \sim\sim r)$	m, D.N.
$n+1$	$p \land (q \supset r)$	n, D.N.

The next replacement rule is Implication:

$$A \supset B \quad : \quad \sim A \lor B$$

Examples of employing it from left to right are given below:

$$m \qquad p \supset [q \supset (\sim r \supset s)]$$

n	$\sim p \lor [q \supset (\sim r \supset s)]$	m, Imp.
$n+1$	$\sim p \lor [\sim q \lor (\sim r \supset s)]$	n, Imp.
$n+2$	$\sim p \lor [\sim q \lor (\sim\sim r \lor s)]$	$n+1$, Imp.

Now, from right to left:

$$m \qquad \sim p \lor [q \land (\sim r \lor s)]$$

n	$p \supset [q \land (\sim r \lor s)]$	m, Imp.
$n+1$	$p \supset [q \land (r \supset s)]$	n, Imp.

The rule of Transposition has the following form:

$$A \supset B \quad : \quad \sim B \supset \sim A$$

It is employed in both directions in the following incomplete deduction:

$$m \qquad p \supset [\sim q \supset (\sim r \supset \sim s)]$$

n	$\sim[\sim q \supset (\sim r \supset \sim s)] \supset \sim p$	m, Trans.
$n+1$	$\sim[\sim q \supset (s \supset r)] \supset \sim p$	n, Trans.
$n+2$	$\sim[\sim(s \supset r) \supset \sim\sim q] \supset \sim p$	$n+1$, Trans.

We turn now to the rule of Commutation, which has the following two forms:

4a $A \wedge B$: $B \wedge A$
4b $A \vee B$: $B \vee A$

This rule states that both conjunction and disjunction are *commutative*. That is, this rule states, in effect, that the order of the conjuncts in a conjunction, or the order of the disjuncts in a disjunction, doesn't really matter. Although conjunctions and disjunctions are commutative, the horseshoe is not. Consequently, it is incorrect to infer, for instance, $q \supset p$ from $p \supset q$ in a deduction. The following incomplete deduction makes several uses of the rule of Commutation:

$$
\begin{array}{lll}
m & (\sim p \vee q) \wedge [(\sim q \wedge r) \vee (r \vee s)] & \\
\\
n & [(\sim q \wedge r) \vee (r \vee s)] \wedge (\sim p \vee q) & m, \text{ Com.} \\
n + 1 & [(r \vee s) \vee (\sim q \wedge r)] \wedge (\sim p \vee q) & n, \text{ Com.} \\
n + 2 & [(r \vee s) \vee (r \wedge \sim q)] \wedge (\sim p \vee q) & n + 1, \text{ Com.}
\end{array}
$$

Now, let's take a look at the rule of Distribution:

5a $A \wedge (B \vee C)$: $(A \wedge B) \vee (A \wedge C)$
5b $A \vee (B \wedge C)$: $(A \vee B) \wedge (A \vee C)$

This rule is used several times in the following incomplete deduction:

$$
\begin{array}{lll}
m & (p \vee q) \wedge [r \vee (p \vee t)] & \\
\\
n & [(p \vee q) \wedge r] \vee [(p \vee q) \wedge (p \vee t)] & m, \text{ Dist.} \\
n + 1 & [(p \vee q) \wedge r] \vee [p \vee (q \wedge t)] & n, \text{ Dist.}
\end{array}
$$

The next replacement rule is Association:

6a $A \wedge (B \wedge C)$: $(A \wedge B) \wedge C$
6b $A \vee (B \vee C)$: $(A \vee B) \vee C$

Obviously, this rule permits any of the following steps:

$$
\begin{array}{lll}
m & p \vee [q \vee (r \vee \sim s)] & \\
\\
n & p \vee [(q \vee r) \vee \sim s] & m, \text{ Assoc.} \\
n + 1 & [p \vee (q \vee r)] \vee \sim s & n, \text{ Assoc.}
\end{array}
$$

The rule of Biconditionalization is also a rather straightforward replacement rule:

7 $A \equiv B$: $(A \supset B) \land (B \supset A)$

Its use is illustrated below:

m $[(p \equiv q) \supset (r \supset s)] \land [(r \supset s) \supset (p \equiv q)]$

n $(p \equiv q) \equiv (r \supset s)$ m, Bic.

$n + 1$ $[(p \supset q) \land (q \supset p)] \equiv (r \supset s)$ n, Bic.

Turning now to DeMorganization, we see that, like some of the other replacement rules, it has two forms:

8a $\sim(A \land B)$: $\sim A \lor \sim B$
8b $\sim(A \lor B)$: $\sim A \land \sim B$

Examples of the use of this rule follow:

m $\sim p \lor [\sim q \land \sim\sim(r \land t)]$

n $\sim p \lor \sim [q \lor \sim(r \land t)]$ m, DeM.
$n + 1$ $\sim\{p \land [q \lor \sim(r \land t)]\}$ n, DeM.

The rule of Exportation has the following form:

9 $(A \land B) \supset C$: $A \supset (B \supset C)$

It is used in the following partial deduction:

m $p \supset [(q \land \sim r) \supset s]$

n $p \supset [q \supset (\sim r \supset s)]$ m, Exp.
$n + 1$ $(p \land q) \supset (\sim r \supset s)$ n, Exp.

Finally, we turn to the rule of Repetition, which has the following form:

10a $(A \land A)$: A
10b $(A \lor A)$: A

Employing this rule is quite easy, as the following incomplete deduction shows:

$$m \quad (\sim p \lor \sim p) \supset q$$

$$n \quad \sim p \supset q \qquad\qquad m, \text{Rep.}$$
$$n + 1 \quad \sim p \supset (q \land q) \qquad n, \text{Rep.}$$

Now that we have become acquainted with each of the replacement rules, let's illustrate the use of the rules of inference we have learned so far. We begin by constructing a deduction for the following valid argument form:

$$(p \land q) \supset r$$
$$q$$

___

$$p \supset r$$

The completed deduction looks like this:

1   $(p \land q) \supset r$
2   q
_____ / $p \supset r$
3   $(q \land p) \supset r$ 1, Com.
4   $q \supset (p \supset r)$ 3, Exp.
5   $p \supset r$ 4, 2, M.P.

Now, consider the following argument form:

$$\sim p \supset q$$
$$r \supset \sim q$$
$$\sim(\sim r \land \sim p)$$

___

$$p$$

We construct a deduction for it in the following way:

1    $\sim p \supset q$
2    $r \supset \sim q$
3    $\sim(\sim r \land \sim p)$
_____ / p
4    $\sim\sim r \lor \sim\sim p$ 3, DeM.
5    $\sim r \supset \sim\sim p$ 4, Imp.
6    $\sim r \supset p$ 5, D.N.
7    $\sim\sim q \supset \sim r$ 2, Trans.
8    $q \supset \sim r$ 7, D.N.
9    $\sim p \supset \sim r$ 1, 8, H.S.
10   $\sim p \supset p$ 9, 6, H.S.
11   $\sim\sim p \lor p$ 10, Imp.
12   $p \lor p$ 11, D.N.
13   p 12, Rep.

Before concluding this section, we might remark on the *intuitiveness* of the replacement rules. With the possible exception of the rules of Double Negation and Repetition, these rules, unlike the transformation rules, do not appear to have a secure intuitive foundation. We have shown how the transformation rules are based on simple argument patterns whose validity is beyond question, so far as our logical intuitions are concerned. Making the same claim for the replacement rules is not quite as plausible. However, we can provide a justification for them once we look to the semantic theory of S. It's easy to show that each replacement rule authorizes replacing a statement form with one semantically equivalent to it. That is, the two metalinguistic expressions on either side of the colon in each rule always refer to equivalent statement forms.

EXERCISE 7.3.2

1   Show that the metalinguistic expressions on each side of the colon of each replacement rule are logically equivalent.
2   Annotate the following deductions.

(a)

1   $(p \vee q) \supset r$
2   $(r \vee q) \supset [p \supset (s \equiv t)]$
3   $p \wedge s$ _____ / $t \supset s$

4   p
5   $p \vee q$
6   r
7   $r \vee q$
8   $p \supset (s \equiv t)$
9   $s \equiv t$
10   $(s \supset t) \wedge (t \supset s)$
11   $t \supset s$

(b)

1   $p \supset q$
2   $q \supset r$
3   $r \supset p$
4   $p \supset \sim r$ _____ / $\sim p \wedge \sim r$

5   $r \supset \sim r$
6   $\sim r \vee \sim r$
7   $\sim r$
8   $\sim q$
9   $\sim p$
10   $\sim p \wedge \sim r$

*(c)

1. $\sim r \lor (s \lor t)$
2. $r \land p$
3. $s \supset t$
   _____ / t
4. r
5. $r \supset (s \lor t)$
6. $s \lor t$
7. $t \lor s$
8. $\sim\sim t \lor s$
9. $\sim t \supset s$
10. $\sim t \supset t$
11. $\sim\sim t \lor t$
12. $t \lor t$
13. t

(d)

1. $\sim(p \land q) \equiv \sim r$
2. $(s \lor t) \supset r$
   _____ / $t \supset p$
3. $[\sim(p \land q) \supset \sim r] \land [\sim r \supset \sim(p \land q)]$
4. $\sim(p \land q) \supset \sim r$
5. $r \supset (p \land q)$
6. $(s \lor t) \supset (p \land q)$
7. $\sim(s \lor t) \lor (p \land q)$
8. $(\sim s \land \sim t) \lor (p \land q)$
9. $(p \land q) \lor (\sim s \land \sim t)$
10. $[(p \land q) \land \sim s] \land [(p \land q) \lor \sim t]$
11. $(p \land q) \lor \sim t$
12. $\sim t \lor (p \land q)$
13. $(\sim t \lor p) \land (\sim t \lor q)$
14. $\sim t \lor p$
15. $t \supset p$

3 Complete the following deductions in accordance with the justifications provided at the right.

(a)

1.	$(p \lor q) \supset r$	
	_____ / $(p \supset r) \land (q \supset r)$	
2.		1, Imp.
3.		2, DeM.
4.	$r \lor (\sim p \land \sim q)$	3, Com.
5.		4, Dist.
6.		5, Com.
7.		6, Com.
8.		7, Imp.
9.		8, Imp.

*(b)

1.	$p \supset q$	
2.	$q \supset r$	
3.	$p \lor q$	
4.	$(q \supset s) \land \sim s$	
	_____ / $t \supset r$	

5.		4, Com.	10.	3, 9, D.S.
6.		5, Simp.	11.	2, 10, M.P.
7.		4, Simp.	12.	$\sim t \lor r$	11, Add.
8.		7, 6, M.T.	13.	12, Imp.
9.		1, 8, M.T.		

(c)

```
 1  ~p ⊃ ~q
 2  (r ∨ ~p) ∨ s
─────────────────────────────── / ~s ⊃ (q ⊃ r)
 3  s ∨ (r ∨ ~p)                  2, Com.
 4                                3, Assoc.
 5  ~~(s ∨ r) ∨ ~p                4, D.N.
 6                                5, Imp.
 7                                6, 1, H.S.
 8                                7, Imp.
 9                                8, D.N.
10                                9, Assoc.
11  s ∨ (~q ∨ r)                  10, Com.
12  ~~s ∨ (~q ∨ r)               11, D.N.
13                                12, Imp.
14                                13, Imp.
```

4 Construct deductions for the following valid argument forms.

*(a) $(p \wedge q) \vee r$

$\overline{}$

$\sim p \supset r$

(b) $\sim (p \wedge \sim q)$

$\overline{}$

$p \supset q$

(c) $(p \supset q) \supset (p \supset r)$
q

$\overline{}$

$p \supset r$

(d) $(p \vee q) \supset (r \wedge s)$
$\sim r$

$\overline{}$

$\sim q$

*(e) $\sim (p \supset q)$
$\sim q \supset r$

$\overline{}$

r

(f) $p \supset (q \supset \sim p)$

$\overline{}$

$q \supset \sim p$

(g) $(\sim p \supset \sim q) \wedge (\sim q \supset p)$
$(p \wedge t) \supset r$
t

$\overline{}$

$r \vee q$

(h) $\sim (p \vee \sim q)$
$r \supset p$

$\overline{}$

$r \supset q$

(i) $\sim p \vee \sim q$
$\sim r \supset q$

$\overline{}$

$p \supset r$

(j) $(p \vee q) \supset r$
$s \supset (t \wedge u)$

$\overline{}$

$(p \supset r) \wedge (s \supset t)$

(k) $r \supset s$
$t \supset p$
$\sim s \vee \sim p$

$\overline{}$

$\sim (r \wedge t)$

(l) $-\!-(p \wedge q)$
$r \supset p$
$s \supset q$

$\overline{}$

$\sim s \vee \sim r$

(m) $p \supset q$
$r \supset s$
$\sim q \vee \sim s$

$\overline{}$

$p \supset \sim r$

(n) $p \supset (q \vee r)$
$\sim (q \vee r) \vee \sim s$
$t \supset s$

$\overline{}$

$\sim p \vee \sim t$

(o) $(p \vee q) \supset (r \wedge s)$
$r \supset \sim s$
$\sim p \supset t$

$\overline{}$

$t \wedge \sim q$

7.3.3 Using the Assumption Rules

Consider the following argument:

If roses are red, then violets are blue.

Therefore, if roses are red, then both roses are red and violets are blue.

This argument is obviously valid. Its formalization is

$$\frac{p \supset q}{p \supset (p \wedge q)}$$

Unfortunately, if we use only the rules considered so far, we'll never be able to show that $\{p \supset q\} \vdash p \supset (p \wedge q)$. Consequently, our system of logic will be inadequate without introducing additional rules, since there will be some intuitively valid argument forms for which no deductions exist. We include the assumption rules among the rules of inference of $\mathfrak{D}$ in order to eliminate this problem. These rules also help to reduce the amount of trial and error involved in the construction of deductions. In fact, they often (but not always) shorten the length of deductions.

As their name suggests, the assumption rules involve the use of *assumptions*. This difference renders them slightly more complicated. Let's consider each of them in turn.

7.3.3.1 The Deduction Rule

As we see from Section 7.1, the Deduction rule looks like this:

$$
\begin{array}{lll}
i \quad m & A & ai \\
i \quad n & B & \\
i \quad n+1 & A \supset B & m\text{—}n, \text{ Ded.}
\end{array}
$$

This rule states: if we can, by *assuming* a statement form A at some step of a deduction, deduce another statement form B at some later step, then we may add the statement form $A \supset B$ as a subsequent step. This rule actually has a great deal of intuitive appeal. Suppose, for instance, that someone were to say to you: "I can prove B on the assumption that A." Wouldn't that person be entitled to conclude that if A, then B?

The principal difficulty with this rule is understanding the restrictions on its use. As you might expect from our brief explanation, you are entitled to add the step $A \supset B$ *only if* you have succeeded in deducing B *after* first assuming A. What's more, all the steps in the deduction which follow your assumption that A are actually unjustified unless you eventually succeed in deducing B.

We introduce two other devices into our notation for deductions involving assumption rules. First, in order to indicate that a given step is being assumed in the hope of deducing something else from it and applying an assumption rule, we write a followed by a number i to the right of the assumed step. This is a justification for writing that step only if we eventually succeed in deducing what we want. The number simply tells us which assumption this is in the deduction. Next, we write a *dependency numeral* in front of the assumption and in front of *every subsequent step in the deduction until the assumption is discharged,* that is, until we deduce what we want. This is to remind us that until we accomplish what we aim to by making an assumption, we're not really entitled to leave anything that depends on it in the deduction. The dependency numeral is simply the number after *a* in the annotation. We use a different number each time we introduce a new assumption into a deduction.

When we finally reach the statement form that we want to deduce from an assumption, we apply the rule and infer the statement form which it authorizes us to add. When we do this, we say we have *discharged* the assumption. To indicate that an assumption has been discharged, we write its dependency numeral in front of the step which discharges it and draw a line through it. Afterward, that dependency numeral never occurs again in that deduction (if we make another assumption, we use a different dependency numeral). Obviously, if we allowed the last step of a deduction to depend on an assumption, we could deduce anything from anything, which we certainly don't want. *Therefore, no completed deduction can end with any assumptions not discharged.* Notationally, this means that the last step of a finished deduction cannot have any dependency numerals before it.

Notice also that in giving the justification for the step which discharges the assumption, we write "*m—n,* Ded." This is to indicate that the application of the Deduction rule depends on the *entire series of steps from m to n.*

Perhaps the best way to learn how to use this rule is to look at a few examples. Let's first consider the argument form given in the last section:

$$\frac{p \supset q}{p \supset (p \wedge q)}$$

We assume the antecedent p of the conclusion and attempt to deduce the consequent of the conclusion, which in this case is $p \wedge q$, at some later step. In this case, it's fairly easy to find the required steps:

	1	$p \supset q$	
1	2	p	$a1$
1	3	q	1, 2, M.P.
1	4	$p \wedge q$	2, 3, Conj.

(with $/\ p \supset (p \wedge q)$ written to the right of step 1)

Now that we have deduced the consequent of the conclusion, namely $p \wedge q$, we are in a position to discharge the assumption. This is done at step 5 by writing the assumption p, placing a horseshoe after it, and then writing what was to be deduced. Thus, we obtain the following:

```
    1  p ⊃ q
                                            / p ⊃ (p ∧ q)
  1  2  p                                   a1
  1  3  q                                   1, 2, M.P.
  1  4  p ∧ q                               2, 3, Conj.
  ⫫  5  p ⊃ (p ∧ q)                         2—4, Ded.
```

This completes the deduction of $p \supset (p \wedge q)$ from $p \supset q$. Note that we place a diagonal line through the dependency numeral at step 5 to indicate that the assumption has been discharged. Also note that, in using the Deduction rule, we always introduce a horseshoe (rather than some other connective) between the assumption and the step we deduce from it.

Let's consider another example:

$$p \supset [(q \vee r) \supset s]$$
$$(s \vee t) \supset u$$

$$p \supset (r \supset u)$$

Now, let's use the Deduction rule. Obviously, since the antecedent of the conclusion is p, we will assume p and attempt to deduce the consequent, namely, $r \supset u$. However, since the main connective of $r \supset u$ is a horseshoe, we can also, if we wish, make a second assumption, namely r. If we do this, then we will have reduced our problem to a matter of finding a deduction of u from the premises and the assumptions p and r. Our deduction proceeds as follows:

```
        1  p ⊃ [(q ∨ r) ⊃ s]
        2  (s ∨ t) ⊃ u
                                            / p ⊃ (r ⊃ u)
   1    3  p                                a1
 2, 1   4  r                                a2
 2, 1   5  (q ∨ r) ⊃ s                      1, 3, M.P.
 2, 1   6  q ∨ r                            4, Add.
 2, 1   7  s                                5, 6, M.P.
 2, 1   8  s ∨ t                            7, Add.
 2, 1   9  u                                2, 8, M.P.
 ⫫, 1  10  r ⊃ u                            4—9, Ded.
  ⫫    11  p ⊃ (r ⊃ u)                      3—10, Ded.
```

This deduction can be done without the Deduction rule, but it requires at least twice as many steps.

It is important to take notice of two points about the above deduction. First, note that we placed different dependency numerals to the left of each assumption: "1" in front of the first, "2, 1" in front of the second. As we stated earlier, you must always add a new dependency numeral with each new assumption. Following this practice allows us to keep track of which assumptions are still in force. Notice that we write "2, 1" rather than "1, 2." We always place the number of the more recent assumption to the left. The second point to notice here concerns the order in which the assumptions are discharged. Notice that here the *second* assumption is discharged first, whereas the *first* assumption is discharged *last*. It is often convenient to discharge assumptions in reverse order, beginning with the last and ending with the first, but it is unnecessary. However, if we had discharged the assumptions here in the other order, we would have gotten $r \supset (p \supset u)$, which is not what we wanted.

Although we placed the assumptions in the above deduction one after the other, it isn't necessary to do this. Assumptions may be made at any step in a deduction. Also, it is permissible to assume anything you please provided that whatever is assumed is eventually discharged. In practice, of course, you only want to assume something which will help you get to where you want to go. Actually, there are a number of imaginative ways to choose assumptions when employing the Deduction rule. Consider, for example, the following deduction:

1		$p \supset [(q \lor r) \supset s]$	
2		$(s \lor t) \supset u$	/ $p \supset (r \supset u)$
1	3	$p \land r$	a1
1	4	p	3, Simp.
1	5	r	3, Simp.
1	6	$(q \lor r) \supset s$	1, 4, M.P.
1	7	$q \lor r$	5, Add.
1	8	s	6, 7, M.P.
1	9	$s \lor t$	8, Add.
1	10	u	2, 9, M.P.
$\cancel{1}$	11	$(p \land r) \supset u$	3—10, Ded.
	12	$p \supset (r \supset u)$	11, Exp.

Note that step 12 doesn't have a dependency numeral attached to it, since it follows from step 11. When we draw a line through a dependency numeral, we're saying that that dependency numeral is no longer to be present in the deduction because its assumption has been discharged: we place the crossed-out numeral in front of step 11 to indicate the step at which the assumption was discharged.

Now consider this way of constructing the deduction:

1		$p \supset [(q \lor r) \supset s]$	
2		$(s \lor t) \supset u$	/ $p \supset (r \supset u)$
1	3	$\sim(r \supset u)$	a1
1	4	$\sim(\sim r \lor u)$	3, Imp.
1	5	$\sim\sim r \land \sim u$	4, DeM.
1	6	$\sim u$	5, Simp.

1	7	$\sim(s \lor t)$	2, 6, M.T.
1	8	$\sim s \land \sim t$	7, DeM.
1	9	$\sim s$	8, Simp.
1	10	$[p \land (q \lor r)] \supset s$	1, Exp.
1	11	$\sim[p \land (q \lor r)]$	10, 9, M.T.
1	12	$\sim p \lor \sim(q \lor r)$	11, DeM.
1	13	$\sim\sim r$	5, Simp.
1	14	r	13, D.N.
1	15	$q \lor r$	14, Add.
1	16	$\sim\sim(q \lor r)$	15, D.N.
1	17	$\sim p$	12, 16, D.S.
✗	18	$\sim(r \supset u) \supset \sim p$	3—17, Ded.
	19	$p \supset (r \supset u)$	18, Trans.

What we have done here is assume the negation of the consequent of the conclusion with an eye to deducing the negation of the antecedent of the conclusion. We knew that this would be a viable strategy because we also knew that we could arrive at our goal by the rule of Transposition.

Our examples so far might suggest that the Deduction rule is applicable only to argument forms whose conclusions have horseshoes for their main connectives. However, the Deduction rule may be employed for other argument forms as well. Consider, for example, the following argument form:

$p \supset \sim q$
$\sim q \supset p$
$(p \land r) \supset s$
r
_____

$q \lor s$

In this case, the main connective of the conclusion is a wedge. The best strategy here is to assume the negation of either disjunct and attempt to deduce the other disjunct. In this case, we assume the negation of the first disjunct:

	1	$p \supset \sim q$	
	2	$\sim q \supset p$	
	3	$(p \land r) \supset s$	
	4	r	

/ $q \lor s$

1	5	$\sim q$	a1
1	6	p	2, 5, M.P.
1	7	$p \land r$	4, 6, Conj.
1	8	s	3, 7, M.P.
✗	9	$\sim q \supset s$	5—8, Ded.
	10	$\sim\sim q \lor s$	9, Imp.
	11	$q \lor s$	10, D.N.

The Deduction rule can also be used to construct deductions for argument forms whose conclusions are conjunctions of two conditionals, as in the following argument form:

$(p \lor q) \supset r$
$s \supset (t \land u)$
_____

$(p \supset r) \land (s \supset t)$

The strategy involved, however, is slightly more complicated. We proceed as illustrated below:

	1	$(p \lor q) \supset r$	
	2	$s \supset (t \land u)$	$/ \ (p \supset r) \land (s \supset t)$
1	3	p	$a1$
1	4	$p \lor q$	1, Add.
1	5	r	1, 4, M.P.
$\cancel{1}$	6	$p \supset r$	3—5, Ded.
2	7	s	$a2$
2	8	$t \land u$	2, 7, M.P.
2	9	t	8, Simp.
$\cancel{2}$	10	$s \supset t$	7—9, Ded.
	11	$(p \supset r) \land (s \supset t)$	6, 10, Conj.

Our strategy here was to construct first a deduction of $p \supset r$ and then a deduction of $s \supset t$, after which we simply conjoined them by Conjunction. Note that we used the dependency numeral "2" instead of "2, 1" at step 7. This is because the assumption p (step 3) was already discharged at step 6. Remember that we always use a new number for each new assumption.

In all the cases before the last example in which we made use of two assumptions, both assumptions were made before either assumption was discharged. Then, using both assumptions, we proceeded to deduce some statement form. We can regard this structure as, in effect, a deduction within a deduction. First, we assume one statement form; next, we assume another, having made that first assumption; then, we deduce some statement form from that second assumption *and* the first; then, we discharge the second assumption by means of the Deduction rule; finally, we discharge the first assumption. The structure is this: if you assume A, then if you assume B, you can deduce C; therefore, if you assume A, you can deduce B ⊃ C; therefore, you can deduce A ⊃ (B ⊃ C).

In the last deduction, however, we proceeded in the following fashion: if you assume A, then you can deduce B; therefore, you can deduce A ⊃ B. Furthermore, if you assume C, then you can deduce D; therefore, you can deduce C ⊃ D. These two parts of the deduction (the deduction of A ⊃ B and the deduction of C ⊃ D) are completely independent of each other. The first part of the deduction makes use of an assumption, A, which is no longer in force by the second part. Consequently, we are not entitled to use that assumption in the second part. Moreover, we cannot use anything which we got before discharging that assumption, once it has been discharged. Consequently, it's not permissible to use an assumption, or any step having that assumption's dependency numeral, at any step in a deduction *after* that assumption has been discharged. Thus, once we have discharged an assumption, the steps in the deduction with its dependency numeral are, in effect, closed off for the rest of the deduction.

Since A ≡ B is equivalent to (A ⊃ B) ∧ (B ⊃ A), we can use the above strategy with one additional step for argument forms whose conclusions are biconditionals. We could also add here a general strategy for using the Deduction rule with conclusions that are conjunctions, but it would be considerably more complicated than a strategy not using the Deduction rule.

We summarize the strategies for using the Deduction rule. If the conclusion of an argument is of the form:

1   A ⊃ B, then
    (*a*)   Assume A and attempt to deduce B.
    (*b*)   Then deduce A ⊃ B by the Deduction rule.
2   A ∨ B, then
    (*a*)   Assume ~A and attempt to deduce B.
    (*b*)   Then deduce ~A ⊃ B by the Deduction rule.
    (*c*)   Next, deduce ~~A ∨ B by the rule of Implication.
    (*d*)   Finally, deduce A ∨ B by the rule of Double Negation.
    or
    (*a'*)   Assume ~B and attempt to deduce A.
    (*b'*)   Then deduce ~B ⊃ A by the Deduction rule.
    (*c'*)   Next, deduce ~~B ∨ A by the rule of Implication.
    (*d'*)   Deduce B ∨ A by the rule of Double Negation.
    (*e'*)   Finally, deduce A ∨ B by the rule of Commutation.
3   (A ⊃ B) ∧ (C ⊃ D), then
    (*a*)   Assume A and attempt to deduce B.
    (*b*)   Then deduce A ⊃ B by the Deduction rule.
    (*c*)   Assume C and attempt to deduce D.
    (*d*)   Deduce C ⊃ D by the Deduction rule.
    (*e*)   Finally, deduce (A ⊃ B) ∧ (C ⊃ D) by the rule of Conjunction.
4   A ≡ B, then
    (*a*)   Assume A and attempt to deduce B.
    (*b*)   Deduce A ⊃ B by the Deduction rule.
    (*c*)   Assume B and attempt to deduce A.
    (*d*)   Deduce B ⊃ A by the Deduction rule.
    (*e*)   Deduce (A ⊃ B) ∧ (B ⊃ A) by the rule of Conjunction.
    (*f*)   Finally, deduce A ≡ B by the rule of Biconditionalization.

EXERCISE 7.3.3.1

1 Construct deductions using the Deduction rule for the following argument forms in Exercise 7.3.2: 4(a) through (c), (f) through (j), and (l) through (n).

2 Construct deductions using the Deduction rule for the following argument forms.

(a) $p \supset (q \supset r)$
     $r \supset (s \wedge t)$
     _____
     $p \supset (q \supset s)$

*(b) $(p \supset q) \wedge (r \supset s)$
     $t \supset (p \vee r)$
     _____
     $t \supset (q \vee s)$

(c) $p \supset q$
     $r \supset p$
     $r \vee (q \vee s)$
     $\sim q$
     _____
     $s \vee p$

(d) $p \supset (q \supset r)$
     $\sim s \supset (p \vee r)$
     $\sim r \supset q$
     _____
     $s \vee r$

(e) $(p \supset q) \supset (p \supset r)$
     q
     _____
     $p \supset r$

*(f) $p \supset [(q \wedge r) \vee s]$
     $(q \wedge r) \supset \sim p$
     $t \supset \sim s$
     _____
     $p \supset \sim t$

(g) $p \equiv q$
     $(p \wedge r) \equiv \sim (q \wedge r)$
     _____
     $\sim p \supset r$

(h) $p \supset \sim q$
     $(p \wedge r) \supset (q \vee s)$
     _____
     $(p \wedge \sim s) \supset \sim r$

*(i) $(p \vee q) \supset (p \supset r)$
     $(\sim s \supset r) \supset \sim (q \vee s)$
     $\sim p \supset q$
     _____
     $(s \vee r) \equiv p$

(j) $(p \vee q) \vee r$
     $q \equiv r$
     _____
     $r \vee p$

(k) $(p \vee q) \supset r$
     _____
     $[(r \vee s) \supset t] \supset (p \supset t)$

*(l) $p \supset q$
     $r \supset s$
     _____
     $(p \vee r) \supset (\sim q \supset s)$

7.3.3.2   The Reductio Ad Absurdum Rule

The rule of Reductio ad Absurdum has the following form:

i m A a1

i n $B \wedge \sim B$
$\dot{\div}$ $n+1$ $\sim A$ m—n, R.A.

The Latin phrase *reductio ad absurdum* literally means *reduction to the absurd*. In effect, this rule asserts that if from a certain assumption it is possible to deduce a contradiction (an absurdity), then that assumption must be false. Thus, we might say, at step m, "Assume that A is the case." At step n, we discover that the assumption of A leads to a contradiction. Consequently, we reject A (that is, we deny it) at step $n + 1$. This rule is sometimes called *indirect proof*, and it is used often in mathematics. The i to the left of each line is, as you might expect, a dependency numeral. The $\dot{i}$ in front of step $n + 1$ indicates, of course, that the assumption has been discharged. In discharging a Reductio assumption, we merely write the assumption itself preceded by a tilde. Note that it is permissible to discharge a Reductio assumption only after a contradiction (a statement form of the form $A \wedge \sim A$) has been obtained.

Let's see how this rule works by considering the following valid argument form:

$p \supset q$
$q \supset r$
$q \supset s$
$\sim r \vee \sim s$
———
$\sim p$

A deduction that employs Reductio ad Absurdum is as follows:

1	$p \supset q$	
2	$q \supset r$	
3	$q \supset s$	
4	$\sim r \vee \sim s$	$/ \quad \sim p$
1	5	p	$a\,1$
1	6	q	1, 5, M.P.
1	7	r	2, 6, M.P.
1	8	s	3, 6, M.P.
1	9	$r \wedge s$	7, 8, Conj.
1	10	$\sim (r \wedge s)$	4, DeM.
1	11	$(r \wedge s) \wedge \sim (r \wedge s)$	9, 10, Conj.
$\dot{\jmath}$	12	$\sim p$	5—11, R.A.

Our strategy, obviously, is to assume the negation of the conclusion (the negation of $\sim p$ is $\sim\sim p$, which is equivalent to p) and then try to deduce a contradiction.

Let's consider another example:

$p \supset (q \supset r)$
$\sim s \supset (p \vee r)$
$\sim r \supset q$
———
$s \vee r$

Using Reductio ad Absurdum, we construct a deduction for this argument form in the following way:

	1	$p \supset (q \supset r)$	
	2	$\sim s \supset (p \lor r)$	
	3	$\sim r \supset q$	/ $s \lor r$
1	4	$\sim (s \lor r)$	a1
1	5	$\sim s \land \sim r$	4, DeM.
1	6	$\sim s$	5, Simp.
1	7	$\sim r$	5, Simp.
1	8	q	3, 7, M.P.
1	9	$p \lor r$	2, 6, M.P.
1	10	p	7, 9, D.S.
1	11	$q \supset r$	1, 10, M.P.
1	12	r	8, 11, M.P.
1	13	$r \land \sim r$	7, 12, Conj.
⨉	14	$\sim\sim(s \lor r)$	4—13, R.A.
	15	$s \lor r$	14, D.N.

Since using the Reductio ad Absurdum rule involves assuming the negation of the conclusion, we seldom need more than one Reductio assumption. However, nothing prevents us from employing a combination of both Reductio ad Absurdum and the Deduction rule. To see how this might work, consider the following argument form:

$p \supset q$
$q \supset [(r \supset r) \supset s]$
___
$p \supset s$

We construct a deduction for this argument form, using both assumption rules, in the following way:

	1	$p \supset q$	
	2	$q \supset [(r \supset r) \supset s]$	/ $p \supset s$
	3	$p \supset [(r \supset r) \supset s]$	1, 2, H.S.
1	4	p	a1
1	5	$(r \supset r) \supset s$	3, 4, M.P.
2, 1	6	$\sim s$	d2
2, 1	7	$\sim(r \supset r)$	5, 6, M.T.
2, 1	8	$\sim(\sim r \lor r)$	7, Imp.
2, 1	9	$\sim\sim r \land \sim r$	8, DeM.
2, 1	10	$r \land \sim r$	9, D.N.
⨉, 1	11	$\sim\sim s$	6—10, R.A.
1	12	s	11, D.N.
⨉	13	$p \supset s$	4—12, Ded.

Notice that our strategy here was to assume p and then try to deduce s. But, in order to deduce s, we reasoned that it might help to assume $\sim s$ and then attempt to deduce a contradiction on the basis of that assumption. Also notice that we discharged our assumptions in reverse order.

As with the Deduction rule, it is possible to employ assumptions independently with the rule of Reductio ad Absurdum. This is illustrated in the following deduction:

	1	$(p \lor q) \supset (r \land s)$	
	2	$r \supset \sim s$	
	3	$\sim p \supset t$	/ $t \land \sim q$
1	4	$\sim t$	$a1$
1	5	$\sim\sim p$	3, 4, M.T.
1	6	p	5, D.N.
1	7	$p \lor q$	6, Add.
1	8	$r \land s$	1, 7, M.P.
1	9	s	8, Simp.
1	10	r	8, Simp.
1	11	$\sim s$	2, 10, M.P.
1	12	$s \land \sim s$	9, 11, Conj.
✗	13	$\sim\sim t$	4—12, R.A.
	14	t	13, D.N.
2	15	q	$a2$
2	16	$p \lor q$	15, Add.
2	17	$r \land s$	1, 16, M.P.
2	18	r	17, Simp.
2	19	$\sim s$	2, 18, M.P.
2	20	s	17, Simp.
2	21	$s \land \sim s$	19, 20, Conj.
✗	22	$\sim q$	15—21, R.A.
	23	$t \land \sim q$	14, 22, Conj.

EXERCISE 7.3.3.2

Construct deductions using the rule of Reductio ad Absurdum for the argument forms listed in Exercise 7.3.2, problem 4.

7.3.3.3 The Reiteration Rule

The last of our assumption rules isn't exactly an assumption rule, since it doesn't involve introducing an assumption. In fact, we introduce this rule only to deal with certain technical problems more simply. The rule of Reiteration is stated as follows:

$$i_1, \ldots, i_k \qquad m \qquad A$$

$$j_1, \ldots, j_l, i_1, \ldots, i_k \qquad n \qquad B$$
$$j_1, \ldots, j_l, i_1, \ldots, i_k \qquad n+1 \qquad A \qquad m, \text{Reit.}$$

What this rule says is this: we may at any time repeat any line of a deduction as a later line, if (1) every assumption in force at the earlier line is still in force and (2) we add all the additional dependency numerals which are attached to the step immediately before the line we add. Although our notation makes this look a bit complicated, it's really quite simple. If A appears at step m with the dependency numerals $i_1, \ldots, i_k$, then we can add A after any other step n if n is preceded by *all* the $i_1, \ldots, i_k$. When we add it, we also add any new dependency numerals $j_1, \ldots, j_l$ which appear at step n.

To explain why we need this rule, consider the following argument form, which happens to be valid:

$$\frac{p}{q \supset p}$$

However, suppose we attempted to use the Deduction rule. We would begin by assuming q:

	1	p	
			$/\ q \supset p$
1	2	q	a1

At this point, if we can deduce p, then we can discharge our assumption to get $q \supset p$. But we already have p as a premise. Unfortunately, since p occurs *before* q, we can't use it in discharging our assumption. Now, we obviously *ought* to be able to add p after q. After all, since p is a premise, we have it even *without* any assumption. Therefore, we certainly ought to be able to get it *with* an assumption. The rule of Reiteration just lets us do that:

	1	p	
			$/\ q \supset p$
1	2	q	a1
1	3	p	1, Reit.
1	4	$q \supset p$	2—3, Ded.

In effect, Reiteration simply allows us to add dependency numerals to something we already have and place it where we need it. It's only a technical convenience, but sometimes it can save repeating a lot of steps. In the example above, we could have proceeded as follows:

$$
\begin{array}{lll}
1 & p & \\
\hline
& & \qquad\qquad\qquad\qquad\qquad / \; q \supset p \\
1 & 2 \quad q & a1 \\
1 & 3 \quad p \wedge p & 1,\ \text{Rep.} \\
1 & 4 \quad p & 3,\ \text{Simp.} \\
\cancel{} & 5 \quad q \supset p & 2\text{—}4,\ \text{Ded.}
\end{array}
$$

In this case, we have to perform an extra step (and a rather silly one) in order to get the dependency numeral 1 on p. Since this is only a technical trick, it's simpler to have an explicit rule of Reiteration.

7.3.4 Natural Deduction as a Decision Procedure

If we can construct a deduction in $\mathfrak{D}$ of the conclusion of an argument form from the set of its premises, then the argument form is valid in the syntactic sense. However, if we are not able to construct a deduction for a given argument form, should we conclude that it is invalid? Before answering this question, let's consider how we would define an invalid argument. Given the way we defined validity in the syntactic sense, we should expect that an argument form is invalid (in the syntactic sense) with respect to statement logic if it is impossible to find a deduction of its conclusion from the set of its premises in $\mathfrak{D}$. However—and this is important—the fact that *we* can't find a deduction for a particular argument form doesn't conclusively prove that the argument form is invalid. After all, as you no doubt realize by now, finding deductions is sometimes difficult. Sometimes a particular person might never succeed in finding a deduction of the conclusion of some argument form from the set of its premises. Now, we obviously don't want our definition of valid argument form to depend on the skill anyone (or even everyone) happens to have in constructing deductions: we said that an argument form is valid if and only if it is *possible* to construct a deduction of its conclusion from the set of its premises; likewise, an argument form is invalid if and only if it is *impossible* to construct a deduction of its conclusion from the set of its premises. If *we* cannot come up with a deduction of the conclusion of an argument form from its premises, that really doesn't prove anything. It could be that it's really impossible to construct such a deduction, in which case the argument form would be invalid. However, perhaps we're just not clever enough to come up with a deduction, even though it really is possible to construct one. This seems to indicate that, unlike semantic methods, the syntactic approach given by $\mathfrak{D}$ is not a decision procedure with respect to validity. As a matter of fact, this is true of $\mathfrak{D}$ as it stands, since constructing deductions is largely a trial-and-error procedure. Consequently, it obviously isn't mechanical; and, since we don't always get a definite answer, it isn't effective either.

  This is a shortcoming of $\mathfrak{D}$ which can be overcome. We can specify procedures for constructing deductions in $\mathfrak{D}$ which are both mechanical and effective, but unfortunately the resulting deductions are extremely long and tedious. As it stands, although $\mathfrak{D}$ is for all *practical* purposes undecidable, once we construct a deduction for a valid argument form, we have shown (syntactically) not only *that* it is valid, but also *why* it is valid: we have shown on what logical principles the validity of that argument form rests.

EXERCISE 7.3.4

Show that the following arguments are valid in the syntactic sense.

1. At this point in the game, it is obvious that if the Chiefs decide to punt and the Patriots fumble, then the Chiefs will win. Unfortunately, however, the Chiefs can't win if they punt and the Patriots don't fumble. Therefore, assuming that the Chiefs do punt, they'll win if and only if the Patriots fumble.

*2. If Alice didn't commit the murder, then either Luis did it or someone has tampered with the evidence. However, if Luis didn't commit the murder, then Sam must be lying. Now Sam's not lying unless Alice is the murderer, in which case Phyllis has already left town. Consequently, if Phyllis hasn't left town yet, then Alice isn't the murderer but Luis is.

3. If Tom's book is about witchcraft or about sex, then the publisher will put it out in paperback and it will have a lurid cover. If it has a lurid cover, then Fred won't like it but Mary will. If Fred likes it or it is too long, then it will be about witchcraft and they'll make it into a bad movie. Therefore, Fred won't like it.

4. If I don't stop smoking, then I'll get lung cancer, in which case I'll die young. On the other hand, in view of my unbalanced personality, if I do quit smoking, then I'm sure that I'll take up drinking to excess. Of course, if I do that, then I'll either kill myself in a car wreck or develop cirrhosis of the liver. In the first case, I'll die young, while in the second case, I'll die young. Therefore, I'm quite sure that I'll die young, whether or not I quit smoking.

*5. Either hedonism is the correct moral theory or else ethical theorizing is worthless. But it is equally unquestionable that either persons don't act in accordance with selfish motives or hedonism is incorrect. So, without doubt, it follows that either people do not act in accordance with selfish motives or the actions of human beings are determined by external factors. After all, either ethical theorizing is not worthless or human actions are determined by external influences.

6. Aristotle, that great philosopher of ancient Greece, cannot be accused of being a proponent of slavery since he believed that the victors of war were not entitled to the enslavement of a defeated population. Nevertheless, he did contend that slavish individuals were incapable of governing their own lives. But even if that were so, he cannot be accused of being a proponent of slavery provided that either he did not himself own slaves or he did not attempt to oppose legislation benefiting slaves. Furthermore, if he believed that the victors of war were not entitled to the enslavement of a defeated population, then he did not own slaves although he did often attempt to oppose legislation benefiting them.

DEDUCTIVE CONSISTENCY

The concept of deductive consistency can easily be defined in terms of deducibility, as follows:

> **Definition of *Deductive Consistency*:** A set S of statement forms is *deductively consistent* if and only if for every statement form A it is not the case that $S \vdash A \wedge \sim A$.

In other words, a set of statement forms is consistent just in case it is not possible to deduce a contradiction from it.

As we would expect, defining the concept of *deductive inconsistency* is straightforward:

> **Definition of *Deductive Inconsistency*:** A set S of statement forms is *deductively inconsistent* if and only if it is not consistent, that is, if and only if for some statement form A, $S \vdash A \wedge \sim A$.

In other words, a set of statement forms is deductively inconsistent if and only if a contradiction is deducible from it.

Consider the following set of statement forms:

$$\{\sim p \vee q, r \supset \sim q, r \wedge p\}$$

We can easily demonstrate that this set is inconsistent by deducing a contradiction from it:

1	$\sim p \vee q$	
2	$r \supset \sim q$	
3	$r \wedge p$	
4	r	3, Simp.
5	p	3, Simp.
6	$p \supset q$	1, Imp.
7	q	6, 5, M.P.
8	$\sim q$	2, 4, M.P.
9	$q \wedge \sim q$	7, 8, Conj.

Since we have demonstrated that $\{\sim p \vee q, r \supset \sim q, r \wedge p\} \vdash q \wedge \sim q$, it follows that $\{\sim p \vee q, r \supset \sim q, r \wedge p\}$ is deductively inconsistent.

Now, what if we cannot deduce a contradiction from a set of statement forms? Can we then conclude that the set is consistent? Since $\mathcal{D}$ does not, in practice, provide a decision procedure, we must answer this question in the negative: the fact that we are unable to deduce a contradiction from a given set may be due only to our lack of ingenuity in constructing deductions rather than to the set's being consistent. Once again, therefore, we can only decide halfway with respect to a certain syntactic property.

The concept of syntactic validity (deducibility) is intimately connected to the concept of deductive inconsistency, as indicated in the following metatheorem:

> **Metatheorem:** If S is a set of statement forms and A is a statement form, then $S \vdash A$ if and only if $S \cup \{\sim A\}$ is deductively inconsistent.

What this metatheorem asserts is this: if a statement form A is deducible from a set of statement forms S, then if we add the negation of A to the set S, the resulting set is inconsistent (we will express this by saying that S *is inconsistent with* the negation of A); and, conversely, if S is inconsistent with the negation of a statement form A, then A is deducible from S. It should be obvious why this metatheorem is true. If we can deduce A from S, then we can deduce A from S together with $\sim A$. In other words, $S \cup \{\sim A\} \vdash A$. Now, since obviously we can deduce $\sim A$ from S and $\sim A$, by conjunction we can get $A \wedge \sim A$ from $S \cup \{\sim A\}$, so that set is inconsistent. Now, to prove that if $S \cup \{\sim A\}$ is inconsistent, then $S \vdash A$, note that if we can deduce a contradiction from $S \cup \{\sim A\}$, then we can deduce A from S by using Reductio ad Absurdum. All we need to do is assume $\sim A$. Then, since $S \cup \{\sim A\} \vdash A \wedge \sim A$ (the set is inconsistent), we can discharge the assumption to get A.

EXERCISE 7.4

1 Show that the following sets of statement forms are deductively inconsistent.

    (a) $\{\sim p \vee q, p, (\sim q \supset \sim p) \supset \sim p\}$
    (b) $\{\sim[\sim(p \wedge q) \equiv \sim q], \sim(q \supset \sim p)\}$
  *(c) $\{(p \supset q) \supset (q \supset r), q, \sim r\}$
    (d) $\{p \supset q, r \supset s, \sim q \vee r, p \wedge \sim s\}$
    (e) $\{p \supset q, \sim q, \sim r, p \vee r\}$
    (f) $\{p, q \wedge r, (q \wedge p) \supset s, \sim s\}$
  *(g) $\{p \vee (r \wedge \sim q), q \vee \sim r, \sim p\}$
    (h) $\{p \vee q, p \supset r, q \supset s, \sim r, \sim s\}$
    (i) $\{p \supset \sim q, q \supset \sim r, s \supset q, s, p \vee r\}$

2 Given that the set $\{p \supset q, q \supset \sim p, p, \sim r\}$ is inconsistent, is $\{p \supset q, q \supset \sim p, p\} \vdash r$ true? Why?

7.4.1 Trivial Validity

We've already become familiar with the concept of trivial validity in the semantic sense in Section 6.5.1. Not surprisingly, a similar relation-

---

ship holds from the syntactic standpoint. Consider the following argument form:

$(p \supset q) \supset r$
$\sim r \wedge \sim s$
$(p \supset q) \vee t$
$t \supset (r \vee q)$
_____

s

Obviously, this argument form will be valid if we can demonstrate that $\{(p \supset q) \supset r, \sim r \wedge \sim s, (p \supset q) \vee t, t \supset (r \vee q)\} \vdash s$. However, in order to show that the argument form is trivially valid, it suffices to show that a contradiction is deducible from $\{(p \supset q) \supset r, \sim r \wedge \sim s, (p \supset q) \vee t, t \supset (r \vee q)\}$:

1	$(p \supset q) \supset r$	
2	$\sim r \wedge \sim s$	
3	$(p \supset q) \vee t$	
4	$t \supset (r \vee q)$	
5	$\sim r$	2, Simp.
6	$\sim(p \supset q)$	1, 5, M.T.
7	t	3, 6, D.S.
8	$r \vee q$	4, 7, M.P.
9	q	8, 5, D.S.
10	$\sim(\sim p \vee q)$	6, Imp.
11	$\sim\sim p \wedge \sim q$	10, DeM.
12	$\sim q$	11, Simp.
13	$q \wedge \sim q$	9, 12, Conj.

EXERCISE 7.4.1

Show that the following arguments, although valid, should not be taken seriously; that is, show that the following arguments are trivially valid.

1   If pollution increases, then pollution control will be enacted even though the manufacturers will be opposed to it. Although many environmentalists are concerned about pollution, the fact of the matter is that pollution is still increasing. Now, it appears very unlikely that pollution control will be enacted. As a result, it simply isn't true that many environmentalists are concerned about pollution.

2   If murder is always wrong, then abortion is morally impermissible and constitutes an act of murder. Therefore, abortion is morally impermissible. After all, isn't murder always wrong? Clearly, if abortion is murder, then the fetus must be a person and have a right to life. Now, in view of the many controversies on this subject, I will concede that the fetus is not a person. Nevertheless, I maintain that it has a right to life.

DEDUCTIVE EQUIVALENCE

There is, of course, a syntactic as well as a semantic side to the concept of logical equivalence, and the purpose of this section is to investigate the syntactic side of the concept, for which the technical term is *deductive equivalence*. We can define deductive equivalence in terms of deducibility as follows:

> **Definition of *Deductive Equivalence*:** Two statement forms A and B are *deductively equivalent* if and only if both {A} ⊢ B and {B} ⊢ A.

What this definition says is this: two statement forms A and B are deductively equivalent just in case B is deducible from the set whose only element is A and A is deducible from the set whose only element is B. When two statement forms A and B are deductively equivalent, we will express this in symbols as A ↔ B. Thus, the above definition could also have been written

A ↔ B if and only if {A} ⊢ B and {B} ⊢ A

In Section 3.2.1, we demonstrated that the following two statements were semantically equivalent:

If Jim attends the meeting, then Tom will attend the meeting.
It is false that both Jim will attend the meeting and Tom won't.

We can now show that they are deductively equivalent. They will be deductively equivalent with respect to statement logic provided that their corresponding statement forms are deductively equivalent. Hence, we formalize them:

$p \supset q$
$\sim(p \wedge \sim q)$

Obviously, $p \supset q \leftrightarrow \sim(p \wedge \sim q)$ if and only if both $\{p \supset q\} \vdash \sim(p \wedge \sim q)$ and $\{\sim(p \wedge \sim q)\} \vdash p \supset q$. We first show that $\{p \supset q\} \vdash \sim(p \wedge \sim q)$:

1	$p \supset q$	/ $\sim(p \wedge \sim q)$
2	$\sim p \vee q$	1, Imp.
3	$\sim p \vee \sim\sim q$	2, D.N.
4	$\sim(p \wedge \sim q)$	3, DeM.

Now, we show that $\{\sim(p \wedge \sim q)\} \vdash p \supset q$:

$$\begin{array}{lll} 1 & \sim(p \wedge \sim q) & \\ & \underline{\hspace{4cm}} & / \ p \supset q \\ 2 & \sim p \vee \sim\sim q & \text{1, DeM.} \\ 3 & \sim p \vee q & \text{2, D.N.} \\ 4 & p \supset q & \text{3, Imp.} \end{array}$$

Clearly, then, $\{p \supset q\} \vdash \sim(p \wedge \sim q)$, and so the two statements cited above are deductively equivalent.

EXERCISE 7.5

Show that the following metalinguistic statements are all true.

1 $p \wedge q \leftrightarrow \sim(p \supset \sim q)$
2 $p \equiv q \leftrightarrow (p \wedge q) \vee (\sim p \wedge \sim q)$
3 $p \supset q \leftrightarrow p \supset (p \wedge q)$
*4 $p \supset (q \supset r) \leftrightarrow q \supset (p \supset r)$
5 $p \leftrightarrow (q \supset p) \wedge (\sim q \supset p)$
6 $\sim p \leftrightarrow (p \supset q) \wedge (p \supset \sim q)$
7 $p \equiv q \leftrightarrow \sim p \equiv \sim q$
8 $\sim p \supset p \leftrightarrow p$
9 $p \vee q \leftrightarrow \sim q \supset p$
*10 $p \leftrightarrow p \wedge (p \vee q)$

7.6
LOGICAL THEOREMS OF $\mathfrak{D}$

The semantic side of the concept of logical law is called *logical truth*. In Section 3.2.4 we also called logical truths *tautologies*. Actually, this applies only to those logical truths which are logical truths with respect to statement logic. As we shall see in Chapter 8, although all tautologies are logical truths, some logical truths are not tautologies. Moreover, the concept of a tautology is actually a semantic concept, since a tautology is a statement that is true under all truth-functional combinations of its constituent statements. In this section, we will investigate the syntactic aspect of laws of logic with respect to statement logic.

Generally, from a syntactic viewpoint, we call a law of logic a *logical theorem*. For statement logic, we offer the following definition:

Definition of *Logical Theorem*: A statement form A is a *logical theorem* of $\mathfrak{D}$ if and only if $\varnothing \vdash A$ in $\mathfrak{D}$.

In other words, a statement form is a logical theorem of $\mathfrak{D}$ just in case it is deducible from the null set. In other, but equivalent, words, a statement form is a theorem just in case it can be deduced from no premises. In a sense, we could regard a logical theorem as a valid argument form with no premises. (You may remember that in Chapter 4 we briefly mentioned the fact that our definitions of *argument* and *argument form* do not require that either have any premises.)

We often write ⊢ A to indicate that A is a logical theorem. Using this symbol, we could have written our definition as follows:

⊢ A if and only if ∅ ⊢ A in 𝔇

Consider the following statement form:

$[(p \wedge q) \supset r] \supset [p \supset (\sim r \supset \sim q)]$

According to our definition, this will be a law of logic in the syntactic sense just in case it is a logical theorem of 𝔇. We demonstrate this as follows:

			/ $[(p \wedge q) \supset r] \supset [p \supset (\sim r \supset \sim q)]$
1	1	$(p \wedge q) \supset r$	a1
2, 1	2	p	a2
3, 2, 1	3	$\sim r$	a3
3, 2, 1	4	$p \supset (q \supset r)$	1, Exp.
3, 2, 1	5	$q \supset r$	4, 2, M.P.
3, 2, 1	6	$\sim q$	5, 3, M.T.
3, 2, 1	7	$\sim r \supset \sim q$	3—6, Ded.
2, 1	8	$p \supset (\sim r \supset \sim q)$	2—7, Ded.
1	9	$[(p \wedge q) \supset r] \supset [p \supset (\sim r \supset \sim q)]$	1—8, Ded.

Now, we demonstrate that ⊢ $(\sim p \supset p) \equiv p$ as follows:

			/ $(\sim p \supset p) \equiv p$
1	1	$\sim p \supset p$	a1
1	2	$\sim \sim p \vee p$	1, Imp.
1	3	$p \vee p$	2, D.N.
1	4	p	3, Rep.
1	5	$(\sim p \supset p) \supset p$	1—4, Ded.
2	6	p	a2
2	7	$p \vee p$	6, Rep.
2	8	$\sim \sim p \vee p$	7, D.N.
2	9	$\sim p \supset p$	8, Imp.
2	10	$p \supset (\sim p \supset p)$	6—9, Ded.
	11	$[(\sim p \supset p) \supset p] \wedge [p \supset (\sim p \supset p)]$	5, 10, Conj.
	12	$(\sim p \supset p) \equiv p$	11, Bic.

Finally, we show that $\vdash (p \supset q) \lor (q \supset r)$ in the following way:

$$\underline{\hspace{5.5cm}} / \ (p \supset q) \lor (q \supset r)$$

1	1	$\sim(p \supset q)$	$a1$
1	2	$\sim(\sim p \lor q)$	1, Imp.
1	3	$\sim\sim p \land \sim q$	2, DeM.
1	4	$\sim q$	3, Simp.
1	5	$\sim q \lor r$	4, Add.
1	6	$q \supset r$	5, Imp.
✗	7	$\sim(p \supset q) \supset (q \supset r)$	1—6, Ded.
	8	$\sim\sim(p \supset q) \lor (q \supset r)$	7, Imp.
	9	$(p \supset q) \lor (q \supset r)$	8, D.N.

We also introduce a syntactic definition of contradictory statement form:

> **Definition of *Contradictory Statement Form*:** A statement form A is *contradictory* (in the syntactic sense) *with respect to statement logic* if and only if the set {A} is deductively inconsistent.

In other words, a statement form A is contradictory (in the syntactic sense) just in case the set whose only member is A is inconsistent. In turn, given the definition of *deductively inconsistent*, this means that A is contradictory just in case {A} $\vdash$ B $\land$ $\sim$B for some statement form B.

Consider the following statement form:

$$[p \supset (q \supset r)] \land \sim[(p \supset r) \lor (p \land \sim q)]$$

This is contradictory just in case it can be demonstrated that $\{[p \supset (q \supset r)] \land \sim[(p \supset r) \lor (p \land \sim q)]\}$ is inconsistent. This is demonstrated as follows:

1	$[p \supset (q \supset r)] \land \sim[(p \supset r) \lor (p \land \sim q)]$	
2	$p \supset (q \supset r)$	1, Simp.
3	$\sim[(p \supset r) \lor (p \land \sim q)]$	1, Simp.
4	$\sim(p \supset r) \land \sim(p \land \sim q)$	3, DeM.
5	$\sim(p \supset r)$	4, Simp.
6	$\sim(p \land \sim q)$	4, Simp.
7	$\sim p \lor \sim\sim q$	6, DeM.
8	$\sim p \lor q$	7, D.N.
9	$\sim(\sim p \lor r)$	5, Imp.
10	$\sim\sim p \land \sim r$	9, DeM.
11	$\sim r$	10, Simp.
12	$\sim\sim p$	10, Simp.
13	q	8, 12, D.S.
14	p	12, D.N.
15	$q \supset r$	2, 14, M.P.
16	$\sim q$	11, 15, M.T.
17	$q \land \sim q$	13, 16, Conj.

It is also possible to define *contingent statement form* in the syntactic sense. We will call such statement forms *independent*:

> **Definition of *Independent Statement Form:*** A statement form A is *independent* in 𝒟 if and only if A is neither a logical theorem of 𝒟 nor contradictory (in the syntactic sense) in 𝒟.

Unfortunately, it is difficult to put this definition to work because of the practical undecidability of 𝒟. After all, we can never be sure that a statement form A is neither a theorem nor contradictory, since our failure to find the appropriate deductions may be due only to our own lack of ingenuity.

EXERCISE 7.6

1 Show that the following statement forms are theorems of 𝒟.

- (a) $(p \supset q) \supset [(\sim p \supset q) \supset q]$
- (b) $p \supset (q \supset p)$
- (c) $\sim(p \equiv q) \equiv (\sim p \equiv q)$
- (d) $[(p \supset q) \supset q] \supset (p \lor q)$
- (e) $p \lor (p \supset q)$
- *(f) $[(p \supset q) \supset p] \supset p$
- (g) $(p \supset q) \lor (p \supset \sim q)$
- (h) $(p \supset q) \lor (\sim p \supset q)$
- (i) $\sim p \supset (p \supset q)$
- (j) $(p \supset q) \supset [(r \lor p) \supset (r \lor q)]$
- (k) $(p \supset q) \supset \{(p \supset r) \supset [p \supset (q \land r)]\}$
- (l) $(p \supset q) \supset \{(r \supset s) \supset [(p \land r) \supset (q \land s)]\}$
- (m) $(p \supset q) \lor (q \supset p)$
- *(n) $(p \supset r) \supset \{(q \supset r) \supset [(p \lor q) \supset r]\}$
- (o) $p \equiv [p \lor (p \land q)]$
- (p) $(p \supset q) \supset [\sim(q \land r) \supset \sim(r \land p)]$
- *(q) $\sim p \supset [(p \supset q) \land (p \supset \sim q)]$
- (r) $[(p \lor q) \supset r] \supset \{[(r \lor s) \supset t] \supset (p \supset t)\}$

2 Show that the following statement forms are contradictory in 𝒟.

- (a) $(p \supset \sim p) \land (\sim p \supset p)$
- *(b) $[\sim(p \supset q) \land \sim(\sim p \supset r)]$
- (c) $[p \lor (p \land q)] \land \sim p$
- (d) $(p \land q) \land (\sim p \lor \sim q)$
- (e) $(\sim p \land q) \land (\sim q \lor p)$

7.7

THE RELATION BETWEEN SEMANTICS AND SYNTACTICS

By now it should be apparent that there is a certain close relation between the syntactic and the semantic correlates of the concept of validity, at least so far as statement logic is concerned. In fact, this correspondence is exact: in $\mathfrak{D}$, an argument is valid syntactically if and only if it is valid semantically, and so deducibility and entailment are really two sides of the same coin. In Chapter 1, we said that we should expect this sort of result for logic in general, and indeed our logical intuitions lead us to suppose that deducibility and entailment are related in this manner. However, intuitions are nothing to rely on in so complex a matter as this. Our purpose in studying the two sides of validity in different chapters has been, in part, in order to show the correspondence between semantics and syntactics.

We can, in fact, prove that there is a correspondence between semantics and syntactics in statement logic. The correspondence is described by the following two metatheorems:

Strong Soundness Metatheorem: If $S \vdash A$, then $S \Vdash A$.

Strong Semantic Completeness Metatheorem: If $S \Vdash A$, then $S \vdash A$.

The first of these metatheorems says that if a statement form is deducible from a set, then it is entailed by that set. The second says that if a statement form is entailed by a set, then it is deducible from that set. We call a system of logic *sound* if (speaking loosely) we can deduce only what we want to in it and never anything we shouldn't be able to. If this holds under all possible circumstances (that is, if for any set S we can never deduce anything from S except what we should be able to), we call the system *strongly sound*. The test of what we *should* or *shouldn't* be able to deduce from a given set is a semantic one: we never want to be able to deduce a false conclusion from true premises. Obviously, this requirement will be met if, whenever we can deduce a statement form from a set of statement forms, the set entails the statement form we've deduced. Therefore, if $S \Vdash B$ whenever $S \vdash B$, then our system will be *strongly sound*.

Completeness is the converse of soundness. We call a logical system *complete* (again, loosely speaking) if we can deduce everything we should be able to. Roughly, this means: if we can deduce the conclusion of every valid argument from its premises. Here again, the test of what we *should* be able to deduce is a semantic one: we call a system complete if we can deduce the conclusion of any *semantically* valid argument from its premises. If we can do this under all circumstances whatsoever, we call the system *strongly complete*. Again, this obviously means that a system is strongly complete if, whenever a set of statement forms entails a statement form, we can deduce that statement form from that set. Therefore, if $S \vdash B$ whenever $S \Vdash B$, our system will be *strongly complete*.

The proof of the strong soundness metatheorem is actually not difficult. We need only prove that all the rules of inference are *sound:* that is, they never allow us to infer a false conclusion from true premises. For the Transformation and Replacement rules, this is easily demonstrated by means of truth tables or semantic trees. The Deduction and Reductio ad Absurdum rules require a more complex procedure. To show that the Deduction rule is sound, suppose that we have been able to deduce B by assuming A and using only the Transformation and Replacement rules. Then, since all these rules are sound, this means that if A and the premises are true, then B must also be true. Therefore, if all the premises are true, then B cannot be false if A is true. Thus according to the truth table definition of the horseshoe, $A \supset B$ must be true. A similar argument for the Reductio ad Absurdum rule shows that if we can deduce a contradiction from the premises and assumption A, then if all the premises are true, A must be false and $\sim A$ must be true. The rule of Repetition is obviously sound: it's always safe to infer anything from itself. Then we can complete our proof by showing that any deduction using all these rules together is necessarily sound: if its premises are all true on any interpretation, then its conclusion must also be true on that interpretation.

The proof of strong completeness is more complex. Essentially, we must show how to construct a deduction for every semantically valid argument form. We can do this by presenting a method for converting any completed semantic tree for a valid argument form into a deduction in $\mathfrak{D}$. All that we need to do is show what steps we introduce into the deduction for each of the semantic tree rules. However, although the procedure is simple in concept, the details are very cumbersome. We give a sketch of the procedure in the Appendix.

It follows from these two metatheorems that certain other semantic concepts will exactly match up with their syntactic counterparts. For instance, if we make S the null set, we immediately get the following:

Weak Soundness Metatheorem: If ⊢ A, then ⊩ A.

Weak Semantic Completeness Metatheorem: If ⊩ A, then ⊢ A.

The first of these says that every logical theorem of $\mathfrak{D}$ is a tautology, while the second says that every tautology is a logical theorem of $\mathfrak{D}$. We call these *weak* soundness and *weak* semantic completeness because, although they follow from strong soundness and strong semantic completeness, respectively, the latter concepts do not follow from them. There are, in fact, logical systems which are weakly sound or weakly semantically complete without being strongly sound or strongly complete.

We can also prove the following metatheorems concerning consistency and logical equivalence:

Consistency Metatheorem: A set S of statement forms is deductively consistent if and only if S is semantically consistent.

Logical Equivalence Metatheorem: $A \leftrightarrow B$ if and only if $A \Leftrightarrow B$.

These metatheorems assert, respectively, that deductive consistency is exactly correspondent to semantic consistency and that deductive equivalence is exactly correspondent to semantic equivalence.

Taken together, these metatheorems show that the semantic and syntactic aspects of all the logical concepts in which we are interested correspond exactly for $\mathfrak{D}$. We could, then, completely characterize all the logical properties of $\mathfrak{D}$ either syntactically or semantically with the same results. This is, as we indicated in Chapter 1, exactly what we want.

The significance of this discovery is that we had no reason to be certain beforehand that it would be the case. The notions of deducibility and entailment are, in fact, fundamental parts of our intuitions about logic, and we certainly would want them to align themselves in this way. However, intuitions alone are no guarantee that things will turn out as we want them to here, and in fact there are other systems of logic in which they do not, even though our intuitions would never have led us to believe this. To take one particularly famous case, it turns out that elementary arithmetic is *incomplete*. What this means is that the concept of *theorem* of arithmetic (which corresponds to the concept of logical theorem as we have used it in $\mathfrak{D}$) can be proved to fall short of the concept of *mathematical truth* of arithmetic (roughly equivalent, for this purpose, to the concept of tautology). When this fact was first discovered by Kurt Gödel, logicians and mathematicians were quite startled, and no wonder: our intuitions about the relation between syntactics and semantics in elementary arithmetic seem just as secure as those concerning statement logic. Yet it turns out to be *impossible* to construct a deductive system for arithmetic in which every mathematical truth will be a theorem.

This brings our study of statement logic to a close. By constructing Symbolic Language $\mathfrak{S}$, we have been able to describe the logical forms of statements and of arguments with respect to statement logic. Moreover, we have given a generalized semantic theory for $\mathfrak{S}$ which enables us to produce a semantic account of the notion of validity. Finally, by extending $\mathfrak{S}$ to $\mathfrak{D}$, we have given a syntactic account of the notion of validity which is in accordance with our logical intuitions. As we have seen, our study of validity with respect to statement logic was able to reach particularly strong results: the syntactic and semantic sides of validity for statement logic turn out to be exact reflections of each other. This result is not nearly so easy to obtain for other systems of logic, and as we have mentioned, it cannot be obtained at all in such strength for some systems. Nevertheless, we may take our study of $\mathfrak{S}$ and its extension $\mathfrak{D}$ as a paradigm of the goal of all logical theorizing: to obtain as complete an account as possible of the relation between the syntactic and semantic properties of a logical system.

REVIEW EXERCISES FOR CHAPTER 7

1 Define the following.
   (a) Deduction
   (b) Deducibility
   (c) Deductive consistency
   (d) Trivial validity
   (e) Deductive equivalence
   (f) Logical theorem

2 In your own words, explain what each of the following metatheorems means.
   (a) $S \vdash A$ if and only if $S \cup \{\sim A\}$ is deductively inconsistent.
   (b) If S is deductively inconsistent, then for any statement form A, $S \vdash A$.
   (c) $\vdash A$ if and only if $\{\sim A\}$ is deductively inconsistent.
   (d) $\{A\} \vdash B$ if and only if $\vdash A \supset B$.
   (e) $A \leftrightarrow B$ if and only if $\vdash A \equiv B$.

3 Show that the following argument forms are valid in the syntactic sense by constructing deductions for them.

(a) $p \equiv q$
    $(r \supset p) \wedge (s \vee r)$
    $\sim s$
    —————
    q

(b) $(p \supset q) \wedge (s \supset \sim q)$
    $(r \vee s) \wedge (r \supset \sim q)$
    —————
    $\sim p$

(c) $(p \wedge q) \equiv (q \vee p)$
    $r \equiv p$
    r
    —————
    $q \wedge p$

(d) $(p \supset q) \wedge (p \vee r)$
    $(r \supset q) \wedge (\sim q \vee s)$
    —————
    $s \wedge q$

*(e) $p \wedge q$
    $q \supset r$
    $p \supset (r \supset s)$
    —————
    s

(f) $(p \supset q) \supset r$
    $p \supset (p \supset q)$
    —————
    $p \supset (r \vee s)$

(g) $(p \supset q) \supset (q \supset r)$
    $\sim s \supset (p \supset q)$
    $(p \supset r) \supset [t \supset (r \supset u)]$
    $t \wedge \sim s$
    —————
    $q \supset u$

(h) $(p \wedge q) \supset \sim r$
    $q \wedge (s \vee t)$
    $t \supset r$
    $s \supset u$
    $p \equiv q$
    —————
    s

*(i) $p \supset (q \wedge r)$
    $(p \supset s) \equiv \sim r$
    $(q \wedge r) \supset s$
    —————
    $\sim r$

(j) $p \wedge q$
    $(q \wedge r) \supset s$
    $(\sim t \vee p) \supset r$
    —————
    $p \wedge s$

(k) $(p \supset q) \supset q$
    $p \supset r$
    $r \supset q$
    —————
    q

(l) $p \vee q$
    $p \supset r$
    s
    $q \supset t$
    —————
    $p \vee t$

*(m) $p \supset (q \supset r)$
    $q \supset (r \supset s)$
    —————
    $p \supset (q \supset s)$

(n) $(p \supset \sim q) \wedge (q \supset r)$
    $r \supset p$
    $\sim s \supset q$
    —————
    s

*(o) $p \wedge q$
    $(q \equiv r) \supset (s \vee t)$
    r
    —————
    $t \vee s$

(p) $(p \vee q) \supset (r \wedge s)$

$\dfrac{\sim r}{\sim q}$

(q) $(p \wedge q) \supset r$
$\sim q \vee s$
$\dfrac{(p \supset r) \supset t}{q \supset (t \wedge s)}$

(r) $(p \supset q) \supset (r \supset s)$
$p \supset r$
$(p \supset s) \supset t$
$\dfrac{r \supset q}{t}$

(s) $(p \supset q) \wedge (r \supset s)$
$(q \supset t) \wedge (s \supset u)$
$(\sim p \supset t) \wedge (\sim q \supset s)$
$\dfrac{\sim t}{\sim q \vee \sim r}$

(t) $[(p \vee q) \vee r] \supset (s \vee t)$
$(s \vee t) \supset \sim p$
$(u \vee v) \supset (p \vee q)$
$q \supset \sim s$
$\dfrac{u}{t}$

4 Show that each of the following statements is true.

(a) $\{p \supset q, p \vee (q \vee \sim r), \sim q\} \vdash \sim r \wedge \sim q$
(b) $\{(p \vee q) \supset (r \supset s), [(s \supset r) \vee \sim p] \wedge p\} \vdash r \equiv s$
(c) $\{(p \equiv \sim p) \wedge p\} \vdash q$
*(d) $\{p \supset r, p \supset \sim r\} \vdash p \supset q$
(e) $\{p \equiv (p \supset q)\} \vdash p$

5 Show that each of the following sets of statement forms is deductively inconsistent.

(a) $\{(p \vee r) \supset s, r, \sim s\}$
*(b) $\{p \supset q, p \supset r, p, q \supset \sim r\}$
(c) $\{\sim (p \vee q), \sim q \supset \sim r, \sim s \vee p, s \vee r\}$
(d) $\{p \supset (q \wedge r), (q \vee s) \supset t, s \vee p, \sim t\}$
(e) $\{p \vee q, \sim r, (s \vee t) \supset r, p \supset s, q \supset t\}$

6 Show that the following argument forms are trivially valid in the syntactic sense.

(a) $\dfrac{\sim [p \equiv (p \vee p)]}{q}$

*(b) $(p \vee q) \wedge \sim r$
$q \supset r$
$\dfrac{p \supset r}{\sim s}$

(c) $(p \vee q) \supset (r \wedge s)$
$(r \vee t) \supset (\sim u \wedge v)$
$(u \vee w) \supset (p \wedge x)$
$\dfrac{u}{p \supset \sim v}$

(d) $p \supset q$
$r \supset s$
$\sim q \vee \sim s$
$\sim p \vee \sim q$
$\dfrac{p \wedge r}{\sim r \supset (s \supset \sim q)}$

7 Show that each of the following statements is true.

(a) $p \leftrightarrow (q \supset q) \supset p$
*(b) $p \supset (p \supset q) \leftrightarrow p \supset q$
(c) $(p \wedge \sim q) \vee (\sim p \wedge q) \leftrightarrow p \equiv \sim q$
*(d) $\sim p \supset (\sim q \supset r) \leftrightarrow (\sim r \supset \sim q) \supset (\sim r \supset p)$
(e) $(p \equiv p) \equiv q \leftrightarrow q$

8 Show that each of the following statements is true.

(a) $\vdash [(p \equiv q) \wedge (q \equiv r)] \supset (p \equiv r)$
(b) $\vdash (p \supset q) \supset [(p \vee r) \supset (q \vee r)]$
*(c) $\vdash (p \supset q) \supset [(p \wedge r) \supset (q \wedge r)]$
(d) $\vdash (p \supset q) \supset [(p \vee q) \supset q]$
(e) $\vdash (p \equiv q) \supset (q \equiv p)$
*(f) $\vdash (p \supset q) \supset [(r \supset p) \supset (r \supset q)]$
(g) $\vdash [(p \supset q) \supset r] \supset (q \supset r)$
(h) $\vdash (p \vee q) \supset [(p \supset q) \supset q]$
*(i) $\vdash \sim(p \equiv \sim p)$
(j) $\vdash \sim(p \supset q) \equiv \sim(\sim q \supset \sim p)$

9 Show that each of the following arguments is valid in the syntactic sense.

(a) If Rodriquez enters the primary, then he will be elected, provided that he campaigns vigorously. Now, as everybody knows, if he wins the nomination and receives the endorsement of the AFL-CIO, then no doubt he will be elected. Consequently, if he enters the primary and campaigns vigorously, then he will have to come out against tax reform. After all, if he doesn't come out against tax reform, he won't be elected even if he receives the support of the AFL-CIO.

(b) Apparently Mary doesn't care what happens to me. After all, if she did, would she treat me the way she does? However, she loves me if she loves anybody. But then again, if she loves me, perhaps she would treat me the way she does. And obviously, if she didn't treat me the way she does, then she would love anybody.

(c) If you don't lend me $5, I won't have any lunch, in which case I'll spend the afternoon hungry. Now, as you must realize, if I spend the afternoon hungry, I'll have one of my attacks. Moreover, unless the police are on hand to restrain me, I'll maim scores of people if I have an attack. But do you really think the police will be on hand to restrain me? Consequently, then, you surely must see that I'll maim a great many unfortunate souls if you don't lend me $5.

(d) Mayor Jones will win the election unless either she fails to attract the union vote or she antagonizes the governor. Now, considering her record, she certainly won't lose the union vote provided that unemployment doesn't go up. On the other hand, she will antagonize the governor if and only if unemployment goes up. Consequently, either Mayor Jones will win the election or unemployment will go up.

(e) It seems appropriate to conclude that it was the butler who killed poor Mrs. Flanagan. I suspect that the butler did not like her, although he in fact liked her if, as everybody claims, he was always kind to her. Furthermore, even though he was always being kind to her, he never spoke well of her.

(f) As you probably realize by now, you won't pass this course unless the instructor likes you. However, the instructor will like you only if you laugh at his jokes. From this, it follows that you won't pass this course. After all, how could you possibly laugh at those miserable jokes?

(g) It's quite obvious that I won't lose weight unless I either go on a strict diet or contract some awful disease. On the other hand, if I do get some terrible disease, then I certainly won't be able to go on a very strict diet. However, if I don't lose weight, then I'll certainly catch some serious disease anyway, in which case I'll lose weight. Consequently, even if I don't go on a diet, I'll lose weight.

(h) I'm either going to flunk out of college or shoot myself. Now, if I flunk out of college, obviously I won't go to law school, in which case I'll disappoint my parents terribly. Furthermore, I'd definitely be unable to go to law school if I shot myself. On the other hand, my parents will also be disappointed if I shoot myself. But then again, if I disappoint my parents, I'll shoot myself. Taking all these facts into consideration, I conclude that I'll go to law school if I don't shoot myself.

(i) The Big Bad Wolf will succeed in eating all the Three Little Pigs just in case either he is able to catch them all off guard or the first Little Pig (Cyril) cannot complete his brick house in time. However, even if Cyril does complete his brick house in time, the Big Bad Wolf will be able to consume all three pigs if either the second Little Pig (Porcina) continues to live in her straw house or the third Little Pig (Hogarth) keeps up the foolish habit of riding his unicycle late at night. Unfortunately for the Three Little Pigs, if Porcina stops living in her straw house, then Hogarth will be sure to continue his nighttime unicycle rides. As a result, it appears that the Big Bad Wolf will succeed in his ghastly plans.

(j) I'll lose weight on the condition that I stop eating ice cream sundaes. However, I'll also lose weight if I'm forced to live on prison food. Now, considering my fondness for ice cream sundaes, I'll never stop eating them unless I find an acceptable substitute unless I take to crime. As a matter of fact, on my salary I can't even afford ice cream sundaes, and so unless I take to crime, I'll stop eating ice cream sundaes. However, considering my general ineptitude, if I take to crime, I'll certainly be caught, in which case I'll be forced to eat prison food. From all these circumstances, it clearly follows that I am going to lose weight.

chapter 8
Predicate Logic I

8.1
THE LIMITATIONS OF STATEMENT LOGIC

In Chapter 1, we pointed out that the notion of logical form is relative to a particular system of logic. In the previous chapters, our aim has been to study the logical forms of statements and arguments with respect to statement logic, that is, with respect to combination by means of truth-functional connecting words. We noted several times that some important aspects of language are just beyond the scope of this kind of analysis. Here, we want to explore briefly one of these aspects, the area called *predicate logic*. In effect, we'll be adding another step to our analysis of statements. Before, we stopped at the level of the atomic statement: from the standpoint of statement logic, all atomic statements have the same logical form. Now, we're going to see what structure we can find inside atomic statements.

We need to look for structures of this sort because there are many arguments that intuitively seem valid but which aren't valid from the standpoint of statement logic. Take this example:

> Every citizen has a right to vote.
> John, however, is a citizen.
> Therefore, John has a right to vote.

None of these statements is truth-functionally compound. Consequently, the formalization of this argument in S is

$$p$$
$$q$$
$$\overline{}$$
$$r$$

and that's obviously invalid. Intuitively, however, the argument is obviously valid. If John is a citizen, and if every citizen has a right to vote, then it follows that John has a right to vote. Consequently, what we have here is an argument that our intuitions tell us is valid but that our system of logic tells us is invalid. This indicates that statement logic has its limitations.

Actually, we can say a little more about this example. Not only is it valid, but also there are arguments that resemble it syntactically which likewise are intuitively valid. Here's one:

> Every person is mortal.
> Jane is a person.
> Therefore, Jane is mortal.

And, here's another:

> Every member of the Communist block officially espouses Marxist economic theory.
> Czechoslovakia is a member of the Communist bloc.
> Therefore, Czechoslovakia officially espouses Marxist economic theory.

And, by this point, you can probably imagine all sorts of other examples, all intuitively valid, which resemble our first one in the same way these do. This suggests that something about the logical form of these arguments makes them valid. In this chapter we'll identify the elements of a new notion of logical form to accommodate these arguments, sketch a way of modifying $ so as to incorporate this extended concept of logical form, and look at a few of the new rules that govern validity in this extended system, which we call *predicate logic*.

8.2
PREDICATION

Let's see just what the above arguments do have in common. If we remove everything from our examples except the words they have in common, we get the following:

Every _____.

_____.

Therefore, _____.

This isn't much—the only actual word they have in common (except for the conclusion indicator *therefore*) is *every*, and that's obviously not the only thing that they have in common. So, let's look at the relationships among the parts of the different statements in each of the examples. You'll remember that we found it was important, in statement logic, to note occurrences of the same atomic statement as a constituent of different statements in an argument. We can't find that sort of thing here, since all these statements are atomic, but we can see some common parts to these different statements. Here's how we might analyze the first example:

Every <u>citizen</u> <u>has a right to vote</u>
      1   2

<u>John</u> is a <u>citizen</u>.
  3   1

Therefore, <u>John</u> <u>has a right to vote</u>.
          3   2

As the numbers indicate, the different statements in this argument do have certain phrases in common. For instance, the word *citizen* occurs in both premises, while the phrase *has a right to vote* is in the first premise and the conclusion. Let's try the same process with our other two examples:

Every <u>person</u> <u>is mortal</u>.
      1   2

<u>Jane</u> is a <u>person</u>.
  3   1

Therefore, <u>Jane</u> <u>is mortal</u>.
        3   2

Every <u>member of the Communist bloc</u>
             1
<u>officially espouses Marxist economic theory</u>.
          2

<u>Czechoslovakia</u> is a <u>member of the Communist bloc</u>.
    3   1

Therefore, <u>Czechoslovakia</u> <u>officially espouses Marxist economic theory</u>.
        3   2

On the basis of this analysis, we can see that that these statements all have a certain form in common. We might represent this form by leaving out the phrases underlined, retaining only blanks with numbers to indicate which blanks are filled with the same phrases. That would give us the following:

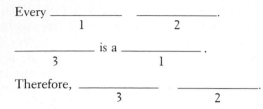

Unfortunately, this won't tell us yet what the logical form of this argument is, because we haven't yet said what sorts of things are appropriate for filling in the blanks. We certainly can't fill them with statements, as in the case of statement logic, since the result is nonsense (try it). What we need here is some way of classifying the different sorts of things that fill these blanks. We'll begin by singling out a certain sort of atomic statement for study: the *simple predication*.

8.2.1 Simple Predications

Look again at the conclusion of our first example: *Therefore, John has a right to vote*. If we omit the conclusion indicator word *therefore*, this statement consists of two parts: *John* and *has a right to vote*. The first of these is, grammatically, a proper name; in a particular context, it would be the name of some specific person called John. We'll have a bit more to say about proper names later, but for now let us just note that a proper name is an expression that corresponds in a way to a unique individual. Turning to the second part of this statement, we find the phrase *has a right to vote*. This phrase doesn't correspond to anything in the way that the proper name *John* does. It does, however, have a certain relationship to the sorts of things to which proper names correspond. We might express this relationship by saying that the phrase *says something about* the person named *John* in our example. In other words, both the name *John* and the phrase *has a right to vote* could be said to apply to a certain individual person, but they apply in different ways. The name simply *picks out*, or *refers to*, or *designates*, that individual; the phrase, however, *says something about* the individual to which it applies.

We will find that this distinction between expressions that just designate some individual person or thing and expressions that say something about people and things is of fundamental importance. Accordingly, let's introduce a term for each of these classes of expressions. We'll call those expressions that simply designate things *names* and those expressions that say something about things *predicate expressions*.

Now, we can return to the analysis of our example. The conclusion of that first argument is a statement consisting of a name and a predicate expression in a certain relationship. Grammatically, the name is the subject of the sentence, and the predicate expression is (grammatically) the predicate. We will call statements with this structure *simple predications*.

The conclusions of our other two examples are also simple predications. In the second argument, it consists of the name *Jane* and the predicate expression *is mortal*. In the third, the subject is *Czechoslovakia*: this, too, is a name, since it designates a single thing. The predicate of the conclusion of the third argument is *officially espouses Marxist economic theory*, and that lengthy phrase is a single predicate expression. Consequently, we've been able to see at least one common element of form among our three arguments: in each of them, the conclusion is a simple predication.

Simple predications are, in a way, the foundation of our study of predicate logic. Consequently, we need to understand just how these statements work. Let's review just what a simple predication is before we pass on to the next stage of our analysis. A *simple predication* is an *atomic* statement consisting of a *name* and a *predicate expression*. A *name* is an expression which *refers to* or *designates* a single object. A predicate expression *applies to*, or *says something about*, or *is true of* something.

EXERCISE 8.2.1

Identify the names and predicate expressions in the following simple predications.
1 Water is a liquid.
°2 My brother Jorge hates okra.
3 Alice was born in the capital of Utah.
*4 Love makes the world go round.
5 Shakespeare wrote many plays.
*6 Seven is an odd number.
7 The Washington Monument is an imposing structure.
*8 Mount Everest is taller than any other mountain in the world.

8.2.2 Individual Variables

Now, we can return to a subject we already dealt with at one level in Chapters 2 and 3. Consider the following expression:

It is painted green.

In isolation, it's not all that clear whether this is a statement. We want to ask, "*What* is painted green? What do you mean by *it*?" In an appropriate context, however, we'd have no trouble understanding this as

---

a statement. In fact, we already learned how to interpret expressions of this sort in Chapter 2:

Jane's house is made of concrete blocks, and it is painted green.

In this example, *it* obviously could be replaced by *Jane's house* without affecting the meaning of the sentence. Grammatically, the word *it* is a pronoun, that is, a word used to take the place of a noun. As the last two examples show, a pronoun like this doesn't really mean anything unless we know what to substitute for it. Here, we substituted the expression *Jane's house*, which is a name (it refers to exactly one object). Consequently, in our second example, when we substitute *Jane's house* for *it*, of course, we get a simple predication. What, then, about the expression *it is painted green*? That has the form of a simple predication, in a way, but it really isn't one: *it* is not a name. Instead, *it is painted green* is something which becomes a simple predication when you substitute a name for the word *it*.

There are a number of words in English which, like *it*, simply indicate places where names can be substituted. The most common examples are the personal pronouns *it, he, she, her, him, they, them*. Some of these have certain restrictions on what can be substituted. For instance, you can't substitute the names of people for *it*, but you can *only* substitute the names of people for *he, her, him*, and *she*. Aside from these restrictions, however, you can't tell what is meant by one of these words outside some particular context. We will call these words *variable words*.

Now, let's return to the expression *it is painted green*. As we said, this isn't exactly a statement, although it could be interpreted as some particular statement if the context told us what to substitute for the word *it*. We will call a sentence of this type, which contains a variable word without any indication of what is to be substituted for it, an *open sentence*. Open sentences become statements only when there is some indication in context of what is to be substituted for the variable words. We've seen how this is accomplished within compound statements and within arguments in the previous chapters, and we don't need to explore all the details of that here. Instead, we're going to propose a rather artificial way we might make use of open sentences to give some indications of the logical structures of statements.

If an open sentence is like a simple predication with a variable word in place of the name, then we could reverse this and say that a simple predication is, in effect, an open sentence with some name substituted for the variable word. We can show this by using the expression *is true of*, as in the following statement, which means about the same thing as *John is a citizen*:

Of John, it is true that he is a citizen.

What we've done here is to take the statement *John is a citizen* and rewrite it as the open sentence *he is a citizen* together with the name *John* and the words *it is true that*. The effect of those words here is to indicate that we're to substitute *John* for the variable word *he* to make a statement out of the open sentence. Using somewhat artificial constructions like this helps make clear something about the logical forms of simple predications (at least, it makes it clear what is the name and what is the predicate expression). Let's agree to use a somewhat abbreviated form that isn't quite correct English. Instead of the example as written above, we'll write

Of John: he is a citizen.

We've simply separated the name from the predicate expression by writing the name first, preceded by *of* and followed by a colon (:), and then the predicate expression with an appropriate variable word (in this case *he*) where the name should go, giving us an open sentence. We'll call these artificial constructions *standard forms* for predications. A few examples of statements and their corresponding standard forms will make the procedure clear:

Statement	Standard Form
John speaks French.	Of John: he speaks French.
California is larger than Utah.	Of California: it is larger than Utah.
I saw Mary at the office.	Of Mary: I saw her at the office.
The Vice President presides over the Senate.	Of the Vice President: he (or she) presides over the Senate.

8.2.3 Truth-Functional Compounds of Predications: More Standard Forms

Simple predications are all atomic from the standpoint of statement logic, but we can imagine truth-functional compounds of them. If we take the two simple predications *Mary is home* and *John is out* and combine them with *and*, we get *Mary is home and John is out*. We can also produce truth-functional compounds of statements that have the same names in them or the same predicate expressions. For instance, we can combine *Mary is home* and *Mary is out* into *Either Mary is home or Mary is out*; and we can combine *Mary is home* and *John is home* into *If Mary is home, then John is home*. As we've noted in previous chapters, when the constituents of a compound statement share a common subject or predicate, we usually abbreviate them. We'd normally contract the last two examples to *Either Mary is home or she's out* and *If Mary is home, then John is*. Let's take a closer look at these contractions in the light of what we've just learned about simple predications. First, consider a compound statement in which the constituents have a common subject:

Either Mary is home or Mary is out.

Let's rewrite the constituents of this statement in standard form, leaving everything else the same:

Either of Mary: she is home or of Mary: she is out.

The same name is indicated for substitution in front of each constituent. Let's take the name out and put it in front of the entire sentence, like this:

Of Mary: either she is home or she is out.

Now, we've developed a new type of open sentence, exemplified by *she is home or she is out*. This open sentence is compound: it contains two open sentences as constituents. If we prefix *Of Mary:* to it, we indicate that *Mary* is to be substituted for *each* occurrence of the variable word *she*. It's really not so unnatural to see this as involved in the way we make up contracted forms for compound statements like this. For instance, if we substitute *Mary* for only the first occurrence of *she*, we get *Mary is home or she is out*, which is a perfectly good sentence meaning the same thing as our standard form. Ordinarily, this is how we indicate what is to be substituted for a variable word in ordinary language: we just assume that the nearest available appropriate word is what goes there. Our standard forms are simply explicit specifications of how substitutions work.

Now let's consider a compound of two simple predications with the same predicate expression but different names:

Mary is at home and John is at home.

Rewriting the constituents as standard forms gives us

Of Mary: she is at home and of John: he is at home.

The open sentences we get here aren't exactly the same, since one contains the variable word *she* and the other contains the word *he*. This is, of course, required by the fact that *Mary* is a feminine name and *John* a masculine name, but otherwise it's of no significance. We'd want to say that the two open sentences are really the same except for that point of gender. As a matter of fact, these distinctions of gender are a little inconvenient for our logical analysis, just as they sometimes are in ordinary language. If we want to use a pronoun referring to a single person, we have to make a choice of gender, even if we don't happen to know the sex of the person. Should the teacher tell the class "Anyone who missed the last test should see me about *his* grade"? Or "*her* grade"? Or perhaps "*his or her* grade"? Or, lacking grammatical correctness, "*their* grade"? None of these is fully satisfactory: even "his or her," which is perhaps all right with respect to gender, is awkward. We're going to get around this problem later by constructing an artificial language for predicate logic. For the present, however, we'll just use the forms *he* and *she* (and likewise *her* and *him*, *her* and *his*) completely interchangeably. So, for our purposes, the open sentences *she is at home* and *he is at home* are completely interchangeable. Now, with this in mind, let's return to our example. That compound statement consists of two statements joined by *and*. Those two statements, in standard form, each consist of the same open sentence with different names substituted. Let's take the names and again place them in front, this time placing the connecting word *between the names*:

Of John and Mary: she is at home.

Notice that we could equally well have written *Of John and Mary: he is at home*. Some more examples will indicate how we put statements into standard form.

Statement	Standard Form
Paris is the capital of France.	Of Paris: it is the capital of France.
Alice and Jane both speak German.	Of both Alice and Jane: she speaks German.
Mark went home and went to bed.	Of Mark: he went home and he went to bed.
John, Fred, Alice, George, Mary, and Julio live in that house.	Of John, Fred, Alice, George, Mary, and Julio: he lives in that house.
Either Martha, or Tom, or Sam, or Luis was the one who bought lunch.	Of Martha or Tom or Sam or Luis: she was the one who bought lunch.

8.3
QUANTIFICATION

The last examples of the previous section illustrated how we might have quite a long list of names prefixed to an open sentence in a standard form. If the list got very long, we might find it more convenient to specify the names on it in some shorter way. We can illustrate this by referring to the examples we considered in Section 8.2. The first premise of the last argument was

Every member of the Communist bloc officially espouses Marxist economic theory.

Let's consider what this says. The Communist bloc is a certain group of countries, primarily in Eastern Europe and Asia, including the Soviet Union, Poland, Czechoslovakia, Hungary, Yugoslavia, Rumania, Albania, Bulgaria, and (depending on how you want to define it) China and some other Asian countries. Our example resembles a simple predication except that, instead of a name, it contains the expression *every member of the Communist bloc*. It's not hard to see that this amounts to the same thing as *Albania and Bulgaria and Czechoslovakia and Hungary and Poland and the Soviet Union and* . . . and so on for all the members of the Communist bloc. Of course, it's a lot easier to say *every member of the Communist bloc* than it is to recite that long list, but there's no difference of meaning. We could, then, rewrite that sentence as

Of Albania and Bulgaria and Czechoslovakia and . . . (and so on): it officially espouses Marxist economic theory.

However, we can say the same thing more concisely as follows:

Of every member of the Communist bloc: it officially espouses Marxist economic theory.

Now that we've done that, we can see a similarity in logical form between this statement and the conclusion of the argument, which is the statement *Czechoslovakia officially espouses Marxist economic theory*. If we write that in standard form, it is

Of Czechoslovakia: it officially espouses Marxist economic theory.

Thus, the open sentence occurring in these two standard forms is the same. However, that's not to say that these two statements are the same in logical form. In fact, as we've interpreted it, that first premise is a long conjunction, something like *Albania officially espouses Marxist economic theory and Bulgaria officially espouses Marxist economic theory and* . . . and so on, with one conjunct for each member of the Communist bloc. The conclusion, however, is a simple predication; in fact, it's one of the conjuncts of that long conjunction. Here, we've been able to see both the similarity and difference in logical form between these two statements.

We're not done analyzing this long conjunction yet, however. First let's take a look at the corresponding premises in the other two examples in Section 8.1. The first premise of the first example is *Every citizen has a right to vote*, which we might turn into standard form as follows:

Of every citizen: he (or she) has a right to vote.

Here, the expression *every citizen* would be a sort of shorthand for a list of all the names of all the people who are citizens, joined by *and*. Obviously, that would be an enormously long conjunction if we were to write it out (if we were talking about United States citizens, we'd have something around 200 million conjuncts). This shows that we're not just talking about a convenient sort of abbreviation here: nobody could ever make practical use of a sentence that is hundreds of millions, or perhaps billions, of words long (we'd never get through saying anything). Instead, the word *every* makes it possible to say something that we couldn't say practically with simple predications and truth-functional compounds alone. Now consider the first premise of the second example, *Every person is mortal*. Its standard form will be

Of every person: she (or he) is mortal.

In this sentence, *every person* has to be understood as shorthand for a list of all the names of all the human beings that ever have lived or ever will live. How long is that list? The answer is that there's no way to tell. If we say that every person is mortal, presumably we're talking about all the people that used to be alive but have since died, including whoever didn't have names and haven't been born yet. Of course, we could imagine that they all have names, or at least that they could be given names, but it should be evident that this word *every* is beginning to go beyond what could be accomplished by a simple list of names, no matter how long.

There's another point we need to notice. The word *person*, which goes with *every* in that last example, is a part of the predicate of the second premise in that same argument: *Jane is a person*. This is a simple predication, and its standard form would be

Of Jane: she is a person.

Our analysis so far doesn't say anything about how this word *person* can occur as a part of the predicate in one statement and as a part of the subject of the other. It's to that problem that we need to turn next. To explain it, we'll need to examine more thoroughly the way that the word *every* and a great many related words work. To do that, we'll introduce the notion of a *quantifier*.

Let's begin by looking at a word that has some connections with *every*, namely the word *everything*. It looks like a name, and so we might want to treat it as one. Now consider its use in the following statement:

Everything has a cause.

In standard form, this is

Of everything: it has a cause.

If we took this as a simple predication, we'd have to take *everything* as the name of some thing, and that clearly isn't what it is. The statement doesn't say that some object or other named *everything* has a cause: it says that everything has a cause. We could best express that, perhaps, by listing all the things that there are and saying of each of them that it has a cause. Consequently, what *everything* does here is to allow us to assert the *conjunction* of *all possible* statements that we can get by substituting names in the open sentence *it has a cause*. The word *everything* (and certain other expressions) functions in a special way to tell what sorts of names to substitute—it simply says substitute *all the names that there are* in the open sentence and form the *conjunction* of *all the simple predications* that result. Thus, we don't need some specific list of names, determined by a word like *citizen* or *person* to know what to substitute. We'll call an expression that directs us to perform all possible substitutions a quantifying expression. In fact, *everything* is a particular sort of quantifying expression which we call a *universal quantifying expression*. Let's turn now to the two sorts of quantifying expressions we'll distinguish, the ways in which they are expressed, and how we can use them to simplify our standard forms and to understand the validity of arguments.

8.3.1 Universal Quantifications

We've just indicated what a universal quantification is: it's an expression which asserts *the conjunction of all possible statements formed by substitution from some one open sentence*. In the example we considered, *everything* simply occupied the place of a name in a simple predication. Sometimes *everything* is used that way, but more often it occurs in statements like this:

> Everything that is made of glass is fragile.

If we try to write this in standard form by replacing *everything* with *it* and putting the quantifying expression in front of the open sentence, we get nonsense:

> Of everything: it is made of glass is fragile.

However, let's think about what the statement says. It says, of each thing that is made of glass, that it is fragile. What about the things that aren't of glass—does it say anything about them? On the surface, it might not seem so, but there's another way to look at it. We could see it as saying that *if* a thing is made of glass, *then* it is fragile. With this in mind, we can rewrite its standard form as a *conditional* open sentence with *everything* prefixed:

> Of everything: *if* it is made of glass, *then* it is fragile.

Doing it this way lets us make another point. The expression *is made of glass* is a predicate expression, and if we analyze our example as a conditional open sentence, we can see that expression functioning as a predicate. Consequently, *everything* here tells us to substitute all possible names in the open sentence *if it is made of glass, then it is fragile*.

The word *everything* simply tells us to form all the substitutions from the open sentence that we can. Some words that act as quantifying expressions are not so general; the most obvious example is *everybody*:

Everybody has a mother.

This doesn't tell us to make every possible substitution we can in the open sentence *it has a mother*: that would include such things as *Uranium has a mother* and *Mount Everest has a mother*, and we don't want that. Instead, *everybody* tells us to form all substitutions using names of *persons*. We could just remember this rule, but we can make our system a little simpler if we note that only people have names of persons. So, we can use the same device we used above: we can write this statement as a conditional open sentence with *everything*:

Of everything: if it is a person, then it has a mother.

This is beginning to sound artificial, but that's really a sort of advantage. We want to come up with a system that will reveal to us the logical forms of statements in a way that explains validity in predicate logic, and it will be a lot easier to do that if we can limit ourselves to a few quantifying expressions (two will do) rather than many. Incidentally, it will also enable us to get around clumsy expressions like *he or she*: we can now get by with the single variable word *it*. Some more examples will help:

Statement	*Standard Form*
Everyone is either male or female.	Of everything: if it is a person, then either it is male or it is female.
I knew everybody at the party.	Of everything: if it is a person, then if it was at the party, then I knew it.
Anyone who has been to college can read.	Of everything: if it is a person, then if it has been to college, then it can read.

Here, we've considered some ways in which words that indicate a sort of limited universal quantification can be rewritten with a single, standard, universal quantifying expression. Let's extend this now to the examples we took in our arguments in Section 8.2. First, consider *Every citizen has a right to vote*. Here, we have the word *every* together with the predicate expression *citizen*. Before, we imagined a list of all the citizens. Now, however, we can find a more insightful analysis:

Of everything: if it is a citizen, then it can vote.

The same sort of analysis can be applied to the first premises of the other two arguments:

Of everything: if it is a person, then it is mortal.
Of everything: if it is a member of the Communist bloc, then it officially espouses Marxist economic theory.

The word *each* functions much like *every*.

Another word indicating universal quantification is *all*. This word normally goes with a plural expression:

All citizens have a right to vote.

In putting such statements into standard form, we convert plurals to singulars where appropriate. Thus, this example would also become

Of everything: if it is a citizen, then it has a right to vote.

There are other English words which indicate universal quantification in a different manner. One such word is *nothing*, as in

Nothing is on the other side of the moon.

If we want to put this in standard form, we might first think of the following:

Of nothing: it is on the other side of the moon.

It's fairly obvious what this sentence means: it means that there isn't any thing which is on the other side of the moon. In other words, this means that the open sentence *it is on the other side of the moon* isn't true no matter what you substitute for *it*. In this way, we could treat *nothing* as an example of a new quantifying expression. However, we can make our account simpler by observing that the open sentence *it is not on the other side of the moon* is, in effect, the negation of the open sentence *it is on the other side of the moon*. That is, if we substitute the same thing for *it* in both these open sentences, one will become a true statement and the other a false statement. Consequently, we can regard *Nothing is on the other side of the moon* as equivalent to the following standard form:

Of everything: it is not on the other side of the moon.

A quantifier word closely related to *nothing* is *nobody*: the only difference is that it applies only to persons. We can show how to put sentences containing *nobody* (and *no one*) into standard form with an example. The statement

> Nobody knows the trouble I've seen.

becomes

> Of everything: if it is a person, then it doesn't know the trouble I've seen.

The word *no* often indicates universal quantification plus a negation, as in the following example:

> No hen has teeth.

In standard form, this becomes

> Of everything: if it is a hen, then it does not have teeth.

8.3.2 Existential Quantifications

A universal quantifying expression tells us two things: (1) form *all possible substitutions* from the open sentence; (2) join all those by *conjunction*. There are other statements which are like universal quantifications in step 1 but not in step 2. Consider the word *something* as in the following example:

> Something is in the next room.

Now, what exactly does this mean? It doesn't, of course, mean that a certain object, the name of which is *something*, is in the next room. To see what it means, consider what would make it true. It would be true if Uncle George's rocking chair were in the next room. Also, it would be true if Plymouth Rock were in the next room. A third thing that would make it true would be if Sam's pet elephant Sarah were in the next room. Obviously, we could keep going like this indefinitely; so let's state a general rule: the statement *Something is in the next room* would be true if *any* statement that we could get by substituting a name into the open sentence *it is in the next room* were true. Of course, it would also be true if two, or three, or some other number of such statements were true, just as long as *at least one* such statement were true. Now, let's think about this in terms of statement logic. If we combine a number of atomic statements by inclusive disjunctions, the resulting compound will be true if and only if *at least one* of the disjuncts is true. Consequently, what *something* tells us is this: (1) form *all possible sub-*

stitutions from the open sentence; (2) join them all by *disjunction*. We could then interpret the standard form of this last example, which we might write

Of something: it is in the next room.

as equivalent to the extremely long disjunction

Either Uncle George's rocker is in the next room *or* Plymouth rock is in the next room *or* Sam's pet elephant Sarah is in the next room *or* . . . (and so on for all the things there are).

The word *something* is thus a quantifying expression, like *everything*, because it tells us to substitute all possible names for a variable word. However, it tells us then to form the *disjunction*, rather than the conjunction, of the resulting statements. We call a statement of this sort an *existential quantification:* an existential quantification asserts *the disjunction of all possible statements formed by substitution from some one open sentence*. Like universal quantifying expressions, some words that indicate existential quantification have restrictions built in, for instance, *someone*. We can substitute only names of persons for this word. We might think we could rewrite sentences using this expression as we handled *everyone* in the last section, perhaps as

Of something: if it is a person, then it is in the next room.

However, if we treat the open sentence in this statement as a material conditional, then it will be true if there is something which isn't a person (that makes the antecedent of the conditional false and so the conditional is automatically true). A more accurate way to treat this statement is the following:

Of something: it is a person *and* it is in the next room.

This will be true just in case there is some person who is in the next room.

Again, just as quantifying expressions like *every* go with predicate expressions, as in *Every citizen has a right to vote*, there are existential quantifying expressions that function similarly, such as *some:*

Some people are irrational.

In standard form, this would be

Of something: it is a person and it is irrational.

For another example, consider the statement

Some mushrooms are not edible.

In standard form, this is

Of something: it is a mushroom and it is not edible.

Another expression that often indicates existential quantification is *there is (are)*, as in

There is a cure for this disease.

In standard form, this becomes

Of something: it is a cure for this disease.

However, the expression *there is no* is better treated as universal quantification, as in the following example:

There's no free lunch.

In standard form, this is

Of everything: it is not a free lunch.

The expressions *there aren't any*, *there isn't any*, etc., are treated similarly.

EXERCISE 8.3.2

Rewrite the following statements in standard form.
   1 Some ugly dogs have ugly owners.
  *2 All animals with hearts have kidneys.
   3 No one who has ever eaten my home-cooked avocado pudding will forget it.
  *4 Some books are not worth reading.
   5 Some rich people are miserable.
  *6 Nothing is harder than diamond.
   7 Alice knows everything worth knowing.
  *8 Every cloud has a silver lining.
   9 Everybody goes to college these days.
 *10 There is a tree in the middle of the garden.

FORMALIZING IN PREDICATE LOGIC

Now that we're familiar with the structure of simple predications and quantified predications, we can devise an artificial language, which we will call ℘, to represent logical forms with respect to predicate logic. All we need to do is make certain modifications to S. We need four kinds of new symbols:

1   Individual constants: $a, b, c, d, \ldots$
2   Individual variables: $x, y, z, \ldots$
3   Predicate variables: $F, G, H, \ldots$
4   Quantifiers: the universal quantifier $\forall$ and the existential quantifier $\exists$

We use individual constants to formalize names, individual variables to formalize individual variable words, predicate variables to formalize predicate expressions, and the two quantifiers to formalize the corresponding quantifying expressions. We no longer make use of statement variables. We'll explain just how the process of formalizing works in stages, beginning with the formalization of simple predications. A simple predication consists of a name and a predicate expression, and so we formalize it with a *predicate variable* and an *individual constant*. We write the predicate variable *first*, then the individual constant, with no punctuation between, as

Fa

We'll call a statement form consisting of a predicate variable and an individual constant a *simple predicate form*. Thus, if we formalize a simple predication, for instance,

The earth is round.

we always get a simple predicate form. In this case, formalizing *The earth* with a and *is round* with F, we get the formalization

Fa

You may use any predicate variable to formalize any predicate expression and any individual constant to formalize any name, as long as you always use the same predicate variable for the same predicate expression and the same individual constant for the same name within a given context. As with our rules for formalizations in statement logic, *same context* normally means *within a single argument*.

Now, simple predicate forms are like statement variables in $\mathcal{S}$: they can be combined with connectives in the same way that simple predications can be combined with connecting words. We formalize in $\mathcal{P}$ just as we did in $\mathcal{S}$ except that we use simple predicate forms instead of statement variables. For instance, consider

John speaks German and Mary speaks French.

To make the process of formalizing clearer, we'll change the process of symbolic abbreviation. Instead of replacing atomic statements with statement constants, we'll formalize them directly with simple predicate forms. Here, formalizing *John* and *Mary* with a and b, and *speaks German* and *speaks French* with F and G, we get

Fa and *Gb*.

Now, we finish formalizing this quasi-statement form as

$Fa \wedge Gb$

Some examples will illustrate how we handle compounds of simple predications in which the same name, or the same predicate expression, appears more than once:

Mary speaks both German and French.	$Fa \wedge Ga$
John and Mary both speak German.	$Fa \wedge Fb$
Mary speaks French but John doesn't.	$Fa \wedge {\sim}Fb$
If John and Mary both speak French, then either Tom or Sue speaks German.	$(Fa \wedge Fb) \supset (Gc \vee Gd)$

Now, let's consider the quantifiers and the individual variables. First, remember that we analyzed universal quantifications as long conjunctions and existential quantifications as long disjunctions. That's roughly the way we treat them in $\mathcal{P}$. Suppose, for instance, that we wanted to formalize *Everything has a cause*. If we treat this as the conjunction of all the simple predications which have the predicate *has a cause*, then we ought to formalize it as the conjunction of all the simple predicate forms with a certain predicate variable, for instance F:

$Fa \wedge Fb \wedge Fc \wedge Fd \wedge Fe \wedge \ldots$

However, just as in the case of natural-language quantified predications, we couldn't actually write down such an expression. So, we'll introduce the quantifiers to avoid this problem. First, we need to introduce the notion of an *open form*. An open form is the formalization of an open sentence. The simplest sort of open form is a simple predicate form with an individual variable in place of the individual constant:

Fx

Like an open sentence, an open form isn't really well formed by itself. However, together with a quantifier, it can be used to produce a statement form. Let's begin with the *universal quantifier* ∀. If we want to assert the endless conjunction $Fa \land Fb \land Fc \land Fd \land \ldots$ mentioned above, we can do so by indicating that we are asserting simultaneously every statement form that would result from the open form Fx if an individual constant were substituted for the variable x. To do this, we write

(∀x)Fx

Notice that we've written the variable x after the universal quantifier ∀ and that the result is enclosed in parentheses. The syntax of $\mathcal{P}$ requires this: *a quantifier must always be followed by an individual variable and enclosed in parentheses.*

This example illustrates the significance of the universal quantifier. In general, we could say that the result of prefixing a universal quantifier followed by a certain individual variable to an open form is equivalent to the conjunction of all the statement forms that result when an individual constant is substituted for that individual variable in that open form. Let's consider some further examples, for instance, *Every man is mortal*. In standard form, this is

Of everything: if it is a man, then it is mortal.

First, we formalize the atomic constituents *it is a man* and *it is mortal:*

Of everything: if Fx, then Gx.

Notice that we've formalized the variable word *it* with the individual variable x and that we've used the same variable both times. We've formalized the predicate expressions *is a man* and *is mortal* with F and G. We'll also use the variable x with the quantifier. Let's do this in stages also, first separating *everything* into *every* and *thing* and replacing *thing* with x:

Of every x: if Fx, then Gx.

Now, we formalize the open form:

Of every x: $Fx \supset Gx$

And finally, we formalize the quantifier word *every*:

$(\forall x)(Fx \supset Gx)$

Notice here that we enclosed $Fx \supset Gx$ in parentheses. The reason is that we need to indicate just how much of the statement form the quantifier governs. Actually, this is just an extension of the concept of scope that we introduced in Chapter 3: the parentheses indicate the *scope* of the quantifier $(\forall x)$.

Given the way we analyze statements containing *nothing*, *nobody*, and *no* alone, it's fairly obvious how to formalize them. First consider this statement:

Nothing is on the other side of the moon.

In standard form this is

Of everything: it is not on the other side of the moon.

Introducing a variable and formalizing predicate expressions, we get

Of every x: not Fx.

where F formalizes *is on the other side of the moon*. Formalizing the open form gives us

Of every x: $\sim Fx$

And finally, formalizing the quantifier word gives us

$(\forall x)\sim Fx$

Let's consider one more example:

No job is both easy and rewarding.

In standard form, we have

Of everything: if it is a job, then it is not both easy and rewarding.

Formalizing will give us

$(\forall x)[Fx \supset \sim(Gx \wedge Hx)]$

The *existential quantifier* $\exists$ works similarly to the universal quantifier. As you might expect, the result of prefixing $(\exists x)$ to an open form is equivalent to the *disjunction* of every statement form that results from the open form when an individual constant is substituted for the individual variable x. Thus, (∃x) Fx is equivalent to the endless disjunction

$$Fa \lor Fb \lor Fc \lor Fd \lor \ldots$$

Formalizing statements involving existential quantification is similar to the process involving universal quantification. The statement

Something is in the next room.

becomes, in standard form,

Of something: it is in the next room.

Introducing individual variables and formalizing atomic constituents, we get

Of some x: Fx

and formalizing the quantifier gives us

(∃x) Fx

Likewise, *Some people are irrational* is formalized in the following steps:

Of something: it is a person and it is irrational.
Of some x: Fx and Gx.
Of some x: Fx ∧ Gx
(∃x) (Fx ∧ Gx)

Now, let's formalize the three examples in Section 8.1. The first, in standard form, would be

Of everything: if it is a citizen, then it has a right to vote.
John is a citizen.
_____

John has a right to vote.

Formalizing *is a citizen* with F, *has a right to vote* with G, and *John* with a, we first get

Of every x: if Fx, then Gx.
Fa.
_____

Ga.

Completing the formalization gives us

$(\forall x) (Fx \supset Gx)$
Fa
_____

Ga

Now, we formalize the second example, which in standard form is

Of everything: if it is a person, then it is mortal.
Jane is a person.
_____

Jane is mortal.

Here, formalizing *is a person* and *is mortal* with F and G and *Jane* with a, we reach the formalization

$(\forall x) (Fx \supset Gx)$
Fa
_____

Ga

Note that this is exactly the same as the formalization of the first argument. In fact, we also get the same argument form for the third example, if we formalize *is a member of the Communist bloc* with F, *officially espouses Marxist economic theory* with G, and *Czechoslovakia* with a. Our methods of formalization thus show us the logical form that these arguments have in common, and so they give us some explanation of why they're all valid.

_____

EXERCISE 8.4

Formalize the statements in Exercise 8.3.2.

8.4.1 More Complex Statements

Since universal and existential quantifications are statements, they can, of course, appear as constituents of compound statements. For instance, consider the following:

If John can't solve this problem, then no one can.

This is obviously a conditional. Its antecedent is *John can't solve this problem*, and its consequent is equivalent to *No one can solve this problem*. Here, the antecedent is the negation of a simple predication, while the consequent is a quantification. It will help in formalizing if we first put the consequent into standard form:

_____

If John can't solve this problem, then of everything: if it is a person, then it can't solve this problem.

Now, formalizing *John* with *a*, *can solve this problem* with *F*, *is a person* with *G*, and *it* with *x*, and introducing the appropriate quantifier, we arrive at the following formalization:

$$\sim Fa \supset (\forall x)(Gx \supset \sim Fx)$$

Notice here that the universal quantification $(\forall x)(Gx \supset \sim Fx)$ is a constituent of the entire statement form. Consequently, the *scope* of the quantifier $(\forall x)$ here is only the open form $(Gx \supset \sim Fx)$. It is important to determine exactly the scopes of quantifiers, just as it was important to determine the scopes of connectives in formalizing in statement logic. For instance, consider the following statement:

1a If anyone can do that, then Mary can.

Now, this is also a conditional, with antecedent *anyone can do that* and consequent *Mary can (do that)*. Obviously, the antecedent is a quantification, but we must be careful in analyzing it. In isolation, the statement *anyone can do that* would naturally be taken as a universal quantification:

Of anyone: she (or he) can do that.

However, there is a peculiarity about *anyone* here. To see what it is, note what happens to our example if we replace *anyone* with another universal quantifying expression, *everyone*:

2a If everyone can do that, then Mary can.

This obviously doesn't mean the same thing as our example. What's the difference? We could describe it as follows. Statement (1a) says, of each person, that if that person can do that, then Mary can. However, statement (2a) says that if it is true of each person that he (she) can do that, then Mary can. The difference is one of scope. In (1a), the universal quantifying expression has as its scope the entire statement, while in (2a) the universal quantifying expression takes only the antecedent of the conditional as its scope. We might symbolically abbreviate as follows:

1b Of everything: if it is a person, then if it can do that, then Mary can.
2b If (of everything: if it is a person, then it can do that), then Mary can.

Formalizing *Mary* with *a*, *is a person* with *F*, *can do that* with *G*, and the variable word *it* with *x*, we get the following formalizations:

1c　$(\forall x)\,[Fx \supset (Gx \supset Ga)]$
2c　$(\forall x)\,(Fx \supset Gx) \supset Ga$

Notice that the scope of the universal quantifier in (1a) is the open form $Fx \supset (Gx \supset Ga)$ while in (2a) the scope is open form $Fx \supset Gx$. Thus, according to our analysis, (2a) is really a conditional while (1a) is actually a universal quantification having a conditional open form as its constituent.

We can generally distinguish universal quantifying expressions into two groups: those which, like *anyone*, always take a large scope, and those which, like *everyone*, always take a small scope. Words functioning similarly to *anyone* include *any*, *anything*, and other compounds of *any*. Words functioning similarly to *everyone* include *everything*, *every*, the compounds of *every*, *each*, and *all*. Normally, these distinctions of scope apply only to quantifying expressions which appear in conditionals. However, the distinction sometimes appears in negations also. Consider these two examples:

3a　I didn't see anything in the room.
4a　I didn't see everything in the room.

The first of these says, of each thing in the room, that I didn't see it; the second is a negation of *I saw everything in the room*. We might, then, with a little twisting, put them into standard form as follows:

3b　Of everything: if it is in the room, then I didn't see it.
4b　Not (of everything: if it is in the room, then I saw it).

Thus, (3a) is a universal quantification, while (4a) is a negation of a universal quantification. Formalizing *I saw* with *F* and *was in the room* with *G*, we can formalize as follows:

3c　$(\forall x)\,(Gx \supset \sim Fx)$
4c　$\sim(\forall x)\,(Gx \supset Fx)$

Existential quantifying expressions generally do not fall into two classes in this way: they all take the shortest possible scope, as *every* does.

Certain other expressions can be formalized with quantifiers in somewhat more complex ways. Consider the following statement:

Nothing except water would quench his thirst.

To put this in standard form, we might first rewrite it as

Of everything except water: it would not quench his thirst.

Now, to bring this into line with our usual standard forms, note that this says the same thing as

Of everything: either it is water or it would not quench his thirst.

Thus we would formalize it as

$(\forall x)(Fx \lor \sim Gx)$

Other expressions that function similarly are *nothing but* and *only*. The expressions *not but* and *none except* are similar except that they usually apply only to persons. Thus

None but the wise are happy.

is, in standard form,

Of everything: if it is a person, then either it is wise or it is not happy.

Formalizing gives us

$(\forall x)[Fx \supset (Gx \lor \sim Hx)]$

Plural subjects often function as if universally quantified:

Dogs are carnivorous.

This means the same as *All dogs are carnivorous*, and so we formalize it as $(\forall x)(Fx \supset Gx)$.

Sometimes we encounter quantified statements of more complex structure, such as

All citizens can vote if they are registered.

In standard form, this would be

Of everything: if it is a citizen, then it can vote if it is registered.

Formalizing, then, gives us

$(\forall x)[Fx \supset (Hx \supset Gx)]$

Another example is

All men and women have moral obligations.

Since this is equivalent to *All men have moral obligations and all women have moral obligations,* we could put it into standard form:

> Of everything: if it is a man, then it has moral obligations and if it is a woman, then it has moral obligations.

which we would formalize as

$$(\forall x)[(Fx \supset Gx) \wedge (Hx \supset Gx)]$$

However, a shorter and equivalent form is

> Of everything: if it is a man or it is a woman, then it has moral obligations.

This is formalized as follows:

$$(\forall x)[(Fx \vee Gx) \supset Hx]$$

Notice, however, that we cannot formalize this as

$$(\forall x)[(Fx \wedge Gx) \supset Hx]$$

This would be the formalization of the following standard form:

> Of everything: if it is a man and it is a woman, then it has moral obligations.

Obviously, this doesn't mean the same thing as the original example (few things, if any, are both men and women).

8.4.2 Complex Predicates

By *complex predicates*, we mean predicate expressions that must be formalized with more than one predicate variable. An example occurs in the following statement:

> Some American cities are seaports.

The expression *American cities* is, we might say, like a conjunction of two predicates: *American* and *city*. We can make this clearer by putting our example into standard form:

> Of something: it is American and it is a city and it is a seaport.

Formalizing would then give us

$$(\exists x)[(Fx \wedge Gx) \wedge Hx]$$

Note that $(Fx \wedge Gx)$ formalizes *American cities.*

Not everything which appears to be a complex predicate of this sort is one, however. Consider the following:

Some athletes are football players.

If we follow the style of analysis used on our last example, we might try to put this in standard form as

Of something: it is an athlete and it is a football and it is a player.

Obviously, this isn't what the example means (almost no athletes are footballs). Instead, the expression *football player* is best treated as a single predicate expression. Thus, its standard form is

Of something: it is an athlete and it is a football player.

How do we know when to break up a predicate expression into parts? The answer is that we must rely on our intuitive understanding of the sentence. Usually, an expression can be broken up whenever it makes sense to do so. There are, however, some cases in which breaking up a predicate expression might change its meaning rather than making it nonsense. Consider this example:

Some English professors specialize in Shakespeare.

If we treat the predicate expression *English professors* as a complex predicate, we would get the following standard form:

Of something: it is English and it is a professor and it specializes in Shakespeare.

Obviously, this standard form treats *English professor* as meaning *professor who is English.* If, however, we meant to say that some professors of English specialize in Shakespeare, then this standard form would be incorrect: we should instead treat *English professor* as a single predicate.

Sometimes we may find the same complex predicate several times in an argument. Under these circumstances, we may find it more convenient to formalize this complex predicate with a single predicate variable. We can get away with this if no part of the complex predicate appears separately elsewhere in the argument, either alone or as a part of another complex predicate. However, even if a complex predicate appears several times, we must separate its parts in formalizing if any one of its parts appears separated elsewhere.

EXERCISE 8.4.2

Formalize the following statements.
*1   Everybody means well.
2   There are people who are amoral.
*3 Tom is tall only if everybody is.
*4 All cats are animals.
5   Some bacteria are not infectious.
*6 All football players are either failing this course or not taking it.
*7 Some hairy spiders make good pets.
8   All happy people are interesting.
*9 All competent logicians are philosophers.
10 Nothing is worth doing.
*11 Nobody will attend the ceremony.
12 Marijuana will get you high only if it is smoked.
*13 No marijuana is worth smoking unless it has desirable effects.
14 Not every carpenter who is in the union is on strike.
*15 Only doctors are qualified medical practitioners.
16 All analytical philosophers find the writings of Wittgenstein interesting.
*17 Some artists paint nudes.
18 There are some artists who are creative but not successful.
19 No philosophers are taken seriously unless they deserve to be.
*20 All psychologists and sociologists are good researchers or good theoreticians.
21 None, except fools, are cowards.
*22 Not every philosopher who is an existentialist is a Marxist.
23 Anyone can petition the government.
*24 If anything is in the drawer, it will be my watch.
25 Murphy can fix your car if anyone can.

8.5

SYMBOLIC LANGUAGE $\mathcal{P}$

Here we will give a formal treatment of the syntax of $\mathcal{P}$. First, we need to introduce the additional metalinguistic variables for individual constants and individual variables. We will use the boldface letters s, t, u, s_1, t_1, u_1, . . . as metavariables for individual constants and the boldface letters x, y, z, x_1, y_1, z_1, . . . as metavariables for individual variables. We will let the quantifiers $\forall$ and $\exists$ serve as names for themselves, as we did with the connectives of $\mathcal{S}$. We also need a new sort of notation. Let A be any expression formed from the symbols of language $\mathcal{P}$ (as we will specify them below). The expression A(x/t), then, is a name of the expression which results from A if every occurrence of the individual constant t in A is replaced with the individual variable x. Thus, if A is the expression $Fa \wedge (Ga \supset Fb)$, and if we let t refer to a and x refer to x, A(x/t) will refer to $Fx \wedge (Gx \supset Fb)$. Notice that we substituted x for both occurrences of a and that we did not substitue x for b here. We sometimes also use our substitution notation when we want to indicate the result of substituting an individual constant for an individual variable. If we let s refer to a with x still referring to *x*, and if B is the open form $Fx \wedge (Gx \supset Fb)$, then B(s/x) is $Fa \wedge (Ga \supset Fb)$. There are two further details concerning this notation. First, if the individual constant or variable for which we are supposed to substitute something doesn't occur in the expression, then the notation, in effect, tells us not to do anything (we call it *vacuous* in that case). Thus, with the same example, if A is $Fa \wedge (Ga \supset Fb)$ and t is *c*, A(x/t) is simply A (*c* does not occur in A). Second, if an individual variable occurs within the scope of a quantifier containing the same variable, we do not substitute *anything* for it. Thus, if C is $Fa \supset (\exists y)(Gy \vee Fy)$, then C(t/y) is $Fa \supset (\exists y)(Gy \vee Fy)$. Since *y* occurs within the scope of $(\exists y)$, we do not substitute anything for it.

Now, we can give a formal account of the syntax of $\mathcal{P}$. First, we specify the vocabulary of $\mathcal{P}$ as the following five sets:

$\mathbf{T} = \{a, b, c, \ldots a_1, b_1, c_1, \ldots\}$ (individual constants)

$\mathbf{V} = \{x, y, z, w, x_1, y_1, z_1, w_1, \ldots\}$ (individual variables)

$\mathbf{R} = \{F, G, H, \ldots, F_1, G_1, H_1, \ldots\}$ (predicate variables)

$\mathbf{C} = \{\sim, \wedge, \vee, \supset, \equiv, \forall, \exists\}$ (connectives and quantifiers)

$\mathbf{M} = \{ \quad (,), [,], \{, \} \quad \}$ (punctuation)

The sets **T**, **V**, and **R** replace the set **P** of Chapter 5, and the set **C** now has two additional members, $\forall$ and $\exists$. **M** remains the same as in Chapter 5. We now define a set **F** of statement forms with the following formation rules:

1   If $A \in \mathbf{R}$ and $s \in \mathbf{T}$, then $As \in \mathbf{F}$.
2 to 6   Exactly as in Chapter 5.
7   If $A \in \mathbf{F}$ and $x \in \mathbf{V}$ and $t \in \mathbf{T}$, then $(\forall x)(A(x/t)) \in \mathbf{F}$.
8   If $A \in \mathbf{F}$ and $x \in \mathbf{V}$ and $t \in \mathbf{T}$, then $(\exists x)(A(x/t)) \in \mathbf{F}$.
9   Nothing else is in **F**.

Part 1 of this definition says that any expression consisting of a predicate variable followed by an individual constant is a statement form. Parts 2 through 6 include the truth-functional connectives in $\mathcal{P}$ just as they are included in $\mathcal{S}$. Parts 7 and 8 introduce quantifiers and individual variables into $\mathcal{P}$. In effect, they say this: if you take a statement form, replace all the occurrences of some individual constant in it by some individual variable, and then place a quantifier containing that variable in front of the result, the expression you get is a statement form. Notice that we enclose the expression after the quantifier with parentheses, just as we enclose compound statement forms produced with dyadic connectives in parentheses in $\mathcal{S}$; this is to avoid ambiguity in our rules. Also, notice that nothing in parts 7 or 8 requires that the individual constant **t** occur in A. This means that according to our rules, $(\forall x)(Fa \vee Gb)$ is a statement form, even though the quantifier is, in a sense, not doing anything. We call quantifiers of this sort *vacuous*, and it's harmless to permit them into the statement forms of $\mathcal{P}$.

8.6
FORMAL SEMANTICS FOR PREDICATE LOGIC

Now, we are in a position to extend the semantics given for $\mathcal{S}$ in Chapter 6 into a semantics for $\mathcal{P}$. Just as we did with the formation rules, we will keep the interpretation rules of Chapter 6 and add some new ones. First, however, let's note a slight difference. In statement logic, we define an interpretation by assigning truth values to all the statement variables of the language. Here, we assign truth values instead to all *simple predicate forms*. Let's call the set of all such expressions **A**. Then, **A** has the following infinite list of members:

$Fa, Fb, Fc, \ldots, Fa_1, Fb_1, Fc_1, \ldots, Fa_2, \ldots$

$Ga, Gb, Gc, \ldots, Ga_1, Gb_1, Gc_1, \ldots, Ga_2, \ldots$

$Ha, Hb, Hc, \ldots, Ha_1, Hb_1, Hc_1, \ldots, Ha_2, \ldots$

$\cdot \quad \cdot \quad \cdot$

Accordingly, we change IR0 slightly:

IR0: For any interpretation I, if $A \in \mathbf{A}$, then either $I(A) = T$ or $I(A) = F$, and not both.

The next five rules, for the connectives of statement logic, remain unchanged. We need two additional rules for the quantifiers, however:

IR6a: For any interpretation I, $I[(\forall x)A] = T$ if and only if, for every individual constant **s**, $I[A(s/x)] = T$.

IR6b: For any interpretation I, $I[(\forall x)A] = F$ if and only if, for some individual constant **s**, $I[A(s/x)] = F$.

The first of these rules could be explained as follows. A universal quantification $(\forall x)A$ is true on an interpretation I if and only if *every* statement form which can be formed from A by substituting an individual constant for the variable **x** is true on I. This is in accordance with our view of universally quantified statements as long conjunctions, since a conjunction is true only if *all* its conjuncts are true; thus, IR6a is effectively an extension of IR2a. Likewise, IR6b says that the universally quantified statement form $(\forall x)A$ is false just in case *at least one* statement form we could get from A by substituting an individual constant for **x** in it is false. Notice here that if **x** does not occur in A, $I[(\forall x)A]$ is the same as $I(A)$.

Our final interpretation rules govern the existential quantifier:

IR7a: For any interpretation I, $I[(\exists x)A] = T$ if and only if, for at least one individual constant **s**, $I[A(s/x)] = T$.

IR7b: For any interpretation I, $I[(\exists x)A] = F$ if and only if, for every individual constant **s**, $I[A(s/x)] = F$.

Here, the first rule says, in effect, that an existential quantification is true on an interpretation just in case *at least one* statement form which results from it by dropping the quantifier and replacing the individual variable with an individual constant is true on that interpretation. This corresponds, of course, to IR3a, since we regard existential quantifications as long disjunctions: a disjunction is true if at least one of its disjuncts is true. Similarly, IR7b is an extension of IR3b: a disjunction is false if and only if every one of its disjuncts is false.

We can develop semantic tree rules from these interpretation rules for determining the validity of argument forms. There are two modifications in the method. The first, obviously, is that we now close off a branch of a tree if we find the same *simple predicate form* both slashed and unslashed in it. The second modification is somewhat more complex. Consider what we should do to extend a true universal quantification. If we regard it as an infinite conjunction, then by analogy with the tree rules for Chapter 6 we should add all the conjuncts to every open branch of the tree. Unfortunately, since there is no end to the list of conjuncts for a universal quantification, we'd never finish this. However, we can get around this if we remember the purpose of semantic trees: we're trying to find whether each branch closes. A branch will close only if we find the same simple predicate form both slashed and unslashed, and so the only conjuncts of a universal quantification that matter are those which we might run into elsewhere in the tree. We can take care of this by what we call *covering*: when you encounter a universal quantification $(\forall x)A$ in some branch, add $A(s/x)$ for every term **s** that occurs in any open branch in the tree to that branch. There is another restriction on this rule: in a sense, we never get done extending a universal quantification that is unslashed. Consequently, whenever we extend a statement form, we must always check to see if any new individual constants have been introduced in any branch. If so, then we must go back to every universal quantification in that branch and add the appropriate statement form for each such new individual constant. A similar procedure governs slashed existential quantifications.

For unslashed existential quantifications, we have another problem.

If an existential quantification is true on an interpretation, that means that at least one of the statement forms we get from it by substitution is true on that interpretation. Which one? It doesn't matter, as far as IR7a is concerned. However, it makes a big difference as far as the tree method is concerned. If it's a statement form which occurs slashed somewhere else in the same branch of the tree, then that branch closes. However, we could always construct *another* tree just like the first one in which we used a different individual constant, and so that branch wouldn't close, at least not for that reason. To avoid this, we make the *weakest* assumption we can about an interpretation in constructing our trees: in extending an unslashed existential quantification (∃x)A, we pick some individual constant s which doesn't occur anywhere in that branch before and add A(s/x) unslashed to the branch. A similar rule applies to slashed universal quantifications.

We may now state the four additional tree rules:

6a (∀x)A
   A(s/x)
   s is any individual
   constant occurring
   in the same branch[1]
	6b (∀̶x̶)̶A̶
	   A̶(̶s̶/̶x̶)̶
	   s does not already
	   occur in the same
	   branch as (∀̶x̶)̶A̶

7a (∃x)A
   A(s/x)
   s does not already
   occur in the same
   branch as (∃x)A
	7b (∃̶x̶)̶A̶
	   A̶(̶s̶/̶x̶)̶
	   s is any individual
	   constant occurring
	   in the same branch[1]

Since we never get through with unslashed universal quantifications and slashed existential quantifications, we shouldn't place a check mark after them when we extend them. Instead, we place a star (*) to indicate that we must always refer to them. Each time a new individual constant is introduced, we must return to every starred statement form above it in that branch and reapply rule 6a or 7b as appropriate (unless, of course, the branch closes).

The definitions of *entailment*, *semantic consistency*, etc., given in Chapter 6 can now be applied without change to 𝒫. Furthermore, since we have extended the tree method to 𝒫, we can use it in exactly the same was in testing for these concepts.

Now, let's illustrate the use of these rules by showing that the argument form we arrived at for the examples in Section 8.1 is valid. We start by assuming the premises are true and the conclusion false on an interpretation:

---

[1] If no individual constant occurs in the branch, any constant may be chosen.

$(\forall x)(Fx \supset Gx)$
Fa
~~Ga~~

Now, since a occurs in the tree, we extend the first premise by 6a:

$(\forall x)(Fx \supset Gx)^*$
Fa
~~Ga~~
$Fa \supset Ga$

We now extend $Fa \supset Ga$ by 4a:

$(\forall x)(Fx \supset Gx)^*$
Fa
~~Ga~~
$Fa \supset Ga$✓

    Fa Ga
    x   x

The left branch contains both Fa and ~~Fa~~, so it closes; the right branch contains both Ga and ~~Ga~~, so it closes. Therefore, the argument form is valid.

Now, let's consider a slightly more complicated argument:

Some hippopotamuses are unruly.
Moreover, all hippopotamuses are mammals.
Therefore, some mammals are unruly.

Formalizing this argument gives us

$(\exists x)(Fx \wedge Gx)$
$(\forall x)(Fx \supset Hx)$
———————————
$(\exists x)(Hx \wedge Gx)$

We show that this is valid with the following semantic tree:

1   $(\exists x)\ (Fx \wedge Gx)$ ✓
3   $(\forall x)\ (Fx \supset Hx)^*$
5   ~~$(\exists x)\ (Hx \wedge Gx)$~~*
2       $Fa \wedge Ga$ ✓
          Fa
          Ga

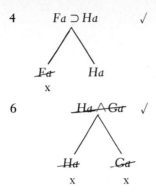

4      $Fa \supset Ha$ ✓

The numerals here indicate the order in which the premises were extended. Note that although we only extended the second premise and the conclusion one time each, we could have extended them again if we encountered more individual constants before the tree closed.

An example of a semantic tree involving more than one extension is the one for the following argument:

> Some philosophers are wise, but some are not.
> Now, the wise philosophers are also logicians.
> However, some logicians aren't wise.
> Therefore, some logicians aren't philosophers.

We formalize this as follows:

$(\exists x)\ (Fx \wedge Gx) \wedge (\exists y)\ (Fy \wedge \sim Gy)$
$(\forall x)\ [(Fx \wedge Gx) \supset Hx]$
$(\exists x)\ (Hx \wedge \sim Gx)$
_____
$(\exists x)\ (Hx \wedge \sim Fx)$

Note that we used the variable y in formalizing the second conjunct of the first premise. We could have used x just as well, but this helps make it clear that this premise is the conjunction of two existential quantifications. To construct the tree for this argument form, we begin by extending this conjunction and then extend the first unslashed existential quantification:

1   $(\exists x)\ (Fx \wedge Gx) \wedge (\exists y)\ (Fy \wedge \sim Gy)$ ✓
     $(\forall x)\ [(Fx \wedge Gx) \supset Hx]$
2   $(\exists x)\ (Hx \wedge \sim Gx)$ ✓
     $\cancel{(\exists x)\ (Hx \wedge \sim Fx)}$
     $(\exists x)\ (Fx \wedge Gx)$
     $(\exists y)\ (Fy \wedge \sim Gy)$
     $Ha \wedge \sim Ga$

Next, we cover all unslashed universal and slashed existential quantifications for the constant *a*:

1 (∃x) (Fx ∧ Gx) ∧ (∃y) (Fy ∧ ~Gy) √
3 (∀x) [(Fx ∧ Gx) ⊃ Hx]*
2 (∃x) (Hx ∧ ~Gx) √
4 ~~(∃x) (Hx ∧ ~Fx)*~~
   (∃x) (Fx ∧ Gx)
   (∃y) (Fy ∧ ~Gy)
   Ha ∧ ~Ga
   (Fa ∧ Ga) ⊃ Ha
   ~~Ha ∧ ~Fa~~

We proceed in this manner until we have extended every existential quantification and covered for every new constant:

1 (∃x) (Fx ∧ Gx) ∧ (∃y) (Fy ∧ ~Gy) √
3, 6, 9 (∀x) [(Fx ∧ Gx) ⊃ Hx]***
2 (∃x) (Hx ∧ ~Gx) √
4, 7, 10 ~~(∃x) (Hx ∧ ~Fx)***~~
5 (∃x) (Fx ∧ Gx) √
8 (∃y) (Fy ∧ ~Gy) √
   Ha ∧ ~Ga
   (Fa ∧ Ga) ⊃ Ha
   ~~Ha ∧ ~Fa~~
   Fb ∧ Gb
   (Fb ∧ Gb) ⊃ Hb
   ~~Hb ∧ ~Fb~~
   Fc ∧ ~Gc
   (Fc ∧ Gc) ⊃ Hc
   ~~Hc ∧ ~Fc~~

Notice that we have now covered with the second and fourth premises three times each. Having extended all quantifications, we now proceed with the unquantified statement forms:

1 (∃x) (Fx ∧ Gx) ∧ (∃y) (Fy ∧ ~Gy) √
3,6,9 (∀x)[(Fx ∧ Gx) ⊃ Hx]***
2 (∃x) (Hx ∧ ~Gx) √
4, 7, 10 ~~(∃x) (Hx ∧ ~Fx)***~~
5 (∃x) (Fx ∧ Gx) √
8 (∃y) (Fy ∧ ~Gy) √
11 Ha ∧ ~Ga √
22 (Fa ∧ Ga) ⊃ Ha √
20 ~~Ha ∧ ~Fa~~ √
13 Fb ∧ Gb √
16 (Fb ∧ Gb) ⊃ Hb √
18 ~~Hb ∧ ~Fb~~ √

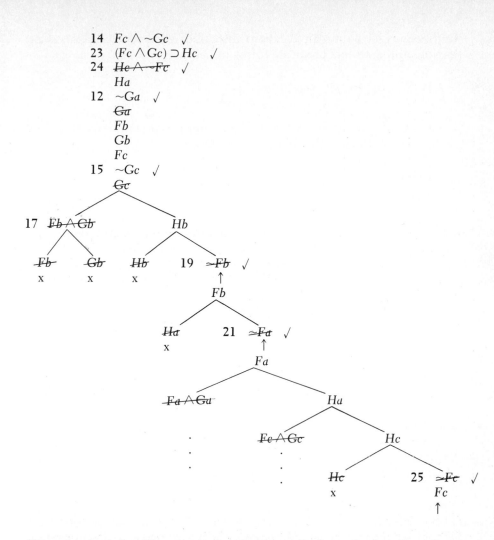

Here, for the sake of brevity, we've simply omitted any further extensions in the open paths under *E̶a̶ ̶∧̶ ̶G̶a̶* and *Fc ∧ Gc*; nothing in these branches will affect what happens in the branches we do consider. Finally, we reach a point at which every compound statement form has been extended, every unslashed existential quantification has been extended, and every unslashed universal or slashed existential quantification has been covered for all individual constants already present in the tree. We could, if we wished, go on adding statement forms to this path forever by covering with (∀x) [(Fx ∧ Gx) ⊃ Hx] and (∃̶x̶)̶ ̶(̶H̶x̶ ̶∧̶ ̶∼̶F̶x̶)̶ for other constants, but the path would obviously never close. Consequently, we've discovered that this argument form is invalid.

Retrieving a counterinterpretation from this open path proceeds just as it did in the case of trees for statement logic except that we now find truth values for atomic predications instead of statement variables. Collecting all the atomic predicate forms in this path, we find

$$Fa, Ga, Ha, Fb, Gb, Hb, Fc, Gc, Hc$$

Consequently, an interpretation I is a counterinterpretation for this argument form if it meets the following conditions:

$$I(Fa), I(Ha), I(Fb), I(Gb), I(Hb), I(Fc), I(Hc) = T$$
$$I(Ga), I(Gc) = F$$

Actually, this isn't quite enough to identify the counterinterpretations: we must also have $I((\forall x) [(Fx \wedge Gx) \supset Hx]) = T$ and $I((\exists x) (Hx \wedge \sim Fx)) = F$. Of course, we can never completely spell out the conditions for either of these in full. However, we don't need to do this. A check of our counterinterpretation will show that it makes both $(\exists x)(Fx \wedge Gx) \wedge (\exists y)$ $(Fy \wedge \sim Gy)$ and $(\exists x)(Hx \wedge \sim Gx)$ true and also that it doesn't *necessarily* make either $(\forall x)[(Fx \wedge Gx) \supset Hx]$ false or $(\exists x)(Hx \wedge \sim Fx)$ true. Consequently, we simply assume that the rest of the counterinterpretation is consistent with these truth values. As a matter of fact, it can be proved that this assumption is justifiable: if a tree is ever going to close, then it will be enough only to extend all the slashed universal and unslashed existential quantifications and then cover for all the constants we get, until there are no more extensions to do that require new constants.

Another thing you might note about this tree is that it's extremely long. This quite frequently happens with predicate logic trees. As a matter of fact, as we'll see in Section 9.4.1, it's possible to get a tree that literally never ends even without covering for constants not already introduced. Notice that this tree would have been considerably longer if we'd shown all the extensions in the branches we left out. We can't avoid long trees like this in general, but sometimes it's possible to make a good guess that we need to cover only for certain constants to get a tree to close. For example, consider the following argument:

> Some philosophers are wise, and so are some logicians.
> Now, all wise logicians are philosophers.
> Therefore, some philosophers are logicians.

Using predicate variables as before, we formalize as

$$(\exists x)(Fx \wedge Gx) \wedge (\exists y)(Hy \wedge Gy)$$
$$(\forall x)[(Hx \wedge Gx) \supset Fx]$$
$$\overline{}$$
$$(\exists x)(Hx \wedge Fx)$$

Setting up the tree as usual, we begin by extending all truth-functional compounds and existential quantifications:

$(\exists x)(Fx \land Gx) \land (\exists y)(Hy \land Gy)$ ✓
$(\forall x)[(Hx \land Gx) \supset Fx]$
$\cancel{(\exists x)(Hx \land Fx)}$
$(\exists x)(Fx \land Gx)$ ✓
$(\exists y)(Hy \land Gy)$ ✓
$Fa \land Ga$
$Hb \land Gb$

Notice that we haven't yet covered for any of these constants. Now, we could proceed to cover for a and b; but notice that in the case of b, when we cover for the second premise, we'll get a conditional with $Hb \land Gb$ as its antecedent. We already have $Hb \land Gb$ in the tree, so let's try first covering only for b and check if the tree closes:

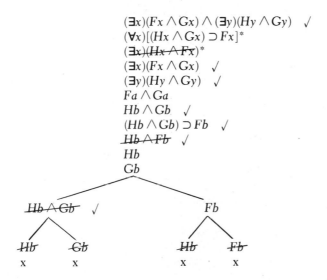

Since all branches close, the argument form is valid. Notice that the tree would have been much longer if we had covered with $(\forall x)[(Hx \land Gx) \supset Fx]$ and $\cancel{(\exists x)(Hx \land Fx)}$ for all constants. With experience, often it becomes possible to make guesses like these about covering that shortens trees. However, there are no easy rules for this, and in the case of an invalid argument we can't be sure a tree won't close until we've covered for every constant present.

Now, we use semantic trees to show that the following two statements are semantically equivalent:

Some trees do not produce fruit.
It's not true that every tree produces fruit.

We may formalize these as

$(\exists x)(Fx \wedge \sim Gx)$
$\sim(\forall x)(Fx \supset Gx)$

To show semantic equivalence, we need to construct two trees. First, we assume that the first statement form is true and the second false, producing the following tree:

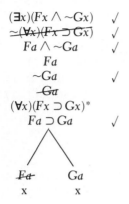

Now, we construct a tree, supposing that the first is false and the second true:

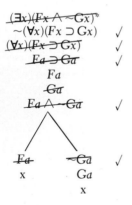

Consequently, the two statements are semantically equivalent.

Notice here that we usually extend slashed universal quantifications and unslashed existential quantifications before extending unslashed universal quantifications and slashed existential quantifications. This generally results in shorter trees. Sometimes, however, we must extend unslashed universal quantifications or slashed existential quantifications before any individual constants have been introduced. In such cases, we simply pick *any* constant and cover for it (it's convenient to start with *a*). To illustrate this, we construct a tree to see if the following set of statement forms is semantically consistent:

$$\{(\forall x)(Fx \supset Gx), (\forall x)(\sim Gx \lor Hx), \sim(\exists x)\sim(Fx \land Hx)\}$$

Its tree is as follows:

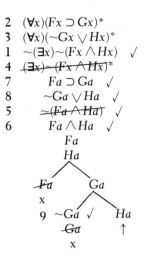

Notice that the right-hand branch remains open; therefore, there is an interpretation on which all these statement forms are true, namely, any interpretation I such that $I(Fa) = T$, $I(Ha) = T$, and $I(Ga) = T$ [and, of course, likewise $(\forall x)(Fx \supset Gx)$, $(\forall x)(\sim Gx \lor Hx)$, and $\sim(\exists x)\sim(Fx \land Hx)$].

We can also apply the tree method to determine whether statement forms of $\mathcal{P}$ are logical truths, contradictions, or contingencies. Consider the following statement form:

$$(\exists x)Fx \supset Fa$$

To see if it is a logical truth, we construct a tree assuming it is false:

$$(\exists x)Fx \supset Fa \quad \checkmark$$
$$(\exists x)Fx \quad \checkmark$$
$$\sim Fa$$
$$Fb$$

Notice that we extended $(\exists x)Fx$ with Fb, since a already occurred in the same branch. Here, the tree remains open, and so $(\exists x)Fx \supset Fa$ is not a logical truth: it is false on an interpretation I if $I(Fa) = F$ and $I(Fb) = T$. (We could have used any other individual constant except a for x.) We now test to see if it is a contradiction:

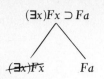

$$(\exists x)Fx \supset Fa$$

~~$(\exists x)Fx$~~ Fa

Notice that neither of these branches will ever close (we stop after one step, since the right-hand branch will never close). According to this tree, $(\exists x)Fx \supset Fa$ is true on any interpretation I if $I(Fa) = T$. As a result, $(\exists x)Fx \supset Fa$ is contingent.

EXERCISE 8.6

1 Determine whether the following argument forms are valid. If not, list a counterinterpretation.

(a) $(\forall x)(Fx \supset Gx)$
     $(\exists x)(Hx \wedge Fx)$
     _____
     $(\exists x)(Hx \wedge Gx)$

(b) $(\forall x)(Fx \supset Gx)$
     $(\forall x)[(Fx \wedge Gx) \supset Hx]$
     _____
     $(\forall x)(Fx \supset Hx)$

*(c) $(\exists x)(Fx \wedge \sim Gx)$
     $(\forall x)(Fx \supset Gx)$
     _____
     $(\forall x)(Gx \supset Fx)$

(d) $(\exists x)(Fx \wedge \sim Gx)$
     $(\forall x)(Hx \supset Gx)$
     $(\exists x)(Fx \wedge Gx)$
     _____
     $(\forall x)(Hx \supset Fx)$

(e) $(\forall x)(Fx \supset Gx)$
     $(\forall x)[(Gx \wedge Fx) \supset Hx]$
     _____
     $(\forall x)[Fx \supset (Gx \wedge Hx)]$

*(f) $(\exists x)(Fx \wedge Gx)$
     Fa
     _____
     Ga

(g) $(\forall x)[(Fx \vee Gx) \supset (Hx \wedge Ix)]$
     $(\forall x)[Hx \vee Ix) \supset (Fx \wedge Gx)]$
     _____
     $(\forall x)(Fx \equiv Hx)$

(h) $(\forall x)(Fx \supset Gx)$
     $(\exists x)(Hx \wedge Gx)$
     _____
     $(\forall x)(Fx \supset Hx)$

(i) $(\forall x)(Fx \wedge Gx)$
     $(\exists x)\sim Gx$
     _____
     $(\exists x)\sim Fx$

*(j) $(\exists x)(\sim Fx \vee \sim Gx)$
     $(\forall x)[(Gx \vee Fx) \supset Hx]$
     $(\exists x)\sim (Ix \vee \sim Fx)$
     _____
     $(\exists x)Hx$

(k) $(\forall x)[(Fx \vee Gx) \supset Hx]$
     $(\forall x)[Ix \supset (Jx \vee Fx)]$
     _____
     $(\forall x)[(Ix \wedge \sim Jx) \supset Hx]$

*(l) $(\forall x)(Fx \supset Gx)$
     $(\exists x)(Gx \wedge \sim Hx)$
     _____
     $(\exists x)(Fx \wedge \sim Hx)$

2 Determine whether the following sets of statement forms are semantically consistent. If consistent, provide an interpretation on which all the members of the set are true.

*(a) {(∀x)(Fx ⊃ Gx), (∃x)(~Gx ∧ Hx), (∀x)(~Hx ∨ Fx)}
 (b) {(∀x)[(Fx ∧ Gx) ⊃ Hx], Ga, ~Ha, (∀x)Fx}
 (c) {(∃x)(Fx ∧ ~Gx), (∀x)(Fx ⊃ Hx), (∀x)(Gx ⊃ Hx)}
 (d) {(∀x)(Fx ⊃ Gx), Fb, ~Hb, (∀x)(Hx ⊃ Gx)}
*(e) {(∀x)(Fx ⊃ Gx), ~(∀x)Gx, (∀x)Fx}

3 Determine whether the following pairs of statement forms are semantically equivalent. Provide interpretations for the pairs which are not.

 (a) (∀x)(Fx ⊃ Gx), ~(∃x)(Fx ∧ ~Gx)
 (b) (∀x)[Fx ⊃ (Gx ⊃ Hx)], (∀x)[(~Gx ∨ ~Fx) ∨ Hx]
 (c) (∀x)(Fa ⊃ Gx), Fa ⊃ (∀x)Gx
 (d) (∀x)(Fx ∧ Ga), (∀x)Fx ∧ Ga
 (e) (∀x)(Fx ⊃ Ga), (∀x)Fx ⊃ Ga
*(f) (∃x)(Fa ⊃ Gx), Fa ⊃ (∀x)Gx
 (g) (∀x)(Fx ⊃ ~Gx), (∃x)(Fx ∧ ~Gx)

4 Determine whether each of the following statement forms is logically true, contingent, or contradictory.

 (a) (∀x)(Fx ∧ Gx) ⊃ Fa
*(b) Fa ⊃ (∀x)Fx
*(c) Fa ⊃ (∃x)Fx
 (d) (∃x)Fx ⊃ Fb
 (e) (∀x)Fx ⊃ (Fa ∧ Fb)

5. Determine whether the following arguments are valid in the semantic sense. Provide counterinterpretations for the ones which are not.
 (a) Cats and dogs are animals. Some cats are felines. Some felines are ferocious. All animals are ferocious. Therefore, some cats are ferocious.
 (b) No politician who is either associated with the Watergate scandal or is a Nixon sympathizer will either be elected to office or will receive the respect of his or her constituency. After all, some politicians are not only associated with Watergate but also are proud of it. Admittedly, some moral politicians will be unhappy if they are not elected. But, then, none but the moral are politicians. Therefore, some politicians are not unhappy.
 (c) It is undeniable that some religious people are not hypocrites. After all, all religious people are honest. Furthermore, some hypocrites are not honest.
*(d) Logicians and mathematicians are symbol manipulators. Doctors and lawyers send bills. Now, all bill senders are both irritating and unnecessary. But, logicians are neither irritating nor unkind. Consequently, some mathematicians are unkind but not irritating.
 (e) All metaphysicians are in touch with the absolute or are confused. All those in touch with the absolute are Hegelians. Not all metaphysicians are Hegelians. Therefore, some metaphysicians are confused.
 (f) All energy comes from the sun. Some energy is in the form of heat. Some of the things coming from the sun are not in the form of heat. Therefore, not everything coming from the sun is energy.
*(g) All voters are citizens. Some citizens have not registered to vote. Therefore, some voters are not registered to vote.
 (h) No human is perfect. All Presidents are humans. Therefore, no Presidents are perfect.

A NATURAL DEDUCTION SYSTEM FOR PREDICATE LOGIC

To expand ℘ into a natural deduction system, we can proceed just as we did with the semantic theory for ℘: we can take our natural deduction system for statement logic, 𝔇, and add some additional rules of inference for the quantifiers. We will call the resulting system 𝔍. System 𝔍, then, takes as its language Symbolic Language ℘ and as its rules of inference all the rules of inference of 𝔇 plus three new transformation rules, one new replacement rule, and one new assumption rule. The additional rules are as follows.

Additional Transformation Rules

9 Universal Instantiation (U.I.)

m $(\forall x)A$

n $A(s/x)$ m, U.I.

10 Existential Generalization (E.G.)

m A

n $(\exists x)A(x/s)$ m, E.G.

11 Universal Generalization (U.G.)

m A

n $(\forall x)A(x/s)$ m, U.G.

Restrictions: s does not occur in any premise of the deduction or in any assumption in force at step m.

Additional Replacement Rule

11 Quantifier Exchange (Q.E.)

$(\forall x) \sim A$: $\sim(\exists x)A$
$(\exists x) \sim A$: $\sim(\forall x)A$

Additional Assumption Rule

4 Existential Instantiation (E.I.)

l $(\exists x)A$

i m $A(s/x)$ ai

i n B
$\vdash$ $n+1$ B l, m—n, E.I.

Restrictions: s does not occur in any premise of the deduction, in step *l*, in step *n*, or in any assumption already in force at step *m*.

The rules of Universal Instantiation and Existential Generalization are, in fact, quite obvious. U.I. effectively says that from a universal quantification we can deduce any of the conjuncts implicit in that universal quantification. Such a deduction is illustrated in the following argument:

> Every thing had a beginning.
> Therefore, the universe had a beginning.

Likewise, E.G. effectively says that an existential quantification can be derived from any statement form simply by substituting a variable for some constant and prefixing an existential quantifier. This is illustrated in the following argument:

> John is in the kitchen.
> Therefore, something is in the kitchen.

We can also compare U.I. to Simplification, since we are effectively inferring one of the conjuncts of a long conjunction. Similarly, E.G. resembles Addition, since we infer a long disjunction from one of its disjuncts.

The rule of Universal Generalization is somewhat harder to explain. We intend it to reflect a certain pattern of argument we often use, as illustrated in the following argument:

> All the members of the council are both charter members and members in good standing.
> Now, every charter member voted against the resolution. However, only members in good standing were entitled to vote.
> Now, consider a particular member of the council, Jones. Jones is, then, both a charter member and a member in good standing.
> Consequently, Jones voted against the resolution, and Jones was entitled to vote.
> Since this is true of Jones, then it will be true of any member of the council, and so all the members of the council not only voted against the resolution but also were entitled to vote.

The procedure in this argument is as follows. We take some member of the council (Jones) and then, just on the basis of the premises of the argument, we see what we can deduce about Jones. Since nothing in the argument depends on the fact that we chose Jones rather than some other member, we could have gotten the same result for any other member. Therefore, we are entitled to draw the universally quantified conclusion applying to all the members of the council. To show just how this argument involves U.G., let's formalize it and construct a deduction. Omitting all intermediate conclusions, as suggested in Section 4.4.4, we obtain:

$(\forall x)[Fx \supset (Gx \wedge Hx)]$
$(\forall x)(Gx \supset Ix)$
$(\forall x)(Hx \supset Jx)$
(Next three sentences omitted)
───────────────────────
$(\forall x)[Fx \supset (Ix \wedge Jx)]$

Note that only the first three statements and the last have been formalized; the rest are all intermediate steps which we omit. However, we can make use of these intermediate conclusions as a guide in constructing a deduction. The sentence *Now, consider a particular member of the council, Jones* isn't really a premise (in fact, it's not a statement); rather, it's an instruction about how to construct the deduction. What it says is, in effect, *assume* that Jones is a member of the council. We could formalize this assumption as

Fa

We'll use this strategy in our deduction. The next two intermediate conclusions are formalized as

$Ga \wedge Ha$
$Ia \wedge Ja$

In constructing our deduction, we may find it useful to try to get these as intermediate steps. A deduction for this argument form using the strategy suggested is

	1	$(\forall x)[Fx \supset (Gx \wedge Hx)]$	
	2	$(\forall x)(Gx \supset Ix)$	
	3	$(\forall x)(Hx \supset Jx)$	/ $(\forall x)[Fx \supset (Ix \wedge Jx)]$
1	4	Fa	$a1$
1	5	$Fa \supset (Ga \wedge Ha)$	1, U.I.
1	6	$Ga \wedge Ha$	4, 5, M.P.
1	7	Ga	6, Simp.
1	8	Ha	6, Simp.
1	9	$Ga \supset Ia$	2, U.I.
1	10	$Ha \supset Ja$	3, U.I.
1	11	Ia	7, 9, M.P.
1	12	Ja	8, 10, M.P.
1	13	$Ia \wedge Ja$	11, 12, Conj.
⅄	14	$Fa \supset (Ia \wedge Ja)$	4—13, Ded.
	15	$(\forall x)[Fx \supset (Ix \wedge Jx)]$	14, U.G.

Now, let's see how this deduction works. We first construct a deduction of $Fa \supset (Ia \wedge Ja)$ from the premises of the argument form. Notice that this is what we have at line 14. Now, U.G. says that we can infer $(\forall x)A(x/s)$ from A *provided that* (1) s does not occur in the premises and (2) s does not occur in any assumption in force when we reach A in the deduction. By *assumption in force* we mean an assumption which has been made and not yet discharged. There is only one assumption in this deduction (line 4), and this is discharged at line 14; consequently, no assumptions are in force at this point. Therefore, we can apply U.G. With s = a and A = line 14, we infer the conclusion by U.G. Note that the intermediate conclusions $Ga \wedge Ha$ and $Ia \wedge Ja$ appear as lines 6 and 13, respectively.

Universal generalization is most clearly exemplified in mathematical arguments. In geometry, for instance, a proof may begin, "Let *ABC* be a triangle," and afterward various things may be proved about this triangle. Since nothing is assumed about *ABC* except that it is a triangle, we can then infer that what has been proved about it is true of every triangle.

The Quantifier Exchange (Q.E.) rules allow us to replace an existential quantifier with a universal quantifier, and conversely. We can justify them syntactically by comparing them to the DeMorganization rules. If we consider $(\forall x)Fx$, for instance, to be the long conjunction.

$$Fa \wedge Fb \wedge Fc \wedge \cdots$$

then $\sim(\forall x)Fx$ would be the denial of this conjunction. However, by the DeMorganization rule, the denial of a conjunction is the disjunction of the denials of its conjuncts. Therefore, after an appropriate number of uses of DeMorganization and Association, $\sim(\forall x)Fx$ becomes

$$\sim Fa \vee \sim Fb \vee \sim Fc \vee \cdots$$

And, this long disjunction is, of course, $(\exists x) \sim Fx$. The remaining part of Q.E. can be established in a similar way.

The additional assumption rule, Existential Instantiation, is a bit difficult to explain. We'll consider an example:

> Unless Jane is home, there's a burglar in the cellar.
> Now, Jane isn't home.
> Consequently, there's a burglar in the cellar.
> However, I'm quite sure that no one in the cellar can get into the house.
> Now, any burglar who can't get into the house is certainly going to be unhappy.
> It follows, then, that the burglar in the cellar can't get into the house.
> Thus, this burglar is, no doubt, unhappy.
> Consequently, there is an unhappy burglar in the cellar.

In this chained argument, we talk about "the burglar in the cellar," even though we really don't know anything except that there is *some* burglar in the cellar. We conclude that this burglar (whoever it may be) is unhappy, and from this we deduce that there's an unhappy burglar in the cellar. This is the procedure of Existential Instantiation: knowing that there is some burglar in the cellar, we simply assume that it's some particular burglar (say, Light Fingers Muldoon) and then conclude that this burglar is unhappy. Of course, we aren't really entitled to conclude, then, that Light Fingers Muldoon is unhappy, only that there is *some* unhappy burglar in the cellar.

Omitting these intermediate conclusions, we formalize using the following:

F for *is home*
G for *is a burglar*
H for *is in the cellar*
I for *can get into the house*
J for *is happy*
a for *Jane*

The argument form is, then,

$\sim Fa \supset (\exists x)(Gx \wedge Hx)$
$\sim Fa$
(third statement omitted)
$(\forall x)(Hx \supset \sim Ix)$
$(\forall x)[Gx \supset (\sim Ix \supset \sim Jx)]$
(sixth and seventh statements omitted)
_____

$(\exists x)[(Gx \wedge \sim Jx) \wedge Hx]$

Although we don't formalize the three intermediate conclusions, we can use them as a guide in constructing the deduction. The first of them, *Consequently, there's a burglar in the cellar*, is an existential quantification:

$(\exists x)(Gx \wedge Hx)$

We may be able to use this as the $(\exists x)A$ of E.I. The sixth and seventh statements talk about "the burglar in the cellar." Since we'll be using E.I., we can give this burglar a name (such as *Light Fingers Muldoon*) and formalize it with some new individual constant (say b). These statements can be formalized as

$(Gb \wedge Hb) \wedge \sim Ib$

and

$\sim Jb$

(Note that the first of these means something like *b is a burglar and b is in the cellar and b can't get into the house*.) Now, let's see how these appear in a deduction using E.I.:

	1	$\sim Fa \supset (\exists x)(Gx \wedge Hx)$	
	2	$\sim Fa$	
	3	$(\forall x)(Hx \supset \sim Ix)$	
	4	$(\forall x)[Gx \supset (\sim Ix \supset \sim Jx)]$	$/ \ (\exists x)[(Gx \wedge \sim Jx) \wedge Hx]$
	5	$(\exists x)(Gx \wedge Hx)$	1, 2, M.P.
1	6	$Gb \wedge Hb$	a 1
1	7	$Hb \supset \sim Ib$	3, U.I.
1	8	$Gb \supset (\sim Ib \supset \sim Jb)$	4, U.I.
1	9	Gb	6, Simp.
1	10	Hb	6, Simp.
1	11	$\sim Ib$	7, 10, M.P.
1	12	$\sim Ib \supset \sim Jb$	8, 9, M.P.
1	13	$\sim Jb$	11, 12, M.P.
1	14	$Gb \wedge \sim Jb$	9, 13, Conj.
1	15	$(Gb \wedge \sim Jb) \wedge Hb$	10, 14, Conj.
1	16	$(\exists x)[(Gx \wedge \sim Jx) \wedge Hx]$	15, E.G.
⅄	17	$(\exists x)[(Gx \wedge \sim Jx) \wedge Hx]$	5, 6—16, E.I.

Notice that here we first deduce $(\exists x)(Gx \wedge Hx)$, which corresponds to an intermediate conclusion of the argument, and then we assume the result of substituting b for x in the open form $Gx \wedge Hx$. We choose b because it does not occur in any of the premises or any assumption in force when we make the assumption at line 6 (there are none). Now, we deduce the conclusion from this assumption. [Note that although we don't actually use the intermediate conclusion $(Gb \wedge Hb) \wedge \sim Ib$, its conjuncts appear in lines 6 and 11. The intermediate conclusion $\sim Jb$ is line 13.] When we have deduced the conclusion at line 16, we still have a dependency numeral. We are entitled to remove this dependency numeral if the individual constant b which we introduced in the assumption does not occur in (1) any premise, (2) any other assumption in force at line 6, (3) line 16. These conditions are satisfied, and so we can discharge the assumption and repeat line 16 without a dependency numeral as line 17. Note that we could not have stopped at line 16, since no deduction may end with an assumption not discharged. Also note that we could not have used E.I. if we had written $Ga \wedge Ha$ at line 6 (a occurs in a premise).

We can illustrate the use of these rules further with some examples. We first construct a deduction to show that $\{(\exists x)Gx, (\forall x)[(Fx \vee Gx) \supset (Hx \vee Ix)], (\forall x)(\sim Fx \supset Gx), (\forall x)(Gx \supset \sim Ix)\} \vdash (\exists x)Hx$.

	1	$(\exists x)Gx$	
	2	$(\forall x)[(Fx \lor Gx) \supset (Hx \lor Ix)]$	
	3	$(\forall x)(\sim Fx \supset Gx)$	
	4	$(\forall x)(Gx \supset \sim Ix)$	

 / $(\exists x)Hx$

1	5	Ga	$a1$
1	6	$\sim Fa \supset Ga$	3, U.I.
1	7	$\sim \sim Fa \lor Ga$	6, Imp.
1	8	$Fa \lor Ga$	7, D.N.
1	9	$(Fa \lor Ga) \supset (Ha \lor Ia)$	2, U.I.
1	10	$Ha \lor Ia$	8, 9, M.P.
1	11	$Ga \supset \sim Ia$	4, U.I.
1	12	$\sim Ia$	5, 11, M.P.
1	13	Ha	10, 12, D.S.
1	14	$(\exists x)Hx$	13, E.G.
⅄	15	$(\exists x)Hx$	1, 5—14, E.I.

Notice that here the step $(\exists x)A$ to which we appealed in applying E.I. is one of the premises.

So far, we have used natural deduction to show that certain argument forms are valid in the syntactic sense. We can also use the definitions of deductive consistency, deductive equivalence, logical theorem, contradictory statement form, and independent statement form as given in Chapter 7 as definitions for the same concepts in system Ɔ. Here, we show by a deduction that $\{(\forall x)(Fx \supset Hx),\ \sim(\exists x)(Hx \land Gx),\ (\exists x)$ $(Fx \land Gx)\}$ is deductively inconsistent:

1	$(\forall x)(Fx \supset Hx)$	
2	$\sim(\exists x)(Hx \land Gx)$	
3	$(\exists x)(Fx \land Gx)$	

 /

4	$(\forall x) \sim (Hx \land Gx)$	2, Q.E.
5	$Fa \supset Ha$	1, U.I.
6	$\sim(Ha \land Ga)$	4, U.I.
7	$\sim Ha \lor \sim Ga$	6, DeM.
8	$Ha \supset \sim Ga$	7, Imp.
9	$Fa \supset \sim Ga$	5, 8, H.S.
10	$\sim Fa \lor \sim Ga$	9, Imp.
11	$\sim(Fa \land Ga)$	10, DeM.
12	$(\forall x) \sim (Fx \land Gx)$	11, U.G.
13	$\sim(\exists x)(Fx \land Gx)$	12, Q.E.
14	$[(\exists x)(Fx \land Gx)] \land \sim[(\exists x)(Fx \land Gx)]$	3, 13, Conj.

Line 14 is of the form $A \land \sim A$, and so the original set of statement forms is deductively inconsistent.

Now, we show that $(\exists x)Fx \supset Fa \leftrightarrow (\forall x)(Fx \supset Fa)$. First we show that $\{(\exists x)Fx \supset Fa\} \vdash (\forall x)(Fx \supset Fa)$:

```
       1   (∃x)Fx ⊃ Fa                               / (∀x)(Fx ⊃ Fa)
   1   2   ~(∀x)(Fx ⊃ Fa)                    a1
   1   3   (∃x)~(Fx ⊃ Fa)                    2, Q.E.
  2, 1  4   ~(Fb ⊃ Fa)                        a2
  2, 1  5   ~(~Fb ∨ Fa)                       4, Imp.
  2, 1  6   ~~Fb ∧ ~Fa                        5, DeM.
  2, 1  7   Fb ∧ ~Fa                          6, D.N.
  2, 1  8   Fb                                7, Simp.
  2, 1  9   ~Fa                               7, Simp.
  2, 1 10   (∃x)Fx                            8, E.G.
  2, 1 11   Fa                                1, 10, M.P.
  2, 1 12   Fa ∧ ~Fa                          9, 11, Conj.
  2, 1 13   Fa ∧ ~Fa                          3, 4—12, E.I.
   ⅄  14   ~~(∀x)(Fx ⊃ Fa)                   2—13, R.A.
      15   (∀x)(Fx ⊃ Fa)                     14, D.N.
```

Notice that in this deduction we employed two assumption rules, Reductio ad Absurdum and Existential Instantiation. Step 3 is the (∃x)A of E.I. Notice that line 2, an assumption which is in force at line 3, does not contain *b*, so that we can correctly apply E.I.

We finish our demonstration that (∃x)Fx ⊃ Fa ↔ (∀x)(Fx ⊃ Fa) with a deduction to show that {(∀x)(Fx ⊃ Fa)} ⊢ (∃x)Fx ⊃ Fa:

```
       1   (∀x)(Fx ⊃ Fa)                            / (∃x)Fx ⊃ Fa
   1   2   (∃x)Fx                            a1
  2, 1  3   Fb                                a2
  2, 1  4   Fb ⊃ Fa                           1, U.I.
  2, 1  5   Fa                                3, 4, M.P.
  2, 1  6   Fa                                2, 3—5, E.I.
   ⅄   7   (∃x)Fx ⊃ Fa                       2—6, Ded.
```

For our last example, we present a deduction to show that (∃x) (Fx ⊃ Fa) is a logical theorem of ℑ:

```
                                              / (∃x)(Fx ⊃ Fa)
   1   1   ~(∃x)(Fx ⊃ Fa)                     a1
   1   2   (∀x)~(Fx ⊃ Fa)                     1, Q.E.
   1   3   ~(Fa ⊃ Fa)                         2, U.I.
   1   4   ~(~Fa ∨ Fa)                        3, Imp.
   1   5   ~~Fa ∧ ~Fa                         4, DeM.
   1   6   ~Fa ∧ ~~Fa                         5, Com.
   ⅄   7   ~~(∃x)(Fx ⊃ Fa)                    1—6, R.A.
      8   (∃x)(Fx ⊃ Fa)                       7, D.N.
```

EXERCISE 8.7

1 Show that the following argument forms are valid in the syntactic sense.

(a) $(\forall x)(Fx \supset Gx)$
$(\forall x)[Gx \supset (Hx \vee Ix)]$
$(\forall x)(Fx \supset {\sim}Ix)$
___
$(\forall x)(Fx \supset Hx)$

(b) $(\forall x)(Fx \supset Gx)$
$(\exists x)(Fx \wedge Hx)$
___
$(\exists x)(Gx \wedge Hx)$

(c) $(\forall x)(Fx \supset Gx)$
$(\forall x)(Hx \supset Fx)$
___
$(\forall x)(Hx \supset Gx)$

*(d) $(\forall x)[(Fx \vee Gx) \supset Hx]$
$(\forall x)(Hx \supset Ix)$
___
$(\forall x)(Fx \supset Ix)$

(e) ${\sim}(\exists x)Fx$
___
$(\forall x)(Fx \supset Gx)$

(f) ${\sim}(\forall x)(Fx \supset {\sim}Gx)$
___
$(\exists x)(Fx \wedge Gx)$

(g) Fa
$(\exists x)(Fx \wedge Gx)$
$(\forall x)(Gx \supset Hx)$
___
$(\exists x)(Fx \wedge Hx)$

*(h) $(\forall x)(Fx \supset {\sim}Gx)$
$(\forall x)(Fx \wedge Hx)$
___
$(\exists x){\sim}Gx$

(i) $(\forall x)(Fx \supset Gx)$
Fc
___
$Hc \supset Gc$

(j) $(\exists x)(Fx \wedge Gx)$
___
${\sim}(\forall x)(Fx \supset {\sim}Gx)$

*(k) $Fa \supset (\forall x)Gx$
$(\exists x)Gx \supset Fa$
___
$(\forall x)(Fa \equiv Gx)$

(l) $(\forall x)[(Fx \vee {\sim}Gx) \equiv {\sim}Gx]$
$(\exists x)(Hx \equiv Fx)$
$(\forall x)({\sim}Fx \supset Gx)$
___
${\sim}(\forall x)(Hx \equiv Gx)$

2 Show that the following sets of statement forms are deductively inconsistent.

(a) $\{(\forall x)(Fx \supset Gx), (\forall x){\sim}Gx, Fa, Ha\}$
(b) $\{(\forall x)(Fx \supset Gx), {\sim}(\exists x)(Fx \wedge Gx), (\exists x)Fx\}$
*(c) $\{(\forall x)(Fx \supset Gx), (\forall x)(Gx \supset Hx), Fa, (\forall x)(Fx \supset {\sim}Hx)\}$
(d) $\{Fa, {\sim}Ga, (\forall x)[Fx \supset (Hx \vee Ix)], {\sim}Ia, {\sim}(\exists x)(Hx \wedge {\sim}Jx),$
$(\forall x)[(Hx \wedge Jx) \supset Gx]\}$
*(e) $\{(\forall x)(Fx \supset Gx), (\exists x)(Hx \wedge Fx), (\forall x)(Hx \supset {\sim}Fx)\}$

3 Show that the following pairs of statement forms are deductively equivalent.

(a) $(\forall x)(Fa \wedge Gx)$ $Fa \wedge (\forall x)Gx$
(b) $(\forall x)Fx$ $(\forall x)[Fx \wedge (Fx \vee Gx)]$
(c) $(\exists x)Fx$ $(\exists x)[Fx \vee (Fx \wedge Gx)]$
(d) $(\forall x)(Fx \vee Gx)$ $(\forall x)({\sim}Gx \supset Fx)$
(e) $(\forall x)(Fx \supset Ga)$ $(\exists x)Fx \supset Ga$
(f) $(\forall x)[(Fx \vee Gx) \supset Hx]$ $(\forall x)[(Fx \supset Hx) \wedge (Gx \supset Hx)]$

4   Show that the following statement forms are logical theorems of $\mathfrak{I}$.

   (a) $(\forall x)[\sim(Fx \supset Gx) \supset Fx]$
*(b) $\sim(\exists x)(Fx \land \sim Fx)$
   (c) $(\forall x)[Fx \supset (\sim Fx \supset Fx)]$
   (d) $(\forall x)[\sim Fx \lor (Gx \supset Fx)]$
   (e) $(Fa \supset Ga) \supset (\exists x)(Fx \supset Gx)$

5   Show that the following arguments are valid in the syntactic sense.
   (a) All insulated homes not only are warm but also save energy. All recent homes are insulated. Therefore, all recent homes are warm.
*(b) All students take either mathematics or logic. But some students do not take mathematics. Therefore, some students take logic.
   (c) Only doctors can practice medicine. Some medical practitioners are not licensed. Therefore, some doctors are not licensed.
   (d) All idealists deny the reality of matter. No materialist denies the reality of matter. Therefore, no materialist is an idealist.
*(e) All communists are revolutionaries. Some communists are Marxists. All Marxist revolutionaries despise the bourgeoisie. Therefore, some communists despise the bourgeoisie.
   (f) My armadillo, Charlemagne, is exceptionally affectionate. Unfortunately, Charlemagne also has repulsive eating habits. Now, nothing can be a desirable pet if it excites disgust. Moreover, everything with repulsive eating habits is sure to provoke disgust. I suppose, then, that my armadillo isn't a desirable pet.
   (g) Some of those who voted for Sanchez also supported the governor's tax bill. Some members of the union also voted for Sanchez. However, there weren't any union members who backed the governor's tax bill. In consequence, it appears that not everyone who voted for Sanchez also supported the governor's tax bill.

REVIEW EXERCISES FOR CHAPTER 8

1   Define the following concepts.
   (a) Name
   (b) Predicate expression
   (c) Simple predication
   (d) Variable word
   (e) Open sentence
   (f) Standard form

2   Determine whether each of the following argument forms is semantically valid. If it is semantically valid, also show that it is syntactically valid. Provide counterinterpretations for those argument forms which are not semantically valid.

   (a) $(\forall x)(Fx \supset Gx)$ *(b) $\sim(\exists x)(Fx \land \sim Gx)$
        $(\exists x)(Hx \land \sim Gx)$ $\sim(\exists x)(Gx \land Hx)$

        _____   _____
        $(\exists x)(Hx \land \sim Fx)$ $(\forall x)(Hx \supset \sim Fx)$

(c) $(\forall x)[Fx \supset (Gx \wedge Hx)]$
$(\exists x)(Ix \wedge Gx)$
$(\exists x)(Ix \wedge \sim Hx)$
_____
$(\forall x)(Fx \supset Ix)$

(d) $(\forall x)(Fx \supset Gx)$
$(\exists x)(Hx \wedge Gx)$
$(\exists x)(Hx \wedge \sim Gx)$
_____
$(\forall x)(Fx \supset Hx)$

(e) $(\forall x)[Fx \supset (Gx \vee Hx)]$
$(\forall x)(Gx \supset \sim Hx)$
$(\exists x)(Fx \wedge Hx)$
_____
$(\exists x)(Fx \wedge \sim Gx)$

*(f) $(\forall x)[Fx \supset (Gx \wedge Hx)]$
$(\exists x)(Gx \wedge Ix)$
$\sim(\forall x)(Ix \supset Hx)$
_____
$(\forall x)(Fx \supset Ix)$

(g) $(\forall x)[(Fx \wedge Gx) \supset Hx]$
$(\exists x)(Ix \wedge Hx)$
$(\exists x)(Ix \wedge \sim Hx)$
_____
$(\forall x)(Fx \supset Ix)$

*(h) $(\forall x)\{(Fx \vee Gx) \supset [(Hx \vee Ix) \supset Jx]\}$
_____
$(\forall x)[Fx \supset (Hx \supset Jx)]$

(i) $(\forall x)[(Fx \vee Gx) \supset (Hx \vee Ix)]$
$(\forall x)(Gx \equiv Jx)$
$(\forall x)(Jx \supset \sim Ix)$
_____
$(\forall x)(Gx \supset Hx)$

(j) $(\forall x)[(Fx \vee Gx) \supset Hx]$
$(\forall x)[(Hx \vee Ix) \supset Jx]$
$(\forall x)[Jx \supset (Kx \wedge Lx)]$
$(\exists x)[Fx \wedge (\sim Kx \wedge \sim Mx)]$
_____
$(\exists x)[Gx \wedge (Mx \wedge \sim Kx)]$

3 Determine whether each of the following arguments is semantically valid. If so, also show that it is syntactically valid.

*(a) Democrats and Republicans are either politicians or public servants. A person is a liberal if and only if he or she is a Democrat. But, no liberal is a politician. Consequently, liberals are public servants.

(b) No person who is liberal but either a Democrat or Republican is consistent. Therefore, no person who is a consistent liberal is both a Democrat and a Republican.

(c) All persons are mortal. No mortal is perfect. But, Jones is a person. Therefore, Jones is not perfect.

*(d) All plumbers and electricians are union members. Some union members go on strike. Some of those who go on strike are not union members. Therefore, some plumbers go on strike.

(e) All gods are omnipotent and omniscient beings. Some gods are omnibenevolent. Therefore, some omnipotent beings are omnibenevolent.

chapter 9
Predicate Logic II

MANY-PLACE PREDICATES: RELATIONS

So far, the only simple predications we have considered are statements consisting of a name and a predicate expression. There are limits on the logical form we can capture using that analysis. Consider the following three sentences:

 1a John is taller than Mary.
 2a Jane is taller than Mary.
 3a John is taller than Sam.

Statements (1a) and (2a) both contain the expression *is taller than Mary*; in addition, each contains a name (*John* or *Jane*). Consequently, we might see their standard forms as

 1b Of John: he is taller than Mary.
 2b Of Jane: she is taller than Mary.

Hence, we could view them as containing the same predicate expression and different names. Now look at statements (1a) and (3a). Again, there is an obvious similarity of form, but it is a different similarity: each contains something which we can view as a predicate expression (*John is taller than*) and a name (*Mary* or *Sam*). Consequently, we could write the standard forms for (1a) and (3a) as

 1c Of Mary: John is taller than she.
 2c Of Sam: John is taller than he.

This gives us two distinct standard forms for (1a) and two distinct predicate expressions: *is taller than Mary* and *John is taller than*. Which of these is correct? Obviously, the answer is that both are, up to a point. Statements (1a), (2a), and (3a) all have something in common, but it's not something that we can get at with the analysis of predications we've used so far. What they have in common is just the expression *is taller than*. This isn't like the predicate expressions in Chapter 8, since combining it with a name doesn't give a statement. However, combining it with two names does, as our examples indicate. Consequently, we call it a *two-place predicate expression*. The present section deals with two-place (and more) predicate expressions. We'll also use the term *relational expression* to mean *two-place predicate expression*. Also, we now use the phrase *simple relational statement* for any statement consisting of a relational expression and two names.

Obviously, in order to formalize relational expressions, we need some additional elements in the syntax of $\mathcal{P}$. To do this, we simply add *two-place predicate variables* to the predicate variables already in $\mathcal{P}$ (later, we'll add three-place, four-place, etc., variables). In fact, to be precise, we should call our old predicate variables *one-place predicate variables*. We use exactly the same stock of letters for two-place predicate variables as for one-place, but in order to indicate that they're two-place variables, we add a superscript 2 to the upper right of each letter:

$$F^2, F^2_1, F^2_2, \ldots$$
$$G^2, G^2_1, G^2_2, \ldots$$
$$H^2, H^2_1, H^2_2, \ldots$$
$$\cdot \quad \cdot \quad \cdot$$

We need these superscript numbers to tell us how many places the variable requires, that is, how many individual constants or variables go with the predicate variable to make a simple statement form. Thus, these superscripts are needed for the formation rules of $\mathcal{P}$. Consider the two expressions

is tall
is taller than

The first of these would be formalized with a one-place predicate variable, and the second with a two-place variable. This reflects the fact that the first expression combines with *one* name to form a statement (e.g., *John is tall*) while the second requires *two* names (e.g., *John is taller than Jim*). Obviously, it would simply be nonsense to assert *John is tall Jim* or *John is taller than*. In English, we recognize the number of names that a predicate expression requires on the basis of linguistic intuitions. However, in $\mathcal{P}$ we need some explicit syntactic device such as superscripts. (Technically, perhaps we should place superscript 1's on our one-place predicate variables also.)

With these additional predicate variables, then, we're able to formalize simple relational statements. We proceed just as we did with one-place predicates, except that we follow each two-place predicate variable with *two* terms. Thus, to formalize *John is taller than Jim*, we would formalize *John* and *Jim* with individual constants (we'll use a and b) and *is taller than* with a two-place predicate variable (we'll use F^2). The result is then

F^2ab

Notice that in $\mathcal{P}$ the order of the names following a two-place predicate variable is of considerable importance. Consequently, in formalizing it's sometimes useful to note down a *quasi-predicate form*, indicating which name is formalized by which term following the predicate variable. By a *quasi-predicate form* we mean simply an open sentence containing a relational expression or other many-place predicate expression, for instance,

x is taller than y.

To help in formalizing, we then note what predicate variable we use for this expression and in what order the variables appear after it:

x is taller than $y = F^2xy$.

This tells us that we are formalizing *is taller than* with F^2, that the name which goes to the *left* of *is taller than* is formalized by the *first* term after F^2, and that the name which goes to the *right* of *is taller than* is formalized by the *second* term after F^2.

We'll also adopt another convention, at least most of the time. Usually, we can get by without actually writing the superscripts on the predicate variables: we can tell whether a predicate variable is one-place, two-place, etc., simply by looking at the number of terms following it. Of course, this amounts to assuming that every expression is syntactically correct and that nothing is followed by too many or too few terms. In order to make this convention work, we must *never use two predicate variables within the same context that differ only by their superscripts*. Thus, we wouldn't use both F_1 and F_1^2 in formalizing the same argument.

Obviously, we'll also need to modify our standard forms to take account of predicate expressions requiring more than one place. We could try to do this by simply writing the names to be substituted into an open sentence in parentheses before it. Thus, we might put

Los Angeles is larger than San Francisco.

into standard form as

Of (Los Angeles, San Francisco): it is larger than it.

Unfortunately, this doesn't tell us which name to put where, so we don't know whether it's the standard form for *Los Angeles is larger than San Francisco* or *San Francisco is larger than Los Angeles*. Consequently, we'll make use of quasi-predicate forms and variables in our standard forms, noting with an equals sign (=) which name is to be substituted for which variable:

Of (Los Angeles = x, San Francisco = y): x is larger than y.

Using this method of putting statements into standard form will also assist us later when we come to quantifications involving relational expressions.

Words which often indicate relational expressions are prepositions such as *with*, *on*, *in*, as the following illustrate:

Chicago is in Illinois.	Of (Chicago = x, Illinois = y): x is in y.
Mary is with Jane.	Of (Mary = x, Jane = y): x is with y.
The cat is on the mat.	Of (the cat = x, the mat = y): x is on y.

In general, any word that indicates a relation in time or space may be treated as a relational expression. Frequently, words which indicate relations require a preposition, most often *of*:

Albany *is the Capital of* New York.
Miriam *is mayor of* Klopstokia.
Sam *is a friend of* Alice.

Transitive verbs can usually be treated as relational expressions:

John *hit* Mary.
I *have read* the *Iliad*.
Melissa *saw* Mercury.
Phil *hates* Uncle Ezra.

Prepositions often function with verbs to indicate relations:

We *are going to* Denver.
Phyllis *lives in* Idaho.
Alas, poor Elmer *has fallen into* the ocean.

In Chapter 2, we noted that *and* sometimes operates to join two words into a single subject rather than as a truth-functional connecting word.

Ordinarily, when this happens, *and* is functioning as part of a relational expression. For instance, the statement

George and Martha are friends.

is really a relational statement. In standard form, it would be

Of (George = x, Martha = y): x and y are friends.

Some further examples illustrate this use of *and*:

Klopstokia *and* Barbaria *are at war.*
The United States *and* England *share many traditions.*
George *and* Martha *were fighting.*
Mary *and* Jane *are sisters.*

Another form of relational expression to be noted is that involving the possessive. Consider the following statement:

George is Martha's brother.

This is clearly a relational statement about George and Martha. We might put it into standard form as

Of (George = x, Martha = y): x is y's brother.

However, we can also convert a possessive into an expression using *of*: thus, we can change *Martha's brother* into *brother of Martha*.

We have considered here only a few of the more obvious types of relational expressions. However, with these examples and suggestions, generally you should be able to identify English expressions that are best interpreted as indicating relations.

EXERCISE 9.1

Put the following simple relational statements into standard form.
1 Kansas is immediately south of Nebraska.
*2 Leroy is much more intelligent than Alfred.
3 Mount Everest is taller than Mount Whitney.
*4 Michael lives in Switzerland.
5 That coat belongs to Martha.
6 Jones has read *Robinson Crusoe*.
7 The Emperor Claudius was succeeded by Nero.
8 Hortense stole $1 million from the Last National Bank.
*9 Jack and Jill are cousins.
10 Kansas City, Missouri, is larger than Kansas City, Kansas.

9.1.1 Compound Statements with Relational Expressions

Since we already know how to formalize compound statements containing simple predications, we're essentially ready to formalize compound statements involving simple relational statements. We proceed as before, first symbolically abbreviating by formalizing the atomic constituents (predications and relational statements) and formalizing any connectives. For instance, to formalize

Juan and Bill are brothers, but Alice and Mary aren't sisters.

we first formalize the names and the relational expressions:

Fab, but not Gcd.

and finally arrive at the formalization:

$Fab \land \sim Gcd$

Just as with one-place predicates, sometimes we find compounds involving relational expressions which have one or more names in common:

Juan is older than Bill but younger than Mary.

Notice that this means the same as

Juan is older than Bill, but Juan is younger than Mary.

Consequently, we formalize it as

$Fab \land Gac$

where $a = Juan$, $b = Bill$, $c = Mary$, $Fxy = x$ is older than y, and $Gxy = x$ is younger than y. Note how the last example differs from the following:

Juan is older than Bill, but Mary is younger.

This is equivalent to

Juan is older than Bill, but Mary is younger than Bill.

Consequently, using individual constants and predicate variables as before, we formalize it as

$Fab \land Gcb$

Sometimes, two names are joined with a connecting word, just as with simple predications:

Al and Alice both like Dallas.

Using $Fxy = x$ *likes* y, this becomes:

$Fab \land Fcb$

Disjunctions also appear in this form: the statement

Either Tony or Mark hates Julie.

becomes

$Fab \lor Fcb$

Relational expressions may share a name in either place, of course:

George likes New Orleans and San Francisco. $Fab \land Fac$
Leroy knows either Martha or Phyllis. $Fab \lor Fac$

More complex statements may involve several names in each place:

Either Sam or Sid knows both Larry and Mary.
$(Fac \land Fad) \lor (Fbc \land Fbd)$

Sometimes, it's rather difficult to disentangle a complicated compound of relational statements. Take, for instance,

Louis, Louise, and Margaret all know Tom, Dick, or Harry.

To analyze this, it's best to put it into standard form, one step at a time:

Of Louis, Louise, and Margaret: he knows Tom, Dick, or Harry.

Of course, this amounts to the conjunction of the statements we obtain by substituting the names *Louis, Louise, Margaret* into the open sentence *he knows Tom, Dick, or Harry.* Now, let's consider one of those:

Of Louis: he knows Tom, Dick, or Harry.

This can be analyzed into standard form as follows:

Of (Louis = x; Tom, Dick, or Harry = y): x knows y.

Here, we've modified our standard form to indicate the abbreviation of the disjunction of all those statements we get by substituting the names *Tom*, *Dick*, *Harry* into the open sentence *Louis knows him*. Thus, the full statement is the conjunction of all the statements we form by substituting the names *Louis*, *Louise*, *Margaret* for x in the disjunction of all the open sentences we form by substituting the names *Tom*, *Dick*, *Harry* for y in the open sentence *x knows y*. Written out in full, this would be

> Either Louis knows Tom, or Louis knows Dick, or Louis knows Harry; and either Louise knows Tom, or Louise knows Dick, or Louise knows Harry; and either Margaret knows Tom, or Margaret knows Dick, or Margaret knows Harry.

Formalized with *a*, *b*, *c* for *Louis*, *Louise*, *Margaret* and *d*, *e*, *f* for *Tom*, *Dick*, *Harry*, this is

$$[(Fad \lor Fae) \lor Faf] \land [(Fbd \lor Fbe) \lor Fbf] \land [(Fcd \lor Fce) \lor Fcf]$$

In order to clarify the structure of statements like this one, often we use standard forms like the following, which is the standard form for this example:

> Of (Louis, Louise, and Margaret = x; Tom, Dick or Harry = y): x knows y.

When a standard form is presented in this fashion, it is to be interpreted as follows. First, form all substitutions of names in the open form according to the *last* (i.e., *extreme right*) list of names indicated; then, form all substitutions in those open forms according to the *next set of names to the left*; and so on. In this case, we begin by substituting the names *Tom*, *Dick*, *Harry* for y in the open sentence *x knows y* and forming the disjunction of all those resulting open sentences:

> x knows Tom or x knows Dick or x knows Harry.

Then we substitute the names *Louis*, *Louise*, *Margaret* for x in this open sentence and conjoin the results:

> Louis knows Tom or Louis knows Dick or Louis knows Harry; and Louise knows Tom or. . . .

Standard forms of this sort help us to distinguish statements that appear similar at first. For instance, the example just considered resembles

> Either Louis or Louise or Margaret knows Tom, Dick, and Harry.

However, in standard form this becomes

Of (Louis or Louise or Margaret = x;
Tom and Dick and Harry = y): x knows y.

Formalizing this, using the same formalization as above, yields

$[(Fad \wedge Fae) \wedge Faf] \vee [(Fbd \wedge Fbe) \wedge Fbf] \vee [(Fcd \wedge Fce) \wedge Fcf]$

Sometimes, we find the connecting word *or* not functioning as a disjunction, as in

Tom is taller than either Mary or Larry.

This is equivalent not to *Tom is taller than Mary or Tom is taller than Larry*, in most contexts, but to

Tom is taller than Mary *and* Tom is taller than Larry.

Thus, its correct formalization is

$Fab \wedge Fac$

A word often used in combining relational statements is *respectively*, as in the following:

Alice and Al are married to Phil and Phyllis, *respectively*.

This clearly means the same thing as

Alice is married to Phil and Al is married to Phyllis.

Thus, *respectively* allows us to take two relational statements which have different terms in both places and assert their conjunction by putting both terms for one place on one side, joined with *and*, and both terms for the other place on the other side, joined with *and*. Formalizing here will give us

$Fab \wedge Fcd$

Obviously, both one- and two-place predicate expressions may occur in the same compound statement:

If Tom is wise, he won't ignore Mary.

We might put this into standard form as

If of Tom: he is wise, then of (Tom = x, Mary = y): not (x will ignore y).

However, we can also write this standard form as

Of (Tom = x, Mary = y): if x is wise, then x won't ignore y.

The corresponding formalization is

$Fa \supset {\sim}Gab$

Note that here, as the context makes clear, G is a two-place predicate variable while F is one-place. Some further examples, with their formalizations, will illustrate the technique of formalizing relational expressions.

In these examples we use the following formalizations:

Fxy	$= x$ loves y	$a =$ Tom
Gx	$= x$ is thoughtful	$b =$ Dick
Hxy	$= x$ is related to y	$c =$ Harry
Ixy	$= x$ despises y	$d =$ Mary
Jxy	$= x$ and y are friends	$e =$ Jane
Kx	$= x$ is an idiot	$f =$ Alice
Lx	$= x$ is rich	
Mxy	$= x$ is richer than y	

Even though Tom and Dick both love Jane, she doesn't love Tom and despises Dick.	$(Fae \wedge Fbe) \wedge ({\sim}Fea \wedge Ieb)$
Harry is rich, but Alice is richer.	$Lc \wedge Mfc$
Tom, Dick, and Harry are all related.	$[(Hab \wedge Hbc) \wedge Hca] \wedge$ $\quad [(Hac \wedge Hcb) \wedge Hba]$
Dick is an idiot, but his rich friend Mary is thoughtful.	$Kb \wedge [(Jdb \wedge Ld) \wedge Gd]$
That idiot Tom is richer than his friends Harry and Mary.	$[Ka \wedge (Mac \wedge Mad)] \wedge$ $\quad (Jac \wedge Jad)$
Alice loves Harry despite the fact that he despises her friend Jane.	$Ffc \wedge (Ice \wedge Jfe)$
Dick is an idiot unless he loves Jane.	${\sim}Fbe \supset Kb$
Alice is richer than either Jane, who is an idiot, or Harry, whom Jane despises.	$(Mfe \wedge Ke) \wedge (Mfc \wedge Iec)$

EXERCISE 9.1.1

Formalize the following statements.
*1   John loves Marcia, but she doesn't love him.
2   Sam moved to New York, where Julio used to live.
*3   If you don't get out of my yard, I'm going to shoot you.
4   Mary and Martha both live in the Aardvark Arms Apartments, but Mary doesn't know Martha.
*5   Jones and Smith are from North and South Dakota, respectively.
6   You don't really understand French unless you live in France.
*7   New York, California, and Montana are smaller than Texas, but Alaska is larger.
8   If John talks to me, then I'll talk to him; but I won't talk to Arthur unless Mary does.
*9   Bill is mean, but he's not as mean as Freddie.
10   If I see Margaret today, then I'll say hello.
*11   If Martha and Mark both went to the Super Bowl, then so did John.
12   Even though *Moby Dick* is a famous book, I still haven't read it.

9.1.2 Other Many-Place Predicates

In addition to the two-place relational expressions considered so far, there are also predicate expressions with three and more places. A simple three-place predicate expression is *is between . . . and*, as in

> Oregon *is between* California *and* Washington.

To formalize three-, four-, and other many-place predicates, we introduce into $\mathcal{P}$ predicate variables of all numbers of places. Thus, we have collections of three-place predicate variables:

$$F^3, F^3_1, F^3_2, \ldots$$
$$G^3, G^3_1, G^3_2, \ldots$$
$$H^3, H^3_1, H^3_2, \ldots$$
$$\ldots \ldots \ldots$$

four-place predicate variables:

$$F^4, F^4_1, F^4_2, \ldots$$
$$G^4, G^4_1, G^4_2, \ldots$$
$$H^4, H^4_1, H^4_2, \ldots$$
$$\ldots \ldots \ldots$$

and, in general, for any positive integer n, n-place predicate variables:

$$F^n, F^n_1, F^n_2, \ldots$$
$$G^n, G^n_1, G^n_2, \ldots$$
$$H^n, H^n_1, H^n_2, \ldots$$
$$\ldots \ldots \ldots$$

Formalizing, then, proceeds in a way similar to that for two-place relational expressions. Formalizing *x is between y and z* with F^3xyz (or simply $Fxyz$), the example above becomes

> $Fabc$

An example of a four-place predicate expression is *x hit y on z with w*, as in the statement

> Mary hit George on the thumb with the hammer.

By formalizing *x hit y on z with w* with F^4xyzw (or simply $Fxyzw$), this becomes

> $Fabcd$

As this example suggests, four-place (and more) predicates are much less common than one-, two-, and three-place predicate expressions. However, if necessary, we can formalize a predicate expression with any number of places in $\mathcal{P}$.

EXERCISE 9.1.2

Formalize the following statements (it may be necessary to use predicate variables with as many as four places).

1 Alabama is between Mississippi and Georgia.
*2 Sam sat across from Mary, who was between Alice and Jim.
3 Chicago is between Los Angeles and New York in size.
4 Two plus three equals five.
*5 William and Mary are George's parents.
*6 The earth is closer to the moon than Mercury is to the sun.
7 I had lunch yesterday with Hrothgar and Grindl, who are friends of mine.
*8 London is closer to Paris than Los Angeles is to San Francisco.
9 Martinez hired Wilson as her assistant, and she agreed to pay him as much as she pays Stephenson.
*10 Miguel, Carla, and Phil shared the work equally.

9.2

MULTIPLE QUANTIFICATION

Just as with one-place predicate expressions, many-place predicate expressions may occur in quantifications. When they do, we may find more than one quantifier operating on a single predicate form. Multiple quantification of this sort introduces certain new problems: we need to determine with care just which quantifier goes with which predicate position. Let's approach multiple quantification in steps. We've already become familiar with statements like the following:

> John loves Marcia, Alice, and Jane.
> John, William, and Sam love Martha.
> John or Michael loves Margaret.

In putting those into standard form, we followed this procedure:

> Of (John = x; Marcia, Alice, and Jane = y): x loves y.
> Of (John, William, and Sam = x; Martha = y): x loves y.
> Of (John or Michael = x; Margaret = y): x loves y.

Obviously, each of these examples is formed by conjunctions and disjunctions of various substitution instances of the open sentence x *loves* y. Let's consider what happens when we introduce a quantifier. Remember, we treat quantifiers as asserting the conjunction or disjunction of *all* substitution instances of an open sentence. Take, first, the statement

> John loves everybody.

We can formalize this by translating *everybody* in the usual way, arriving at the standard form

> Of (John = x; everything = y): if y is a person, then x loves y.

Formalizing gives us

> $(\forall x)(Fy \supset Gay)$

where $Fx = x$ *is a person*, $Gxy = x$ *loves* y, and $a = John$. Now, let's consider what happens if we generalize *this* statement. First, consider

> John, Fred, or Marcia loves everybody.

In standard form, this becomes

> Of (John, Fred, or Marcia = x; everybody = y): x loves y.

Here, *first* we make all possible substitutions for y in x *loves* y and conjoin the resulting expressions; *then* we substitute the names *John, Fred, Marcia* for x in that resulting long expression and form the *disjunction* of all those statements:

John loves Abigail and John loves Bertha and John loves Charles and . . . ; or, Fred loves Abigail and Fred loves Bertha and Fred loves Charles and . . . ; or, Marcia loves Abigail and Marcia loves Bertha and Martha loves Charles and. . . .

Of course, this is just what we would formalize as

$$[(\forall x)Fax \lor (\forall x)Fbx] \lor (\forall x)Fcx$$

Now, suppose we expand this by substituting *every possible* name for x and forming the disjunction of the resulting statements. The result will be

Abigail loves Abigail and Abigail loves Bertha and . . . ; or Bertha loves Abigail and Bertha loves Bertha and . . . ; or. . . .

Formalizing and introducing a universal quantifier as before, we obtain

$$(\forall x)Fax \lor (\forall x)Fbx \lor (\forall x)Fcx \, . . .$$

Now, a disjunction of all possible substitution instances of an open form is what we interpret as an existential quantification. However, in order to write the last statement form with a quantifier, we need to remember that two different substitutions are going on. *First*, we are substituting for the *right-hand* side, *then* for the *left-hand* side. To indicate this, we need to use a different variable with the second quantifier, as follows:

$$(\exists y)(\forall x)Fyx$$

What this says is: for *at least one term* y, Fyx is true for *every term* x.

Interpreting multiple quantifications can be quite tricky, especially with respect to quantifier order. The fact is that natural language is frequently ambiguous in this area, and sometimes we don't have a clear idea of what we mean by some multiple quantifications. Consider first

John doesn't like Sam, but someone does.

Using $Fxy = x$ *likes* y, $a = $ *John*, $b = $ *Sam*, we formalize it as

$$\sim Fab \land (\exists x)Fxb$$

Note that since x doesn't occur in Fab, the quantifier $(\exists x)$ would be vacuous in operating on it. Consequently, we could also formalize this last example as

$$(\exists x)(\sim Fab \land Fxb)$$

Contrast this example with

John doesn't like Sam, but he does like someone.

Here, the quantifier governs a different position after the predicate variable:

$\sim Fab \land (\exists x)Fax$

Now, consider these two statements:

John likes Sam if anyone does.
If John likes Sam, then anyone does.

The first is equivalent to

If anyone likes Sam, then John likes Sam.

This says that if at least one person likes Sam, then John likes Sam. Consequently, it's an existential quantification. With $Fx = x$ *is a person*, $Gxy = x$ *likes* y, $a = Sam$, $b = John$, we formalize it as

$(\exists x)[(Fx \land Gxa) \supset Gba]$

The second example says that if John likes Sam, then *any* person will like Sam. Here, then, we use a universal quantifier:

$Gba \supset (\forall x)(Fx \supset Gxa)$

Notice that we formalize *anyone* with an existential quantifier in one example and a universal quantifier in the other. This follows the rule we set down in the previous chapter of treating *anyone* as a universal quantifier when in the consequent of a conditional and an existential quantifier in the antecedent.

Relative clauses often provide complicated multiple quantification:

Anyone who likes Sam likes John.

Note that this means

For any person, if that person likes Sam, then that person likes John.

In standard form, this is

For $(x = $ anyone$)$: if x likes Sam, then x likes John.

We can formalize this as

$(\forall x)[(Fx \wedge Gxa) \supset Gax]$

A more complicated example is

John likes everyone who likes him.

This is equivalent to

For every person, if that person likes John, then John likes him.

We can formalize this as

$(\forall x)[(Fx \wedge Gxa) \supset Gax]$

As these two examples show, relative clauses with *who* and similar words (*which*, *that*, etc.) are usually treated as the antecedents of conditionals. The following is a bit more complex:

There is somebody who doesn't like anybody unless that person likes him.

Standard form helps clarify this:

Of (somebody = x; anybody = y): x doesn't like y unless y likes x.

Using predicate variables as above, we can reach a symbolic abbreviation:

Of (something = x; everything = y): Fx and if Fy, then not Gxy unless Gyx.

Formalizing, then, gives us

$(\exists x)(\forall y)\{Fx \wedge [Fy \supset (\sim Gyx \supset \sim Gxy)]\}$

Sometimes, it's convenient to introduce quantifiers in analyzing certain expressions. For instance, instead of treating *horse owner* as a simple predicate, we might treat it as a compound of the simple predicate *horse* and the relational expression *owner:*

x is a horse owner = $(\exists y)y$ is a horse and x owns y.

Frequently, we must use this sort of analysis to explain the validity of arguments. For instance, the following is obviously a valid argument:

All horses are animals.
Therefore, all horse owners own animals.

We can formalize this as follows, using $Fx = x$ *is a horse*, $Gx = x$ *is an animal*, $Hxy = x$ *owns* y:

$$(\forall x)(Fx \supset Gx)$$
$$\overline{(\forall x)[(\exists y)(Fy \wedge Hxy) \supset (\exists z)(Gz \wedge Hxz)]}$$

Notice that we used the variable y in spelling out *horse owners* and the variable z in spelling out *animal owners*. Strictly speaking, this isn't necessary: the open form $(\exists z)(Gz \wedge Hxz)$ is outside the scope of the quantifier $(\exists y)$, and so we could have written this form as $(\exists y)$ $(Gy \wedge Hxy)$. However, we want to avoid things that even appear ambiguous, and so we always use a new variable for each new quantifier, just to be safe.

Another example of implicit existential quantifiers is

We visited all the capital cities of Europe.

We could, of course, treat *capital city* as a one-place predicate expression, but we can express more logical form by noting that *is capital of* is a relational expression. Thus, our example means the same as

We visited every city which is capital of some country in Europe.

Then, using $Fx = x$ *is a city*, $Gxy = x$ *is capital of* y, $Hx = x$ *is a country*, $Ix = x$ *is in Europe*, $Jxy = x$ *visited* y, and $a = we$, we get

$$(\forall x)(\{Fx \wedge (\exists y)[(Hy \wedge Iy) \wedge Gxy]\} \supset Jax)$$

Possessives often give rise to complex forms, as in

Some parents can't stand any of their children's friends.

This sentence says that there are *some* parents who can't stand *any* person who is a friend of *any* of their children: there are thus three quantifiers in its formalization. Using $Fx = x$ *is a parent*, $Gxy = x$ *can stand* y, $Hxy = x$ *is a child of* y, $Ixy = x$ *is a friend of* y, we have

$$(\exists x)\{Fx \wedge (\forall y)[(\exists z)(Hzx \wedge Iyz) \supset \sim Gxy]\}$$

Notice that in effect we formalized y *is a friend of a child of* x as

Of (something $= z$): z is a child of x and y is a friend of z.

which, when formalized, becomes the open form $(\exists z)(Hzx \wedge Iyz)$. Note here that we could have analyzed this differently by treating it as

Of (something $= x$): x is a parent and of (everything $= y$; everything $= z$): if z is a child of x and y is a friend of z, then x can't stand y.

This would then give us the formalization

$$(\exists x)\{Fx \wedge (\forall y)(\forall z)[(Hzx \wedge Iyz) \supset \sim Gxy]\}$$

As a matter of fact, these formalizations are equivalent. Notice that the existential quantifier in the first includes within its scope only $Hzx \wedge Iyz$, while the universal quantifier $(\forall z)$ in the second includes in its scope the longer form $(Hzx \wedge Iyz) \supset \sim Gxy$. As with single quantifications, we often find that an existential quantifier within the antecedent of an expression is equivalent to the corresponding universal quantifier placed in front of the entire conditional.

A different sort of problem appears in the next example:

Nothing is as hard as a diamond.

If we treat *diamond* as a predicate expression here, then this says that nothing is as hard as anything which is a diamond. In standard form, this is

Of (everything = x; anything = y): if y is a diamond, then x is not as hard as y.

Formalizing this gives us

$$(\forall x)(\forall y)(Fx \supset \sim Gxy)$$

Unfortunately, this could be interpreted as saying that nothing, *not even a diamond*, is as hard as a diamond. Since we don't want that, let's interpret the example to mean

Nothing *else* is as hard as a diamond.

We can interpret this as

If something isn't a diamond, then it isn't as hard as a diamond.

Notice that the *it* in this sentence goes with the quantifier word *something*. This sentence doesn't say *If there is something which isn't a diamond, then there is something which isn't as hard as a diamond*. Instead, it says

For anything you like, if it isn't a diamond, then it isn't as hard as a diamond.

We formalize this as

$$(\forall x)(\forall y)[(\sim Fx \wedge Fy) \supset \sim Gxy]$$

Many statements in natural language are ambiguous in ways that we can clarify with the techniques of formalization. Frequently, we encounter ambiguities involving the scopes of quantifying expressions. Consider, for instance, the statement

Everybody loves somebody.

This could mean that there is some person or other whom everybody loves, or it could mean that every person loves some person or other (but not necessarily the same one). These differences in logical form can be brought out in standard form. The first interpretation is

Of (somebody = x; everybody = y): y loves x.

Formalizing gives us

$(\exists x)(\forall y)Fyx$

Notice that this will be true if and only if, for some term a, all substitutions for y in Fya give true statement forms. In standard form, the second interpretation is

Of (everybody = x; somebody = y): x loves y.

Formalizing then gives

$(\forall x)(\exists y)Fxy$

Notice that this will be true if and only if, for *every* term a, there is some term b such that Fab is true. In terms of the corresponding ordinary language statements, the first interpretation will be true only if there is some person (call him Phil) whom everyone including Phil loves. The second interpretation will be true even if no such person as Phil exists, so long as each person loves someone or other. Notice that the only difference between $(\exists x)(\forall y)Fyx$ and $(\forall x)(\exists y)Fxy$ is in the scopes of the quantifiers. In each, there is a universal quantifier associated with the variable in the first position and an existential quantifier associated with the variable in the second position. However, in $(\exists x)(\forall y)Fyx$, the universal quantifier is within the scope of the existential quantifier, while in $(\forall x)(\exists y)Fxy$ the existential quantifier is within the scope of the universal quantifier. This illustrates how differences of scope or differences in the order of quantifiers can create differences in the meanings of statements.

The techniques of formalization we have learned so far are extremely powerful. With them, we can understand the logical forms that explain the validity of a much wider class of arguments than can be dealt with in statement logic. In fact, the language $\mathcal{P}$ is flexible and powerful enough to deal with the great majority of arguments and statements that occur, with the exception of intensional compounds. Skill in formalizing complex quantification statements requires a good deal of familiarity with a wide variety of natural-language idioms, and there is no way that an introductory text can deal with that subject comprehensively. However, it's usually not difficult to figure out ways of handling different sorts of statements for yourself, once you become familiar with the capabilities of $\mathcal{P}$.

EXERCISE 9.2

1 Formalize each of the following statements, revealing as much logical detail as possible.
  *(a) Only a fool trusts everybody.
  (b) Some people don't like rutabagas, but I prefer them to any other vegetable.
  *(c) No dog likes any cat.
  (d) Someone was sitting on my left, and someone else on my right, and they knew each other.
  *(e) Everyone has parents, although not everyone has children.
  (f) Some people who live in France aren't French.
  *(g) Every even number is the product of 2 and some number.
  (h) Anyone may apply for this position, but only those with college degrees will be seriously considered.
  *(i) John doesn't know how to make lasagna, but someone who does know used to live in that house.
  (j) This key will open any door in any house built by the Snazzy Construction Company.
  *(k) There's no fool like an old fool.
  (l) Some people like only philosophers who write obscure and incomprehensible books.
  *(m) Everyone loves a lover.
  (n) Those students who wish to receive master's degrees in January must complete all requirements by the end of November.
  *(o) Every book that Jones wrote is better than any book that Smith wrote but worse than some book which Brown wrote.

2 Formalize the following arguments.
  (a) Someone has stolen my car. Now, anyone who did that is obviously not trustworthy, and if a person isn't trustworthy, I won't lend them my lawn mower. Consequently, if George stole my car, I won't lend him my lawn mower.
  *(b) Any person who was born in the United States or who is the child of a United States citizen is a United States citizen. Now, Felipe was born in the United States. Therefore, even though Alice, who is Felipe's daughter, was born in Canada, she is a United States citizen.
  *(c) Seventeenth-century European philosophers are all either rationalists or empiricists if they are of importance. However, no important ration-

alists lived in England. Therefore, all seventeenth-century English philosophers are empiricists.

(d) Everyone knows someone or other, and there is nobody whom no one knows. Now, some people know only people who know them, but there are others who know people that don't know them. Consequently, if everyone knows himself, someone knows two other people who don't know each other.

9.3
THE FORMAL SYNTAX OF $\mathcal{P}$

We need only make some slight changes in our formal definition of a statement form of $\mathcal{P}$ to accommodate many-place predicates. Essentially, all we need to modify is the definition of the set **A** of atomic statements. We replace the set **R** with a set of sets of predicate variables of different numbers of places. Thus, $\mathbf{R}_1 = \{F^1, G^1, \ldots\}$, $\mathbf{R}_2 = \{F^2, G^2, \ldots\}$, and in general $\mathbf{R}_n = \{F^n, G^n, \ldots\}$. Note that our old **R** is now $\mathbf{R}_1$. Now we redefine the set **A** as follows:

> For every positive integer n, if $F \in \mathbf{R}_n$ and each of $s_1, s_2, \ldots, s_n \in \mathbf{V}$, then $Fs_1s_2 \ldots s_n \in \mathbf{A}$.

All other formation rules for the system $\mathcal{P}$ remain unchanged.

While our formation rules are effective in distinguishing statement forms of $\mathcal{P}$ from unsyntactic strings of symbols, there is a certain ambiguity involved in multiple quantifications which must be removed. To see the difficulty, consider the following expression:

$(\forall x)(\exists x)Fxx$

Since it begins with the quantifier $(\forall x)$, this is a statement form if and only if it follows the appropriate rule, which says: if A is a statement form, then $(\forall x)A(x/s)$ is. Now, when we remove $(\forall x)$ from our example, the result is

$(\exists x)Fxx$

We *could* get this from $(\exists x)Fax$ by substituting x for a. Therefore, $(\forall x)(\exists x)Fxx$ is a statement form if $(\exists x)Fax$ is. That expression, in turn, is a statement form if and only if Fax can be derived from a statement form by substituting x for some individual constant. We *could* get it by substituting x for b in Fab. Fab is atomic and therefore a statement form.

Consequently, so is $(\exists x)Fax$; consequently, so is $(\forall x)(\exists x)Fxx$. The way the statement form is built up, then, is as follows:

Fab	atomic
Fax	$Fab(x/b)$
$(\exists x)Fax$	statement form by rule 8
$(\exists x)Fxx$	$(\exists x)Fax(x/a)$
$(\forall x)(\exists x)Fxx$	statement form by rule 7

Unfortunately, this isn't the only way that we could arrive at $(\forall x)$ $(\exists x)Fxx$. We could also start with Fab, substitute x/a to get Fxb and then quantify to get $(\exists x)Fxb$, and then substitute x/b and quantify to get $(\forall x)(\exists x)Fxx$. Or, we could start with Faa and substitute x/a to get Fxx, add the quantifier to get $(\exists x)Fxx$, and then substitute (vacuously) x/a again and add a vacuous quantifier to get $(\forall x)(\exists x)Fxx$. Or, we could start with Faa, substitute (vacuously) x/b and quantify to get $(\exists x)Faa$, then substitute x/a and quantify for $(\forall x)(\exists x)Fxx$. Obviously, as it stands, $(\forall x)(\exists x)Fxx$ is terribly ambiguous. The problem is, *we don't know which occurrence of x goes with which quantifier*. We can see the difference if we simply go through the same process as above but use x for the first substitution and y for the second. In that case, the four ways of coming up with $(\forall x)(\exists x)Fxx$ will yield, respectively, $(\forall y)(\exists x)Fyx$, $(\forall y)(\exists x)Fxy$, $(\forall y)(\exists x)Fxx$, and $(\forall y)(\exists x)Fyy$. Just to see how different these are, let $Fxy = x$ *loves* y. Then, the first formalizes *Everybody loves somebody*; the second formalizes *Everybody is loved by somebody*; the third formalizes *Somebody loves himself* $[(\forall y)$ is vacuous]; and the last formalizes *Everybody loves himself* $[(\exists x)$ is vacuous]. As it stands, we don't know which of these $(\forall x)(\exists x)Fxx$ is supposed to be formalizing. What's worse, unless we add some restrictions, $(\forall x)(\exists x)Fxx$ would be the logical form of *all* these statements; but they obviously don't mean the same, and we've just given a *different* logical form for each.

Notice that this is a problem about the *meaning* of a certain expression, and thus it is a *semantic* problem. We don't need to change our formation rules at all. Instead, we only need to decide which one of the four possibilities we're going to use in interpreting $(\forall x)(\exists x)Fxx$—in other words, how we'll apply our semantic rules to it. To make the distinction, we need another concept which is syntactic and not semantic: we distinguish between a *free* and a *bound occurrence* of a variable. An occurrence of a variable in an expression is said to be *free* if the variable is *not within the scope of a quantifier containing the same variable*. Thus, an occurrence of x in an expression is a free occurrence if it is not within the scope of an occurrence of either $(\forall x)$ or $(\exists x)$. Note that an occurrence of x could be free even if it occurred with the scope of an occurrence of, say, $(\forall y)$ or $(\exists z)$. A free occurrence of a variable is produced by substituting a variable for a constant in a statement form. Consequently, free occurrences of variables are found only in open forms, never in statement forms. If an occurrence of a variable is not free, we say that it is *bound*. From the definition, it's clear that a bound occurrence of a variable x will always be within the scope of a quantifier containing the same variable.

Now, the rule we adopt to resolve ambiguous expressions like $(\forall x)(\exists x)Fxx$ is the following: *a quantifier is vacuous unless there is a free occurrence of its variable in the expression on which it operates.* In the case of $(\forall x)(\exists x)Fxx$, this makes the first quantifier vacuous. Consider the expression on which $(\forall x)$ operates here: $(\exists x)Fxx$. There are two occurrences of x in this expression, but they're both within the scope of $(\exists x)$. As a result, there are no *free* occurrences of x in $(\exists x)Fxx$, and the addition of $(\forall x)$ is vacuous. In a way, this is an extension of the notion of a vacuous quantifier. In the previous chapter, we noted that a quantifier is vacuous if its variable doesn't occur in the expression on which it operates. Now, we're saying that a bound occurrence of a variable is not available for any other quantifier to operate on. This requires a restriction on our substitution notation: $A(t/x)$ now means the result of substituting t for every *free* occurrence of x. Thus, if $A = (\forall x)(Fx \supset Gxy)$, $A(a/x) = (\forall x)$ $(Fx \supset Gxy)$, since there are no *free* occurrences of x in A. This restriction will affect both our tree rules and our rules of inference, as we will explain later.

The distinction between free and bound occurrences should never cause any difficulties in formalizing. We've adopted the rule of always using a new variable for every new quantifier, and consequently we can never come up with such things as $(\forall x)(\exists x)Fxx$.

EXERCISE 9.3

1 Identify the free occurrences of variables in the following expressions.

    (a) $(\forall x)(Fx \vee \sim Gxy) \supset (\exists y)Gyx$
  *(b) $(\exists x)(Gx \supset \sim Hy) \vee [(\forall x)Hx \equiv Fx]$
    (c) $(\forall x)[Fx \vee (\exists x)Gx] \supset (\exists x)Hyx$
  *(d) $(\exists x)(\exists y)(Fxy \wedge Fyx) \supset \sim Gyx$
  *(e) $(\exists x)Fx \supset Gx$

2 Determine what occurrences of quantifiers, if any, are vacuous in the following statement forms.

  *(a) $(\exists x)[(\forall x)Gx \supset Hx]$
    (b) $(\forall x)(\forall y)(\forall z)[Fxz \wedge (\exists y)(Fzy \vee Fyz]$
  *(c) $Gac \supset (\exists x)(\forall y)(Gxa \equiv Gcx)$
    (d) $(\forall y)[(\exists x)Fx \supset (\forall x)(Gx \vee Hxy)]$
  *(e) $(\forall x)Fx \supset (\exists x)(\exists y)Fxy$

SEMANTIC TREES FOR MULTIPLE QUANTIFICATIONS

We already have all the techniques necessary to construct semantic trees for any argument form composed of statement forms in $\mathcal{P}$, and so we're ready to test arguments with multiple quantification for validity. The formal semantics for $\mathcal{P}$ remains the same except, of course, that we now require an interpretation to assign a truth value to every many-place atomic predicate form. Of course, the rule for determining free and bound occurrences sometimes may affect the results of our extensions. In particular, the result of extending a statement logic form beginning with a vacuous quantifier is simply the same statement form, slashed or un-slashed as before, without the quantifier. This is because $A(t/x) = A$ if $\mathbf{x}$ does not occur free in A. More generally, when using the tree rules for $\forall$ and $\exists$, we perform our substitutions in accordance with the rules of the last section, substituting only for free occurrences of variables. Ordinarily this will cause us no difficulty, since our procedure for formalizing arguments makes it impossible for the same variable to occur both free and bound in the same open form.

Constructing trees proceeds in exactly the same manner. Take as an example the following argument:

All horses are animals.
Consequently, anyone who owns a horse owns an animal.

Using $Fx = x\text{ is a horse}$, $Gx = x\text{ is an animal}$, $Hxy = x\text{ owns }y$, we formalize this as

$$(\forall x)(Fx \supset Gx)$$
$$\overline{(\forall x)[(\exists y)(Fy \land Hxy) \supset (\exists z)(Gz \land Hxz)]}$$

We construct a tree in the usual manner (the numbers at left indicate the order in which statement forms were extended):

$$
\begin{array}{rl}
3, 6 & (\forall x)(Fx \supset Gx)^{**} \\
1 & \cancel{(\forall x)[(\exists y)(Fy \land Hxy) \supset (\exists z)(Gz \land Hxz)]} \;\checkmark \\
2 & \cancel{(\exists y)(Fy \land Hay) \supset (\exists z)(Gz \land Haz)} \;\checkmark \\
5 & (\exists y)(Fy \land Hay) \\
4, 7 & \cancel{(\exists z)(Gz \land Haz)}^{**} \\
& Fa \supset Ga \\
& \cancel{Ga \land Haa} \\
8 & Fb \land Hab \;\checkmark \\
9 & Fb \supset Gb \;\checkmark
\end{array}
$$

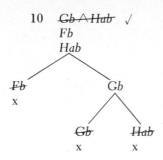

10   ~~Gb∧Hab~~ √
    Fb
    Hab

~~Fb~~
x

Gb

~~Gb~~
x

~~Hab~~
x

Notice that even though this tree is slightly longer than those we encountered in dealing with single quantification, no new principles are involved.
However, the procedure of extending slashed existential and unslashed
universal quantifications often generates many more steps. Here, for instance, four such steps were involved. We give some further examples to
illustrate semantic trees for arguments with multiple quantification, beginning with the following:

> Everyone loves someone. However, some people love only people who do
> not love them in return. Therefore, there are some people who are loved
> by people who do not love themselves.

Formalizing with $Fxy = x$ *loves* y,[1] we get

$$(\forall x)(\exists y)Fxy$$
$$(\exists x)(\forall y)(Fxy \supset \sim Fyx)$$
$$\overline{(\exists x)(\exists y)(Fyx \wedge \sim Fyy)}$$

Now, in constructing a semantic tree for this argument form, we may be
faced with a great many extensions of unslashed universal and slashed
existential quantifications. In order to simplify the procedures, we'll try
to introduce individual constants as slowly as possible. To do this, we
extend some unslashed existential or slashed universal quantifications first
and then instantiate the constant introduced in all available slashed existential or unslashed universal quantifications before we proceed. We continue in this way until we have made use of every premise and of the conclusion at least once before we extend any truth-functional compounds.
Here is a tree for this example:

2, 7 $(\forall x)(\exists y)Fxy$**
   1   $(\exists x)(\forall y)(Fxy \supset \sim Fyx)$ √
3, 8   ~~$(\exists x)(\exists y)(Fyx \wedge \sim Fyy)$~~**
4, 9 $(\forall y)(Fay \supset \sim Fya)$**

---

[1] Since all quantifiers in this argument apply only to persons, we omit the understood
predicate expression *is a person* for convenience.

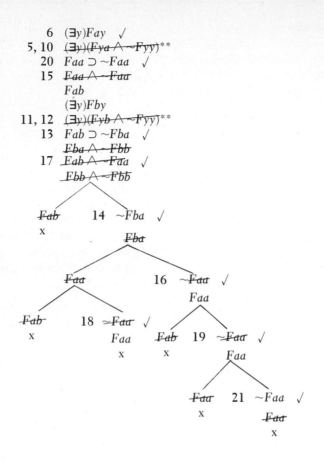

Let's review exactly how this tree is constructed. First, we extended
$(\exists x)(\forall y)(Fxy \supset \sim Fyx)$ to get $(\forall y)(Fay \supset \sim Fya)$. Incidentally, note
that the universal quantifier and its variable y are not affected by the ex-
tension. Then, we extend $(\forall x)(\exists y)Fxy$, $(\exists x)(\exists y)(Fyx \wedge \sim Fyy)$, and
the universal quantification we just added—$(\forall y)(Fay \supset \sim Fya)$—for the
constant a. This gives us $(\exists y)Fay$, $(\exists y)(Fya \wedge \sim Fyy)$, and $Faa \supset$
$\sim Faa$. Since the second of these is a slashed existential quantification,
we extend it for a to get $Faa \wedge \sim Faa$. Now, having extended all available
unslashed universal and slashed existential quantifications with a, we
extend another unslashed existential quantification, $(\exists y)Fay$, to get Fab.
Now, we extend each of the four starred expressions again for b to get
$(\exists y)Fby$, $(\exists y)(Fyb \wedge \sim Fyy)$, $Fab \supset \sim Fba$, and $Fba \wedge \sim Fbb$. Since
the second of these is a slashed existential quantification, we must then
extend it for *both a and b*, getting $Eab \wedge \sim Faa$ and $Ebb \wedge \sim Fbb$. At this
point, we decided to try extending some of the unquantified statement

forms to see if the tree would close. Nine more extensions accomplished this. Notice that although we never extended some of the unquantified truth-functional compounds, nevertheless we needed statements from all stages of our extensions of starred statement forms in order to close the tree.

9.4.1 Infinite Trees

This tree illustrates how multiple quantifications that contain mixed universal and existential quantifiers can generate very lengthy trees. Each time a new constant term is introduced, we must extend all previous starred statement forms, and this may introduce other unslashed universal or slashed existential quantifications which we must extend, in turn, for the new constant. These extensions, in turn, may give rise to new unslashed existential or slashed universal quantifications, which require us to introduce new constant terms. How far can this process continue? The answer, unfortunately, is very far indeed. As a matter of fact, it is possible for a semantic tree to go on forever without either closing or running out of new statement forms to extend. Such a tree can be generated by a single statement, in fact. Consider the following example:

> There is somebody who is happy only if no one is.

Forgetting for the moment about formalizing *someone* with *something* and *is a person*, we can formalize this comparatively innocent statement as

$$(\exists x)(\forall y)(Fx \supset {\sim}Fy)$$

Now, we can use the methods of previous chapters to determine whether this is a logical truth, a contingency, or a contradiction. It is easy to show that it isn't a contradiction:

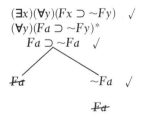

We can extend this tree by extending $(\forall y)(Fa \supset {\sim}Fy)$ for new constants, but obviously that won't get the tree to close. Now, let's see if it is a logical truth:

$(\exists x)(\forall y)(Fx \supset \sim Fy)$***
$(\forall y)(Fa \supset \sim Fy)$ √
$Fa \supset \sim Fb$ √
Fa
$\sim Fb$ √
Fb
$(\forall y)(Fb \supset \sim Fy)$ √
$Fb \supset \sim Fc$ √
Fb
$\sim Fc$ √
Fc
$(\forall y)(Fc \supset \sim Fy)$ √
$Fc \supset \sim Fd$

.
.
.

We've departed slightly from the usual order of extending starred statement forms to show what happens here. Each time we extend $(\exists x)(\forall y)(Fx \supset \sim Fy)$ for a new constant, we get a slashed universal quantification. This gives us another new constant which we must then use to extend $(\exists x)(\forall y)(Fx \supset \sim Fy)$ again. Obviously, the process continues forever, without either the tree's closing or all the extensions being completed.

What we've just illustrated is a major difference between the semantic tree method applied to statement logic and the method applied to predicate logic. Unfortunately, the tree method is not a decision procedure for validity or any of the other semantic notions for the full system of $\mathcal{P}$ with multiple quantification. Unlike statement-logic trees and trees not involving multiple quantifications, there are some trees in predicate logic which neither close nor finish. Now, it is possible to prove that our tree method is still adequate in a limited sense: whenever the premises of an argument form in $\mathcal{P}$ entail its conclusion, then the corresponding semantic tree will close after a finite number of steps. This means that if the tree for an argument form is infinite, then that argument form is invalid. However, there is no mechanical way to tell when we have an infinite tree. The example we just considered is an easy case: after two or three trips through the same circle, we can see that it's not ever going to close. However, we can't give any *mechanical* and *effective* procedure for doing this: any rules that identify some trees as infinite will fail to tell us that some others are. Consequently, although we'll always be able to tell for sure if an argument is valid, we have no effective procedure for telling us that an argument is invalid in predicate logic.

This result is more than an accidental fact about our particular methods. According to a well-known metatheorem, *Church's theorem*, there cannot be *any* mechanical and effective decision procedure for validity and related notions in predicate logic. This is an important result, so let's indicate precisely what it means. In terms of our language $\mathcal{P}$, this means that no *semantic* decision procedure can be produced that will always indicate, after a finite number of steps, whether the premises of any given argument form entail its conclusion. In fact, we can show that our procedure will spot a valid argument (semantically) after a finite number of steps, but we can't always be sure that any particular semantic tree is going to close. This means that we can't determine by any mechanical procedures the difference between an infinite tree and a tree that just hasn't closed *yet*, but will eventually close. Church's theorem says more than this, however. It asserts that *no* mechanical and effective decision procedure of *any* sort exists for predicate logic. Consequently, we must simply give up on one project we might have hoped to accomplish: we can never give a set of procedures that will allow us to determine in every case whether an argument is valid. However, we can still investigate the relationships among various logical notions, including the general question of the relationship between the semantic and the syntactic dimensions of arguments. At least in the case of predicate logic, we will still be able to construct a deductive system that corresponds in the appropriate way to our semantics.

EXERCISE 9.4

1 Determine whether the following argument forms are valid or invalid and give a counterinterpretation for any invalid forms. (None of these examples should yield an infinite tree.)

*(a) $(\exists x)Fxa \supset (\exists y)Fay$
      $(\forall x)(Gbx \supset Fxa)$

      $\overline{(\exists x)Gbx \supset (\exists y)Fay}$

 (b) $(\forall x)(\exists y)(Fxy \supset Fxx)$
      $(\forall x)\{Gx \supset [(\exists z)Fxz \supset (\exists y)Fyx]\}$
      $(\forall x)\sim Fxx$

      $\overline{(\forall x)[Gx \supset \sim(\exists z)Fxz]}$

*(c) $(\forall x)(\forall y)(Fxy \vee \sim Fyy)$
      $(\exists x)(\forall y)Fxy$

      $\overline{(\exists y)(\exists x)(Fxy \wedge Fyx)}$

 (d) $(\forall x)Fax \supset (\exists y)(\exists z)(Gyz \wedge \sim Gay)$
      $(\forall x)(\forall y)\sim Gxy$

      $\overline{\sim(\forall x)Fxx \vee (\exists x)Gxx}$

*(e) $(\exists x)Fx \lor (\exists y)(\forall z)Gyz$
$(\forall x)(\exists y)\sim Gyx$
$(\forall x)[Fx \supset (\exists y)(\forall z)Gzy]$
——————————————————
$(\exists y)(\forall z)Gyz$

(f) $(\forall x)(\forall y)[(Fx \land Gxy) \supset (\exists z)Hxyz]$
$(\forall x)(Gax \supset Fx)$
$(\exists y)Gay$
——————————————————
$\sim (\forall x)(\forall y)(\exists z)(Gaz \lor Hxyz)$

*(g) $(\forall x)Fax \lor (\forall y)(\exists z)(Fya \land \sim Faz)$
$(\exists x)Gxb \supset \sim Fab$
——————————————————
$(\exists x)(\exists y)(Fay \supset Fxa)$

(h) $(\forall x)(\forall y)(Fxy \supset Fyx)$
$(\exists x)(\forall y)Fxy$
——————————————————
$(\exists x)(\forall y)(Fxy \supset Fyx)$

*(i) $(\forall x)\sim Gx$
$(\forall x)(\forall y)(Hxy \supset Fx)$
$(\forall x)(Fx \supset Gx)$
——————————————————
$(\exists x)(\exists y)\sim Hxy$

(j) $(\forall x)(\forall y)Fxy \supset (\exists z)Gz$
——————————————————
$(\exists x)(\exists y)(\exists z)(Fxy \supset Gz)$

*(k) $(\forall x)(\exists y)Fxy$
$(\exists z)(\forall x)[(\exists y)Fxy \supset Fxz]$
——————————————————
$(\exists z)(\forall x)Fxz$

(l) $(\forall x)[Fx \supset (\forall y)(Gxy \supset Hy)]$
$(\forall x)[Ix \supset (\forall y)(Jy \supset Gxy)]$
——————————————————
$(\exists x)(Ix \land Fx) \supset (\forall y)(Jy \supset Hy)$

*(m) $(\exists x)[Fx \land (\forall y)(Fy \supset Gyx)]$
——————————————————
$(\exists x)(Fx \land Gxx)$

(n) $(\forall x)(Fx \supset Gx)$
$(\forall x)(\exists y)(Hy \land Iyx)$
$(\forall x)[(Hx \land Gx) \supset Jx]$
$(\forall x)(\forall y)[(Jy \land Iyx) \supset Jx]$
——————————————————
$(\forall x)(\forall y)[(\sim Fy \supset \sim Ixy) \supset Jx]$

*(o) $(\exists x)(\exists y)[(Fx \land \sim Fy) \land \sim Gxy]$
$(\forall x)(\forall y)[(Fx \land Hy) \supset Gxy]$
——————————————————
$(\exists x)(\sim Fx \land \sim Hx)$

2   Determine whether each of the following arguments is valid or invalid. You may assume that an argument is invalid if you extend some statement form in its tree five or more times without the tree's closing.

*(a)   Any gambler who needs the help of a criminal is desperate. But, then, all gamblers are criminals. Consequently, any gambler who needs his or her own help is desperate.

(b)   Everything in my garage is worth buying. A person who sells anything worth buying performs a great service. Some auctioneer sold some of the lawn mowers in my garage. Therefore, some auctioneer has performed a great service.

*(c)   If any philosopher is wiser than Plato, then she must be more subtle than Aristotle. Now, unless a philosopher is a logician, she must be less subtle than Aristotle. No philosopher alive in 1800, however, was a logician. Consequently, if a philosopher was wiser than Plato, then she wasn't alive in 1800.

(d)   Everyone who came to Philbert's party brought someone else who had never met any of Philbert's friends. However, some people who came also brought friends whom Philbert had already met. Now, Philbert invited all his friends, but some of them didn't come. Hortense didn't go to the party even though she was invited. Consequently, there was someone at the party who had never met Hortense.

3   Determine whether the following statement forms are logically true, contingent, or contradictory.

(a) $(\forall x)[(\exists y)Fxy \supset (\forall z)Fxz] \supset (\forall y)(\forall z)(Fyz \supset Fzy)$
*(b) $(\forall x)Fxx \supset (\forall x)(\exists y)Fxy$
(c) $(\forall x)(Fx \supset Gx) \supset (\forall x)[(\exists y)(Fy \wedge Hxy) \supset (\exists y)(Gy \wedge Hxy)]$
(d) $(\forall x)(\forall y)(\forall z)[(Fxy \wedge Fxz) \supset Fyz] \supset (\forall x)(\forall y)(Fxy \supset Fyx)$
*(e) $(\forall x)Fxx \supset (\forall x)[(\forall y)(Fxy \supset Gy) \supset Gx]$

4   Determine whether the following pairs of statement forms are semantically equivalent.

(a) $(\exists x)[(\exists y)Fxy \supset Gx]$, $(\exists x)(\exists y)(Fxy \supset Gx)$
*(b) $(\forall x)(\forall y)(Fxy \supset Hyx)$, $(\forall y)(\forall x)(Fxy \supset Hyx)$
(c) $(\forall x)[(\exists y)Fxy \supset Gx]$, $(\forall x)(\forall y)(Fxy \supset Gx)$
(d) $(\forall x)[Fx \supset (\exists y)Gyx]$, $(\exists x)(\exists y)(Fx \supset Gyx)$
*(e) $(\forall x)[(\exists y)Fyx \supset Gx]$, $(\forall x)(\forall y)(Fyx \supset Gx)$

9.5

DEDUCTIONS WITH MULTIPLE QUANTIFICATIONS

The rules of inference for system $\mathfrak{I}$ introduced in Section 8.7 are sufficient for deductions involving multiple quantifications. However, certain restrictions must be imposed on the rules of Universal Generalization (U.G.) and Existential Generalization (E.G.) because of difficulties concerning free and bound occurrences of variables. Consider the following two deduction steps, each of which seems to be in accordance with E.G.:

$$m \quad (\forall x)(Fx \supset Gax) \qquad\qquad m \quad (\forall x)(Fx \supset Gax)$$

$$n \quad (\exists y)(\forall x)(Fx \supset Gyx) \qquad n \quad (\exists x)(\forall x)(Fx \supset Gxx)$$

In each case, step n appears to follow from step m by E.G., replacing a with a variable. However, the logical forms of the steps added in the two cases are different. We can see the problem clearly if we consider the steps involved in E.G. First, for some statement A on some line, we form $A(\mathbf{x/s})$. Here, $A = (\forall x)(Fx \supset Gax)$, $\mathbf{s} = a$, and $\mathbf{x} = y$ in one case and x in the other. If we form $A(y/a)$, we get the open form

$$(\forall x)(Fx \supset Gyx)$$

Here, y occurs free. Now, when we add $(\exists y)$, we bind this free occurrence, making the open form a statement form. However, in the second inference, when we form $A(x/a)$, we get the following:

$$(\forall x)(Fx \supset Gxx)$$

This is not an open form: all occurrences of x are within the scope of the initial quantifier $(\forall x)$, so the new occurrence of x is bound. Consequently, when we add the quantifier $(\exists x)$, it is vacuous: the statement form

$$(\exists x)(\forall x)(Fx \supset Gxx)$$

is really equivalent to

$$(\forall x)(Fx \supset Gxx)$$

Technically, what's gone wrong in this second case is this: we tried to use E.G. by first substituting a variable for an occurrence of a constant and then placing an existential quantifier *for that variable* in front of the resulting open form. However, we picked a variable for which a quantifier was already present, and we *substituted that variable for a constant which is inside the scope of that quantifier*. As a result, our substitution immediately became a bound occurrence; and there is no open form, resulting in the vacuous quantifier. We can avoid this problem with a simple device: in using E.G. and U.G., *never substitute a variable for a constant if that variable is already present in the statement form*.[1] In the present case, our first deduction step follows this rule [y doesn't occur in $(\forall x)(Fx \supset Gax)$], but our second step violates it (x does occur).

We modify rules 10 and 11 of 3 as follows:

[1] This is actually a bit stronger than necessary, but it's the easiest rule to follow.

10 Existential Generalization

.   .

m A

.   .

n $(\exists x)A(x/s)$ m, E.G.

Restriction: x does not occur in A.

11. Universal Generalization

.   .

m A

.   .

n $(\forall x)A(x/s)$ m, U.G.

Restrictions: s does not occur in any premise of the deduction or in any assumption in force at step m; x does not occur in A.

Except for these restrictions, deductions proceed exactly as in Chapter 8. As examples, we give deductions for the valid arguments in the previous section.

	1	$(\forall x)(Fx \supset Gx)$	/ $(\forall x)[(\exists y)(Fy \wedge Hxy) \supset (\exists z)(Cz \wedge Hxz)]$
1	2	$(\exists y)(Fy \wedge Hay)$	$a1$
2, 1	3	$Fb \wedge Hab$	$a2$
2, 1	4	Fb	3, Simp.
2, 1	5	$Fb \supset Gb$	1, U.I.
2, 1	6	Gb	4, 5, M.P.
2, 1	7	Hab	3, Simp.
2, 1	8	$Gb \wedge Hab$	6, 7, Conj.
2, 1	9	$(\exists z)(Gz \wedge Haz)$	8, E.G.
2, 1	10	$(\exists z)(Gz \wedge Haz)$	2, 3—9, E.I.
1	11	$(\exists y)(Fy \wedge Hay) \supset (\exists z)(Gz \wedge Haz)$	2—10, Ded.
	12	$(\forall x)[(\exists y)(Fy \wedge Hxy) \supset (\exists z)(Gz \wedge Haz)]$	11, U.G.

The strategy here was to assume the antecedent of an instance of the open form in the conclusion, deduce the consequent, deduce the entire instance of the open form by the Deduction rule, and then deduce the conclusion by U.G. Note that we used the variable y in the assumption at step 2; this is in order to match the variables in the conclusion. Likewise, we introduced z at step 9 and x at step 12 in order to match the variables in the conclusion. In general, we may introduce any variables we please into a deduction so long as we don't violate the restrictions on U.G. and E.G. However, it's often important (as it is here) to make sure that we get the variables we want in the conclusion.

	1	$(\forall x)(\exists y)Fxy$	
	2	$(\exists x)(\forall y)(Fxy \supset \sim Fyx)$	/ $(\exists x)(\exists y)(Fyx \wedge \sim Fyy)$
1	3	$(\forall y)(Fay \supset \sim Fya)$	a1
1	4	$Faa \supset \sim Faa$	3, U.I.
1	5	$\sim Faa \vee \sim Faa$	4, Imp.
1	6	$\sim Faa$	5, Rep.
1	7	$(\exists y)Fay$	1, U.I.
2, 1	8	Fab	a2
2, 1	9	$Fab \wedge \sim Faa$	8, 6, Conj.
2, 1	10	$(\exists y)(Fyb \wedge \sim Fyy)$	9, E.G.
2, 1	11	$(\exists x)(\exists y)(Fyx \wedge \sim Fyy)$	10, E.G.
2̸, 1	12	$(\exists x)(\exists y)(Fyx \wedge \sim Fyy)$	7, 8—11, E. I.
⊬ 13	13	$(\exists x)(\exists y)(Fyx \wedge \sim Fyy)$	2, 3—12, E.I.

The strategy here is similar to that of the previous example. However, we made two uses of E.I., once with the premise $(\exists x)(\forall y)(Fxy \wedge \sim Fyx)$ as $(\exists x)A$ of the rule and once with step 7, $(\exists y)Fay$, as $(\exists x)A$.

EXERCISE 9.5

1 Construct deductions to show that each of the following is valid in Ⱥ.

(a) $(\forall x)(\forall y)(Fx \supset Gy)$
$(\exists x)\sim Hx \supset (\exists y)Fy$
$\sim(\forall x)Hx$

$(\exists x)Gx$

*(b) $\sim(\exists x)(\forall y)Fxy$
$(\forall x)(\exists y)Fyx$

$(\exists x)(\exists y)(\exists z)(Fxy \wedge \sim Fxz)$

(c) $(\forall x)(\exists y)Fxy$
$\sim(\forall x)(\exists y)Fyx$

$(\exists x)(\exists y)(Fxy \wedge \sim Fyx)$

*(d) $(\forall x)[Fx \supset (\exists y)Gxy]$
$(\exists x)(\forall y)(Fy \supset Gyx)$

$(\exists x)(\forall y)(\forall z)[(Fz \wedge Gzy) \supset Gzx]$

(e) $(\forall x)(Fxa \supset Fxb)$
$(\forall x)\sim Fxx$

$\sim Fba$

*(f) $(\forall x)(Fx \supset Gx) \wedge (\forall y)[Gy \supset (\exists x)Hyz]$
$(\forall x)(\forall y)(Hxy \supset Fy)$

$(\exists x)Fx \supset (\exists y)(\exists z)[(Fy \wedge Fz) \wedge Hyz]$

(g) $(\forall x)[Gax \supset (Gbx \lor \sim Gxc)]$
    $(\forall x)(Gxc \supset Gxb)$
    _____
    $(\exists x)[(Gbx \land Gxc) \supset (Gxb \land Gbx)]$

(h) $(\forall x)(\forall y)(Fxy \lor Fyx)$
    $(\forall x)(\forall y)(Fxy \equiv \sim Gxy)$
    _____
    $(\forall x)(\forall y)(Gxy \supset Fyx)$

(i) $(\forall x)(\forall y)[\sim Hxy \supset (\forall z)(Fxz \land \sim Gxz)]$
    $\sim (\exists x)(\exists y)Hxy$
    _____
    $(\forall x)[(\exists y)Fxy \supset (\forall z)\sim Gxz]$

(j) $(\exists x)(\forall y)\{[Fy \land (\exists z)Gzy] \supset Hxy\}$
    $(\forall x)[(\exists y)Hxy \supset \sim Fx]$
    _____
    $(\exists x)(\exists y)Gxy \supset (\exists z)\sim Fz$

2 Construct a deduction to show the validity of the following.
   (a) All George's friends hate Ethel. Likewise, Ethel's friends all hate George. Now, people's friends don't hate them. Consequently, no one is a friend of both Ethel and George.
   *(b) Arthur's friends all either live in San Francisco or prefer Los Angeles to San Francisco. Now, no one who lives in San Francisco prefers Los Angeles to that city. Arthur, however, has no friends living in Los Angeles except for people who prefer San Francisco to Los Angeles. Now, it's obvious that no one can both prefer Los Angeles to San Francisco and prefer San Francisco to Los Angeles. It's also obvious that no one lives in both these cities. Consequently, if Arthur has any friends at all, they live in San Francisco.
   (c) Every great philosopher is either speculative or analytical. The speculative ones are always incomprehensible, while the analytical ones are always boring. Philo hates anything if it's either boring or incomprehensible. Consequently, the only philosophers Philo doesn't hate are the ones that aren't great.
   *(d) Anything worth doing is worth doing well. Of course, all things are worth doing well only if they're profitable. Now, in general, nothing is profitable unless someone is willing to do it without anyone else forcing him or her. However, no one will do this logic exercise unless someone forces him or her. Consequently, some things aren't worth doing.

9.5.1 Deduction Schemata

A *deduction schema* is not an actual deduction but a deduction performed with metavariables. The value of a deduction schema is that it shows us how to deduce any statement form of a given form from any class of statement forms of certain forms. We'll use deduction schemata only in order to show that all statement forms of certain forms are theorems. Thus, the conclusions of our deduction schemata will be *theorem schemata*. The following example illustrates how a deduction schema works:

			/ $[(\exists x)A \supset B] \supset (\forall x)(A \supset B)$
1	1	$(\exists x)A \supset B$	$a1$
2, 1	2	$A(s/x)$	$a2$ (note: s does not occur in B)
2, 1	3	$(\exists x)A$	2, E.G. (replacing s with x)
2, 1	4	B	1, 3, M.P.
2, 1	5	$A(s/x) \supset B$	2—4, Ded.
1	6	$(\forall x)(A \supset B)$	5, U.G. ($[A(s/x) \supset B](x/s)$ is just $A \supset B$)
7	7	$[(\exists x)A \supset B] \supset (\forall x)(A \supset B)$	1—6, Ded.

This deduction schema shows us that any statement form of the form $[(\exists x)A \supset B] \supset (\forall x)(A \supset B)$ is a theorem of Ⅎ. It does this not by an actual deduction, but by giving us a *schema* for a deduction—in effect, a recipe for producing deductions. If we substitute appropriate expressions for A and B in this deduction schema, the result will be a correct deduction. Note that we must occasionally add a note about how to carry out the deduction. For instance, at step 2 we make an assumption. Our plan is to deduce B from this assumption and then introduce introduce a universal quantifier at step 6 by U.G. However, in order to get this to work right, we must introduce a constant into step 2 that doesn't occur in B, so that B(x/s) will be B and B won't be affected by the quantifier introduced at step 6. Such restrictions are no problem, since we can always find an appropriate constant for any actual deduction. We call any deduction we can get by substituting actual statement forms in a deduction schema an *instance* of that schema. When we can deduce a metalinguistic expression in a deduction schema from the null set, as in this case, we call it a *theorem schema*, and we call anything that we get by substituting in a theorem schema an *instance* of that schema. Obviously, all instances of theorem schemata are theorems of Ⅎ.

We give deduction schemata for two further theorem schemata of Ⅎ, together with an instance for each, in order to illustrate the technique further.

			/ $(\forall x)(A \supset B) \supset [(\exists x)A \supset B]$ (x does not occur in B)
1	1	$(\forall x)(A \supset B)$	$a1$
2, 1	2	$(\exists x)A$	$a2$
3, 2, 1	3	$A(s/x)$	$a3$ (s does not occur in B)
3, 2, 1	4	$A(s/x) \supset B$	1, U.I. (x does not occur in B)
3, 2, 1	5	B	3, 4, M.P.
3, 2, 1	6	B	2, 3—5, E.I. (s does not occur in B)
2, 1	7	$(\exists x)A \supset B$	2—6, Ded.
1	8	$(\forall x)(A \supset B) \supset [(\exists x)A \supset B]$	1—7, Ded.

Here, we have a restriction in the theorem schema: $(\forall x)(A \supset B) \supset [(\exists x)A \supset B]$ is a theorem only if x doesn't occur in B. However, this isn't a severe restriction, since if **x** did occur in B, it would be a free occurrence in (∃x)A ⊃ B and hence the schema wouldn't be a statement form. Here's an instance of this deduction schema:

```
                                                    / (∀x)[(∃y)Fxy ⊃ Ga] ⊃
                                                      [(∃x)(∃y)Fxy ⊃ Ga]
     1   1   (∀x)[(∃y)Fxy ⊃ Ga]                     a1
   2, 1   2   (∃x)(∃y)Fxy                           a2
  3, 2, 1   3   (∃y)Fby                             a3
  3, 2, 1   4   (∃y)Fby ⊃ Ga                        1, U.I.
  3, 2, 1   5   Ga                                  3, 4, M.P.
  3, 2, 1   6   Ga                                  2, 3—5, E.I.
     2, 1   7   (∃x)(∃y)Fxy ⊃ Ga                    2—6, Ded.
        1   8   (∀x)[(∃y)Fxy ⊃ Ga] ⊃               1—7, Ded.
                [(∃x)(∃y)Fxy ⊃ Ga]
```

Here A = (∃y)Fxy and B = Ga. Note that since *a* occurs in B, we chose *b* for s at step 2. Otherwise, as you can see, the deduction is simply a matter of substitution in the schema. We give one further example:

```
                                                    / (∃x)(∃y)A ⊃ (∃y)(∃x)A
     1   1   (∃x)(∃y)A                              a1
   2, 1   2   (∃y)A(s/x)                            a2 (s does not occur in A)
  3, 2, 1   3   A(s/x)(t/y)                         a3 (t does not occur in A)
  3, 2, 1   4   (∃x)A(t/y)                          3, E.G.
  3, 2, 1   5   (∃y)(∃x)A                           4, E.G.
  3, 2, 1   6   (∃y)(∃x)A                           2, 3—5, E.I.
     2, 1   7   (∃y)(∃x)A                           1, 2—6, E.I.
        1   8   (∃x)(∃y)A ⊃ (∃y)(∃x)A              1—7, Ded.
```

The following deduction of (∃x)(∃y)(Fx ⊃ Gyx) ⊃ (∃y)(∃x)(Fx ⊃ Gyx) is an instance of this schema:

```
                                    / (∃x)(∃y)(Fx ⊃ Gyx) ⊃ (∃y)(∃x)(Fx ⊃ Gyx)
     1   1   (∃x)(∃y)(Fx ⊃ Gyx)                     a1
   2, 1   2   (∃y)(Fa ⊃ Gya)                        a2
  3, 2, 1   3   Fa ⊃ Gba                            a3
  3, 2, 1   4   (∃x)(Fx ⊃ Gbx)                      3, E.G.
  3, 2, 1   5   (∃y)(∃x)(Fx ⊃ Gyx)                  4, E.G.
  3, 2, 1   6   (∃y)(∃x)(Fx ⊃ Gyx)                  2, 3—5, E.I.
     2, 1   7   (∃y)(∃x)(Fx ⊃ Gyx)                  1, 2—6, E.I.
        1   8   (∃x)(∃y)(Fx ⊃ Gyx) ⊃ (∃y)(∃x)(Fx ⊃ Gyx)   1—7, Ded.
```

The technique of deduction schemata gives us a more powerful means of discovering theorems, since we can now give "proofs" in the metalanguage for whole classes of theorems as theorem schemata. Incidentally, note that we could also make use of theorem schemata in the more limited system 𝒟 (or indeed in any natural deduction system at all).

1 Show that each of the following is a theorem schema of ℑ.

(a) $[(\forall x)A \land (\forall x)B] \equiv (\forall x)(A \land B)$
$^*(b)$ $(\exists x)(A \land B) \supset [(\exists x)A \land (\exists x)B]$
(c) $[(\forall x)A \lor (\forall x)B] \supset (\forall x)(a \lor B)$
$^*(d)$ $[(\exists x)A \lor (\exists x)B] \equiv (\exists x)(A \lor B)$
$^*(e)$ $[(\forall x)A \supset B] \equiv (\exists x)(A \supset B)$ (Note: x does not occur in B.)
(f) $[(\exists x)A \land (\exists x)B] \equiv (\exists x)(\exists y)[A \land B(y/x)]$ (Note: y does not occur in A or B.)
$^*(g)$ $(\forall x)A \supset (\exists x)A$
(h) $(\forall x)(A \supset B) \supset [(\forall x)A \supset (\forall x)B]$

9.6
SOME PROPERTIES OF TWO-PLACE RELATIONS

Logicians often find it important to distinguish certain properties of two-place relations. As we will see, the properties in question are *semantic:* they concern the truth values of statements in which those relational expressions occur. However, it's possible to express all these properties with statement forms in ℘. We'll later make use of the properties to explain how certain arguments work (see Section 9.7).

The first group of properties concerns relational statements in which the same term is in first and second places, for instance, *Arthur knows himself* or *Seven is equal to seven*. These properties are known as *reflexive* properties. There are some relational expressions which produce true statements whenever their first and second terms are the same, for instance, *is equal to, is the same as, is in the same place as*. Such relations are said to be *totally reflexive*. In other words, a relation is totally reflexive if everything is in that relation to itself. In ℘, we can say that F is totally reflexive as follows:

F is totally reflexive = $(\forall x)Fxx$

Some relational expressions are reflexive in a more limited way, which we may explain with an example. Consider the expression *has the same color of eyes as*. Everyone obviously has the same color of eyes as himself or herself—that is, everyone who has eyes at all. Those people (and things) who do not have eyes do not have the same color of eyes as anyone. However, it still remains true that if someone has the same color of eyes as anyone, then he or she has the same color of eyes as himself or herself. A relation with this property is said to be *reflexive*. More precisely, a relation F is reflexive if, whenever a relational statement with F is true for a given term occurring in either place, then that statement is true with that same term in both places. In $\mathcal{P}$, we express this as follows:

F *is reflexive* $= (\forall x)[(\exists y)(Fxy \lor Fyx) \supset Fxx]$

Note that any totally reflexive relation is reflexive. Further properties are *irreflexivity* and *nonreflexivity*. A relation is irreflexive if nothing has it to itself. In other words, a relation is irreflexive if every simple statement form made with it and containing the same name in both places is false. In $\mathcal{P}$, this is expressed as

F *is irreflexive* $= (\forall x)\sim Fxx$

Obvious examples of irreflexive relational expressions are *is different from*, *is older than*, *is a child of*. It's also obvious that no relation is both reflexive and irreflexive. However, some relations are neither reflexive nor irreflexive: these are known as *nonreflexive* relations. A nonreflexive relation, then, is one which some things have to themselves and some things don't. We can express this in $\mathcal{P}$ by negating the definitions for total reflexivity and for irreflexivity and conjoining them: this would give us $\sim(\forall x)Fxx \land \sim(\forall x)\sim Fxx$. However, two uses of Q.E. gives us the following form, which expresses nonreflexivity more clearly:

F *is nonreflexive* $= (\exists x)\sim Fxx \land (\exists x)Fxx$

Note that every relational expression is reflexive, irreflexive, or nonreflexive and that no expression has more than one of these properties.

A second group of properties concerns what happens to the truth values of relational statements when we interchange their first and second terms. For certain expressions, the truth value of an expression will not change if we switch its terms in this way, e.g., *is equal to*, *is different from*, *has the same color of eyes as*. If John has the same color of eyes as Bill, then Bill has the same color of eyes as John. When a relational expression has this property, we say that it is *symmetrical*. In the language $\mathcal{P}$, we express this as

F *is symmetrical* $= (\forall x)(\forall y)(Fxy \supset Fyx)$

As you may check for yourself, this is equivalent to $(\forall x)(\forall y)(Fyx \supset Fxy)$. Some relations have what we might call precisely the reverse of this property: if a relational statement with them is true, then it becomes false when we switch the terms. Thus, if the statement *Jane is taller than Mary* is true, then the statement *Mary is taller than Jane* must be false. Relations having this property are called *asymmetrical*. Other examples of asymmetrical relations include most comparative adjective forms like *is older than*, *is heavier than*, etc., as well as many other expressions, including *is to the right of*, *is inside of*, *is a child of*. In $\mathcal{P}$ we express asymmetry as follows:

F is asymmetrical $= (\forall x)(\forall y)(Fxy \supset \sim Fyx)$

Obviously, no relational expression is both symmetrical and asymmetrical, but some are neither. For instance, *is a brother of* is neither symmetrical (sisters are not brothers of their brothers) nor asymmetrical (brothers are brothers of their brothers). When an expression is neither symmetrical nor asymmetrical, we say that it is *nonsymmetrical*. Obviously, we may define this term precisely by simply denying the definitions of symmetry and asymmetry and then conjoining them. Appropriately transformed, this definition can be expressed in $\mathcal{P}$ as

F is nonsymmetrical $= (\exists x)(\exists y)(Fxy \wedge Fyx) \wedge (\exists x)(\exists y)(Fxy \wedge \sim Fyx)$

Reflexive properties concern single relational statements with a single term repeated; and symmetry, asymmetry, etc., concern pairs of relational statements which are alike except that their terms are reversed. The third group of properties we will consider concerns pairs of relational statements having one term in common. Some relations are such that if one thing has them to another and that other has them to a third, then the first thing has them to the third. An example of an expression with this property is *is taller than*: if John is taller than Jane and Jane is taller than Jim, then it follows that John is taller than Jim. Whenever a relational expression has this property, we say that it is *transitive*. In $\mathcal{P}$, we express this as follows:

F is transitive $= (\forall x)(\forall y)(\forall z)[(Fxy \wedge Fyz) \supset Fxz]$

Many comparative adjectives provide transitive relations, such as *it is taller than* in our example. Other transitive relational expressions include *is a descendant of*, *is within*, *is equal to*, *weighs less than*, *contains*. A property contrasted with transitivity is intransitivity. A relational expression is *intransitive* if whenever one thing has that relation to another and the other thing has it to a third, the first thing does *not* have it to a third. An example of such a relational expression is *is a child of*: if John is a child of Jane and Jane is a child of Jim, then John is not a child of Jim (under most circumstances outside Greek tragedy). We can express intransitivity in $\mathcal{P}$ as

F is intransitive $= (\forall x)(\forall y)(\forall z)[(Fxy \wedge Fyz) \supset \sim Fxz]$

Other intransitive relational expressions include *is twice as big as, is mother of, is a different sex from*. As in the case of our other concepts, we find that no relation is both transitive and intransitive, although some relations are neither, for example, *is different from*: if A is different from B and B is different from C, nothing follows about whether A is different from C. Relations which are neither transitive nor intransitive are said to be *nontransitive*. A definition of this term in $\mathcal{P}$ is

> F *is nontransitive* =
> $(\exists x)(\exists y)(\exists z)[(Fxy \wedge Fyz) \wedge Fxz] \wedge (\exists x)(\exists y)(\exists z)[(Fxy \wedge Fyz) \wedge {\sim}Fxz]$

The properties of reflexivity, symmetry, and transitivity are all independent of one another: a relational expression may have any one of them either with or without having either of the others. Thus, *is larger than* is transitive but not symmetrical or reflexive; *is at least as tall as* is reflexive and transitive but not symmetrical; *is a sibling of* is symmetrical and transitive but not reflexive; and *is equal to* is reflexive, symmetrical, and transitive. When a relation has all three properties of reflexivity, symmetry, and transitivity, it is said to be an *equivalence relation*. The following are equivalence relations:

> is identical to
> is the same as
> equals

We can often demonstrate that relations which have certain properties also have others. For instance, we can demonstrate that if a relation is transitive and irreflexive, then it is asymmetrical. Suppose F is transitive and irreflexive. In $\mathcal{P}$, this is

> $(\forall x)(\forall y)(\forall z)[(Fxy \wedge Fyz) \supset Fxz]$
> $(\forall x){\sim}Fxx$

To show that F is asymmetrical, we must show that $(\forall x)(\forall y)(Fxy \supset {\sim}Fyx)$ follows from these premises. The following deduction shows this:

1	$(\forall x)(\forall y)(\forall z)[(Fxy \wedge Fyz) \supset Fxz]$	
2	$(\forall x){\sim}Fxx$ / $(\forall x)(\forall y)(Fxy \supset {\sim}Fxx)$	
3	$(\forall y)(\forall z)[(Fay \wedge Fyz) \supset Faz]$	1, U.I.
4	$(\forall z)[(Fab \wedge Fbz) \supset Faz]$	3, U.I.
5	$(Fab \wedge Fba) \supset Faa$	4, U.I.
6	${\sim}Faa$	2, U.I.
7	${\sim}(Fab \wedge Fba)$	5, 6, M.T.
8	${\sim}Fab \vee {\sim}Fba$	7, DeM.
9	$Fab \supset {\sim}Fba$	8, Imp.
10	$(\forall y)(Fay \supset {\sim}Fya)$	9, U.G.
11	$(\forall x)(\forall y)(Fxy \supset {\sim}Fyx)$	10, U.G.

Similarly, we can show that relations with certain combinations of properties are impossible, e.g., intransitivity and total reflexivity. We need only show that the set

$$\{(\forall x)(\forall y)(\forall z)[(Fxy \wedge Fyz) \supset {\sim}Fxz], \ (\forall x)Fxx\}$$

is inconsistent. The following tree demonstrates this:

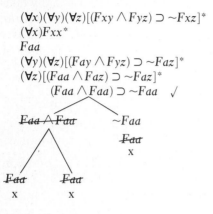

9.6.1 Converses and Relative Products

Frequently, we find two relational expressions with the following characteristic: when something has the first relation to something else, then that other thing has the second relation to the first. Thus, consider the expressions *is a parent of* and *is a child of*. Whenever *a* is a parent of *b*, *b* is a child of *a*. When two relational expressions are related in this way, they are said to be *converses* of each other. Thus, *is a parent of* is the converse of *is a child of*, and *is a child of* is the converse of *is a parent of*. Notice, incidentally, that the relation of being the converse of a relation is symmetrical. In $\mathcal{P}$, we may express the fact that one relational expression is the converse of another as follows:

F is the converse of G = $(\forall x)(\forall y)(Fxy \equiv Gyx)$

Many relational expressions have special terms as converses:

is a grandparent of	is a grandchild of
is in front of	is behind
includes	is part of
precedes	follows

Converses of verbs can usually be formed with the passive voice:

hits	is hit by
includes	is included in
owns	is owned by
knows	is known by

Notice, incidentally, that some expressions which you might initially take to be converses are only partly converses. Thus, *is mother of* and *is a child of* are not converses. If *a* is mother of *b*, then *b* is a child of *a*; but if *a* is a child of *b*, it doesn't follow that *b* is mother of *a* (*b* could also be father of *a*). Usually, in cases like these, it's possible to treat one of the relational expressions as an implicit compound of two or more other predicates. We could, for instance, treat *is mother of* as a combination of *is a parent of* and *is female*. Likewise, we could treat *is a son of* as compounded from *is a child of* and *is male*. It sometimes is necessary to analyze expressions in this way to get at the logical form of an argument.

In formalizing, it's convenient to formalize a relational expression and its converse with the same predicate variable, reversing the order of the terms in one case. Thus, we would formalize both *is a parent of* and *is a child of* with the same predicate letter—let's say F—but formalize *x is a parent of y* as Fxy and *x is a child of y* as Fyx. Incidentally, note that a symmetrical relation is its own converse. Relational expressions may also be compounded in another way: one may be the *relative product* of two others. It's easiest to explain this notion with an example. Consider the meaning of the term *aunt*. Except for aunts by marriage, a person's aunt is a sister of his or her parent. Therefore, we could replace *is an aunt of* with *is a sister of a parent of*. To formalize this, we can introduce an implicit existential quantifier by noting that the last expression amounts to *is a sister of someone who is a parent of*. Then, *x is an aunt of y* could be formalized as the following open form, where Gxy = *x is a parent of y* and Fxy = *x is a sister of y*:

$$x \text{ is an aunt of } y = (\exists z)(Fxz \wedge Gzy)$$

In general, to say that one relational expression A is the *relative product* of two others B and C means this: *x* has A to *y* if and only if there is some other thing *z* such that *x* has B to *z* and *z* has C to *y*. In $\mathcal{P}$, we express this as

$$F \text{ is the relative product of } G \text{ and } H = (\forall x)(\forall y)[Fxy \equiv (\exists z)(Gxz \wedge Hzy)]$$

Many relations are relative products of others. A large class of examples is the terms for family relationships: *is a grandparent of* = *is a parent of a parent of*, *is a cousin of* = *is a child of an aunt or uncle of*, *is a father-in-*

law of = *is a father of a spouse of,* and so on. In fact, many of these can be analyzed as relative products of relative products several times repeated.

In formalizing, it's sometimes convenient to note when one expression is the relative product of two others. Thus, if the expressions *parent* and *child* were common in an argument, we might treat *grandparent* in that argument as the relative product of *parent* with itself.

EXERCISE 9.6

1   For each of the following relational expressions, tell whether it is reflexive, symmetrical, or transitive.
   (a) Is longer than
   *(b) Loves
   (c) Is at least as wise as
   (d) Is no longer than
   *(e) Is divisible by
   (f) Is a subset of
   *(g) Has been married to
   (h) Is consistent with
   (i) Outruns
   *(j) Entails

2   Find an expression which is a converse for each of the following relational expressions.
   (a) Loves   *(e) Is worse than
   *(b) Is an ancestor of   (f) Is to the left of
   (c) Comes before   *(g) Is the square root of
   (d) Is under   (h) Is east of

3   Express each of the following as a relative product of two relations.
   *(a) Is a granddaughter of
   (b) Is a father-in-law of
   *(c) Is a fellow employee with
   (d) Is a maternal grandparent of
   *(e) Is a subdivision of

4   Prove (either semantically or syntactically) the following claims.
   (a) If F is an asymmetrical relation, then it is also irreflexive.
   (b) If F is an intransitive relation, then it is also irreflexive.
   (c) If F is an irreflexive and transitive relation, then it is also asymmetrical.

5   Prove (either semantically or syntactically) that no relation F can be:
   (a) Asymmetrical and nonreflexive
   (b) Totally reflexive and asymmetrical
   (c) Transitive, nonsymmetrical, and irreflexive

6   A relation F is said to be *serial* if $(\forall x)(\exists y)Fxy$, that is, if everything bears the relation F to something. Prove (either semantically or syntactically) that if a relation F is serial, transitive, and symmetrical, then it is totally reflexive.

ENTHYMEMES

Consider the following argument:

> Fred is taller than Harry.
> Harry is taller than Jim.
> Therefore, Fred is taller than Jim.

Undoubtedly, we are inclined to say this argument is valid. If we let $a = Fred$, $b = Harry$, $c = Jim$, and $Fxy = x$ *is taller than* y, then this argument would be formalized as

> Fab
> Fbc
> ———
> Fac

Its tree, of course, will look like this:

> Fab
> Fbc
> ~~Fac~~

Now this tree apparently indicates that, contrary to our logical intuitions, the argument is invalid. What are we to make of this? We have seen on several occasions that when an argument *seems* valid to us but yet cannot be shown to be, generally it has been due to some limitation in our artificial language. In an effort to overcome such limitations, we have often found it necessary to enlarge our artificial language. Fortunately, however, the problem here is not one whose resolution requires an extension of our symbolic apparatus. Rather, the problem is that the argument contains a "suppressed" premise. By a suppressed premise we mean a premise which, because it contains a piece of common knowledge, is left unmentioned. Sometimes, we say that the premise is *tacitly assumed* by the argument. We call such an argument an *enthymeme*.

In general, an enthymeme is an argument which is incompletely expressed on the grounds that anyone can reasonably be expected to supply what has been left out. More often than not, the premise which is left out in an enthymeme is a well-known, and sometimes even trivial, piece of information. Because an enthymeme is incomplete, we must explicitly state the suppressed premise or premises when checking it for validity. Now, the argument given above is valid on the condition that we explicitly state the missing premise, which is that the relation *taller than* is transitive. We have seen that a relation F is transitive if and only if the following is true:

$$(\forall x)(\forall y)(\forall z)[(Fxy \wedge Fyz) \supset Fxz]$$

Consequently, the logical structure of the argument given above, once it is recognized that it is an enthymeme, is this:

Fab
Fbc
$(\forall x)(\forall y)(\forall z)[(Fxy \wedge Fyz) \supset Fxz]$

Fac

Its tree will now show that the argument is valid:

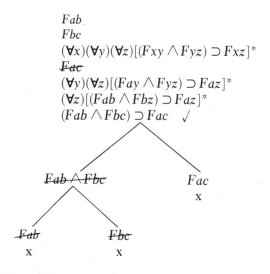

If we do not supply the suppressed premise that the relation *taller than* is transitive, then the above argument is, strictly speaking, invalid. However, it would be unfair to the person who presented this argument to insist that it is invalid if she or he intended, but did not express, the suppressed premise, especially if the person could have expected almost anyone to supply it. Admittedly, not just anybody would use the term *transitive* to characterize the property of the relation *taller than* (after all, it's a technical term), but that doesn't mean that once it is explained to him or her, he or she would not accept it. Notice that a suppressed premise is not just any missing premise you might want to add, but a premise which expresses, under the appropriate circumstances, something almost anybody could be expected to know. Just imagine how lifeless and boring many discussions would be if we were expected to make explicit all those trivial tidbits which everybody already knows. Accordingly, as long as the suppressed premise is either common knowledge or a trivial truth, we may regard such enthymematic arguments as valid.

Sometimes the suppressed premises of enthymemes involve trivial generalizations, as in the following argument:

Some senators are clever. Furthermore, all clever politicians campaign effectively. Therefore, some senators are effective campaigners.

This is an argument that's intuitively valid, but its tree won't close. Therefore, it's an enthymeme. But what is the suppressed premise? Even though a suppressed premise usually expresses a trivial truth, it isn't always obvious what this premise is. In order to determine what it is, first let's formalize it:

$(\exists x)(Fx \wedge Gx)$
$(\forall x)[(Gx \wedge Hx) \supset Ix]$
—————————————
$(\exists x)(Fx \wedge Ix)$

Here $Fx = x$ *is a senator*, $Gx = x$ *is clever*, $Hx = x$ *is a politician*, and $Ix = x$ *is an effective campaigner*. The tree for this enthymeme is constructed as follows:

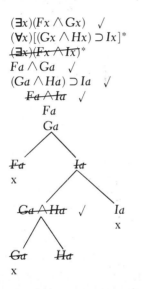

Clearly, if this argument is valid, it must be an enthymeme. But, again, what is the suppressed premise? Another way of asking this question is: What would make the open branch close? Any of the following would: Fa, Ga, Ia, Ha. Now, let's consider the actual predicate expressions in this argument. Are there any obvious connections among *is a senator*, *is clever*, *is a politician*, and *is an effective campaigner*? One likely possibility is this: *all senators are politicians*. That statement is, in fact, an obviously trivial generalization. If we formalize this, we get $(\forall x)(Fx \supset Hx)$. As the following tree shows, this premise will indeed make this argument valid. Let's insert $(\forall x)(Fx \supset Hx)$ in the open branch. Now we obtain the following tree:

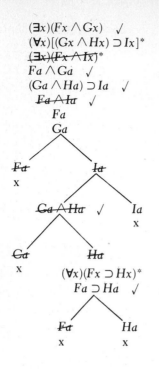

$(\exists x)(Fx \wedge Gx)$ ✓
$(\forall x)[(Gx \wedge Hx) \supset Ix]^*$
$\overline{(\exists x)(Fx \wedge Ix)}^*$
$Fa \wedge Ga$ ✓
$(Ga \wedge Ha) \supset Ia$ ✓
$\overline{Fa \wedge Ia}$ ✓
Fa
Ga

$\overline{Fa}$ $\overline{Ia}$
x

          $\overline{Ga \wedge Ha}$ ✓ Ia
                                              x

$\overline{Ga}$ $\overline{Ha}$
x $(\forall x)(Fx \supset Hx)^*$
          $Fa \supset Ha$ ✓

          $\overline{Fa}$ Ha
          x   x

Looking for obvious connections in this way usually enables you to find the suppressed premises of enthymemes.

It is also possible for the suppressed premises of an enthymeme to express that a certain relation is the converse of another relation. For example, consider this argument:

> New York is east of Chicago. However, Los Angeles is west of Chicago. Therefore, New York is east of Los Angeles.

As far as our logical intuitions are concerned, there is absolutely no doubt that this argument is valid. Nevertheless, without the additional premises that *being west of* is the converse of *being east of* and *being east of* is a transitive relation, the tree for this argument will reveal that it is invalid. It is formalized as

Fab
Gcb
$\overline{}$
Fac

where $Fxy = x$ *is east of* y, $Gxy = x$ *is west of* y, $a = New\ York$, $b = Chi$-cago, and $c = Los\ Angeles$. However, adding the suppressed premises, which are respectively formalized as

$$(\forall x)(\forall y)(Fxy \equiv Gyx)$$
$$(\forall x)(\forall y)(\forall z)[(Fxy \wedge Fyz) \supset Fxz]$$

yields a valid argument form, as the following tree verifies:

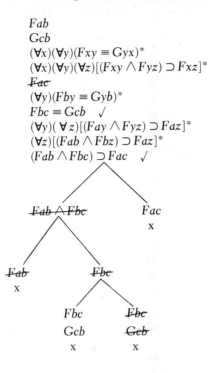

Obviously, enthymemes may also possess various combinations of suppressed premises that express trivial generalizations, that certain relations have various properties, or that a certain relation is the converse of some other given relation.

EXERCISE 9.7

Show that the following enthymemes are valid by adding the requisite suppressed premises.

1 All domestic cats are lovable animals. Therefore, some felines are lovable animals.

*2 A dog is more intelligent than any cat even though some Siamese are more intelligent than all laboratory mice. Hence, any dog is more intelligent than any laboratory mouse.

*3 Fred does not live in the suburbs since he is a bachelor. You see, only married people live in the suburbs.

4　Tom failed his logic course. Therefore, he failed a philosophy course.
5　Fred is the same age as Tom. Juan is not the same age as Fred. So, Tom is not the same age as Juan.
*6　All Ferd's descendants are ugly. Now, Ferd is an ancestor of Mary who, in turn, is an ancestor of Tom. Therefore, Tom is ugly.
7　All small cars get better gas mileage than any expensive car. Therefore, no small car is an expensive car.

9.8

IDENTITY

There are at least three different uses of *is* and related words in natural language. To see this, consider the following statements:

1　Fred *is* angry.
2　There *is* a God.
3　Tricky Dick *is* Richard Nixon.

The first statement simply attributes the property of being angry to Fred and so, as we already know, is formalized as Fa. Since this statement is simply composed of a name and a predicate, the *is* in this statement is called the *is of predication*. The *is* in the second statement is called the *is of existence* since this statement is equivalent to *God exists* and is therefore formalized as $(\exists x)Fx$.

The third statement can be analyzed in at least two different ways. The first involves viewing the *is* as an *is* of predication. Thus, on this analysis, statement (3) would be viewed as a compound of the name *Tricky Dick* and the predicate expression *is Richard Nixon*. There is, however, a shortcoming to this analysis which the following argument illustrates:

Tricky Dick wrote A *Heartbeat from the Presidency*.
Tricky Dick is Richard Nixon.
Therefore, Richard Nixon wrote A *Heartbeat from the Presidency*.

Now this argument is obviously valid; however, let's test its formalization. By letting $Fxy = x$ *wrote* y, $Gx = is\ Richard\ Nixon$, $a = Tricky\ Dick$, $b = A\ Heartbeat\ from\ the\ Presidency$, and $c = Richard\ Nixon$, this argument is formalized in the following way:

Fab
Ga
$\overline{}$
Fcb

As the following tree shows, this argument form is invalid:

> *Fab*
> *Ga*
> ~~*Fcb*~~

Clearly, this analysis doesn't reveal enough logical form. Perhaps the statement *Tricky Dick is Richard Nixon* should be analyzed as follows:

> Of *(Tricky Dick = x, Richard Nixon = y)*: *x* is *y*.

Here we've treated *is* as a two-place predicate expression meaning *is identical to* and which is therefore called the *is of identity*. Letting $Ixy =$ *x is identical to y*, we now would formalize the above argument in the following way:

> *Fab*
> *Iac*
> ———
> *Fcb*

Unfortunately, however, a semantic tree for this still won't close:

> *Fab*
> *Iac*
> ~~*Fcb*~~

In order to get this tree to close, we must stipulate the appropriate truth conditions for statements of identity. This will be done in Section 9.11. For the present, we will keep our discussion of the semantics of identity at an intuitive level.

What does it mean to say that Tricky Dick is Richard Nixon? At least this much: there is a unique individual in the world who happens to have two names—Tricky Dick and Richard Nixon. It doesn't matter which name you choose; either will pick out (refer to) this same individual. Hence, whatever properties are attributed to the individual referred to by one name will apply equally to the very same individual referred to by the other name. In other words, although two different names are involved, there is only one unique individual. Clearly, then, to say *Tricky Dick wrote* **A Heartbeat from the Presidency** is equivalent to saying (given that Tricky Dick is Richard Nixon) *Richard Nixon wrote* **A Heartbeat from the Presidency.** Thus *Tricky Dick is Richard Nixon* will be true under the following circumstances: if we can substitute *Richard Nixon* for *Tricky Dick* in any statement whatever without changing its truth value. When we turn to the semantics for $\mathcal{P}$, this will become something like this: if $Iab = T$ on an interpretation I, then we can substitute *b* for *a* in any statement form A and get a new statement form with the same truth value on I as A.

Returning to our tree, we have

Fab
Iac
~~*Fcb*~~

This tree represents an interpretation I where I(*Fab*) = T, I(*Iac*) = T, and I(*Fcb*) = F. Now, in view of the above discussion, since we have I(*Iac*) = T, we may substitute *c* for *a* in any statement form A without changing its truth value on I. We already have I(*Fab*) = T; substituting, then, we get I(*Fcb*) = T. If we add this to our tree, it closes:

Fab
Iac
~~*Fcb*~~
Fcb
  x

More will be said about the use of semantic trees on arguments containing statements of identity in Section 9.11.1. All that we wish to establish here is that the proper analysis of statements of identity not only requires the recognition that more logical form is involved, but also requires us to take account of the truth conditions of the identity predicate. We include an analysis of these truth conditions because they are extremely general and can be expressed in terms of language $\mathcal{P}$.

From now on, let's agree to use the symbol = instead of *I* for formalizing the predicate *is identical to*. Thus, instead of writing *Iac*, we write $a = c$. Let's also agree to write $a \neq c$ instead of $\sim a = c$.

We can introduce this new symbol into $\mathcal{P}$ as follows. First, we add the symbol = to the set **C**:

$$\mathbf{C} = \{\sim, \wedge, \vee, \supset, \equiv, \forall, \exists, =\}$$

Next, we add the following clause to the definition of the set **A** of simple predicate forms:

If s, t ∈ **T**, then s = t ∈ **A**.

9.9

FORMALIZING STATEMENTS OF IDENTITY

We find that = is necessary in capturing the full logical form of many statements which do not explicitly contain the predicate expression *is identical to* or any equivalent. The following subsections show how to formalize several classes of such statements.

9.9.1 Statements Involving *At Least*

Consider the following statement:

There is at least one God.

This statement can be formalized as $(\exists x)Fx$ where F formalizes the predicate *is God*. Obviously to say that something is God is to say that there is at least one God.

Now consider this statement:

There are at least two Gods.

It might seem appropriate to formalize this statement as

$(\exists x)(\exists y)(Fx \wedge Fy)$

But this is not correct; after all, the x and y referred to might be the same object, in which case it would not capture what the statement asserts. The statement says there are at least two *different* Gods, not that there *might* also be only one. The only way to formalize this statement correctly is to employ the identity symbol:

$(\exists x)(\exists y)[(Fx \wedge Fy) \wedge x \neq y]$

This statement form says that there is an x which is a God and a y which is a God, and x is not identical to y.

It is also possible to formalize the statement *There are at least three Gods* in similar fashion:

$(\exists x)(\exists y)(\exists z)\{[(Fx \wedge Fy) \wedge Fz] \wedge [(x \neq y \wedge x \neq z) \wedge y \neq z]\}$

It's obvious how to formalize the phrases *at least four*, *at least five*, and so on.

9.9.2 Statements Involving *At Most*

Now consider the following statement:

There is at most one God.

It is formalized in this way:

$(\forall x)[Fx \supset (\forall y)(Fy \supset x = y)]$

What this statement form says is this: for all x, if x is God, then for all y, if y is God, then x is identical to y. In other words, there is at most one

God. Note that we use the *universal* quantifier and not the existential quantifier in formalizing this statement. The reason is that although the statement says there is at most one God, it doesn't say that *there is* one. In other words, this statement would be true if there were no God at all, as well as if there were only one.

We can similarly formalize the statement *There are at most two Gods* in the following way:

$$(\forall x)(\forall y)\{[(Fx \land Fy) \land x \neq y] \supset (\forall z)[Fz \supset (z = x \lor z = y)]\}$$

Statements containing the phrases *at most three*, *at most four*, and so on can be handled similarly. It should be noted that the phrase *no more than* functions similarly to *at most*.

9.9.3 Statements Involving *Exactly*

Now that we know how to formalize statements containing *at least* and *at most*, it is a simple matter to formalize those containing *exactly*. To see this, consider this statement:

There is exactly one God.

This statement says that there is *at least* one God and *at most* one God. Accordingly, it is formalized as follows:

$$(\exists x)[Fx \land (\forall y)(Fy \supset x = y)]$$

This statement form simply says that there is at least one thing such that it is a god and for anything else whatsoever, if it is also a god, then they are the same thing. In other words, there is exactly one god.

To formalize the statement *There are exactly two gods* we proceed similarly:

$$(\exists x)(\exists y)\{[(Fx \land Fy) \land x \neq y] \land (\forall z)[Fz \supset (z = x \lor z = y)]\}$$

This statement form says there is a thing x which is a god and another *distinct* thing y which is god, and furthermore, if anything else is a god then it is either the same thing as x or the same thing as y. In other words, there are exactly two gods.

We proceed similarly for the locutions *exactly three*, *exactly four*, and so on. We might note that the word *only* is often handled in the same way as *exactly*. Obviously, the statement *There is only one God* is equivalent to *There is exactly one God*.

9.9.4 Statements Involving Exceptions

Consider the following statement:

1a Fred is uglier than everybody except Ferd.

Here the word *except* serves to exempt somebody from the statement being made. In other words, this statement says this: consider the open sentence *Fred is uglier than him*. This open sentence becomes true for any name you substitute for *him* so long as it isn't Ferd. Keeping this in mind, we can easily formalize this statement as

1b $(\forall x)[(Fx \wedge x \neq a) \supset Gbx]$

where $Fx = x$ *is a person*, $a = Ferd$, $b = Fred$, and $Gxy = x$ *is uglier than y*. What this formalization says, of course, is this: for all x, if both x is a person and x is not identical to Ferd, then Fred is uglier than x.

It should be noted that (1a) is ambiguous. Normally, it would probably be viewed as saying this:

2a Fred is uglier than everybody *else* except Ferd.

However, this is not literally what (1a) means. Rather, (1a) asserts that Fred is uglier than anyone you pick so long as you don't pick Ferd. But this would entail that Fred is uglier than himself if he isn't the same person as Ferd. Clearly (2a) does not entail this last possibility. It says only that Fred is uglier than everybody other than himself except for Ferd. We can formalize it as

2b $(\forall x)\{[(Fx \wedge x \neq b) \wedge x \neq a] \supset Gbx\}$

In view of the above discussion, it is obvious that we would formalize

3a Fred is uglier than everybody else.

simply as

3b $(\forall x)[(Fx \wedge x \neq a) \supset Gax]$

In this formalization, $a = Fred$.

There are other words besides *except* and *else* which are employed in statements expressing exceptions, for example, *but*, *besides*, *other than*, and so on. Thus any of the following statements would be formalized like (1a):

4 Fred is uglier than everybody but Ferd.
5 Besides Ferd, Fred is uglier than everybody.
6 Fred is uglier than everybody other than Ferd.

Another word which often is used in statements expressing exceptions is *only*, as in

7a   The only thing that Tom likes is football.

This statement asserts two things: that Tom likes football and that he doesn't like anything else. It is formalized thus:

7b $Fab \wedge (\forall x)(x \neq b \supset {\sim}Fax)$

where $Fxy = x$ *likes* y, $a = Tom$, and $b = football$.

9.9.5   Statements Involving Superlatives

Superlative statements involve such words as *ugliest, tallest, wisest*, and so on. The identity symbol is also useful in formalizing such statements. As an example of how this is done, consider the following statement:

1a   Ferd is the ugliest person.

This statement asserts a conjunction of two statements:

Ferd is a person and Ferd is uglier than everybody else.

In view of our discussion in the last section, it is formalized as

1b $Fa \wedge (\forall x)[(Fx \wedge x \neq a) \supset Gax]$

where $Fx = $ *is a person*, $a = Ferd$, and $Gxy = x$ *is uglier than* y.
The negation of (1a), namely,

2a   Ferd is not the ugliest person.

will, of course, be formalized as

2b ${\sim}Fa \vee {\sim}(\forall x)[(Fx \wedge x \neq a) \supset Gax]$

Sometimes statements involving superlatives are expressed with a qualification, as in the following:

3a   Fred is one of the ugliest people.

This statement doesn't require the use of the identity symbol in its formalization. It means the same as

4   Fred is a person and no person is uglier than he.

Statement (4) rules out the possibility that anyone is uglier than Fred, although it certainly does not rule out the possibility that at least one person is as ugly. Thus (4) and consequently (3a) are formalized in the following fashion:

3b $Fa \wedge (\forall x)(Fx \supset \sim Gxa)$

Of course, the negation of (3a), namely,

5a Fred is not one of the ugliest people.

will be formalized as

5b $\sim Fa \vee \sim (\forall x)(Fx \supset \sim Gxa)$

However, a qualified superlative like the following does require the identity symbol in its formalization:

6a Fred and Ferd are two of the ugliest people.

Again, this statement is equivalent to

7 Both Fred and Ferd are persons and nobody is uglier than either of them.

This is formalized as

6b $[(Fa \wedge Fb) \wedge a \neq b] \wedge (\forall x)[Fx \supset \sim(Gxa \vee Gxb)]$

EXERCISE 9.9

Formalize each of the following statements.
1   There are at least two dollars in my pocket.
2   There are at most two ugly people in the world.
*3   There is exactly one brave man.
4   Pedro is taller than everybody else.
*5   With the exception of Tim, Peter is taller than everybody.
6   Mary is brighter than everybody else besides Tom.
7   Only Mary loves Tom.
8   Tom loves nobody but Mary.
*9   Maria is the smartest student of the class.
10   Ferd is one of the dumbest students in the class.
11   Pedro is taller than everyone except Molly and Jane.
*12   Everyone likes someone else.
13   Someone likes everyone else.
*14   Tom and Mary are two of the fastest runners.
15   Peter gave a book to everybody but Alice.
16   Only Sharon received a book from everybody else.

17 Paul is the biggest "pothead" on campus.
*18 Nobody else but Tom was at home.
19 Mary didn't receive a book from everybody else.
*20 Mars has exactly two moons.
21 There are at least two prime numbers.
22 Cicero is Tully.
23 There was only one student in the class.
*24 The smallest number is zero.
25 At least two flies are in my kitchen.
*26 Nobody wants to be somebody else.
27 Everybody wants to be somebody else.
28 Fred is not taller than anybody else other than Tim.
29 Tom loves only Mary.
30 One is smaller than every number but zero.

9.10
FORMALIZING DESCRIPTIONS

We have already mentioned that one defining characteristic of names is that they refer to one unique individual or object. However, names are not the only kinds of expressions which have this function. There are expressions which, strictly speaking, are not names and yet also have this function: they are called *definite descriptions*, and they include such expressions as *the Attorney General of the United States*, *the author of **Dune**, the director of **Star Wars**,* and *the tallest building in the world.* Formalizing statements employing definite descriptions requires that we only make use of the skills of formalization which we have already acquired.

Consider the following statement:

1a The Attorney General of the United States is honest.

This statement says two things:[2]

2a There is exactly one Attorney General of the United States.
3a He (or she) is honest.

We already know how to formalize (2a):

2b $(\exists x)[Fx \land (\forall y)(Fy \supset x = y)]$

Here $Fx = x$ *is an Attorney General of the United States.* The open sentence (3a), of course, is formalized in the following way:

---

[2] This analysis of definite descriptions was first proposed by Bertrand Russell in his paper "On Denoting," *Mind* 14 (1905).

3b Gx

Here $Gx = x$ *is honest*. Now all that we have to do is conjoin (2b) and (3b):

1b $(\exists x)\{Fx \wedge (\forall y)[(Fy \supset x = y) \wedge Gx]\}$

Notice that we have conjoined them in such a way that the x in (3b) falls within the scope of the existential quantifier in (1b).

Now consider this statement:

4a The Vulcan on The[3] Star Ship *Enterprise* is both witty and logical.

Again this statement says two things:

5a There is exactly one Vulcan on The Star Ship *Enterprise*.
6a He is both witty and logical.

We formalize (5a) in this way:

5b $(\exists x)\{(Fx \wedge Gxa) \wedge (\forall y)[(Fy \wedge Gya) \supset x = y]\}$

where $Fx = x$ *is a Vulcan*, $Gxy = x$ *is on* y, and $a = $ *The Star Ship Enterprise*. The formalization of (6a) is straightforward:

6b $Ix \wedge Jx$

Here I stands for *is witty* and J for *is logical*. Putting them together yields

4b $(\exists x)\{(Fx \wedge Gxa) \wedge (\forall y)[(Fy \wedge Gya) \supset x = y] \wedge (Ix \wedge Jx)\}$

Some definite descriptions are also superlatives:

7a The fastest runner on the team is injured.

This statement asserts the following:

8a There is exactly one fastest runner on the team.
9a He (or she) is injured.

We already know how to deal with superlatives of the following form:

10a John is the fastest runner on the team.

---

[3] Here *The* is part of a proper name rather than part of a definite description.

It is formalized as

$$\text{10b} \quad Fa \wedge (\forall x)[(Fx \wedge x \neq a) \supset Gax]$$

where $Fx = x$ *is a runner on the team*, $Gxy = x$ *is faster than* y, and $a = John$. Now (8a) is a variant of (10a); instead of saying that a given person named so-and-so is the fastest runner on the team, it simply asserts the existence of such a runner. Consequently, (8a) is formalized as

$$\text{8b} \quad (\exists x)\{Fx \wedge (\forall y)[(Fy \wedge x \neq y) \supset Gxy]\}$$

Here F and G are the same as in (10b). Formalizing (9a) is easy:

$$\text{9b} \quad Hx$$

where $Hx = x$ *is injured*. Putting (8b) and (9b) together in the appropriate fashion now yields

$$\text{7b} \quad (\exists x)(Fx \wedge (\forall y)\{[(Fy \wedge x \neq y) \supset Gxy] \wedge Hx\})$$

Some statements often assert the identity of a definite description with a name:

11   The captain of The Star Ship *Enterprise* is James Kirk.

The meaning of this statement is captured by the following two statements:

12a   There is exactly one captain of The Star Ship *Enterprise*.
13a   He is James Kirk.

We formalize (12a) as

$$\text{12b} \quad (\exists x)[Fxa \wedge (\forall y)(Fya \supset x = y)]$$

where $Fxy = x$ *is captain of* y and $a = The\ Star\ Ship\ Enterprise$. Statement (13a) is formalized in this way:

$$\text{13b} \quad x = b$$

where $b = James\ Kirk$. Putting (12b) and (13b) together in the appropriate way now yields

$$\text{14b} \quad (\exists x)\{Fxa \wedge (\forall y)[(Fya \supset x = y) \wedge x = b]\}$$

Some statements often assert the identity of two definite descriptions, as in the following example:

15a   Fred's mother is the mayor of Klopstokia.

Note that *Fred's mother* is a definite description since it is equivalent to *the mother of Fred*. This statement makes the following three assertions:

16a   There is exactly one mother of Fred.
17a   There is exactly one mayor of Klopstokia.
18a   One is identical to the other.

We formalize (16a) thus:

16b $(\exists x)[Fxa \wedge (\forall y)(Fya \supset x = y)]$

where $Fxy = x$ *is the mother of* y and $a = Fred$. We formalize (17a) similarly:

17b $(\exists z)[Gzb \wedge (\forall w)(Gwb \supset z = w)]$

Here $Gxy = x$ *is mayor of* y and $b = Klopstokia$. (18a) is formalized in this way:

18b $x = z$

We now conjoin (16b), (17b), and (18b) in the following way:

15b $(\exists x)(\exists z)(\{[Fxa \wedge (\forall y)(Fya \supset x = y)] \wedge [Gzb \wedge (\forall w)(Gwb \supset z = w)]\} \wedge$
       $x = z)$

Now consider this statement:

19a   Everybody voted for Fred's mother.

This makes the following two assertions:

16a   There is exactly one mother of Fred.
20a   Everybody voted for her.

We have already formalized (16a), so we turn to the formalization of (20a):

20b $(\forall z)(Gz \supset Hzx)$

where $Gx = x$ *is a person* and $Hxy = x$ *voted for* y. Putting (16b) and (20b) together in the appropriate way yields

19b $(\exists x)\{[Fxa \land (\forall z)(Fya \supset x = y)] \land (\forall z)(Gz \supset Hzx)\}$

We now present a few more statements along with their formalizations. Almost all are slight variants on some of the things we have already learned.

21 Fred is uglier than everybody except the person who resembles Ferd.

$(\exists x)(\{(Fx \land Gxa) \land (\forall y)[(Fy \land Gya) \supset x = y]\} \land (\forall z)[(Fz \land z \neq x) \supset Hbz])$

Here $Fx = x$ *is a person*, $Gxy = x$ *resembles* y, $Hxy = x$ *is uglier than* y, $a = Ferd$, and $b = Fred$.

22 The mayor of Transylvania likes everybody who voted for her.

$(\exists x)\{[Fxa \land (\forall y)(Fya \supset x = y)] \land (\forall z)[(Gz \land Hzx) \supset Ixz]\}$

Here $Fxy = x$ *is mayor of* y, $a =$ Transylvania, $Gx = x$ *is a person*, $Hxy = x$ *voted for* y, and $Ixy = x$ *likes* y.

23 Fred's father likes only Fred's friends.

$(\exists x)\{[Fxa \land (\forall y)(Fya \supset x = y)] \land (\forall z)(Gxz \supset Hza)\}$

Here $Fxy = x$ *is a father of* y, $a = Fred$, $Gxy = x$ *likes* y, and $Hxy = x$ *is a friend of* y.

24 The woman most loved by Fred is also loved by Ferd.

$(\exists x)(\{Fx \land (\forall y)[(Fy \land x \neq y) \supset Gaxy]\} \land Hbx)$

Here we use $Fx = x$ *is a woman*, $Gxyz = x$ *loves* y *more than* z, $Hxy = x$ *loves* y, $a = Fred$, and $b = Ferd$.

We would like to note two difficulties concerning the formalization of statements containing definite descriptions. The first is concerned with the negations of these kinds of statements since they are often ambiguous. To see what is meant here, consider the following statement:

25 The King of the United States is not just.

Depending on the context, this statement might mean either

26a There is exactly one King of the United States and he is not just.

or

27a It is not true that the King of the United States is just.

If (26a) is the intended meaning of (25), then of course it would be formalized as

26b $(\exists x)\{[Fx \wedge (\forall y)(Fy \supset x = y)] \wedge \sim Gx\}$

where $Fx = x$ *is a King of the United States* and $Gx = x$ *is just*. However, if (27a) is the intended meaning of (26a), then it would be formalized as

27b $\sim(\exists x)\{[Fx \wedge (\forall y)(Fy \supset x = y)] \wedge Gx\}$

The other difficulty concerns what are often called *generic descriptions*. These are phrases which appear to be definite descriptions but are really universal quantifications. The following statement is an example:

28   The whale is a mammal.

Although the word *whale* is preceded by the definite article *the*, this is not enough to make the phrase *the whale* a definite description since this phrase doesn't *necessarily* pick out or refer to one unique object. As a matter of fact, (28) is really equivalent to *All whales are mammals*. Notice we said that *the whale* doesn't necessarily refer to a unique object. Of course, it might in a given context. The kind of ambiguity being discussed here might be better illustrated by the following statement:

29   The ape is an intelligent creature.

Now, more often than not, this statement would mean *All apes are intelligent creatures*. Nevertheless, we can certainly imagine possible contexts where the phrase *the ape* would, in fact, single out a unique object. For example, we might employ (29) to pick out a certain ape among the other animals in a given zoo. In any event, it is clear that such ambiguities can be resolved only by the context.

EXERCISE 9.10

Formalize the following statements.
1   Plato was the teacher of the great Greek philosopher whose name was Aristotle.
*2   The theory of forms was advocated by Plato.
3   At least two people voted for the mayor of Transylvania.
*4   If Descartes isn't the father of early modern philosophy, then nobody else is.
5   The man who corrupted Hadleyburg is the man whom Twain disliked.
*6   Nobody likes the leader of the Third Reich.
7   The student who received the highest grade on the logic examination is presently helping Alice.
*8   Alfred is the dog that bit Fred.

9   Everybody admires the person most liked by everybody else.
*10   The director of *Star Wars* is one of the best directors.
11   The dog is a domesticated animal.
*12   Nobody likes the person who likes everybody.
13   Janice is the person who likes everybody.
*14   Tom is the person who likes nobody but himself.
15   Tom and Janice are two of the best students.
16   The person who received the highest grade on the logic examination failed chemistry.

9.11
SEMANTIC ANALYSIS OF IDENTITY

In order to provide semantics for identity, we need only introduce two more interpretation rules into the semantic theory of $\mathcal{P}$. As you might expect, we must stipulate the truth conditions for statement forms having the following structure:

$$s = t$$

We state them as follows:

IR8a: For any interpretation I, $I(s = t) = T$ if and only if for every $A \in F$, $I[A(t/s)] = I(A)$.

IR8b: For any interpretation I, $I(s = t) = F$ if and only if for some $A \in F$, $I[A(t/s)] \neq I(A)$.

Now IR8a says that any statement form $s = t$ is true on an interpretation I just in case for every statement form A containing occurrences of s, if all the occurrences of s are replaced by t, then the truth value of A remains unchanged. What this means, in particular, is that if $I(a = b) = T$, then if, say, we have

$I(Fa) = T$
$I(Gabc) = T$
$I(Fa \supset Gca) = F$

then we would also have

$I(Fb) = T$
$I(Gbbc) = T$
$I(Fb \supset Gcb) = F$

In other words, when an identity $a = b$ is true, replacing one of these constants with an another in a statement form will not change its truth value. Clearly, if *John* and *Jack* refer to the same individual, then you do not change the truth value of the statement *Mary loves John* when you replace *John* by *Jack*. If John is Jack, then the truth value of *Mary loves John* is the same as the truth value of *Mary loves Jack*.

Interpretation Rule 8b, on the other hand, tells us that s = t is false on an interpretation I just in case there is some statement form A such that when t replaces s in A, the truth value of A is changed. Undoubtedly, if I(*Fa*) = T but I(*Fb*) = F, then I(*a* = *b*) = F. In such a circumstance, we want to say that *a* is not identical to *b*.

It might appear as though the formulations of interpretation rules 8a and 8b are circular. After all, in defining s = t semantically, we also make use of the identity symbol in the expressions I[A(t/s)] = I(A) and I[A(t/s)] ≠ I(A). Strictly speaking, however, the identity symbol in s = t is a name which is being used to mention the identity symbol in the object language. What is being defined by 8a and 8b is the identity symbol in the object language. The identity symbol in the expressions I[A(t/s)] = I(A) and I[A(t/s)] ≠ I(A), on the other hand, is not a name, but rather a symbol of the metalanguage. Accordingly, then, the latter identity symbol is a different symbol from the one being defined in the object language. To insist that 8a and 8b are circular is to disregard the object language–metalanguage distinction.

9.11.1 Semantic Trees for Identity

It has been our practice to select extension rules for semantic trees which reflect structurally the interpretation rules of the semantic theory. Now, if we continue this practice with identity, the extension rules will look something like this:

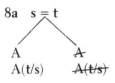

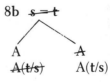

A is any statement form
occurring in the same branch
as s = t.

A is a statement form
which does not already
occur in the same branch
as s = t.

In constructing a tree, we would employ 8a in very much the same way that 6a is used except that instead of covering individual constants, we would now cover statement forms. Extension rule 8b, on the other hand, would be employed in similar fashion to 6b except, of course, instead of introducing a new individual constant, we would introduce a new statement form not already occurring in a given branch of a tree.

The justification for rule 8a is obvious: if s = t is true, then substituting t for s in any statement for A will not change A's truth value. We make this a branching rule simply because we might have a tree in which no statement form A containing s occurs. Here, we would pick any arbitrary statement form. Obviously, if A already occurs, slashed or unslashed, one branch will close. Rule 8b is a little harder to explain. If s = t is false on I, then I[A(t/s)] ≠ I(A) for *some* A. However, we don't know which A this might be. So, we proceed as we did with (∃x)A and (∀x)A: we make the minimum assumption about I. Here, this is to assume that A is not one of the statement forms already in the tree (this resembles introducing new constants in rules 6b and 7a).

Now, although extension rules 8a and 8b are correct, they make tree construction unnecessarily cumbersome. In order to appreciate this point, consider the following argument form:

$$\frac{Fa \supset Fb}{a = b}$$

Proceeding as usual, we would set up as follows:

$Fa \supset Fb$
~~a = b~~

Extending by means of extension rule 4a, we would obtain

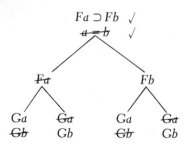

Employing 8b would now result in the following completed tree:

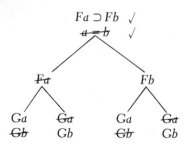

None of the paths close; and so, as we would expect, the argument form is invalid. Notice that we introduced the statement form Ga in the two paths under ~~Fa~~ and Fb. This was because rule 8b stipulated that we introduce any statement form not already occurring in the same branch as

$a = b$. Now, it may not appear to you that the above semantic tree is all that cumbersome, but, as we shall see, it really is compared to the tree that would be generated from an alternative set of extension rules.

Actually, our alternative is a single extension rule:

8 $s = t$
   A
   A(t,s)

Here we introduce the notation A(t,s), which means the result of replacing *some* (possibly all) occurrences of s in A with t. If there is a statement form of the form $s = t$ in an open branch, take any other statement form A which occurs in that branch, replace some of the occurrences of s in A with t, and write the result A(t,s) at the bottom of the open branch.

So far, it has been our practice to close a branch of a tree only when one kind of circumstance obtains, namely, when at least one atomic statement form occurs in that branch both slashed and unslashed. We have said that such a branch is impossible since it represents an interpretation on which a given statement form is both true and false (a violation of IR0). Now we are going to stipulate another kind of circumstance under which we may close the branch of a tree: namely, when a statement form of the form $s = s$ occurs slashed. The reason is because it represents an impossible interpretation, one which violates Interpretation Rules 8b and O. Let's imagine we have a branch of a tree in which $a = a$ is slashed:

.
.
~~$a = a$~~
.
.
.

Now since extension rule 8b structurally represents IR8b, let's extend 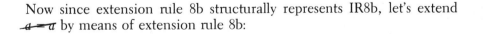 ~~$a = a$~~ by means of extension rule 8b:

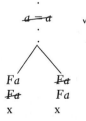

Clearly, the two branches generated by extending ~~$a = a$~~ by 8b are inconsistent, and so they both close.

From now on, then, let's agree never to use extension rules 8a and 8b. Instead, we shall use extension rule 8 only, agreeing that we always close the branch of a tree which contains a statement form of the form s = s slashed.

Let's now return to the following invalid argument form:

$$Fa \supset Fb$$
$$\overline{a = b}$$

Its completed tree will now look like this:

Notice that $a = b$ doesn't get extended since we no longer have an extension rule that will permit us to extend it. (Anyway, it's an *atomic* statement form.) Nor do we close either of the open branches since $a = b$ is not an instance of $s = s$, but rather of $s = t$. If we select the open branch at the left, then a counterinterpretation for this argument form will be

$$I(Fa) = F$$
$$I(a = b) = F$$
$$I(Fb) = T$$

As usual, since Fb doesn't occur in the open branch at the left, we may assign it either value.

Now consider the following argument:

At least one God exists. But there is at most one God. Therefore, there is exactly one God.

This argument is formalized as

$$(\exists x)Fx$$
$$(\forall x)(\forall y)[(Fx \wedge Fy) \supset x = y]$$
$$\overline{(\exists x)[Fx \wedge (\forall y)(Fy \supset x = y)]}$$

where $Fx = x$ *is a God*. (In the second premise, we used an alternative formalization for *at most one*.) We construct a tree for this argument form in the following way:

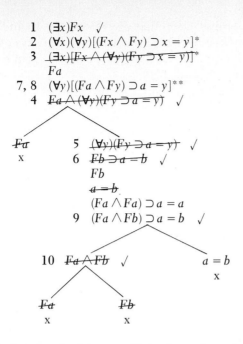

1 $(\exists x)Fx$ $\checkmark$
2 $(\forall x)(\forall y)[(Fx \wedge Fy) \supset x = y]^*$
3 $\cancel{(\exists x)[Fx \wedge (\forall y)(Fy \supset x = y)]}^*$
   Fa
7, 8 $(\forall y)[(Fa \wedge Fy) \supset a = y]^{**}$
4 $\cancel{Fa \wedge (\forall y)(Fy \supset a = y)}$ $\checkmark$

$\cancel{Fa}$
x

5 $\cancel{(\forall y)(Fy \supset a = y)}$ $\checkmark$
6 $\cancel{Fb \supset a = b}$ $\checkmark$
   Fb
   $\cancel{a = b}$
   $(Fa \wedge Fa) \supset a = a$
9 $(Fa \wedge Fb) \supset a = b$ $\checkmark$

10 $\cancel{Fa \wedge Fb}$ $\checkmark$

$a = b$
x

$\cancel{Fa}$
x

$\cancel{Fb}$
x

Notice that in this tree all the branches closed by simply using the extension rules we had already learned before taking up the topic of identity.
Now consider this argument:

Everybody likes Mary. But Mary is Frieda.
Therefore, everybody likes Frieda.

It is formalized as

$(\forall x)(Fx \supset Gxa)$
$a = b$
___
$(\forall x)(Fx \supset Gxb)$

where $Fx = x$ *is a person*, $Gxy = x$ *likes* y, $a = Mary$, and $b = Frieda$. We begin constructing the tree as follows:

3 $(\forall x)(Fx \supset Gxa)^*$
   $a = b$
1 $\cancel{(\forall x)(Fx \supset Gxb)}$ $\checkmark$
2 $\cancel{Fe \supset Gcb}$ $\checkmark$
   Fc
   $\cancel{Gcb}$
4 $Fc \supset Gca$ $\checkmark$

$\cancel{Fe}$
x

Gca

Notice that, at this point, the branch at the right remains open. However, extension rule 8 permits us to close it:

$(\forall x)(Fx \supset Gxa)^*$
$a = b$
$\cancel{(\forall x)(Fx \supset Gxb)}$ $\checkmark$
$\cancel{Fe \supset Gcb}$ $\checkmark$
Fc
$\cancel{Gcb}$
$Fc \supset Gca$ $\checkmark$

$\cancel{Fc}$ Gca
x Gcb
               x

We have both $a = b$ and Gca in the same open branch; hence rule 8 permits us to write Gcb, thereby closing the branch.

Now we demonstrate that

$(\forall x)(\forall y)(x = y \supset y = x)$

is a logical truth:

$\cancel{(\forall x)(\forall y)(x = y \supset y = x)}$ $\checkmark$
$\cancel{(\forall y)(a = y \supset y = a)}$ $\checkmark$
$\cancel{a = b \supset b = a}$ $\checkmark$
$a = b$
$\cancel{b = a}$
$\cancel{b = b}$
x

Here we have both $a = b$ and $\cancel{b = a}$ in the same open branch; hence rule 8 permits us to write $\cancel{b = b}$, which in turn allows the branch to close. Note the fact that $(\forall x)(\forall y)(x = y \supset y = x)$ is a logical truth shows that the identity relation is symmetrical. Actually, identity is also a transitive relation since

$(\forall x)(\forall y)(\forall z)[(x = y \land y = z) \supset x = z]$

is a logical truth. Its tree looks like this:

$\cancel{(\forall x)(\forall y)(\forall z)[(x = y \land y = z) \supset x = z]}$ $\checkmark$
$\cancel{(\forall y)(\forall z)[(a = y \land y = z) \supset a = z]}$ $\checkmark$
$\cancel{(\forall z)[(a = b \land b = z) \supset a = z]}$ $\checkmark$
$\cancel{(a = b \land b = c) \supset a = c}$ $\checkmark$
$a = b \land b = c$ $\checkmark$
$\cancel{a = c}$
$a = b$
$b = c$
$a = c$
x

Here we have both $a = b$ and $b = c$ in the same open branch; hence rule 8 permits us to replace b in $a = b$ by c, and so we write $a = c$, thereby allowing the branch to close.

Finally, we note that the identity relation is also totally reflexive by demonstrating that

$$(\forall x)x = x$$

is a logical truth:

Clearly, then, the identity relation is an equivalence relation.

EXERCISE 9.11.1

1 Show whether the following argument forms are valid in the semantic sense. If not, produce at least one counterinterpretation.

*(a) $(\forall x)(Fx \supset Gx)$
      $\sim(Fa \supset Hb)$
      $(\forall x)(Gx \supset Hx)$
      ─────────
      $a \neq b$

(b) $(\exists x)(Fx \wedge Gx)$
     $Fa \wedge (\forall x)(Fx \supset x = a)$
     ──────────────────
     Ga

*(c) $(\exists x)(Fx \wedge Gx)$
      $(\exists x)[Fx \wedge (\forall y)(Fy \supset x = y)] \wedge Hx\}$
      ──────────────────
      $(\exists x)(Gx \wedge Hx)$

(d) Fa
     ──────────
     $(\exists x)(x = a \wedge Fx)$

(e) $(\exists x)(\exists y)(\forall z)(z = x \vee z = y)$
     $Fa \wedge Fb$
     $a \neq b$
     ──────────────
     $(\forall x)Fx$

*(f) Fa
      $(\exists x)(\forall y)x = y$
      ──────────────
      $(\exists x)(\forall y)(Fy \equiv x = y)$

*(g) $(\forall x)(x = a \supset Fx)$
      $a \neq b$
      ────────
      $\sim Fb$

(h) $(\forall x)(x = a \supset Fx)$
     $a = b$
     ────────
     Fb

2 Determine whether the following statement forms are logical truths, contradictions, or contingencies.

(a) $(\exists x)x = a$
(b) $(\forall x)Fx \equiv (\exists y)(x = y \wedge Fy)$
*(c) $Fa \equiv (\forall x)(x = a \supset Fx)$
(d) $(\forall x)a = x$
*(e) $(\forall x)[a = x \supset (Fx \supset Fa)]$
(f) $(\exists x)(\exists y)(\forall z)(z = x \vee z = y)$
(g) $(\forall x)(\forall y)(\forall z)[(x = y \wedge x = z) \supset y = z]$
*(h) $(\exists x)\{(Fx \wedge Gx) \wedge (\forall y)[(Fy \wedge Gy) \supset x = y] \supset (\forall x)Fx\}$

3 Determine whether the following arguments are valid.

    (a) Nobody likes the person who likes Mary. Jane is the person who likes Mary. Consequently, nobody likes Jane.

  *(b) Only one person was able to perform the task. The man who loves Mary was able to perform the task. Moreover, the person who knows Fred was able to perform the task. Therefore, the person who knows Fred is the man who loves Mary.

    (c) Zero is less than every other number. Therefore, no number is less than zero.

    (d) The President of the United States is a Democrat. Fred is not a Democrat. Therefore, Fred is not President of the United States.

  *(e) John is an Olympic athlete. All Olympic athletes are well disciplined. The best swimmer in the world is not well disciplined. As a consequence, the best swimmer in the world is not John.

    (f) The director of *Close Encounters of the Third Kind* is Spielberg. But Spielberg is also the director of *Jaws*. Evidently, then, the director of *Close Encounters of the Third Kind* is the director of *Jaws*.

  *(g) Everybody is mortal. Therefore, the kindest person in the world is mortal.

    (h) Everybody is mortal. There is exactly one kind person. Therefore, the kindest person in the world is mortal.

    (i) Every senator at the reception was a Democrat. Now, not only was every Democrat campaigning, but at most two people were campaigning. Moreover, there were at least two senators at the reception. As a result, there were exactly two Democrats.

  *(j) Anyone who knows Ferd likes him better than anyone who doesn't know him. Only the ugliest person that I know knows Ferd. Now, every ugly person that I know is interesting. Therefore, the person who likes Ferd most is interesting.

9.12

SYNTACTIC ANALYSIS OF IDENTITY

In order to deal with deductions involving identity, we need only introduce three additional transformation rules to Natural Deduction System Ⴢ. We will call the resulting system Ⴢ⁼. The additional rules are as follows.

Additional Transformation Rules

12 Positive Identity Exchange (P.I.E.)

$$
\begin{array}{lll}
 & \cdot & \cdot \\
l & s = t & \\
 & \cdot & \\
m & A & \\
 & \cdot & \\
n & A(t,s) & l, m, \text{P.I.E.} \\
 & \cdot &
\end{array}
$$

13 Negative Identity Exchange (N.I.E.)

$$
\begin{array}{lll}
 & \cdot & \cdot \\
l & A & \\
 & \cdot & \\
m & {\sim}A(t,s) & \\
 & \cdot & \\
n & s \neq t & l, m, \text{N.I.E.} \\
 & \cdot &
\end{array}
$$

m $s = s$ T.R.I.

The rules of Positive Identity Exchange and Negative Identity Exchange are structurally similar to Interpretation Rules 8a and 8b, respectively. P.I.E. effectively says that if we have $s = t$, then we may replace one occurrence of s with t in any line of a deduction and write the result A(t,s) as the next line. N.I.E., on the other hand, states that if we have in a deduction both a statement form A and its negation with some occurrence of s replaced by t, then we may add $s \neq t$. Notice, incidentally, that these rules still hold (although vacuously) when s does not occur in A. In that case, A(t,s) is just A and so P.I.E. amounts to reiteration. However, in such a case the premises of N.I.E. amount to A and $\sim$A. T.R.I. simply states that the identity relation is totally reflexive. That anything whatsoever is itself and not some other thing is perhaps the most venerable truism. Surely, nothing could be more intuitive. However, since this rule is our first and only one-step transformation rule, it deserves further comment. You will recall that in Section 9.11 we proved that $s = s$ is a law of logic. Accordingly, we should expect that $\varnothing \vdash s = s$ and so $\vdash s = s$. Therefore, T.R.I. simply stipulates that this is the case.

We now demonstrate how these rules are to be used by constructing a few deductions. Let's first look at the following argument form:

$(\forall x)[Fx \supset (x = a \lor x = b)]$
$(\exists x)(Fx \land Gx)$

$Ga \lor Gb$

We construct a deduction for it in the following way:

	1	$(\forall x)[Fx \supset (x = a \lor x = b)]$	
	2	$(\exists x)(Fx \land Gx)$	/ $Ga \lor Gb$
1	3	$Fc \land Gc$	$a1$
1	4	Fc	3, Simp.
1	5	Gc	3, Simp.
1	6	$Fc \supset (c = a \lor c = b)$	1, U.I.
1	7	$c = a \lor c = b$	6, 4, M.P.
2, 1	8	$\sim(Ga \lor Gb)$	$a2$
2, 1	9	$\sim Ga \land \sim Gb$	8, DeM.
2, 1	10	$\sim Ga$	9, Simp.
2, 1	11	$c \neq a$	5, 10, N.I.E.
2, 1	12	$c = b$	7, 11, D.S.
2, 1	13	$\sim Gb$	9, Simp.
2, 1	14	Gb	5, 12, P.I.E.

2, 1	15	$Gb \wedge \sim Gb$	14, 13, Conj.
~~2~~, 1	16	$\sim\sim(Ga \vee Gb)$	8—15, R.A.
1	17	$Ga \vee Gb$	16, D.N.
~~1~~	18	$Ga \vee Gb$	2, 3—17, E.I.

We have already observed that the identity relation is symmetrical since $(\forall x)(\forall y)(x = y \supset y = x)$ is a logical truth. We now show that it is a theorem of $\mathfrak{J}^=$:

			/ $(\forall x)(\forall y)(x = y \supset y = x)$
1	1	$a = b$	a1
1	2	$a = a$	T.R.I.
1	3	$b = a$	2, 1, P.I.E.
1	4	$a = b \supset b = a$	1—3, Ded.
	5	$(\forall y)(a = y \supset y = a)$	4, U.G.
	6	$(\forall x)(\forall y)(x = y \supset (y = x)$	5, U.G.

We now show that Fa is deductively equivalent to $(\exists x)(x = a \wedge Fx)$. First, we show that $\{Fa\} \vdash (\exists x)(x = a \wedge Fx)$:

	1	Fa	
			/ $(\exists x)(x = a \wedge Fx)$
1	2	$\sim(\exists x)(x = a \wedge Fx)$	a1
1	3	$(\forall x)\sim(x = a \wedge Fx)$	2, Q.E.
1	4	$\sim(a = a \wedge Fa)$	3, U.I.
1	5	$a \neq a \vee \sim Fa$	4, DeM.
1	6	$\sim\sim Fa$	1, D.N.
1	7	$a \neq a$	5, 6, D.S.
1	8	$a = a$	T.R.I.
1	9	$a \neq a \wedge a = a$	8, 7, Conj.
~~1~~	10	$\sim\sim(\exists x)(x = a \wedge Fx)$	2—9, R.A.
	11	$(\exists x)(x = a \wedge Fx)$	10, D.N.

Next, we show that $\{(\exists x)(x = a \wedge Fx)\} \vdash Fa$:

	1	$(\exists x)(x = a \wedge Fx)$	
			/ Fa
1	2	$b = a \wedge Fb$	a1
1	3	$b = a$	2, Simp.
1	4	Fb	2, Simp.
1	5	Fa	3, 4, P.I.E.
~~1~~	6	Fa	1, 2—5, E.I.

Clearly, $Fa \leftrightarrow (\exists x)(x = a \wedge Fx)$.

In Section 9.6, some of the properties of relations were discussed. A property that wasn't mentioned there but now can be mentioned since we have been introduced to identity is called *antisymmetry*. A relation, F is antisymmetrical if and only if

$(\forall x)(\forall y)[(Fxy \wedge Fyx) \supset x = y]$

Obviously, the identity relation is antisymmetrical since

$$(\forall x)(\forall y)[(x = y \land y = x) \supset x = y]$$

is no doubt a theorem of $\mathfrak{I}$. A well-known antisymmetrical relation is *being a subset of*. Undoubtedly, if a is a subset of b and b is a subset of a, then a is the same set as b.

A very curious fact is that there is only one relation which can be totally reflexive, symmetrical, and antisymmetrical, and that is the identity relation. This means that the identity relation is *unique* in this respect. Now, how is it possible to prove that the identity relation is the only relation that can be totally reflexive, symmetrical, and antisymmetrical? Quite simply. Where F is any totally reflexive, symmetrical, and antisymmetrical relation, we must show that Fab is equivalent to $a = b$. In other words we must show

$$(\forall x)(\forall y)(Fxy \equiv x = y)$$

More specifically, we must show that

$$\{(\forall x)Fxx, \ (\forall x)(\forall y)(Fxy \supset Fyx), \ (\forall x)(\forall y)[(Fxy \land Fyx) \supset x = y]\} \vdash$$
$$(\forall x)(\forall y)(Fxy \equiv x = y)$$

is true. This way of stating what we want to prove ensures that the relation F has the desired properties. The deduction proceeds in the following fashion:

	1	$(\forall x)Fxx$	
	2	$(\forall x)(\forall y)(Fxy \supset Fyx)$	
	3	$(\forall x)(\forall y)[(Fxy \land Fyx) \supset x = y]$ ____/ $(\forall x)(\forall y)(Fxy \equiv x = y)$	
1	4	Fab	$a1$
1	5	$(\forall y)(Fay \supset Fya)$	2, U.I.
1	6	$Fab \supset Fba$	5, U.I.
1	7	Fba	4, 6, M.P.
1	8	$Fab \land Fba$	4, 7, Conj.
1	9	$(\forall y)[(Fay \land Fya) \supset a = y]$	3, U.I.
1	10	$(Fab \land Fba) \supset a = b$	9, U.I.
1	11	$a = b$	10, 8, M.P.
✗	12	$Fab \supset a = b$	4—11, Ded.
2	13	$a = b$	$a2$
2	14	Faa	1, U.I.
2	15	Fab	14, 13, P.I.E.
✗	16	$a = b \supset Fab$	13—15, Ded.
	17	$(Fab \supset a = b) \land (a = b \supset Fab)$	12, 16, Conj.
	18	$Fab \equiv a = b$	17, Bic.
	19	$(\forall y)(Fay \equiv a = y)$	18, U.G.
	20	$(\forall x)(\forall y)(Fxy \equiv x = y)$	19, U.G.

EXERCISE 9.12

1 Show that the following argument forms are valid in the syntactic sense.

(a) $(\forall x)(Fx \supset Gx)$
Fa
$a = b$
_____
Gb

*(b) $(\forall x)[Fx \supset (\forall y)(Fy \supset x = y)]$
Fa
$a \neq b$
_____
$\sim Fb$

(c) $(\forall x)(Fx \supset \sim Gx)$
Fa
Gb
_____
$a \neq b$

*(d) $a = b$
_____
$c = a \equiv c = b$

*(e) $(\forall x)(\forall y)[(Fx \wedge Fy) \supset x = y]$
$(\exists x)Fx$
_____
$(\exists x)[Fx \wedge (\forall y)(Fy \supset x = y)]$

(f) $(\exists x)[Fx \wedge (\forall y)(Fy \supset y = x)]$
$(\forall x)(Gx \supset Fx)$
$(\exists x)Gx$
_____
$(\exists x)[Gx \wedge (\forall y)(Gy \supset y = x)]$

*(g) $(\forall x)(Fx \supset x = a)$
Fb
_____
$a = b$

(h) $(\forall x)(Fx \supset x = a)$
$(\forall x)(Fx \supset Gx)$
Fb
_____
$(\exists x)(Fx \wedge Gx)$

2 Show that the following statement forms are theorems of $\mathfrak{F}^{=}$.

(a) $(\forall x)(\forall y)(Fxy \supset x = y) \supset (\forall x)[Gx \supset (\forall y)(Fxy \supset Gy)]$
*(b) $Fa \supset (\exists x)(x = a \wedge Fx)$
(c) $(\forall x)[Fx \supset (\exists y)(y = x \wedge Fy)]$
(d) $(\forall x)(\exists y)[x = y \wedge (\forall z)(x = z \supset z = y)]$
*(e) $(\forall x)Fxx \supset (\forall x)(\exists y)Fxy$

3 Show that the following pair of statement forms is deductively equivalent in $\mathfrak{F}^{=}$.

$(\exists x)[Fx \wedge (\forall y)(Fy \supset y = x)]$
$(\exists x)(\forall y)(Fy \equiv y = x)$

4 Show that each of the following arguments is valid in the syntactic sense.
*(a) Everyone knows Jack even though he is John. John is a good friend. Therefore, there is a good friend whom everyone knows.
(b) Tom is the only person who likes Mary. Fred is the only person who likes everybody. Some of those who like Mary also like everybody. Consequently, Tom is Fred.
(c) Jim is the fastest runner on the team. However, Jim is not faster than Sam. But, then, Sam is a runner on the team. Therefore, Jim is Sam.
*(d) The logician at Dumple University is a philosopher. Therefore, every logician at Dumple University is a philosopher.

THE SOUNDNESS AND COMPLETENESS OF Ɔ AND Ɔ⁼

Although Ɔ is not decidable, it is possible to prove the following meta-theorems:

> **Soundness Metatheorem:** For any set **S** of statement forms and any statement form A, **S** ⊢ A only if **S** ⊩ A.

> **Strong Semantic Completeness Metatheorem:** For any set **S** of statement forms and any statement form A, **S** ⊩ A only if **S** ⊢ A.

To prove the soundness metatheorem, we need to prove only that the additional rules U.I., U.G., E.I., and Q.E. are sound, i.e, never allow us to infer a false conclusion from true premises. The demonstration of the soundness of all the other rules for 𝔇 will carry over to Ɔ unchanged. For U.I. and E.G., this is easily accomplished. Consider first U.I. We regard $(\forall x)$ A as the conjunction of all the statement forms $A(s/x)$ for all constants s. Thus if $(\forall x)$A is true on an interpretation, then each of these conjuncts must be true. Therefore, we may correctly infer any one of them. In effect, U.I. is a generalized form of Simplification. A similar situation holds for E.G. If $A(s/x)$ is true for any term s, then $(\exists x)$A, which we regard as the disjunction of all statement forms $A(s/x)$ for every term s, will also be true, since a disjunction is true if one of its disjuncts is true. Again, we might compare E.G. to an extended form of Addition. The two Q.E. rules can be derived from the DeMorganization rules. If we write $\sim(\forall x)$A as

$$\sim[A(a/x) \wedge A(b/x) \wedge A(c/x) \wedge \cdots]$$

we can then apply DeMorganization to transform this into

$$\sim A(a/x) \vee \sim A(b/x) \vee \sim A(c/x) \vee \cdots$$

And, as we regard it, this is simply $(\exists x)\sim$A. A similar transformation can be performed on $\sim(\exists x)$A and $(\forall x)\sim$A. Since we already know that the DeMorganization rules are sound, Q.E. is sound.

The soundness of the two remaining rules of Ɔ, U.G. and E.I., is somewhat harder to prove. Speaking in terms of deducibility, U.G. in effect says: if s does not occur in any statement form in **S** and if **S** ⊢ A, then **S** ⊢ $(\forall x)$A(x/s). Let's show the soundness of this rule in stages. Suppose that we can deduce A from **S** without using either U.G. or E.I. In that case, since all the other rules of Ɔ are sound, **S** ⊩ A. However, nothing about that deduction can possibly depend on the fact that s occurs in A, since s doesn't occur in anything in **S**. Thus, we could have constructed a deduction for any other statement form A(t/s) instead. Therefore, given the soundness of all these deductions, we have S ⊩ A(t/s) for all constants t that don't occur in S. As a matter of fact, we can show that S ⊩ A(t/s) even for constants that do occur in A, if S is consistent. Therefore, if S ⊢ A where a term s occurs in A that doesn't occur in any statement form in S, then S ⊩ A(t/s) for every constant t. This means that each of the infinitely many conjuncts of (∀x)A(x/s) is entailed by S, and so S ⊩ (∀x)A(x/s), which is what U.G. tells us. We might compare U.G. to infinitely many applications of Conjunction.

The soundness of E.I. is related in a less direct way to Constructive Dilemma. E.I. tells us that if we have constructed a deduction of (∃x)A from S, we may then assume A(s/x), deduce some other statement form B, and then discharge our assumption if s doesn't occur in the premises, in any assumptions in force, or in B. To see why this is sound, suppose that we have a deduction of (∃x)A from S that doesn't use E.I. This deduction will then be sound, and so S ⊩ (∃x)A. We now assume A(s/x), since we can, of course, assume whatever we wish. If we now are able to deduce B, we could discharge the assumption with Deduction to get A(s/x) ⊃ B. Now, we could repeat this deduction infinitely many times, once for each statement form A(t/x) that is one of the implicit disjuncts of (∃x)A, leaving out those containing constants already in the deduction. Each time, we will get a conditional A(t/x) ⊃ B. Now, if we conjoin these, we will get something like this:

$$[A(a/x) \supset B] \land [A(b/x) \supset B] \land [A(c/x) \supset B] \land \cdots$$

Thus, we could get infinite conjunctions by infinitely many uses of Conjunction. Now, we already have a long disjunction of all the antecedents of these conditionals implicit in (∃x)A:

$$A(a/x) \lor A(b/x) \lor A(c/x) \lor \cdots$$

These resemble the premises for Constructive Dilemma, and so we can infer

$$B \lor B \lor B \lor B \lor \cdots$$

And, by applications of Repetition, this becomes simply B. Consequently, E.I. is sound. In effect, it tells us this: if you can get B from every disjunct implicit in (∃x)A, then you can get it from (∃x)A.

The soundness of Ⅎ= follows quickly from the soundness of Ⅎ. P.I.E. lets us infer A(t,s) from A and s = t. IR8a tells us that if I(s = t) = T, then I[A(t/s)] = I(A). We need only show that if I(s = t) = T, then I[A(t,s)] = I(A). Note that the only difference between A(t/s) and A(t,s) is that in the first t replaces *every* occurrence of s while in the second it might replace only *some* occurrences of **s**. Now, if I(**s** = **t**) = T, then I[A(**t**/**s**)] = I(A) for every statement form A. Consider, then, some statement form A(**t**,**s**) formed by replacing some occurrences of **s** with **t**. If **s** = **t** is true, then I[A(**t**,**s**)(**t**/**s**)] = I[A(**t**,**s**)], since the truth value of every statement form is unchanged by substituting **t** for **s**. However, since the only difference between A and A(**t**,**s**) is that A(**t**,**s**) has **t**'s in some places where A has **s**'s, A(**t**,**s**)(**t**/**s**) will be the same as A(**t**/**s**)—we just replace the rest of the **s**'s with **t**'s. So I[A(**t**/**s**)] = I[A(**t**,**s**)]. However, since I(**s** = **t**) = T, we also have I(A) = I[A(**t**/**s**)]. Consequently, I[A(**t**,**s**)] = I(A). Therefore, if I(**s** = **t**) = T and I(A) = T, then I[A(**t**,**s**)] = T. Thus, P.I.E. is sound. A similar argument shows that N.I.E. is sound. The soundness of T.R.I. follows from the fact that every statement form of the form **s** = **s** is a logical truth, which is easily shown. If I(**s** = **s**) = F, then according to IR8b, for some statement form A, I(A) and I[A(**s**/**s**)] are not the same. However, A(**s**/**s**) is just A, and so I(A) is both T and F, contradicting IR0.

The completeness of ℑ and ℑ= is more difficult to prove, and a strict proof is well beyond the scope of this book. However, we can at least indicate the structure of a possible proof. Our proof depends on the following claim:

> A semantic tree for an argument form closes if and only if the argument form is valid.

To show this, we need to show that every infinite tree corresponds to an invalid argument form. Remember that an argument form is invalid if and only if it has a counterinterpretation. Now, if a tree closes at some step, we can find a counterinterpretation for its argument form. What if it never closes? In that case, we can still retrieve a counterinterpretation from it, but it will be an *infinite* counterinterpretation. In a sense, of course, every interpretation is infinite, since each interpretation must specify truth values for infinitely many statement forms. Moreover, as we have noted, if a counterinterpretation includes true universal or false existential quantifications, it must include infinitely many specifications of truth values of atomic predications. With an infinite tree, the situation is simply more complex: the counterinterpretation is infinite, and we never get finished with a presentation of it in any simple way. Thus, an infinite tree would yield an infinite counterinterpretation if we could ever finish it. We could also express this in another way: if the tree for an argument form is infinite, then however far we develop it, we still have an interpretation that makes the premises true and the conclusion false. Of course, we never get all the details of this interpretation, but if the tree is *in fact* infinite, we can be sure that we'll never run into a contradiction in supposing that the argument form has a counterinterpretation. Now, since an infinite tree always means that an argument is invalid, consequently every valid argument form has a finite tree that closes. Therefore, we will eventually come up with a finite closed tree for any valid argument form. From this, it's a mechanical matter to retrieve a deduction in ℑ corresponding to a valid argument form (the details are sketched in the Appendix). Consequently, whenever S ⊩ A in ℗, S ⊢ A in ℑ.

To extend this to ℑ⁼ is simple, given the completeness of ℑ (again, the details are in the Appendix).

There is an important limitation on the above proofs, from a theoretical point of view: our proof of the strong completeness theorem holds *only if the set* S *of premises of the deduction is finite*. Of course, this is always the case with argument forms derived from actual arguments, but there is no theoretical reason to exclude the notion of a relation of entailment between an *infinite* set S and a statement form A. In fact, we can easily illustrate such a case. Let S be the following infinite set:

{Fa, Fb, Fc, Fd, . . . (and so on for every individual constant)}

If every member of S is true, then clearly $(\forall x)Fx$ is true. However, we can't possibly construct semantic trees in a meaningful sense for infinite sets. In fact, our semantic theory generally is unable to deal effectively with such sets. In order to establish the completeness of ℑ and ℑ⁼ in general, we would need to introduce more elaborate techniques or an alternative semantic theory.

REVIEW EXERCISES FOR CHAPTER 9

1   Determine whether each of the following argument forms is semantically valid. If it is, also show that it is syntactically valid. Provide counterinterpretations for those argument forms which are not semantically valid.

*(a) $(\forall x)(\forall y)(Fxy \supset Gxy)$
$\sim(\exists x)(\exists y)Gxy$
_____
$(\exists x)(\exists y)Fxy$

(b) $(\forall x)(Fxa \supset Fax)$
$(\exists x)\sim Fax$
_____
$(\exists x)\sim Fxa$

*(c) $(\forall x)(\forall y)Fxy \supset (\exists x)(Fxx \wedge Gx)$
$(\exists x)Fxx$
$(\exists x)(Gx \wedge Hx)$
_____
$(\exists x)Gx \supset (\forall x)(Gx \supset Hx)$

*(d) $(\forall x)(\forall y)(Fxy \supset Gxy)$
$(\forall x)(\exists y)Fyx$
_____
$(\forall x)(\exists y)Gyx$

(e) $(\forall x)(Fax \supset b = x)$
Gab
$b \neq c$
_____
$\sim Fac$

*(f) $(\forall x)(\forall y)[(Fx \wedge x \neq y) \supset Gxy]$
$Fa \wedge \sim Fb$
_____
Gab

*(g) $(\forall x)(Fx \supset Gb)$
_____
$(\exists x)Fx \supset Gb$

(h) $(\forall x)(\forall y)[(\exists z)(Fzy \wedge Fxz) \supset Fyx]$
$\sim(\exists x)Fxx$
_____
$(\forall x)(\forall y)(Fyx \supset \sim Fxy)$

(i) $(\forall x)(\exists y)Fxy$

    $\overline{(\exists y)Fay}$

*(j) $(\forall x)(\forall y)(\exists z)(Fyz \supset Fxy)$

    $\sim Faa$

    $\overline{\sim Fab}$

*(k) $(\forall x)[Fx \supset (\forall y)(Fy \supset Gxy)]$

    $(\exists x)(Fx \wedge (\exists y)\sim Gxy)$

    $\overline{(\exists x)\sim Fx}$

(l) $(\forall x)[(\exists y)(Fyx \supset (\forall z)Fxz]$

    $\overline{(\forall y)(\forall z)(Fyz \supset Fzy)}$

(m) $(\forall x)[Fx \wedge \sim Gx) \supset (\exists y)(Hxy \wedge Iy)]$

    $(\exists x)[(Jx \wedge Fx) \wedge (\forall y)(Hxy \supset Jy)]$

    $(\forall x)(Jx \supset \sim Gx)$

    $\overline{(\exists x)(Jx \wedge Ix)}$

(n) $(\forall x)Fx \supset Ga$

    $(\forall x)(Gx \supset x = b)$

    $\overline{(\forall x)Fx \supset a = b}$

(o) $(\exists x)(\exists y)\{[(Fx \wedge Fy) \wedge x \neq y] \wedge (Gx \wedge Gy)\}$

    $(\forall x)(Gx \supset \sim Hx)$

    $(\exists x)(Fx \wedge Hx)$

    $\overline{(\exists x)\{(Fx \wedge Hx) \wedge (\forall y)[y \neq x \supset (Fy \supset \sim Hy)]\}}$

2 Determine whether each of the following sets of statement forms is semantically consistent. If it is semantically inconsistent, then show that it is also deductively inconsistent. Provide at least one interpretation for those sets which are semantically consistent.

  (a) $\{\sim(\exists x)(\exists y)Fxy,\ Gaa,\ (\exists x)Gxa \supset (\forall x)Fxx\}$
  *(b) $\{\sim(\exists x)(Fx \wedge Gx),\ (\forall x)(Fx \supset Gx),\ (\exists x)Fx\}$
  (c) $\{(\forall x)(\forall y)(\sim Fxy \vee Gxy),\ (\forall x)\sim(\exists y)Fxy,\ \sim(\exists x)(\exists y)Gxy\}$
  *(d) $\{(\exists x)[(\exists y)Fy \equiv (\exists y)Gxy],\ (\forall x)(Gax \equiv Fx)\}$
  (e) $\{(\forall x)(Fx \supset x = a),\ Fb,\ a = b\}$

3 Determine whether each of the following statement forms is logically true, contingent, or contradictory. If it is logically true, show that it is also a theorem.

  *(a) $[(\exists x)Fx \supset (\exists x)Gx] \supset (\exists x)(Fx \supset Gx)$
  (b) $(\exists x)[(\exists y)Fy \supset Fx]$
  (c) $(\forall x)(\forall y)Fxy \supset (\exists x)Fxx$
  (d) $(\forall x)[(\forall y)(y = x \supset Fy) \supset Fx]$
  (e) $(\exists x)(\forall y)Fxy \supset (\forall y)(\exists x)Fxy$

4 Construct deductions for the following theorem schemata.

  (a) $(\forall \mathbf{x})(A \wedge B) \equiv [(\forall \mathbf{x})A \wedge (\forall \mathbf{x})B]$
  (b) $(\exists \mathbf{x})(A \vee B) \supset (\exists \mathbf{x})A \vee (\exists \mathbf{x})B$
  (c) $\sim(\exists \mathbf{x})A \supset (\forall \mathbf{x})(A \supset B)$
  (d) $(\forall \mathbf{x})[A \vee B) \supset C] \supset [(\forall \mathbf{x})(C \supset D) \supset (\forall \mathbf{x})(A \supset D)]$

5 Determine whether each of the following pairs of statement forms is semantically equivalent. If a given pair is semantically equivalent, also show that it is deductively equivalent.

(a) $(\forall x)(\forall y)Fxy$ $(\forall y)(\forall x)Fxy$
(b) $(\exists x)(\exists y)Fxy$ $(\exists y)(\exists x)Fxy$
*(c) $(\exists x)Fx \supset (\exists y)Gy$ $(\forall x)(\exists y)(Fx \supset Gy)$
(d) $Fa \wedge (\exists x)(\forall y)x = y$ $(\exists x)(\forall y)(Fy \equiv x = y)$
*(e) Fa $(\forall x)(Fx \equiv x = a)$

6 Determine whether each of the following arguments is semantically valid.
Show that each of those which is semantically valid is also syntactically valid.
(a) Tom isn't the only one who wishes to be elected. Therefore, somebody
besides Tom wishes to be elected.
(b) Some logicians are known by all logicians. Therefore, some logicians are
known by themselves.
(c) No number is larger than itself. Therefore, any number larger than every
number is not a number.
(d) Ferd is uglier than John. Ferd is not uglier than anyone who is more
handsome than he. Therefore, John is not more handsome than Ferd.
(e) Jim is the only drunk in town. However, Fred is the only "pothead" in
town. Now, it is evident that some drunks are potheads. Therefore, Jim
is Fred.

APPENDIX

A SKETCH OF A PROOF OF COMPLETENESS
FOR 𝔇, 𝔍, AND 𝔉

In order to prove strong semantic completeness for 𝔇, we must give a procedure for converting any finished semantic tree into a deduction of 𝔇. Now, the semantic tree method begins by assuming that the premises of an argument form are all true and the conclusion false on some interpretation; then, the method tries to show that this assumption is impossible. We convert this into a deduction by assuming the negation of the conclusion of the argument form and then deducing a contradiction. To explain the strategy further, we need to introduce the notion of a *deduction sketch*. A deduction sketch is a fragment of a deduction (with some steps missing) which we obtain from a semantic tree in a certain way. Obviously, we begin with the same premises as the tree. Then, as we indicated, we assume the negation of the conclusion as the first step. For a tree that doesn't branch, we obtain the remaining steps of the deduction sketch quite simply: we write every unslashed statement form unchanged and replace every slashed statement form with its negation. The following example illustrates the process:

$$
\begin{array}{lllll}
\sim(p \vee q) \;\; \checkmark & & 1 & \sim(p \vee q) & \\
r \wedge s \;\; \checkmark & & 2 & r \wedge s & \\
\cline{4-4}
\sim\!p\supset\!s \;\; \checkmark & 1 & 3 & \sim(\sim p \supset s) & \quad\;\; /\; \sim p \supset s \\
& & & & a\,1 \\
p\vee q \;\; \checkmark & & & \sim(p \vee q) & \\
r & & & r & \\
s & & & s & \\
p & & & \sim p & \\
q & & & \sim q & \\
\sim p & & & \sim p & \\
s & & & \sim s & \\
\text{x} & & & &
\end{array}
$$

Now, what we have here are the beginnings of a deduction of $\sim p \supset s$ from $\{\sim(p \vee q), r \wedge s\}$. We start by assuming the negation of the conclusion, and we continue until we arrive at a contradiction. We know that we can get a contradiction since the tree closes and therefore contains some statement variable both slashed and unslashed: our deduction sketch consequently contains both a statement variable and its negation. We can then conjoin these two deduction steps to get a contradiction and discharge our assumption by R.A. to get $\sim\sim(\sim p \supset s)$ and, finally, the conclusion by D.N. Now we must show how to fill in the necessary steps and justifications to make this deduction sketch into a deduction. We can do this by specifying certain deduction steps to be added with each application of a tree rule. First, consider the rule for the inverted wedge: if we have $A \wedge B$, we extend it by writing A and then B below it. This corresponds to two uses of Simplification, as follows:

$A \wedge B$	m	$A \wedge B$	
	.		
A	n	A	m, Simp.
B	$n+1$	B	m, Simp.

Here, all we needed to do was to add justifications to steps already in the deduction sketch. We can treat every other nonbranching tree rule in this way, except that first we must introduce some steps involving replacement rules to transform the initial statement form into a conjunction. For example, the rule $\cancel{A \supset B}$ requires the following strategy (we mark new steps with an asterisk):

$\cancel{A \supset B}$ ✓	m	$\sim(A \supset B)$	
	.	.	
	*n	$\sim(\sim A \vee B)$	m, Imp.
	*$n+1$	$\sim\sim A \wedge \sim B$	n, DeM.
	*$n+2$	$A \wedge \sim B$	$n+1$, D.N.
A	$n+3$	A	$n+2$, Simp.
$\cancel{B}$	$n+4$	$\sim B$	$n+2$, Simp.

We can define a similar strategy for each nonbranching rule. Then, we can convert the deduction sketch given above into a complete deduction using these strategies, as follows:

$\sim(p \vee q)$ ✓			1	$\sim(p \vee q)$	
$r \wedge s$ ✓			2	$r \wedge s$	
					$/ \sim p \supset s$
$\cancel{\sim p \supset s}$ ✓		1	3	$\sim(\sim p \supset s)$	a1
$\cancel{p \vee q}$ ✓		1	4	$\sim(p \vee q)$	1, Reit.
r		1	5	r	2, Simp.
s		1	6	s	2, Simp.
		*1	7	$\sim p \wedge \sim q$	4, DeM.
$\cancel{p}$		1	8	$\sim p$	7, Simp.
$\cancel{q}$		1	9	$\sim q$	7, Simp.
		*1	10	$\sim(\sim\sim p \vee s)$	3, Imp.
		*1	11	$\sim\sim\sim p \wedge \sim s$	10, DeM.
		*1	12	$\sim p \wedge \sim s$	11, D.N.
$\sim p$		1	13	$\sim p$	12, Simp.
$\cancel{s}$		1	14	$\sim s$	12, Simp.
x		*1	15	$s \wedge \sim s$	6, 14, Conj.
		*$\cancel{1}$	16	$\sim\sim(\sim p \supset s)$	3–15, R.A.
		*	17	$\sim p \supset s$	16, D.N.

Notice that we sometimes repeat some statement forms using Reiteration. This is, in fact, unnecessary as far as constructing a deduction is concerned; however, we are trying to describe a completely mechanical procedure for converting a tree into a deduction.

For tree rules which branch, we must use a more elaborate strategy. In effect, we treat each branch as introducing a new assumption (namely, the statement form at the head of the branch). Since all branches close, we ultimately deduce contradictions following each such new assumption, and so we discharge each of them with R.A. In order to incorporate these steps into the entire deduction, we must then use the following strategy:

1 Convert the statement form to which the branching rule is applied into a statement form of the form $A \vee B$.
2 Assume A and deduce a contradiction; then infer $\sim A$ by R.A. (this is the first branch).
3 Assume B and deduce a contradiction; then infer $\sim B$ by R.A. (this is the second branch).
4 Deduce $\sim A \wedge \sim B$ by Conjunction, then $\sim(A \vee B)$ by De-Morganization.
5 Using this last step and the original statement form, deduce $(A \vee B) \wedge \sim(A \vee B)$ by Conjunction.

We now have a contradiction, and so we may discharge the assumption on which this part of the deduction depends. If the only assumption in force is the original one (the negation of the conclusion), we are finished with our deduction. If the branch is preceded by some other branching rule, we discharge the assumption made at that branch.

These techniques allow us to produce a deduction from any completed semantic tree for a valid argument form, as illustrated in the following example:

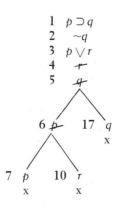

1 $p \supset q$
2 $\sim q$
3 $p \vee r$
4 r
5 q
6 p 17 q
                  x
7 p 10 r
   x   x

$$
\begin{array}{lll}
1 & p \supset q \\
2 & {\sim}q \\
3 & p \vee r \\
\hline
 & & / \; r
\end{array}
$$

dep.		line		justification
1		4	$\sim r$	$a1$
1		5	$\sim q$	2, Reit.
2, 1		6	$\sim p$	$a2$
3, 2, 1	left branch	7	p	$a3$
*3, 2, 1	$p \vee r$	8	$p \wedge \sim p$	6, 7, Conj.
~~3~~, 2, 1		9	$\sim p$	7—8, R.A.
4, 2, 1	right branch	10	r	$a4$
*4, 2, 1	$p \vee r$	11	$r \wedge \sim r$	4, 10, Conj.
~~4~~, 2, 1		12	$\sim r$	10—11, R.A.
* 2, 1		13	$\sim p \wedge \sim r$	9, 12, Conj.
* 2, 1		14	$\sim(p \vee r)$	13, DeM.
* 2, 1		15	$(p \vee r) \wedge \sim(p \vee r)$	3, 14, Conj.
* ~~2~~, 1		16	$\sim\sim p$	6—15, R.A.
5, 1		17	q	$a5$
* 5, 1		18	$q \wedge \sim q$	5, 17, Conj.
* ~~5~~, 1		19	$\sim q$	17—18, R.A.
* 1		20	$\sim\sim p \wedge \sim q$	16, 19, Conj.
* 1		21	$\sim(\sim p \vee q)$	20, DeM.
* 1		22	$\sim(p \supset q)$	21, Imp.
* 1		23	$(p \supset q) \wedge \sim(p \supset q)$	1, 22, Conj.
*		24	$\sim\sim r$	4—23, R.A.
*		25	r	24, D.N.

(Left-margin labels: "left branch $p \supset q$", "left branch $p \vee r$", "left branch" / "right branch"; "right branch $p \supset q$". Assumption $\sim r$ discharged at 24.)

In this deduction, steps 6 to 16 correspond to the left branch obtained by extending $p \supset q$ (note the assumption $\sim p$ at step 6), and steps 17 to 19 correspond to the right branch (q is assumed at 17). Since there is another branch under the left-hand branch, we have two more parts to the proof for each of those branches: 7 to 9 and 10 to 12. After this, we deduce a contradiction to the statement form which created the second branch (we extended $p \vee r$ under p) by Conjunction and DeMorganization and reach a contradiction at step 15. The assumption atop the left branch is discharged at 16, and that over the right branch is discharged at 19. Thus, the negations of both disjuncts of $\sim p \vee q$ have been deduced. Therefore, we can now deduce $\sim(p \supset q)$ by DeMorganization and Implication and derive a contradiction at step 23. From this, we get the conclusion in two steps. The procedure is completely mechanical, but it is highly inefficient; we can easily give a much shorter deduction for this argument form:

$$
\begin{array}{lll}
1 & p \supset q \\
2 & {\sim}q \\
3 & p \vee r \\
\hline
 & & / \; r \\
4 & {\sim}p & \text{1, 2, M.T.} \\
5 & r & \text{3, 4, D.S.}
\end{array}
$$

To prove the completeness of ℑ and ℑ⁼, we must first assume that a tree for a valid argument form in either system will always close after finitely many steps. Then, we can reconstruct a deduction from a finished tree in a manner similar to that given above. All extensions of true universal quantifications correspond directly to applications of U.I. Any extension of a false existential quantification can be handled similarly. First, we will have transformed the slashed statement form (∃x)A into ~(∃x)A. We then arrive at any statement form added to the tree by covering with the steps (∀x)~A (by Q.E.) and ~A(s/x) (by U.I.). Here, ~A(s/x) corresponds to some slashed instance of (∃x)A in the tree. To handle true existential quantifications, we first note that when we extend (∃x)A with A(s/x), we require that s not already occur in that path. In terms of the deduction corresponding to the tree, this will mean that s does not occur in any premise or in any assumption in force at that point (remember that whenever we branch, we effectively make a new assumption). Accordingly, we treat A(s/x), when introduced to extend (∃x)A, as an assumption for E.I. Now, this branch will eventually close, and when it does, we can discharge the assumption at its head with R.A. That assumption cannot be A(s/x), since that step was introduced by extending (∃x)A, which doesn't give a branch. Consequently, when the branch closes, we get ~B for some assumption B. B can't contain s, since it occurs above A(s/x) in the tree, and so neither does ~B. Consequently, we can apply E.I. and discharge the assumption A(s/x). A similar set of procedures will take care of (∀x)A, after first transforming it into (∃x)~A.

Finally, to include the system ℑ⁼, we need only two procedures. The extension rule for s = t corresponds directly to P.I.E., so every statement form added by covering s = t can be added to a deduction by P.I.E. To account for branches which close because of s = s, we need add only the following steps after ~s = s: s = s (by T.R.I.), s = s ∧ ~s = s (by Conjunction), and a discharge of whatever assumption was last introduced by R.A.

SELECTED ANSWERS TO EXERCISES

CHAPTER 1

Review Exercises, p. 18

2 (a) Not a statement (question); (c) not a statement (command); (h) probably meaningless, and so can't be true or false; syntactically appears to be a statement; (j) statement; (k) see answer to (h); but if *Saturday* is a person's name, this is a statement.

CHAPTER 2

Exercise 2.1, p. 24

1 (a) Compound; (b) *Helium is heavier than air*; (c) It is not the case that.
4 (a) Compound; (b) *I like pickles and ice cream*; (c) not.
7 (a) Compound; (b) *I will attend the party, I will attend the picnic*; (c) neither . . . nor.
10 (a) Compound; (b) *I will attend the picnic, Mary attends the picnic*; (c) only if.
13 (a) Compound; (b) *Beethoven was a great composer, Mozart was a great composer*; (c) if . . . then.

Exercise 2.2, p. 27

1 No; 3 Yes; 5 No; 7 Yes; 9 No.

Exercise 2.3.1, p. 31

1 P even though R; 3 If L, then H; 5 Either I or M; 7 A but O; 9 C unless E.

Exercise 2.4, p. 60

1 M only if J, $p \supset q$; 3 Not only E, but also C, $p \wedge q$; 5 E provided that A, $q \supset p$; 7 Not U, $\sim p$; 9 R when L, $q \supset p$; 11 W despite the fact that E, $p \wedge q$.

Review Exercises, p. 61

2 (b) p (counterfactual conditional); (c) $p \wedge q$ (note that *and* in *Mary had a ham and cheese sandwich* is not a connecting word); (f) $p \supset q$; (j) $\sim p$.

chapter 3

Exercise 3.1, p. 69

1 (a) $(p \vee q) \wedge (r \supset s)$; $[(p \vee q) \wedge r] \supset s$; $[p \vee (q \wedge r)] \supset s$; $p \vee [q \wedge (r \supset s)]$; $p \vee [(q \wedge r) \supset s]$
  (c) $(p \supset q) \wedge \sim (r \equiv s)$; $p \supset [q \wedge \sim (r \equiv s)]$
2 (a) $(p \wedge q) \wedge r$; (c) $(p \supset q) \wedge [\sim q \supset (r \wedge s)]$; (e) $q \supset p$; (g) $p \supset (q \vee r)$; (i) $\sim p \wedge (\sim q \wedge r)$; (k) $p \supset (\sim r \supset \sim q)$ (If p, then not q given that not r); (m) $p \supset q$; (o) $\sim q \supset \sim p$ (not p unless q); (q) $(\sim q \supset p) \wedge [r \equiv (q \wedge \sim p)]$ (p provided that

not q, but r if and only if both q and not p); (s) $p \equiv (\sim q \vee r)$ (is false = is not true).

Exercise 3.2, p. 78

Each *column* for a truth table follows the statement form *horizontally* below to save space.

1 (c) p—TTFF; q—TFTF; $\sim p$—FFTT; $q \vee p$—TTTF; $\sim p \wedge (q \vee p)$—FFTF.
(f) p—TTTTFFFF; q—TTFFTTFF; r—TFTFTFTF; $\sim p$—FFFFTTTT; $\sim q$—FFTTFFTT; $p \vee \sim q$—TTTTFFTT; $\sim r$—FTFTFTFT; $\sim q \vee \sim p$—FFTTTTTT; $(p \vee \sim q) \wedge r$—TFTFFFTF; $(\sim q \vee \sim p) \wedge \sim r$—FFFTFTFT; $[(p \vee \sim q) \wedge r] \supset [(\sim q \vee \sim p) \wedge \sim r]$—FTFTTTFT. (g) p—TTFF; q—TFTF; $p \wedge q$—TFFF; $p \supset (p \wedge q)$—TFTF; $\sim p$—FFTT; $[p \supset (p \wedge q)] \supset \sim p$—FTTT.

2 (c) True when any of the statements *Mary will attend the picnic*, *Jim attends the picnic*, and *Tom attends the picnic* is true. (e) Not true under any possible circumstances.

Exercise 3.2.1, p. 80

2 p—TTFF; q—TFTF; $p \supset q$—TFTT; $\sim p$—FFTT; $\sim q$—FTFT; $\sim(p \supset q)$—FTFF; $\sim p \supset \sim q$—TTFT; not logically equivalent.

7 p—TTFF; q—TFTF; $\sim p$—FFTT; $p \equiv q$—TFFT; $\sim(p \equiv q)$—FTTF; $\sim p \equiv q$—FTTF; logically equivalent.

9 p—TTFF; q—TFTF; $\sim p$—FFTT; $\sim q$—FTFT; $\sim p \wedge \sim q$—FFFT; $p \vee q$—TTTF; $\sim(\sim p \wedge \sim q)$—TTTF; logically equivalent.

Exercise 3.2.3, p. 88

1 p—TF; $\sim p$—FT; $p \supset \sim p$—FT; contingent.

3 p—TF; $\sim p$—FT; $p \wedge \sim p$—FF; $\sim p \supset (p \wedge \sim p)$—TF; contingent.

5 p—TTFF; q—TFTF; $p \vee q$—TTTF; $\sim q$—FTFT; $\sim p$—FFTT; $\sim q \supset \sim p$—TFTT; $(p \vee q) \supset (\sim q \supset \sim p)$—TFTT; contingent.

7 p—TTTTFFFF; q—TTFFTTFF; r—TFTFTFTF; $p \wedge q$—TTFFFFFF; $(p \wedge q) \supset r$—TFTTTTTT; $\sim r$—FTFTFTFT; $\sim q$—FFTTFFTT; $\sim r \supset \sim q$—TFTTTFTT; $p \supset (\sim r \supset \sim q)$—TFTTTTTT; $[(p \wedge q) \supset r] \supset [p \supset (\sim r \supset \sim q)]$—TTTTTTTT; tautology.

9 p—TTTTFFFF; q—TTFFTTFF; r—TFTFTFTF; $p \supset q$—TTFFTTTT; $\sim p$—FFFFTTTT; $q \wedge \sim p$—FFFFTTFF; $(q \wedge \sim p) \supset r$—TTTTTFTT; $(p \supset q) \vee [(q \wedge \sim p) \supset r]$—TTTTTTTT; tautology.

Review Exercises, p. 89

1 (b) $[(p \wedge \sim q) \vee r] \wedge \{r \supset [\sim u \supset (s \wedge t)]\}$ (p instead of q unless r, in which case s and t if not u); (c) $\sim r \supset \sim (p \wedge \sim q)$ [not (p without q) unless r]; (f) $p \supset [\sim s \supset (r \supset q)]$ [if p, then (q if r) unless s]; (i) $p \supset \{(q \vee r) \wedge [r \supset (t \supset s)]\}$ (if p, then q unless r, in which case s if t).

2 (b) p—TTTTFFFF; q—TTFFTTFF; r—TFTFTFTF; $\sim p$—FFFFTTTT; $r \supset \sim p$—FTFTTTTT; $\sim(r \supset \sim p)$—TFTFFFFF; $q \wedge \sim(r \supset \sim p)$—TFFFFFFF; $p \equiv [q \wedge \sim(r \supset \sim p)]$—TFFFFTTTT; (d) p—TTFF; q—TFTF; $\sim q$—FTFT; $\sim q \wedge p$—FTFF; $p \supset q$—TFTT; $p \wedge (p \supset q)$—TFFF; $p \wedge (\sim q \wedge p)$—FTFF; $[p \wedge (p \supset q)] \vee [p \wedge (\sim q \wedge p)]$—TTFF.

4 (a) equivalent; (c) equivalent; (e) not equivalent.

5 (a) tautology; (c) contingent; (e) tautology; (g) tautology.

CHAPTER 4

Exercise 4.2, p. 99

1 Conclusion: *There is absolutely no doubt that Mr. Pickwick murdered the butler.*
3 Conclusion: *Consequently, she'll have to find someone else to live there while she's away.*
5 Conclusion: *John probably isn't going to quit his job after all.*

Exercise 4.3, p. 103

2 *Symbolic Abbreviation*
M but N; besides C.
R, even though F.
S and B.
_____

Y.

Formalization
$(p \wedge q) \wedge r$
$s \wedge t$
$u \wedge v$
_____
w

6 *Symbolic Abbreviation*
P assuming that not M.
M if and only if I and U.
I and U unless S.
_____

P so long as S.

Formalization
$\sim q \supset p$
$q \equiv (r \wedge s)$
$\sim t \supset (r \wedge s)$
_____
$t \supset p$

Exercise 4.4, p. 114

2 Note that the conclusion is *I don't think the astronauts actually went to the moon.*

Symbolic Abbreviation
If M, B.
Not B.
_____
Not M.

Formalization
$p \supset q$
$\sim q$
_____
$\sim p$

4 Note that this is a chained argument. Consequently, every conclusion is omitted except for the very last one.

Symbolic Abbreviation
If M, W.
If M, then B and R.
If M, then L; and not L.
_____
Not R.

Formalization
$p \supset q$
$p \supset (r \wedge s)$
$(p \supset t) \wedge \sim t$
_____
$\sim s$

Review Exercises, p. 115

2 Note that in this argument the word *which* is treated as *and*.

Symbolic Abbreviation
E unless P
If E, T, and if T, R.
If R, I.
Not G unless I.
Not I unless T, and not T unless E.
_____
If G, not P.

Formalization
$\sim q \supset p$
$(p \supset r) \wedge (r \supset s)$
$s \supset t$
$\sim t \supset \sim u$
$(\sim r \supset \sim t) \wedge (\sim p \supset \sim r)$
_____
$u \supset \sim q$

4 *Symbolic Abbreviation*   *Formalization*
   Not D unless E. $\sim q \supset \sim p$
   T. r
   ─────────────────────────   ─────────
   D even if not E, so long as T. $r \supset p$
6 *Symbolic Abbreviation*   *Formalization*
   Not H without G unless R. $\sim r \supset (\sim p \wedge \sim q)$
   D if G. $q \supset s$
   (Intermediate conclusion)
   H. p
   ─────────────────────────   ─────────
   D if not R. $\sim r \supset s$

CHAPTER 5

Exercise 5.3, p. 124

2 (*a*) $x \in S$; (*b*) $S \not\subseteq S$; (*c*) $S \cap S' = T$
3 (*b*) False; (*d*) true; (*f*) true.
4 All are.
5 (*b*) True; (*d*) true; (*f*) true.

Exercise 5.4, p. 130

1 (*b*)
2 (*a*)
3 (*b*), (*c*), (*d*), (*e*)

CHAPTER 6

Exercise 6.2.1, p. 135

1 Invalid; counterinterpretation $p =$ T, $q =$ T; **3** valid; **5** valid; **7** valid; **9** valid.

Exercise 6.5, p. 155

2 (*a*) Valid; (*d*) valid; (*g*) valid; (*i*) invalid: counterinterpretation if I(*p*) = T, I(*q*) = T, I(*r*) = T, I(*s*) = F, I(*t*) = T.

Exercise 6.6, p. 157

1 (*a*) Inconsistent; (*c*) consistent; interpretation I(*p*) = T, I(*q*) = T, I(*r*) = T, *or* I(*p*) = T, I(*q*) = F, I(*r*) = T; (*d*) inconsistent.

Exercise 6.6.1, p. 160

1 (*a*) Trivially valid; (*c*) trivially valid; (*f*) nontrivially valid.
2 (*b*) Argument form $p \supset q$, $(r \wedge \sim p) \supset (s \wedge t)$, $(t \vee p) \wedge (p \supset u) \, / \, (u \wedge s) \supset q$; invalid; counterinterpretation if I(*p*) = F, I(*q*) = F, I(*r*) = T or F, I(*s*) = T, I(*t*) = T, I(*u*) = T and I(*t*) = T. (*e*) Argument form $p \supset q$, $q \supset (s \supset r)$, $q \supset \sim s$, $\sim r \supset t / p \supset t$; invalid; counterinterpretation if I(*p*) = T, I(*q*) = T, I(*r*) = T, I(*s*) = F, I(*t*) = F.

Exercise 6.7, p. 164

1 (*b*) Not equivalent: counterinterpretation if I(*p*) = F, I(*q*) = F; (*e*) equivalent; (*h*) not equivalent: counterinterpretation if I(*p*) = T, I(*q*) = F, I(*t*) = F, *or* if I(*p*) = F, I(*q*) = T, I(*r*) = T.

Exercise 6.8, p. 168

3 Contingent: true if I(*p*) = T; 6 tautologous; 9 tautologous; 12 contradictory.

Review Exercises, p. 170

2 (*a*) Valid; (*d*) valid; (*g*) valid; (*j*) valid; (*m*) invalid: counterinterpretation if *pqrstu* = TTTTTF, TTTTFT; (*p*) valid; (*s*) valid.
3 (*a*) Inconsistent; (*c*) consistent: I(*p*) = T, I(*q*) = F, I(*r*) = F, I(*s*) = T, I(*t*) = F; (*e*) inconsistent.
4 (*a*)False; (*c*) false; (*e*) false.
5 (*a*) Tautology; (*c*) tautology; (*e*) tautology; (*g*) contingency; (*i*) contingency; (*k*) tautology; (*m*) contingency; (*o*) tautology.

CHAPTER 7

Exercise 7.3.1, p. 194

1 (*a*): (4) 2, Simp.; (5) 1, 4, M.P.; (6) 3, 5, M.T.; (7) 6, Add.
(*c*): (7) 2, 4, M.P.; (8) 1, Simp.; (9) 7, 8, M.P.; (10) 3, 5, Conj.; (11) 9, 10, C.D.; (12) 6, Simp.; (13) 11, 12, D.S.; (14) 13, Add.; (15) 8, 12, Conj.; (16) 14, 15, Conj.
2 (*b*): (6) ~*s*; (8) (*r* $\lor$ ~*p*) $\supset$ ~*t*; (9) *r* $\lor$ ~*p*; (10) ~*t*; (11) ~*q*; (12) ~*p*.
(*d*): (5) *p* $\land$ *q*; (6) *p*; (7) ~*q* $\lor$ *s*; (8) ~*q* $\supset$ ~*p*; (9) (~*q* $\supset$ ~*p*) $\land$ (*s* $\supset$ *t*); (10) ~*p* $\lor$ *t*.

Exercise 7.3.1.1, p. 199

1 (5) ~*r* / 2, Simp.; (6) ~(*p* $\supset$ *q*) / 1, 5, M.T.; (7) *t* / 6, 3, D.S.; (8) *r* $\lor$ *q* / 7, 4, M.P.; (9) *q* / 5, 8, D.S.
5 (5) *p* / 2, 4, D.S.; (6) *p* $\lor$ *q* / 5, Add.; (7) *r* / 1, 6, M.P.; (8) *r* $\lor$ *s* / 7, Add.; (9) *t* / 8, 3, M.P.
12 (4) (*p* $\lor$ *q*) $\supset$ ~*t* / 1, 3, H.S.; (5) (*p* $\lor$ *q*) $\supset$ ~(*r* $\land$ *s*) / 4, 2, H.S.

Exercise 7.3.2, p. 205

2 (*a*): (4) 3, Simp.; (5) 4, Add.; (6) 1, 5, M.P.; (7) 6, Add.; (8) 2, 7, M.P.; (9) 4, 8, M.P.; (10) 9, Bic.; (11) 10, Simp.
(*c*): (4) 2, Simp.; (5) 1, Imp.; (6) 4, 5, M.P.; (7) 6, Com.; (8) 7, D.N.; (9) 8, Imp.; (10) 3, 9, H.S.; (11) 10, Imp.; (12) 11, D.N.; (13) 12, Rep.
3 (*b*): (5) ~*s* $\land$ (*q* $\supset$ *s*); (6) ~*s*; (7) *q* $\supset$ *s*; (8) ~*q*; (9) ~*p*; (10) *q*; (11) *r*; (13) *t* $\supset$ *r*.
4 (*a*): (2) *r* $\lor$ (*p* $\land$ *q*) / 1, Com.; (3) (*r* $\lor$ *p*) $\land$ (*r* $\lor$ *q*) / 2, Dist; (4) *r* $\lor$ *p* / 3, Simp.; (5) *p* $\lor$ *r* / 4, Com.; (6) ~~*p* $\lor$ *r* / 5, D.N.; (7) ~*p* $\supset$ *r* / 6, Imp.
(*e*): (3) ~(~*p* $\lor$ *q*) / 1, Imp.; (4) ~~*p* $\land$ ~*q* / 3, DeM.; (5) ~*q* / 4, Simp.; (6) *r* / 2, 5, M.P.

Exercise 7.3.3.1, p. 215

2 (b): 1(3) t / a1; 1(4) $p \vee r$ / 2, 3, M.P.; 1(5) $q \vee s$ / 1, 4, C.D.; χ(6) $t \supset (q \vee s)$ / 3—5, Ded.

(f): 1(4) p / a1; 1(5) $(q \wedge r) \vee s$ / 1, 4, M.P.; 1(6) $\sim\sim p$ / 4, D.N. 1(7) $\sim(q \wedge r)$ / 2, 6, M.T.; 1(8) s / 5, 7, D.S.; 1(9) $\sim\sim s$ / 8, D.N.; 1(10) $\sim t$ / 3, 9, M.T.; χ(11) $p \supset \sim t$ / 4—10, Ded.

(i): 1(4) $s \vee r$ / a1; 1(5) $\sim\sim s \vee r$ / 4, D.N.; 1(6) $\sim s \supset r$ / 5, Imp.; 1(7) $\sim(q \vee s)$ / 2, 6, M.P.; 1(8) $\sim q \wedge \sim s$ / 7, DeM.; 1(9) $\sim q$ / 8, Simp.; 1(10) $\sim\sim p$ / 3, 9, M.T.; 1(11) p / 10, D.N.; χ(12) $(s \vee r) \supset p$ 4—11, Ded; 2(13) p / a2; 2(14) $p \vee q$ / 13, Add.; 2(15) $p \supset r$ / 1, 14, M.P.; 2(16) r / 13, 15, M.P.; 2(17) $s \vee r$ / 16, Add.; 2(18) $p \supset (s \vee r)$ / 13—17, Ded; (19) $[(s \vee r) \supset p] \wedge [p \supset (s \vee r)]$ / 12, 18, Conj.; (20) $(s \vee r) \equiv p$ / 19, Bic.

(l): 1(3) $p \vee r$ / a1; 1(4) $(p \supset q) \wedge (r \supset s)$ / 1, 2, Conj.; 1(5) $q \vee s$ / 4, 3, C.D.; 1(6) $\sim\sim q \vee s$ / 5, D.N.; 1(7) $\sim q \supset s$ / 6, Imp.; 1(8) $(p \vee r) \supset (\sim q \supset s)$ / 3—7, Ded.

Exercise 7.3.4, p. 221

2 Argument form: $\sim p \supset (q \vee r)$, $\sim q \supset s$, $(\sim s \vee p) \wedge (p \supset t)$ / $\sim t \supset (\sim p \wedge q)$
1(4) $\sim t$ / a1; 1(5) $p \supset t$ / 3, Simp.; 1(6) $\sim p$ / 5, 4, M.T.; 1(7) $\sim s \vee p$ / 3, Simp.; 1(8) $\sim s$ / 6, 7, D.S.; 1(9) $\sim\sim q$ / 2, 8, M.T.; 1(10) q / 9, D.N.; 1(11) $\sim p \wedge q$ / 6, 10, Conj.; χ(12) $\sim t \supset (\sim p \wedge q)$ / 4—11, Ded.

5 Argument form: $p \vee q$, $\sim r \vee \sim p$, $\sim q \vee s$ / $\sim r \vee s$
1(4) r / a1; 1(5) $\sim\sim r$ / 4, D.N.; 1(6) $\sim p$ / 2, 5, D.S.; 1(7) q / 1, 6, D.S.; 1(8) $\sim\sim q$ / 7, D.N.; 1(9) s / 3, 8, D.S.; χ(10) $r \supset s$ / 4—9, Ded; (11) $\sim r \vee s$ / 10, Imp.

Exercise 7.4, p. 223

1 (c): (4) $\sim p \vee q$ / 2, Add.; (5) $p \supset q$ / 4, Imp.; (6) $q \supset r$ / 1, 5, M.P.; (7) r / 2, 6, M.P.; (8) $r \wedge \sim r$ / 7, 3, Conj.

(g): (4) $r \wedge \sim q$ / 1, 3, D.S.; (5) $\sim q$ / 4, Simp.; (6) r / 4, Simp.; (7) $\sim r$ / 2, 5, D.S.; (8) $r \wedge \sim r$ / 6, 7, Conj.

Exercise 7.5, p. 226

4 First show $\{p \supset (q \supset r)\} \vdash q \supset (p \supset r)$:
(2) $\sim p \vee (q \supset r)$ / 1, Imp.; (3) $\sim p \vee (\sim q \vee r)$ / 2, Imp.; (4) $(\sim p \vee \sim q) \vee r$ / 3, Assoc.; (5) $(\sim q \vee \sim p) \vee r$ / 4, Com.; (6) $\sim q \vee (\sim p \vee r)$ / 5, Assoc.; (7) $\sim q \vee (p \supset r)$ / 6, Imp.; (8) $q \supset (p \supset r)$ / 7, Imp.
Now show $\{q \supset (p \supset r)\} \vdash p \supset (q \supset r)$:
(2) $\sim q \vee (p \supset r)$ / 1, Imp.; (3) $\sim q \vee (\sim p \vee r)$ / 2, Imp.; (4) $(\sim q \vee \sim p) \vee r$ / 3, Assoc.; (5) $(\sim p \vee \sim q) \vee r$ / 4, Com.; (6) $\sim p \vee (\sim q \vee r)$ / 5, Assoc.; (7) $\sim p \vee (q \supset r)$ / 6, Imp.; (8) $p \supset (q \supset r)$ / 7, Imp.

10 First show $\{p\} \vdash p \wedge (p \vee q)$: (2) $p \vee q$ / 1, Add.; (3) $p \wedge (p \vee q)$ / 1, 2, Conj.
Now show $\{p \wedge (p \vee q)\} \vdash p$: (2) p / 1, Simp.

Exercise 7.6, p. 229

1 (n): 1(1) $p \supset r$ / a1; 2, 1 (2) $q \supset r$ / a2; 3, 2, 1 (3) $p \vee q$ / a3; 3, 2, 1 (4) $(p \supset r) \wedge (q \supset r)$ / 1, 2, Conj.; 3, 2, 1 (5) $r \vee r$ / 4, 3, C.D.; 3, 2, 1 (6) r / 5, Rep. $\mathcal{3}$, 2, 1 (7) $(p \vee q) \supset r$ / 3—6, Ded.; $\mathcal{2}$, 1 (8) $(q \supset r) \supset [(p \vee q) \supset r]$ / 2—7, Ded.; χ (9) $(p \supset r) \supset \{(q \supset r) \supset [(p \vee q) \supset r]\}$ / 1—8, Ded.

(q): 1(1) $\sim p$ / a1; 1(2) $\sim p \vee q$ / 1, Add.; 1(3) $p \supset q$ / 2, Imp.; 1(4) $\sim p \vee \sim q$ / 1, Add.; 1(5) $p \supset \sim q$ / 4, Imp.; 1(6) $(p \supset q) \wedge (p \supset \sim q)$ / 3, 5, Conj.; χ(7) $\sim p \supset [(p \supset q) \wedge (p \supset \sim q)]$ / 1—6, Ded.

2 (b): Show that $\{\sim(p \supset q) \wedge \sim(\sim p \supset r)\}$ is deductively inconsistent:
(2) $\sim(p \supset q)$ / 1, Simp.; (3) $\sim(\sim p \supset r)$ / 1, Simp.; (4) $\sim(\sim p \vee q)$ / 2, Imp.;
(5) $\sim\sim p \wedge \sim q$ / 4, DeM.; (6) $\sim\sim p$ / 5, Simp.; (7) p / 6, D.N.; (8) $\sim(\sim\sim p \vee$
$r)$ / 3, Imp.; (9) $\sim(p \vee r)$ / 8, D.N.; (10) $\sim p \wedge \sim r$ / 9, DeM.; (11) $\sim p$ / 10,
Simp.; (12) $p \wedge \sim p$ / 7, 11, Conj.

Review Exercises, p. 233

3 (e): (4) p / 1, Simp.; (5) q / 1, Simp.; (6) r / 2, 5, M.P.; (7) $r \supset s$ / 3, 4, M.P.;
(8) s / 6, 7, M.P.

(i): 1(4) r / a1; 1(5) $[(p \supset s) \supset \sim r] \wedge [\sim r \supset (p \supset s)]$ / 2, Bic.; 1(6) $(p \supset s) \supset$
$\sim r$ / 5, Simp.; 1(7) $\sim\sim r \supset \sim(p \supset s)$ / 6, Trans.; 1(8) $\sim\sim r$ / 4, D.N.; 1(9)
$\sim(p \supset s)$ / 7, 8, M.P.; 1(10) $\sim(\sim p \vee s)$ / 9, Imp.; 1(11) $\sim\sim p \wedge \sim s$ / 10,
DeM.; 1(12) $\sim\sim p$ / 11, Simp.; 1(13) p / 12, D.N.; 1(14) $q \wedge r$ / 1, 13, M.P.;
1(15) s / 3, 14, M.P.; 1(16) $\sim s$ / 11, Simp.; 1(17) $s \wedge \sim s$ / 15, 16, Conj.; $\mathcal{X}$(18)
$\sim r$ / 4—17, R.A.

(m): 1(3) p / a1; 2, 1 (4) q / a2; 2, 1 (5) $q \supset r$ / 1, 3, M.P.; 2, 1 (6) r / 4, 5, M.P.;
2, 1 (7) $r \supset s$ / 2, 4, M.P.; 2, 1 (8) s / 7, 6, M.P.; $\mathcal{Z}$, 1 (9) $q \supset s$ / 4—8, Ded.;
$\mathcal{X}$(10) $p \supset s)$ / 3—9, Ded.

(o): 1(4) $\sim t$ / a1; 1(5) q / 1, Simp.; 1(6) $\sim r \vee q$ / 5, Add.; 1(7) $r \supset q$ / 6, Imp.;
1(8) $\sim q \vee r$ / 3, Add.; 1(9) $q \supset r$ / 8, Imp.; 1(10) $(q \supset r) \wedge (r \supset q)$ / 9, 7,
Conj.; 1(11) $q \equiv r$ / 10, Bic.; 1(12) $s \vee t$ / 2, 11, M.P.; 1(13) s / 4, 12, D.S.;
$\mathcal{X}$(14) $\sim t \supset s$ / 4—13, Ded; (15) $\sim\sim t \vee s$ / 14, Imp.; (16) $t \vee s$ / 15, D.N.

4 (d): (3) $\sim\sim r \supset \sim p$ / 2, Trans.; (4) $r \supset \sim p$ / 3, D.N.; (5) $p \supset \sim p$ / 1, 4, H.S.;
(6) $\sim p \vee \sim p$ / 5, Imp.; (7) $\sim p$ / 6, Rep.; (8) $\sim p \vee q$ / 7, Add.; (9) $p \supset q$ / 8,
Imp.

5 (b): (5) q / 1, 3, M.P.; (6) r / 2, 3, M.P.; (7) $\sim r$ / 3, 5, M.P.; (8) $r \wedge \sim r$ / 6, 7,
Conj.

6 (b): Show that $\{(p \vee q) \wedge \sim r, q \supset r, p \supset r\}$ is deductively inconsistent: (4)
$p \vee q$ / 1, Simp.; (5) $\sim r$ / 1, Simp; (6) $(p \supset r) \wedge (q \supset r)$ / 2, 3, Conj.; (7)
$r \vee r$ / 4, 6, C.D.; (8) r / 7, Rep.; (9) $r \wedge \sim r$ / 8, 5, Conj.

7 (b): To show $\{p \supset (p \supset q)\} \vdash p \supset q$: (2) $\sim p \vee (p \supset q)$ / 1, Imp.; (3) $\sim p \vee$
$(\sim p \vee q)$ / 2, Imp.; (4) $(\sim p \vee \sim p) \vee q$ / 3, Assoc.; (5) $\sim p \vee q$ / 4, Rep.;
(6) $p \supset q$ / 5, Imp. To show $\{p \supset q\} \vdash p \supset (p \supset q)$: (2) $\sim p \vee (p \supset q)$ / 1,
Add.; (3) $p \supset (p \supset q)$ / 2, Imp.

(d): To show $\{\sim p \supset (\sim q \supset r)\} \vdash (\sim r \supset \sim q) \supset (\sim r \supset p)$: 1(2) $\sim r \supset \sim q$ / a1; 2,
1 (3) $\sim r$ / a2; 2, 1 (4) $\sim q$ / 2, 3, M.P.; 2, 1 (5) $\sim\sim p \vee (\sim q \supset r)$ / 1, Imp;
2, 1 (6) $p \vee (\sim q \supset r)$ / 5, D.N.; 2, 1 (7) $p \vee (\sim\sim q \vee r)$ / 6, Imp.; 2, 1 (8)
$p \vee (q \vee r)$ / 7, D.N.; 2, 1 (9) $(p \vee q) \vee r$ / 8, Assoc.; 2, 1 (10) $p \vee q$ / 9, 3,
D.S.; 2, 1 (11) p / 10, 4, D.S.; $\mathcal{Z}$, 1 (12) $\sim r \supset p$ / 3—11, Ded.; $\mathcal{X}$(13)
$(\sim r \supset \sim q) \supset (\sim r \supset p)$ / 2—12, Ded. To show $\{(\sim r \supset \sim q) \supset (\sim r \supset p)\} \vdash$
$\sim p \supset (\sim q \supset r)$: 1(2) $\sim p$ / a1; 2, 1 (3) $\sim q$ / a2; 2, 1 (4) $\sim\sim r \vee \sim q$ / 3, Add.;
2, 1 (5) $\sim r \supset \sim q$ / 4, Imp.; 2, 1 (6) $\sim r \supset p$ / 1, 5, M.P.; 2, 1 (6) $\sim\sim r$ / 6,
2, M.T.; 2, 1 (7) r / 6, D.N.; $\mathcal{Z}$, 1 (8) $\sim q \supset r$ / 3—7, Ded.; $\mathcal{X}$ (9) $\sim p \supset$
$(\sim q \supset r)$ / 2—8, Ded.

8 (c): 1 (1) $p \supset q$ / a1; 2, 1 (2) $p \wedge r$ / a2; 2, 1 (3) p / 2, Simp.; 2, 1, (4) q / 1, 3,
M.P.; 2, 1 (5) r / 2, Simp; 2, 1 (6) $q \wedge r$ / 4, 5, Conj.; $\mathcal{Z}$, 1 (7) $(p \wedge r) \supset (q \wedge r)$
/ 2—6, Ded.; $\mathcal{X}$ (8) $(p \supset q) \supset [(p \wedge r) \supset (q \wedge r)]$ / 1—7, Ded.

(f): 1 (1) $p \supset q$ / a1; 2, 1 (2) $r \supset p$ / a2, 2, 1 (3) $r \supset q$ / 1, 2, H.S.; $\mathcal{Z}$, 1(4) $(r \supset p) \supset$
$(r \supset q)$ / 2—3, Ded.; $\mathcal{X}$ (5) $(p \supset q) \supset [(r \supset p) \supset (r \supset q)]$ / 1—4, Ded.

(i): 1(1) $p \equiv \sim p$ / a1; 1(2) $(p \supset \sim p) \wedge (\sim p \supset p)$ / 1, Bic.; 1(3) $p \supset \sim p$ / 2,
Simp.; 1(4) $\sim p \supset p$ / 2, Simp.; 1(5) $\sim p \vee \sim p$ / 3, Imp.; 1(6) $\sim p$ / 5, Rep.;
1(7) p / 4, 6, M.P.; 1 (8) $p \wedge \sim p$ / 6, 7, Conj.; $\mathcal{X}$ (9) $\sim(p \equiv \sim p)$ / 1—8, R.A.

CHAPTER 8

Exercise 8.2.1, p. 241

2 Name: *My brother Jorge*; predicate expression: *hates okra*.
4 Name: *Love*; predicate expression: *makes the world go round*.
6 Name: *Seven*; predicate expression: *is an odd number*.
8 Name: *Mount Everest*; predicate expression: *is taller than any other mountain in the world*.

Exercise 8.3.2, p. 253

2 Of everything: if it is an animal with a heart, then it has kidneys.
4 Of something: it is a book and it is not worth reading.
6 Of everything: it is not harder than diamond.
8 Of everything: if it is a cloud, then it has a silver lining.
10 Of something: it is a tree and it is in the middle of the garden.

Exercise 8.4.2, p. 265

1 F = is a person, G = means well; $(\forall x)(Fx \supset Gx)$
3 F = is tall, G = is a person, a = Tom; $Fa \supset (\forall x)(Gx \supset Fx)$
4 F = is a cat, G = is an animal; $(\forall x)(Fx \supset Gx)$
6 F = is a football player, G = is failing this course, H = is taking this course; $(\forall x)[Fx \supset (Gx \lor {\sim}Hx)]$
7 F = is a spider, G = is hairy, H = makes a good pet; $(\exists x)[(Fx \land Gx) \land Hx]$
9 F = is a logician, G = is competent, H = is a philosopher; $(\forall x)[(Fx \land Gx) \supset Hx]$
11 F = is a person, G = will attend the ceremony; $(\forall x)(Fx \supset {\sim}Gx)$
13 F = is marijuana, G = is worth smoking, H = has desirable effects; $(\forall x)[Fx \supset {\sim}({\sim}Hx \supset Gx)]$
15 F = is a doctor, G = is a medical practitioner, H = is qualified; $(\forall x)[(Gx \land Hx) \supset Fx]$
17 F = is an artist, G = paints nudes; $(\exists x)(Fx \land Gx)$
20 F = is a psychologist, G = is a sociologist, H = is a good researcher, I = is a good theoretician; $(\forall x)[(Fx \lor Gx) \supset (Hx \lor Ix)]$
22 F = is a philosopher, G = is an existentialist, H = is a Marxist; ${\sim}(\forall x)[(Fx \land Gx) \supset Hx]$
24 F = is in the drawer, a = my watch; $(\exists x)Fx \supset Fa$

Exercise 8.6, p. 278

1. (*c*) (trivially) valid; (*f*) invalid: counterinterpretation if $I(Fa) = T$, $I(Fb) = T$, $I(Ga) = F$, $I(Gb) = T$. (*j*) valid (first premise unnecessary); (*e*) invalid; counterinterpretation if $I(Fa) = F$, $I(Ga) = T$, $I(Ha) = F$. 2. (*a*) inconsistent; (*e*) inconsistent; 3. (*f*) not equivalent: $I(Fa) = T$, $I(Gb) = F$, $I(Gc) = T$; 4. (*b*) contingent; (*c*) logically true; 5. (*d*) invalid; argument form $(\forall x)[(Fx \lor Gx) \supset Hx]$, $(\forall x)[(Ix \lor Jx) \supset Kx]$, $(\forall x)[Kx \supset (Lx \land Mx)]$, $(\forall x)[Fx \supset {\sim}(Lx \lor Nx)] / (\exists x)[Gx \land (Nx \land {\sim}Lx)]$; counterinterpretation if $I(Fa) = F$, $I(Ga) = T$, $I(Ha) = T$, $I(Ia) = F$, $I(Ja) = F$, $I(Ka) = F$, $I(La) = T$, $I(Ma) = T$, $I(Na) = F$ (there are many others); (*g*) invalid: argument form $(\forall x)(Fx \supset Gx)$, $(\exists x)(Gx \land {\sim}Hx) / (\exists x)(Fx \land {\sim}Hx)$: counterinterpretation if $I(Fa) = F$, $I(Ga) = T$, $I(Ha) = F$.

Exercise 8.7, p. 288

1 (*d*): 1(3) Fa / *a*1; 1(4) $Fa \lor Ga$ / 3, Add.; 1(5) $(Fa \lor Ga) \supset Ha$ / 1, U.I.; 1(6) Ha / 4, 5, M.P.; 1(7) $Ha \supset Ia$ / 2, U.I.; 1(8) Ia / 6, 7, M.P.; χ(9) $Fa \supset Ia$ / 3—8, Ded.; (10) $(\forall x)(Fx \supset Ix)$ / 9, U.G.

(*h*): (3) $Fa \land Ha$ / 2, U.I.; (4) Fa / 3, Simp.; (5) $Fa \supset {\sim}Ga$ / 1, U.I.; (6) ${\sim}Ga$ / 4, 5, M.P.; (7) $(\exists x){\sim}Gx$ / 6, E.G.

(*k*): 1(3) Gb / *a*1; 1(4) $(\exists x)Gx$ / 3, E.G.; 1(5) Fa / 2, 4, M.P.; χ(6) $Gb \supset Fa$ / 3—5, Ded.; 2(7)Fa / *a*2;2(8) $(\forall x)Gx$ / 1, 7, M.P.; 2(9)Gb / 8, U.I.; 2(10) $Fa \supset Gb$ / 7—9, Ded.; (11) $(Fa \supset Gb) \land (Gb \supset Fa)$ / 6, 10, Conj.; (12) $Fa \equiv Gb$ / 11, Bic.; (13) $(\forall x)(Fa \equiv Gx)$ / 12, U.G.

2 (*c*): (5) $Ea \supset Ga$ / 1, U.I.; (6) $Ga \supset Ha$ / 2, U.I.; (7) $Fa \supset {\sim}Ha$ / 4, U.I.; (8) Ga / 3, 5, M.P.; (9) Ha / 6, 8, M.P.; (10) ${\sim}Ha$ / 3, 7, M.P.; (11) $Ha \land {\sim}Ha$ / 9, 10, Conj.

(*e*): (4) $Ha \supset {\sim}Fa$ / 3, U.I.; (5) ${\sim}Ha \lor {\sim}Fa$ / 4, Imp.; (6) ${\sim}(Ha \land Fa)$ / 5, DeM.; (7) $(\forall x){\sim}(Hx \land Fx)$ / 6, U.G.; (8) ${\sim}(\exists x)(Hx \land Fx)$ / 7, Q.E.; (9) $(\exists x)(Hx \land Fx) \land {\sim}(\exists x)(Hx \land Fx)$ / 2, 9, Conj.

4 (*b*): 1(1) $Fa \land {\sim}Fa$ / *a*1; χ(2) ${\sim}(Fa \land {\sim}Fa)$ / 1—1, R.A.; (3) $(\forall x){\sim}(Fx \land {\sim}Fx)$ / 2, U.G.; (4) ${\sim}(\exists x)(Fx \land {\sim}Fx)$ / 3, Q.E.

5 (*b*): Argument form: $(\forall x)[Fx \supset (Gx \lor Hx)]$, $(\exists x)(Fx \land {\sim}Gx)$ / $(\exists x)(Fx \land Hx)$; sample deduction: 1(3) $Fa \land {\sim}Ga$ / *a*1; 1(4) $Fa \supset (Ga \lor Ha)$ / 1, U.I.; 1(5) Fa / 3, Simp.; 1(6) $Ga \lor Ha$ / 4, 5, M.P.; 1(7) ${\sim}Ga$ / 3, Simp.; 1(8) Ha / 6, 7, D.S.; 1(9) $Fa \land Ha$ / 5, 8, Conj.; 1(10)$(\exists x)(Fx \land Hx)$ / 9, E.G.; χ(11) $(\exists x)(Fx \land Hx)$ / 2, 3—10, E.I.

(*e*): Argument form: $(\forall x)(Fx \supset Gx)$, $(\exists x)(Fx \land Hx)$, $(\forall x)[(Hx \land Gx) \supset Ix]$ / $(\exists x)(Fx \land Ix)$; sample deduction: 1(4) $Fa \land Ha$ / *a*1; 1(5) Fa / 4, Simp.; 1(6) Ha / 4, Simp.; 1(7) $Fa \supset Ga$ / 1, U.I.; 1(8) Ga / 5, 7, M.P.; 1(9) $Ha \land Ga$ / 6, 8, Conj.; 1(10) $(Ha \land Ga) \supset Ia$ / 3, U.I.; 1(11) Ia / 9, 10, M.P.; 1(12) $Fa \land Ia$ / 5, 11, Conj.; 1(13) $(\exists x)(Fx \land Ix)$ / 12, E.G.; χ(14) $(\exists x)(Fx \land Ix)$ / 2, 4—13, E.I.

Review Exercises, p. 289

2 (*b*) Valid: (3) $(\forall x){\sim}(Fx \land {\sim}Gx)$ / 1, Q.E.; (4) $(\forall x){\sim}(Gx \land Hx)$ / 2, Q.E.; (5) ${\sim}(Fa \land {\sim}Ga)$ / 3, U.I.; (6) ${\sim}(Ga \land Ha)$ / 4, U.I.; (7) ${\sim}Fa \lor {\sim}{\sim}Ga$ / 5, DeM.; (8) ${\sim}Ga \lor {\sim}Ha$ / 6, DeM.; (9) ${\sim}Fa \lor Ga$ / 7, D.N.; (10) $Fa \supset Ga$ / 9, Imp.; (11) $Ga \supset {\sim}Ha$ / 8, Imp.; (12) $Fa \supset {\sim}Ha$ / 10, 11, H.S.; (13) ${\sim}{\sim}Ha \supset {\sim}Fa$ / 12, Trans.; (14) $Ha \supset {\sim}Fa$ / 13, D.N.; (15) $(\forall x)(Hx \supset {\sim}Fx)$ / 14, U.G.

(*f*) Invalid; counterinterpretation if I(Fa) = F, I(Fb) = F, I(Fc) = T, I(Ga) = T, I(Gc) = T, I(Ha) = T, I(Hb) = F, I(Hc) = T, I(Ia) = T, I(Ib) = T, I(Ic) = F, other truth values arbitrary.

(*h*) Valid: 1(2) Fa / *a*1; 1(3) $Fa \lor Ga$ / 2, Add.; 1(4) $(Fa \lor Ga) \supset [(Ha \lor Ia) \supset Ja]$ / 1, U.I.; 1(5) $(Ha \lor Ia) \supset Ja$ / 3, 4, M.P.; 2,1 (6) Ha / *a*2; 2,1 (7) $Ha \lor Ia$ / 6, Add.; 2,1 (8) Ja / 5, 7, M.P.; $\mathbf{2}$,1 (9) $Ha \supset Ja$ / 6—8, Ded.; χ (10) $Fa \supset (Ha \supset Ja)$ / 2—9, Ded.; (11) $(\forall x)[Fx \supset (Hx \supset Jx)]$ / 10, U.G.

3 (*a*) Valid; argument form $(\forall x)[(Fx \lor Gx) \supset (Hx \lor Ix)]$, $(\forall x)(Jx \equiv Fx)$, $(\forall x)(Jx \supset {\sim}Hx)$ / $(\forall x)(Jx \supset Ix)$; sample deduction: (4) $(Fa \lor Ga) \supset (Ha \lor Ia)$ / 1, U.I.; (5) $Ja \equiv Fa$ / 2, U.I.; (6) $Ja \supset {\sim}Ha$ / 3, U.I.; (7) $(Ja \supset Fa) \land (Fa \supset Ja)$ / 5, Bic.; (8) $Ja \supset Fa$ / 7, Simp.; 1(9) Ja / *a*1; 1(10) Fa / 8, 9, M.P.; 1(11) $Fa \lor Ga$ / 10, Add.; 1(12) $Ha \lor Ia$ / 4, 11, M.P.; 1(13) ${\sim}Ha$ / 6, 9, M.P.; 1(14) Ia / 12, 13, D.S.; χ(15) $Ja \supset Ia$ / 9—14, Ded.; (16) $(\forall x)(Jx \supset Ix)$ / 15, U.G.

(*d*) Invalid; argument form $(\forall x)[(Fx \lor Gx) \supset Hx]$, $(\exists x)(Hx \land Ix)$, $(\exists x)(Ix \land {\sim}Hx)$ / $(\exists x)(Fx \land Ix)$; counterinterpretation if I(Fa) = F, I(Fb) = F, I(Ga) = T, I(Gb) = T, I(Ha) = T, I(Hb) = F, I(Ia) = T, I(Ib) = T.

CHAPTER 9

Exercise 9.1, p. 295

2 Of(Leroy = x, Alfred = y): x is much more intelligent than y.
4 Of(Michael = x, Switzerland = y): x lives in y.
8 Of(Hortense = x; the Last National Bank = y): x stole \$1 million from y.
9 Of(Jack = x, Jill = y): x and y are cousins.

Exercise 9.1.1, p. 301

1 Fxy = x loves y, a = John, b = Marcia; $Fab \wedge {\sim}Fba$
3 Fxy = x gets out of y, Gxy = x is going to shoot y, a = you, b = my yard, c = I; ${\sim}Fab \supset Gca$
5 Fxy = x is from y, a = Jones, b = North Dakota, c = Smith, d = South Dakota; $Fab \wedge Fcd$
7 Fxy = x is smaller than y, Gxy = x is larger than y, a = New York, b = Texas, c = California, d = Montana, e = Alaska; $[(Fab \wedge Fcb) \wedge Fdb] \wedge Geb$
9 Fx = x is mean, Gxy = x is as mean as y, a = Bill, b = Freddie; $Fa \wedge {\sim}Gab$
11 Fxy = x went to y, a = Martha, b = Super Bowl, c = Mark, d = John; $(Fab \wedge Fcb) \supset Fdb$

Exercise 9.1.2, p. 302

2 Fxy = x sat across from y, $Gxyz$ = x was between y and z; $Fab \wedge Gbcd$
5 $Fxyz$ = x and y are z's parents: $Fabc$
6 $Fxyzw$ = x is closer to y than z is to w; $Fabcd$
8 $Fxyzw$ = x likes y as much as z likes w; $Fabcd$
10 $Fxyz$ = x, y, and z shared the work equally; $Fabc$

Exercise 9.2, p. 310

1 (a) Fx = x is a person, Gxy = x trusts y, Hx = x is a fool; $(\forall x)[(\forall y)(Fy \supset Gxy) \supset Hx]$
   (c) Fx = x is a dog, Gx = x is a cat, Hxy = x likes y; $(\forall x)(\forall y)[(Fx \wedge Gy) \supset {\sim}Hxy]$
   (e) Fx = x is a person, Gxy = x is a child of y; $(\forall x)[Fx \supset (\exists y)(Fy \wedge Gxy)] \wedge {\sim}(\forall x)[Fx \supset (\exists y)(Fy \wedge Gyx)]$
   (g) Fx = x is a number, Gx = x is even, $Hxyz$ = x is the product of y and z, a = 2; $(\forall x)[(Fx \wedge Gx) \supset (\exists y)(Fy \wedge Hxay)]$
   (i) Fx = x is lasagna, Gxy = x knows how to make y, Hx = x is a person, Ixy = x used to live in y, a = John, b = that house; $(\forall x)(Fx \supset {\sim}Gax) \wedge (\exists y)\{[Hy \wedge (\forall x)(Fx \supset Gyx)] \wedge Iyb\}$
   (k) Fx = x is a fool, Gx = x is old, Hxy = x is like y; ${\sim}(\exists x)\{Fx \wedge (\forall y)[(Fy \wedge Gy) \supset Hxy]\}$
   (m) Fx = x is a person, Gxy = x loves y; $(\forall x)(Fx \supset (\forall y)(\forall z)\{[(Fy \wedge Fz) \wedge Gyz] \supset Gxy\})$
   (o) Fx = x is a book, Gxy = x wrote y, Hxy = x is better than y, Ixy = x is worse than y, a = Jones, b = Smith, c = Brown; $(\forall x)\{(Fx \wedge Gax) \wedge (\forall y)[(Fy \wedge Gby) \supset Hxy]\} \wedge (\forall x)\{(Fx \wedge Gax) \supset (\exists y)[(Fy \wedge Gcy) \wedge Ixy]\}$
2 (b) Fx = x is a person, Gxy = x was born in y, Hxy = x is a citizen of y, Ixy = x is a child of y, Jx = x is a female, a = the United States, b = Felipe, c = Alice, d = Canada; $(\forall x)[(Fx \wedge \{Gxa \vee (\exists y)[(Fy \wedge Hya) \wedge Ixy]\}) \supset Hxy]$; Gba; $Hca \wedge [(Jc \wedge Icb) \wedge Gcd]$

(c) $Fx = x$ is a philosopher, $Gxy = x$ lives in y, $Hx = x$ is important, $Ix = x$ is a rationalist, $Jx = x$ is an empiricist, a = seventeenth century, b = Europe, c = England; $(\forall x)\{[Fx \wedge (Gxa \wedge Gxb)] \supset [Hx \supset (Ix \vee Jx)]\}$; $(\forall x)[(Hx \wedge Ix) \supset {\sim}Gxc]$; / $(\forall x)\{[Fx \wedge (Gxa \wedge Gxc)] \supset Jx\}$.

Exercise 9.3, p. 313

1 [Free occurrences are circled] (b) $(\exists x)(Gx \supset {\sim}H(y)) \vee [(\forall x)Hx \equiv F(x)]$;

2 [Vacuous quantifiers are circled] (a) None; (c) $Gac \supset (\forall x)(\textcircled{\forall y})(Gxa \equiv Gcx)$; (e) none.

Exercise 9.4, p. 319

1 (a) Valid; (c) valid; (e) valid; (g) valid; (i) valid; (k) valid; (m) valid; (o) valid.
2 (a) $Fx = x$ is a gambler, $Gx = x$ is a criminal, $Hxy = x$ needs the help of y, $Ix = x$ is desperate (the argument is valid); $(\forall x)\{[Fx \wedge (\exists y)(Gy \wedge Hxy)] \supset Ix\}$; $(\forall x)(Fx \supset Gx)$ / $(\forall x)[(Fx \wedge Hxx) \supset Ix]$
(c) $Fx = x$ is a philosopher, $Gxy = x$ is wiser than y, $Hxy = x$ is more subtle than y, $Ix = x$ is a logician, $Jxy = x$ is less subtle than y, $Kx = x$ was alive in 1800, a = Plato, b = Aristotle. The argument form is invalid. There are several counterinterpretations for the argument form, but all of them include the following: $I(Fc) = I(Gca) = I(Kc) = I(Hcb) = I(Jcb) = T$ and $I(Ic) = F.]$ $(\forall x)$ $[(Fx \wedge Gxa) \supset Hxb;]$; $(\forall x)[(Fx \wedge {\sim}Ix) \supset Jxb]$; $(\forall x)[(Fx \wedge Kx) \supset {\sim}Ix]$ / $(\forall x)$ $[(Fx \wedge Gxa) \supset {\sim}Kx]$.
3 (b) Logically true; (e) logically true.
4 (b) Semantically equivalent; (e) semantically equivalent.

Exercise 9.5, p. 324

1 (b): (1) ${\sim}(\exists x)(\forall y)Fxy$; (2) $(\forall x)(\exists y)Fxy$; (3) $(\forall x){\sim}(\forall y)Fxy$ / 1, Q.E.; (4) $(\forall x)$ $(\exists y){\sim}Fxy$ / 3, Q.E.; (5) $(\exists y)Fya$ / 2, U.I.; 1 (6) Fba / a1; 1 (7) $(\exists y){\sim}Fby$ / 4, U.I.; 2, 1 (8) ${\sim}Fbc$ / a2; 2, 1 (9) $Fba \wedge {\sim}Fbc$ / 6, 8, Conj.; 2, 1 (10) $(\exists z)$ $(Fba \wedge {\sim}Fbz)$ / 9, E.G.; 2, 1 (11) $(\exists y)(\exists z)(Fby \wedge {\sim}Fbz)$ / 10, E.G.; 2, 1 (12) $(\exists x)(\exists y)(\exists z)(Fxy \wedge {\sim}Fxz)$ / 11, E.G.; 2, 1 (13) $(\exists x)(\exists y)(\exists z)(Fxy \wedge {\sim}Fxz)$ 7, 8—12, E.I.; ⟋(14) $(\exists x)(\exists y)(\exists z)(Fxy \wedge {\sim}Fxz)$ / 5, 6—13, E.I.
(d): (1) $(\forall x)[Fx \supset (\exists y)Gxy]$; (2) $(\exists x)(\forall y)(Fy \supset Gyx)$; 1 (3) $(\forall y)(Fy \supset Gya)$ / a1; 1 (4) $Fb \supset Gba$ / 3, U.I.; 2, 1 (5) $Fb \wedge Gbc$ / a2; 2,1 (6) Fb / 5, Simp.; 2, 1 (7) Gba / 4, 6, M.P.; ⟋, 1 (8) $(Fb \wedge Gbc) \supset Gba$ / 5—7, Ded.; 1 (9) $(\forall z)[(Fz \wedge Gzc) \supset Gza]$ / 8, U.G.; 1 (10) $(\forall y)(\forall z)[(Fz \wedge Gzy) \supset Gza]$ / 9, U.G.; 1 (11) $(\exists x)$ $(\forall y)(\forall z)[(Fz \wedge Gzy) \supset Gzx]$ / 10, E.G.; ⟋ (12) $(\exists x)(\forall y)(\forall z)[(Fz \wedge Gzy) \supset Gzx]$ / 2, 3—11, E.I. Note: premise 1 is superfluous.
2 (b): $Fxy = x$ is a friend of y, $Gxy = x$ lives in y, $Hxyz = x$ prefers y to z, a = Arthur, b = San Francisco, c = Los Angeles. (1) $(\forall x)[Fxa \supset (Gxb \vee Hxcb)]$ / (prem.); (2) $(\forall x)[Gxb \supset {\sim}Hxcb]$ / (prem.); (3) $(\forall x)[(Fxa \wedge Gxc) \supset Hxbc]$ / (prem.); (4) ${\sim}(\exists x)(Hxcb \wedge Hxbc)$ / (prem.); (5) ${\sim}(\exists x)(Gxb \wedge Gxc)$ / (prem.); (6) $(\forall x){\sim}(Hxcb \wedge Hxbc)$ / 4, Q.E.; (7) $(\forall x){\sim}(Gxb \wedge Gxc)$ / 5, Q.E.; 1 (8) $Fda \wedge Gdc$ / a1; 1 (9) $Fda \supset (Gdb \vee Hdcb)$ / 1, U.I.; 1 (10) $Gdb \supset {\sim}Hdcb$ / 2, U.I.; 1 (11) $(Fda \wedge Gdc) \supset Hdbc$ / 3, U.I.; 1 (12) ${\sim}(Hdcb \wedge Hdbc)$ / 6, U.I.; 1 (13) ${\sim}(Gdb \wedge Gdc)$ / 7, U.I.; 1 (14) $Hdbc$ / 8, 11, M.P.; 1 (15) ${\sim}Hdcb \vee {\sim}Hdbc$ /12, DeM.; 1 (16) ${\sim}{\sim}{\sim}Hdbc$ / 14, D.N.; 1 (17) ${\sim}Hdcb$ / 15, 16, D.S.; 1 (18) Fda / 8, Simp.; 1 (19) $Gdb \vee Hdcb$ / 9, 18, M.P.; 1 (20) Gdb / 17, 19, D.S.; 1 (21) ${\sim}Gdb \vee {\sim}Gdc$ / 13, DeM.; 1 (22) $Gdb \supset {\sim}Gdc$ / 21, Imp.; 1 (23)

~Gdc / 20, 22, M.P.; 1 (24) Gdc / 8, Simp.; 1 (25) Gdc ∧ ~Gdc / 23, 24, Conj.; ⅄ (26) ~(Fda ∧ Gdc) / 8—25, R.A.; (27) ~Fda ∨ ~Gdc / 26, DeM.; (28) Fda ⊃ ~Gdc / 27, Imp.; (29) (∀x)(Fxa ⊃ ~Gxc) 28, U.G.

(d): Fx = x is worth doing, Gx = x is worth doing well, Hx = x is profitable, Ixy = x is willing to do y, Jxy = x forces y, a = this logic exercise. (1) (∀x)(Fx ⊃ Gx) / (prem.); (2) (∀x)(Gx ⊃ Hx) / (prem.); (3) (∀x){~Hx ∨ (∃y)[Iyx ∧ ~(∃z)Jzy]} / (prem.); (4) (∀x)[~Ixa ∨ (∃y)Jyx]; 1 (5) Fa / a1; 1 (6) Fa ⊃ Ga / 1, U.I.; 1 (7) Ga ⊃ Ha / 2, U.I.; 1 (8) ~Ha ∨ (∃y)[Iya ∧ ~(∃z)Jzy] / 3, U.I.; 1 (9) Fa ⊃ Ha / 6, 7, H.S.; 1 (10) Ha / 5, 9, M.P.; 1 (11) ~~Ha / 10, D.N.; 1 (12) (∃y)[Iya ∧ ~(∃z)Jzy] / 8, 11, D.S.; 2, 1 (13) Iba ∧ ~(∃z)Jzb / a2; 2, 1 (14) ~(∃z)Jzb / 13, Simp.; 2, 1 (15) (∀z)~Jzb / 14, Q.E.; 2, 1 (16) ~Jcb / 15, U.I.; 2, 1 (17) (∀y)~Jyb / 16, U.G.; 2, 1 (18) ~(∃y)Jyb / 17, Q.E.; 2, 1 (19) Iba / 13, Simp.; 2, 1 (20) Iba ∧ ~(∃y)Jyb / 18, 19, Conj.; 2, 1 (21) ~~Iba ∧ ~(∃y)Jyb / 20, D.N.; 2, 1 (22) ~[Iba ∨ (∃y)Jyb] / 21, DeM.; 2, 1 (23) (∃x)~[~Ixa ∨ (∃y)Jyx] / 22, E.G.; 2, 1 (24) (∃x)~[~Ixa ∨ (∃y)Jyx] / 12, 13 to 23, E.I.; 1 (25) ~(∀x)[~Ixa ∨ (∃y)Jyx] / 24, Q.E.; 1 (26) (∀x)[~Ixa ∨ (∃y)Jyx] ∧ ~(∀x)[~Ixa ∨ (∃y)Jyx] / 4, 26, Conj.; 1 (27) ~Fa / 5—26, R.A.; (28) (∃x) ~Fx / 27, E.G.

Exercise 9.5.1, p. 328

1 (b): 1 (1) (∃x)(A ∧ B) / a1; 2, 1 (2) (A ∧ B)(s/x) / a2 [s does not occur in A or B]; 2, 1 (3) A(s/x) / 2, Simp.; 2, 1 (4) B (s/x) / 2, Simp.; 2, 1 (5) (∃x)A / 3, E.G.; 2, 1 (6) (∃x)B / 4, E.G.; 2, 1 (7) (∃x)A ∧ (∃x)B / 5, 6, Conj.; 2, 1 (8) (∃x)A ∧ (∃x)B / 1, 2—7, E.I.; 1 (9) (∃x)(A ∧ B) ⊃ [(∃x)A ∧ (∃x)B] / 1—8, Ded.

(d): 1 (1) (∃x)A / a1; 2, 1 (2) A(s/x) / a2 [s does not occur in A or B]; 2, 1 (3) A(s/x) ∨ B (s/x) / 2, Add.; 2, 2 (4) (∃x)(A ∨ B) / 3, E.G.; 2, 1 (5) (∃x)(A ∨ B) / 1, 2—4, E.I.; ⅄ (6) (∃x)A ⊃ (∃x)(A ∨ B) / 1—5, Ded.; 3 (7) (∃x)B / a3; 4, 3 (8) B(t/x) / a4 [t does not occur in A or B]; 4, 3 (9) A(t/x) ∨ B(t/x) / 8, Add.; 4, 3 (10) (∃x)(A ∨ B) / 9, E.G.; 4, 3 (11) (∃x) (A ∨ B) / 7, 8—10, E.I.; 3 (12) (∃x)B ⊃ (∃x)(A ∨ B) / 7—11, Ded.; (13) [(∃x)A ⊃ (∃x)(A ∨ B)] ∧ [(∃x)B ⊃ (∃x)(A ∨ B)] / 6, 12, Conj.; 5 (14) (∃x) A ∨ (∃x)B / a5; 5 (15) (∃x)(A ∨ B) ∨ (∃x)(A ∨ B) / 13, 14, C.D.; 5 (16) (∃x) (A ∨ B) / 15, Rep.; 5 (17) [(∃x)A ∨ (∃x)B] ⊃ (∃x)(A ∨ b) / 14—16, Ded.; 6 (18) (∃x)(a ∨ B) / a6; 7, 6 (19) (A ∨ B)(u/x) / a7 [u does not occur in A ∨ B]; 8, 7, 6 (20) (∀x)~A / a8; 8, 7, 6 (21) ~A(u/x) / 20, U.I.; 8, 7, 6 (22) B(u/x) / 19, 21, D.S. [(A ∨ B)(u/x) = A(u/x) ∨ B(u/x)]; 8, 7, 6 (23) (∃x)B / 22, E.G.; 8, 7, 6 (24) (∀x)~A ⊃ (∃x)B / 20—23, Ded.; 7, 6 (25) (∀x)~A ⊃ (∃x)B / 18, 19—24, E.I.; 6 (26) ~(∃x)A ⊃ (∃x)B / 25, Q.E.; 6 (27) ~~(∃x)A ∨ (∃x)B / 26, Imp.; 6 (28) (∃x)A ∨ (∃x)B / 27, D.N.; 6 (29) (∃x)(A ∨ B) ⊃ [(∃x)A ∨ (∃x)B] / 18—28, Ded.; (30) {[(∃x)A ∨ (∃x)B] ⊃ (∃x)(A ∨ B)} ∧ {(∃x)(A ∨ B) ⊃ [(∃x)A ∨ (∃x)B]} / 17, 29, Conj.; (31) [(∃x)A ∨ (∃x)B] ≡ (∃x)(A ∨ B) / 30, Bic.

(e): 1 (1) (∀x)A ⊃ B / a1; 2, 1 (2) (∀x)~(A ⊃ B) / a2; 2, 1 (3) ~(A ⊃ B)(s/x) / 2, U.I. [s does not occur in A or B]; 2, 1 (4) ~(~A ∨ B)(s/x) / 3, Imp.; 2, 1 (5) (~~A ∧ ~B)(s/x) / 4, DeM.; 2, 1 (6) (A ∧ ~B)(s/x) / 5, D.N.; 2, 1 (7) A(s/x) / 6, Simp.; 2, 1 (8) (∀x)A / 7, U.G.; 2, 1 (9) B / 1, 8, M.P.; 2, 1 (10) ~B / 6, Simp. [B(s/x) = B]; 2, 1 (11) B ∧ ~B / 9, 10, Conj.; 2, 1 (12) ~(∀x)~(A ⊃ B) / 2—11, R.A.; 1 (13) ~~(∃x)(A ⊃ B) / 12, Q.E.; 1 (14) (∃x)(A ⊃ B) / 13, D.N.; ⅄ (15) [(∀x)A ⊃ B] ⊃ (∃x)(A ⊃ B) / 1—14, Ded.; 3 (16) (∃x)(A ⊃ B) / a3; 4, 3 (17) (∀x)A / a4; 5, 4, 3 (18) A(t/x) ⊃ B / a5 [t does not occur in A or B: since x does not occur in B, B(t/x) = B]; 5, 4, 3 (19) A(t/x) / 17, U.I.; 5, 4, 3 (20) B / 18, 19, M.P.; 5, 4, 3 (21) B / 16, 18—20, E.I.; 4, 3 (22) (∀x)(A ⊃ B) / 17—21, Ded.; 3 (23) (∃x)(A ⊃ B) ⊃ [(∀x)A ⊃ B] / 16—22, Ded.; (24) {[(∀x)A ⊃ B] ⊃ (∃x)(A ⊃ B)} ∧ {(∃x)(A ⊃ B) ⊃ [(∀x)A ⊃ B]} / 15, 23, Conj.; (25) [(∀x)A ⊃ B] ≡ (∃x)(A ⊃ B) / 24, Bic.

(g): 1 (1) $(\forall x)A$ / $a1$; 1 (2) $A(s/x)$ / 1, U.I. [s does not occur in A]; 1 (3) $(\exists x)A$ / 2, E.G.; $\vdash$ (4) $(\forall x)A \supset (\exists x)A$ / 1—3, Ded.

2 (c) 1 (1) $(\exists y)(\forall x)Fxy$ / $a1$; 2, 1 (2) $(\forall x)Fxa$ / $a2$; 2, 1 (3) Faa / 2, U.I.; 2, 1 (4) $(\exists x)Fxx$ / 3, E.G.; 2, 1 (5)$(\exists x)Fxx$ / 1, 2—4, E.I.; $\vdash$ (6) $(\exists y)(\forall x)Fxy \supset (\exists x)Fxx$ / 1—5, Ded.

(f): 1 (1) $(\exists x)(\forall y)(Fxy \equiv \sim Fyy)$ / $a1$; 2, 1 (2) $(\forall y)(Fay \equiv \sim Fyy)$ / $a2$; 2, 1 (3) $Faa \equiv \sim Faa$ / 2, U.I.; 2, 1 (4) $Faa \wedge (\sim Faa \supset Faa)$ / 3, Bic.; 2, 1 (5) $(\sim Faa \vee \sim Faa) \wedge (\sim Faa \supset Faa)$/4, Imp.; 2, 1(6) $\sim Faa \wedge (\sim Faa \supset Faa)$ / 5, Rep.; 2, 1 (7) $\sim Faa \wedge (\sim\sim Faa \vee Faa)$ / 6, Imp.; 2, 1 (8) $\sim Faa \wedge (\sim\sim Faa \vee \sim\sim Faa)$ / 7, D.N.; 2, 1 (9) $\sim Faa \wedge \sim\sim Faa$ / 8, Rep.; 2, $\vdash$ (10) $\sim(\exists x)(\forall y)(Fxy \equiv \sim Fyy)$ / 1—9, R.A.; $\mathcal{L}$ (11)$\sim(\exists x)(\forall y)(Fxy\equiv\sim Fyy)$ / 1, 2—10, E.I.

Exercise 9.6, p. 334

1 (b) None; (e) reflexive, transitive; (g) symmetrical; (j) reflexive, transitive.
2 (b) is a descendant of; (e) is better than; (g) is the square of.
3 (a) is a daughter of a child of; (c) is an employee of an employer of; (e) is a division of a division of.

Exercise 9.7, p. 339

2 $Fx = x$ is a dog, $Gx = x$ is a cat, $Hxy = x$ is more intelligent than y, $Ix = x$ is a Siamese, $Jx = x$ is a laboratory mouse. The suppressed premises are $(\forall x)$ $(Ix \supset Gx)$ [all Siamese are cats]; $(\forall x)(\forall y)(\forall z)[(Hxy \wedge Hyz) \supset Hxz]$ [the relation *more intelligent than* is transitive]; $(\forall x)[Fx \supset (\forall y)(Gy \supset Hxy)] \wedge (\exists x)[Ix \wedge (\forall y)(Jy \supset Hxy)]$ / $(\forall x)[Fx \supset (\forall y)(Jy \supset Hxy)]$
3 $Fx = x$ is a bachelor, $Gx = x$ is a suburb, $Hxy = x$ lives in y, $Ix = x$ is a person, $Jx = x$ is married, a = Fred. The suppressed premise is $(\forall x)[Fx \supset \sim(Ix \wedge Jx)]$ [no bachelor is a married person]; Fa; $(\forall x)\{Gx \supset (\forall y)[Hyx \supset (Iy \wedge Jy)]\}$ / $(\forall x)(Gx \supset \sim Hax)$
6 $Fxy = x$ is a descendant of y, $Gx = x$ is ugly, $Hxy = x$ is an ancestor of y, a = Ferd, b = Mary, c = Tom. The suppressed premises are $(\forall x)(\forall y)(\forall z)$ $[(Hxy \wedge Hyz) \supset Hxz]$ [*being an ancestor of* is a transitive relation]; $(\forall x)(\forall y)$ $(Fxy \equiv Hxy)$ [*being a descendant of* is the converse of *being an ancestor of*]; $(\forall x)(Fxa \supset Gx)$; $Hab \wedge Hbc$ / Gc

Exercise 9.9, p. 347

3 $Fx = x$ is brave, $Gx = x$ is a man: $(\exists x)\{(Fx \wedge Gx) \wedge (\forall y)[(Fy \wedge Gy) \supset x = y]\}$
5 $Fx = x$ is a person, $Gxy = x$ is taller than y, a = Tim, b = Peter: $(\forall x)[(Fx \wedge x \neq a) \supset Gbx]$
9 $Fx = x$ is a student in the class, $Gxy = x$ is smarter than y, a = Maria: $Fa \wedge (\forall x)[(Fx \wedge x \neq a) \supset Gax]$
12 $Fx = x$ is a person; $Gxy = x$ likes y: $(\forall x)\{Fx \supset (\exists y)[(Fy \wedge x \neq y) \wedge Gxy]\}$
14 $Fxy = x$ is a faster runner than y, a = Tom, b = Mary: $a \neq b \wedge (\forall x)$ $[(x \neq a \wedge x \neq b) \supset (Fax \wedge Fbx)]$
18. $Fx = x$ was at home, a = Tom: $(\forall x) (x \neq a \supset \sim Fx)$
20 $Fxy = x$ is a moon of y, a = Mars: $(\exists x)(\exists y)\{[(Fxa \wedge Fya) \wedge x \neq y] \wedge (\forall z)$ $[Fza \supset (z = x \vee z = y)]\}$
24 $Fx = x$ is a number, $Gxy = x$ is smaller than y, a = zero: $Fa \wedge (\forall x)[(Fx \wedge x \neq a) \supset Gax]$
26 $Fx = x$ is a person, $Gxy = x$ wants to be y: $\sim(\exists x)\exists y)\{[(Fx \wedge Fy) \wedge x = y] \wedge Gxy\}$

Exercise 9.10, p. 353

2 $Fxy = x$ was advocated by y, a = the theory of forms, b = Plato (note that *the theory of forms* is not a description, but rather a name); Fab

4 $Fxy = x$ is a father of y, $Gx = x$ is a person, a = early modern philosophy, b = Descartes; $\sim[Fba \wedge (\forall x)(x \neq b \supset \sim Fxa)] \supset (\forall y)[(Gy \wedge y \neq b) \supset \sim Fya]$

6 $Fxy = x$ is a leader of y, $Gx = x$ is a person, $Hxy = x$ likes y, a = the Third Reich; $(\exists x)\{[Fxa \wedge (\forall y)(Fya \supset x = y)] \wedge (\forall z)(Gz \supset \sim Hzx)\}$

8 $Fx = x$ is a dog, $Gxy = x$ bit y, a = Fred, b = Alfred; $(\exists x)(\{(Fx \wedge Gxa) \wedge (\forall y)[(Fy \wedge Gya) \supset x = y]\} \wedge b = x)$

10 $Fxy = x$ is a director of y, $Gx = x$ is a director, $Hxy = x$ is better than y, a = *Star Wars*; $(\exists x)([Fxa \wedge (\forall y)(Fya \supset x = y)] \wedge [Gx \wedge (\forall z)[(Gz \wedge z \neq x) \supset \sim Hzx])$

12 $Fx = x$ is a person, $Gxy = x$ likes y; $(\exists x)[(\{[Fx \wedge (\forall y)(Fy \supset Gxy)] \wedge (\forall z)[Fz \wedge (\forall w)(Fw \supset Gzw)]\} \supset x = z) \wedge (\forall y)(Fy \supset \sim Gyx)]$

14 $Fx = $ is a person, $Gxy = x$ likes y, a = Tom; $(\exists x)\{[(\{(Fx \wedge (\forall y)[(Fy \wedge x = y) \supset \sim Gxy]\} \wedge (\forall z)\{Fz \wedge (\forall w)[(Fw \wedge w \neq z) \supset \sim Gzw]\}) \supset x = z] \wedge a = x\}$

Exercise 9.11.1, p. 361

1 (a) Valid; (c) valid; (f) valid; (g) invalid: counterinterpretation if I(Fa), I(Fb) = T; I($a = b$) = F.

2 (c) Contingent; (e) logical truth; (h) contingent.

3 (b) $Fx = x$ is a person, $Gx = x$ was able to perform the task, $Hx = x$ is a man, $Ixy = x$ loves y, $Jxy = x$ knows y, a = Mary, b = Fred: $(\forall x)(\forall y)\{(Fx \wedge Fy) \supset [(Gx \wedge Gy) \supset x = y]\}$, $(\exists x)(\{(Hx \wedge Ixa) \wedge (\forall y)[(Hy \wedge Iya) \supset y = x]\} \wedge Gx)$, $(\exists x)(\{(Fx \wedge Jxb) \wedge (\forall y)[(Fy \wedge Jyb) \supset y = x]\} \wedge Gx) / (\exists x)(\exists y)[(\{(Hx \wedge Ixa) \wedge (\forall z)[(Hz \wedge Iza) \supset z = x]\} \wedge \{(Fy \wedge Jyb) \wedge (\forall z)[(Fz \wedge Jzb) \supset z = y]\}) \wedge x = y]$: valid.

(e) $Fx = x$ is an Olympic athlete, $Gx = x$ is well disciplined, $Hxy = x$ is a better swimmer than y, a = John: Fa, $(\forall x)(Fx \supset Gx)$, $(\exists x)(\{(\forall y)(y \neq x \supset Hxy) \wedge (\forall z)[(\forall w)(w \neq z \supset Hzw) \supset z = x]\} \wedge \sim Gx) / (\exists x)(\{(\forall y)(y \neq x \supset Hxy) \wedge (\forall z)[(\forall w)(w \neq z \supset Hzw) \supset z = x]\} \wedge x \neq a)$: valid.

(g) $Fx = x$ is a person, $Gx = x$ is mortal, $Hxy = x$ is kinder than y: $(\forall x)(Fx \supset Gx) / (\exists x)[\{Fx \wedge (\forall y)[(Fy \wedge y \neq x) \supset Hxy]\} \wedge (\forall z)(\{Fz \wedge [(\forall w)(Fw \wedge w \neq z) \supset Hzw]\} \supset z = x) \wedge Gx]$: invalid.

(j) $Fxy = x$ knows y, $Gx = x$ is a person, $Hxyz = x$ likes y better than z, $Ixy = x$ is uglier than y, $Jx = x$ is ugly, $Kx = x$ is interesting, a = Fred, b = I: $(\forall x)\{(Gx \wedge Fxa) \supset (\forall y)[(Gy \wedge Fya) \supset Hxay]\}$, $(\exists x)\{[((Gx \wedge Fbx) \wedge (\forall y)\{[(Gy \wedge Fby) \wedge y \neq x] \supset Ixy\}) \wedge ((\forall z)\{(\forall w)[(Gw \wedge Fbw) \wedge w \neq z] \supset Izw\} \supset z = x)] \wedge (\forall y)(Fya \supset y = x)\}$, $(\forall x)\{[(Gx \wedge Jx) \wedge Fbx] \supset Kx\} / (\exists x)\{[\{Gx \wedge (\forall y)[(Gy \wedge y \neq x) \supset Hxay]\} \wedge ((\forall z)\{Gz \wedge (\forall w)[(Gw \wedge w \neq z) \supset Hzaw]\} \supset z = x)] \wedge Kx\}$: invalid.

Exercise 9.12, p. 366

1 (b): 1(4) Fb / a1; 1(5) $Fa \supset (\forall y)(Fy \supset a = y)$ / 1, U.I.; 1(6) $(\forall y)(Fy \supset a = y)$ / 2, 5, M.P.; 1(7) $Fb \supset a = b$ / 6, U.I.; 1(8) $a = b$ / 4, 7, M.P.; 1(9) $a = b \wedge a \neq b$ / 8, 3, Conj.; 1(10) $\sim Fb$ / 4—9, R.A.

(d): 1(2) $c = a$ / a1; 1(3) $c = b$ / 1, 2, P.I.E.; 1(4) $c = a \supset c = b$ / 2—3, Ded.; 2(5) $c = b$ / a2; 2(6) $a = a$ / T.R.I.; 2(7) $b = a$ / 1, 6, P.I.E.; 2(8) $c = a$ / 5, 7, P.I.E.; 2(9) $c = b \supset c = a$ / 5—8, Ded.; (10) $(c = a \supset c = b) \wedge (c = b \supset c = a)$ / 4, 9, Conj.; (11) $c = a \equiv c = b$ / 10, Bic.

(e): 1(3) *Fa* / *a*1; 1(4) (∀*y*)[(*Fa* ∧ *Fy*) ⊃ *a* = *y*] / 1, U.I.; 1(5) (*Fa* ∧ *Fb*) ⊃ *a* = *b* / 4, U.I.; 2, 1(6) *Fb* / *a*2; 2,1 (7) *Fa* ∧ *Fb* / 3, 6, Conj.; 2,1 (8) *a* = *b* / 5, 7, M.P.; 2,1 (9) *Fb* ⊃ *a* = *b* / 6—8, Ded.; 1(10) (∀*y*)(*Fy* ⊃ *a* = *y*) / 9, U.G.; 1(11) *Fa* ∧ (∀*y*)(*Fy* ⊃ *a* = *y*) / 3, 10, Conj.; 1(12) (∃*x*)[*Fx* ∧ (∀*y*)(*Fy* ⊃ *x* = *y*)] / 11, E.G.; ⊬ (13) (∃*x*)[*Fx* ∧ (∀*y*)(*Fy* ⊃ *x* = *y*)] 2, 3—12, E.I.

(g): (3) *Fb* ⊃ *b* = *a* / 1, U.I.; (4) *b* = *a* / 2, 3, M.P.; (5) *b* = *b* / T.R.I.; (6) *a* = *b* / 4, 5, P.I.E.

2 (b); 1(1) *Fa* / *a*1; 2,1 (2) ~(∃*x*)(*x* = *a* ∧ *Fx*) / *a*2; 2,1 (3) (∀*x*) ~ (*x* = *a* ∧ *Fx*) / 2, Q.E.; 2,1 (4) ~(*a* = *a* ∧ *Fa*) / 3, U.I.; 2,1 (5) *a* = *a* / T.R.I.; 2,1 (6) *a* = *a* ∧ *Fa* / 5, 1, Conj.; 2,1 (7) (*a* = *a* ∧ *Fa*) ∧ ~(*a* = *a* ∧ *Fa*) / 6, 4, Conj; 2,1 (8) ~~(∃*x*) (*x* = *a* ∧ *Fx*) / 2—7, R.A.; 1(9)(∃*x*)(*x* = *a* ∧ *Fx*) / 8, D.N.; ⊬(10) *Fa* ⊃ (∃*x*) (*x* = *a* ∧ *Fx*) / 1—9, Ded.

(e): 1(1)(∀*x*) *Fxx* / *a*1; 2,1(2) ~(∀*x*)(∃*y*)*Fxy* / *a*2; 2,1(3) (∃*x*)~(∃*y*) *Fxy* / 2, Q.E.; 3,2,1 (4) ~(∃*y*)*Fay* / *a*3; 3,2,1 (5) (∀*y*)~*Fay* / 4, Q.E.; 3,2,1 (6) ~*Faa* / 5, U.I.; 3,2,1 (7) *Faa* / 1, U.I.; 3,2,1 (8) *Faa* ∧ ~*Faa* / 7, 6, Conj.; 3,2,1 (9) ~~(∀*x*)(∃*y*)*Fxy* / 2—8, R.A. 2,1 (10) ~~(∀*x*)(∃*y*)*Fxy* / 3, 4—9, E.E.; 1 (11) (∀*x*)(∃*x*)*Fxy* / 10, D.N.; ⊬(12) (∀*x*)*Fxx* ⊃ (∀*x*)(∃*y*)*Fxy* / 1—11, Ded.

4 (a): *Fx* = *x* is a person, *Gxy* = *x* knows *y*; *Hx* = *x* is a good friend, *a* = Jack, *b* = John: (1) (∀*x*) (*Fx* ⊃ *Gxa*) ∧ *a* = *b* (prem.); (2) *Hb* (prem.); (3) *a* = *b* / 1, Simp.; (4) (∀*x*) (*Fx* ⊃ *Gxa*) / 1, Simp.; (5) (∀*x*) (*Fx* ⊃ *Gxb*) / 3,4, P.I.E.; (6) *Hb* ∧ (∀*x*) (*Fx* ⊃ *Gxb*) / 2,5, Conj.; (7) (∃*y*) [*Hy* ∧ (∀*x*) (*Fx* ⊃ *Gxy*)] / 7, E.G.

(d): *Fx* = *x* is a logician, *Gxy* = *x* is at *y*, *Hx* = *x* is a philosopher, *a* = Dumple University: (1) (∃*x*) ({(*Fx* ∧ *Gxa*) ∧ (∀*y*) [(*Fy* ∧ *Gya*) ⊃ *y* = *x*]} ∧ *Hx*) (prem.) 1(2) *Fb* ∧ *Gba* / *a*1; 2,1 (3) {(*Fc* ∧ *Gca*) ∧ (∀*y*)[(*Fy* ∧ *Gya*) ⊃ *y* = *c*]} ∧ *Hc* / *a*2; 2,1 (4) *Hc* / 3, Simp.; 2,1 (5) (*Fc* ∧ *Gca*) ∧ (∀*y*)[(*Fy* ∧ *Gya*) ⊃ *c* = *y*] / 1, 3, Simp.; 2,1 (6) (∀*y*)[(*Fy* ⊃ *Gya*) ⊃ *c* = *y*] / 5, Simp.; 2,1 (7) (*Fb* ∧ *Gba*) ⊃ *c* = *b* / 6, U.I.; 2,1 (8) *c* = *b* / 2, 7, M.P.; 2,1 (9) *Hb* / 4,8, P.I.E.; 2,1 (10) *Hb* / 1, 3—9, E.I.; ⊬ (11) (*Fb* ∧ *Gba*) ⊃ *Hb* / 2—10, Ded.; (12) (∀*x*) [(*Fx* ∧ *Gxa*) ⊃ *Hx*] / 11, U.G.

Review Exercises for Chapter 9, p. 370

1 (a) Invalid: counterinterpretation if I(*Fab*) = F, I(*Gab*) = F, and likewise for all other individual constants.

(c) Invalid: counterinterpretation if I(*Faa*) = T, I(*Ga*) = T, I(*Fbb*) = T, I(*Gc*) = T, I(*Hc*) = T, I(*Gd*) = T, I(*Ge*) = T, I(*He*) = F. [Simpler counterinterpretations are possible, say, I(*Faa*), I(*Ga*), I(*Ha*) = T, I(*Gb*) = T, I(*Hb*) = F.

(d) Valid: (1) (∀*x*)(∀*y*)(*Fxy* ⊃ *Gxy*); (2) (∀*x*)(∃*y*)*Fyx*; (3) (∃*y*)*Fya* / 2, U.I.; 1(4) *Fba* / *a*1; 1(5) (∀*y*)(*Fby* ⊃ *Gby*) / 1, U.I.; 1(6) *Fba* ⊃ *Gba* / 5, U.I.; 1(7) *Gba* / 4, 6, M.P.; 1(8) (∃*y*) *Gya* / 7, E.G.; ⊬ (9) (∃*y*) *Gya* / 3, 4—8, E.I.; (10) (∀*x*)(∃*y*)*Gyx* / 9, U.G.

(f) Valid: (1) (∀*x*)(∀*y*)[(*Fx* ∧ *x* ≠ *y*) ⊃ *Gxy*]; (2) *Fa* ∧ ~*Fb*; (3) *Fa* / 2, Simp.; (4) ~*Fb* / 2, Simp.; (5) *a* ≠ *b* / 3, 4, N.I.E.; (6) *Fa* ∧ *a* = *b* / 3, 5, Conj.; (7) (∀*y*)[(*Fa* ∧ *a* ≠ *y*) ⊃ *Gay*] / 1, U.I.; (8) (*Fa* ∧ *a* ≠ *b*) ⊃ *Gab* / 7, U.I.; (9) *Gab* / 6, 8, M.P.

(g) Valid: (1) (∀*x*)(*Fx* ⊃ *Gb*); (2) *Fa* ⊃ *Gb* / 1, U.I.; 1(3) ~*Gb* / *a*1; 1(4) ~*Fa* / 2, 3, M.T.; 1(5) (∀*x*)~*Fx* / 4, U.G.; 1(6) ~(∃*x*)*Fx* / 5, Q.E.; ⊬ (7) ~*Gb* ⊃ ~(∃*x*)*Fx* / 3—6, Ded.; (8) (∃*x*)*Fx* ⊃ *Gb* / 7, Trans.

(j) Invalid: counterinterpretation if I(*Faa*) = F, I(*Fab*) = T, I(*Fac*) = F.

(k) Valid: (1) (∀*x*)[*Fx* ⊃ (∀*y*)(*Fy* ⊃ *Gxy*)]; (2) (∃*x*)(*Fx* ∧ (∃*y*)~*Gxy*); 1(3) *Fa* ∧ (∃*y*)~*Gay* / *a*1; 1(4) *Fa* / 3, Simp.; 1(5) (∃*y*)~*Gay* / 3, Simp.; 2,1 (6) ~*Gab* / *a*2; 2,1 (7) *Fa* ⊃ (∀*y*)(*Fy* ⊃ *Gay*) / 1, U.I.; 2,1 (8) (∀*y*)(*Fy* ⊃ *Gay*) / 4, 7, M.P.; 2,1 (9)*Fb* ⊃ *Gab* / 8, U.I.; 2,1 (10) ~*Fb* / 6, 9, M.T.; 2,1 (11) (∃*x*)~*Fx* / 10, E.G.; 2,1 (12) (∃*x*)~*Fx* / 5, 6—11, E.I.; 1 (13) (∃*x*)~*Fx* / 2, 3—12, E.I.

(o) Invalid: counterinterpretation if I(Fa), I(Fb), I(Fc), I(Fd), I(Ga), I(Gb), I(Hc), I(Hd) = T, I($a = b$), I($d = c$), I(Gc), I(Ha), I(Hb) = F.

2   (b) Inconsistent: (1) $\sim(\exists x)(Fx \wedge Gx)$; (2) $(\forall x)(Fx \supset Gx)$; (3) $(\exists x)Fx$; (4) $(\forall x)\sim(Fx \wedge Gx)$ / 1, Q.E.; 1(5) Fa / a1; 1(6) $Fa \supset Ga$ / 2, U.I.; 1(7) $\sim(Fa \wedge Ga)$ / 4, U.I.; 1(8) $\sim Fa \vee \sim Ga$ / 7, DeM.; 1(9) Ga / 5, 6, M.P.; 1(10) $\sim\sim Ga$ / 9, D.N.; 1(11) $\sim Fa$ / 8, 10, D.S.; 1(12) $Fa \wedge \sim Fa$ / 5, 11, Conj.; $\cancel{\ell}$ (13) $\sim Fa$ / 5—12, R.A.; (14) $(\forall x)\sim Fx$ / 13, U.G.; (15) $\sim(\exists x)Fx$ / 14, Q.E.; (16) $(\exists x)Fx \wedge \sim(\exists x)Fx$ / 3, 15, Conj.

    (d) Consistent: I(Fa), I(Gaa) = F.

5   (c) Equivalent: $\{(\exists x)Fx \supset (\exists y)Gy\} \vdash (\forall x)(\exists y)(Fx \supset Gy)$: (1)$(\exists x)Fx \supset (\exists y)Gy$; 1(2) $(\forall y)\sim(Fa \supset Gy)$ / a1; 1 (3) $\sim(Fa \supset Gb)$ / 2, U.I.; 1(4) $\sim(\sim Fa \vee Gb)$ / 3, Imp.; 1(5) $\sim\sim Fa \wedge \sim Gb$ / 4, DeM.; 1(6) $\sim Gb$ / 5, Simp.; 1(7) $(\forall y)\sim Gy$ / 6, U.G.; 1(8) $\sim(\exists y)Gy$ / 7, Q.E.; 1(9) $\sim\sim Fa$ / 5, Simp.; 1(10) Fa / 9, D.N.; 1(11) $(\exists x)Fx$ / 10, E.G.; 1(12) $(\exists y)Gy$ / 1, 11, M.P.; 1(13) $(\exists y)Gy \wedge \sim(\exists y)Gy$ / 8, 12, Conj.; $\cancel{\ell}$ (14) $\sim(\forall y)\sim(Fa \supset Gy)$ 2—13, R.A.; (15) $\sim\sim(\exists y)(Fa \supset Gy)$ / 14, Q.E.; (16) $(\exists y)(Fa \supset Gy)$ / 15, D.N.; (17) $(\forall x)(\exists y)(Fx \supset Gy)$ / 16, U.G. $\{(\forall x)(\exists y)(Fx \supset Gy)\} \vdash (\exists x)Fx \supset (\exists y)Gy$: (1) $(\forall x)(\exists y)(Fx \supset Gy)$; 1(2) $(\exists x)Fx$ / a1; 2,1 (3) Fa / a2; 2, 1 (4) $(\exists y)(Fa \supset Gy)$ / 1, U.I.; 3,2,1 (5) $Fa \supset Gb$ / a3; 3,2,1 (6) Gb / 3, 5, M.P.; 3, 2, 1 (7) $(\exists y)Gy$ / 6, E.G.; $\cancel{3}$,2,1, (8) $(\exists y)Gy$ / 4, 5—7, E.I.; $\cancel{2}$,1 (9) $(\exists y)Gy$ / 2, 3—8, E.I.; $\cancel{\ell}$ (10) $(\exists x)Fx \supset (\exists y)Gy$ / 2—9, Ded.

    (e) Not equivalent: counterinterpretation if I(Fa), I(Fb) = T, I($a = b$) = F.

Index

Index

Intersection, 123–124
Intransitive relations, 330–331
Intuition, 26
  linguistic, 45, 51
  logical, 50
Invalid argument, 6
Inverted wedge, 33, 42–45
Irreflexivity, 329

Justification, 2–3, 16

Language, 11–17
  artificial, 17, 32
  levels of, 119–122
  natural, 17
  object, 117–121
Law of logic, 85, 131
  logical theorem, 226–228, 286–287
  logical truth, 85–86, 277
  tautology, 165–166
Linguistics, 12
Logic:
  law of, 85–86, 131
      (See also Law of logic)
  predicate, 237
  statement, 19
  subject of, 1, 35
  as theoretical study, 5
  twentieth-century, 13
Logical equivalence, 78–80, 131
Logical equivalence metatheorem, 231–232
Logical falsehood, 87
Logical form, 22, 27
  of atomic statements, 40
  definition of, 34
Logical theorem, 131, 286, 287
  definition of, 226
Logical truth, 85–86, 131, 277
Logicians:
  ancient Greek, 50
  medieval, 50
  Megarian-Stoic, 50

Material conditional, 54
  connection with entailment, 169–170
  minimal truth-functional meaning of,
      52–53
Mathematical truth, 232
Meaning:
  of connecting words, 35–38
  of connectives, 38–40

Meaning:
  and semantics, 14–15
  and syntax, 15–16
  truth-functional, 44
Mechanicalness, 136
Members (of sets), 122
Mention, 118
Metalanguage, 117–121
Meta-metalanguage, 119–120
Metatheorem:
  consistency, 231–232
  definition of, 158
  logical equivalence, 231–232
  soundness of T and ℑ=, 367–369
  strong semantic completeness for 𝔇, 230
  strong semantic completeness for T and
      ℑ=, 367
  strong soundness, 230, 367
  weak soundness for 𝔇, 231
  weak semantic completeness for 𝔇, 231
Metavariables, 126–127, 129–130
Multiple quantification, 302–311
  interpretation of, 304–305
  relative clauses, 305–306

Name, 240
  definition of, 241
Natural deduction system:
  𝔇, 175, 177–179
  ℑ, 280
  ℑ=, 362–363
Negation, 40–42
Noncontradiction, 86
Nonreflexivity, 329
Nonsense, 11–12
Nonsymmetrical relations, 330
Nontransitive relations, 331
Nothingness, 62, 90, 116, 174

Open form, 256
Open sentence, 242, 244
Ordinal numbers in arguments, 110

Paradox, 54, 120–122
Persuasion, 5
Possessives, 295, 307–308
Predicate expression, 240, 292
  definition of, 241
  with three or more places, 301, 302
  two-place, 292
Predicate logic, 237–238

Standard form, 243, 291–294
Statement:
  atomic, 19, 21
  complex, 63–69
  compound, 19
  constituent, 19–23
  definition of, 4
  self-referential, 120–121
  semantic properties of, 71
Statement constant, 28–29
Statement form, 32, 128, 266, 311
Statement logic, 19, 232
  limitations of, 31, 237–238
Statement variable, 32
Stylistic words, 101
Superscripts, 292–293
Suppressed premises, 335–339
Symbolic abbreviation, 29
  of arguments, 100–103
  of statements, 28–29
Symbolic language $\mathcal{P}$, 254, 265–267, 311–313, 342
Symbolic language $\mathcal{S}$, 32–35, 125–129
Symbols, manipulation of, 8, 17
Symmetrical relations, 329
Syntactics, 12
  connection with semantics, 229–232
Syntax, 12

Tabular notation, 122
Tarski, Alfred, 11n.
Tautology, 85–86
  definition of, 165
Theorem schemata, 325
Tilde, 33, 40–42
Total reflexivity, 328
Transformation rules, 177–178, 280
  use of, 183–194
Transitive relations, 330
Triple bar, 33, 57–58

Trivial validity:
  semantic side, 158–160
  syntactic side, 223–224
Truth:
  concept of, 11
  semantic concept, 13
Truth conditions, 13–15, 36–37
  weakest, 52–53
Truth function, 24–27
Truth tables, 38
  for complex statement forms, 76–84
  for connectives, 39
  construction of, 70–84
  number of rows, 76
  steps for constructing, 76
Truth value, 24
Turnstile, 180, 227

Union, 123–124
Universal quantifier, 256
Universal quantifying expression, 251, 261
  definition of, 248
Unsound argument, 6
Use, 118
Use-mention distinction, 117–118

Vacuous operator, 108–109
Vacuous quantifier, 267, 313
Valid argument, 6
  definition of: in semantic sense, 132
    in syntactic sense, 181
Valid argument form, definition of:
  in semantic sense, 132
  in syntactic sense, 180
Validity, two aspects of, 10
Vocabulary, 11–12

Wedge, 33, 45–48